Supporting Play:
Birth through Age Eight

Join us on the web at

EarlyChildEd.delmar.com

Supporting Play:
Birth through Age Eight

Dorothy Justus Sluss, Ph.D.

Associate Professor of Early Childhood Education

Eugene T. Moore School of Education

Clemson University

THOMSON

DELMAR LEARNING

Australia   Canada   Mexico   Singapore   Spain   United Kingdom   United States

Supporting Play: Birth through Age Eight
Dorothy Justus Sluss

Vice President, Career Education SBU:
Dawn Gerrain

Director of Editorial:
Sherry Gomoll

Acquisitions Editor:
Erin O'Connor

Director of Production:
Wendy A. Troeger

Production Editor:
Joy Kocsis

Director of Marketing:
Wendy E. Mapstone

Cover Design:
Joseph Villanova

Composition:
Pre-Press Company, Inc.

Cover Images:
© Getty Images

Library of Congress Cataloging-in-Publication Data

Sluss, Dorothy Justus.
  Supporting play : birth through age eight / Dorothy Justus Sluss.
     p. cm.
  Includes bibliographical references and index.
  ISBN 1-4018-5143-6
  1. Play--United States. 2. Early childhood education--United States. I. Title.
  LB1140.35.P55S58 2004
  372.21--dc22

                                    2004014334

This book is lovingly dedicated to Roger for providing love, support, and comfort food.

Special thanks to Jim and Amy for graciously dealing with both wedding and book deadlines.

Brief Contents

Table of Contents

Preface

■ The Need to Play

Play is fun and, for most young children, something that occurs naturally. This was recognized by the pioneers of early childhood education. Play formed the basis of programs when early childhood education was in its infancy. Throughout the twentieth century, play has been examined from a variety of disciplines using multiple perspectives. Today we know more about the benefits and value of play for young children than at any other time in history. Play develops the cognitive, social, emotional, and physical domains. Support for play as a medium for learning has been established by scholars such as Piaget, Vygotsky, Bruner, Sutton-Smith, Smilansky, Pelligrini, Reifle, and Smith. Educators who know and understand young children value their play. Play is holistic and creates a euphoric sense of joy. This book was written to support the work of teachers who want to know more about play and the implementation of a play-based program. Those who will want to read this book include:

- ◆ Undergraduate and graduate students in early childhood programs
- ◆ Early childhood educators, directors, and classroom teachers
- ◆ Homeschoolers
- ◆ Parents of young children

More American children are in preschools than at any other time in this country's history. About 60% of children under five are cared for by someone other than their parents for an average of 30 hours a week. As the traditional nursery school changes to become more focused on academic learning, play is at risk in the preschool classroom, yet play is how children learn. Play is also at risk for children over five. Many kindergarten programs are struggling to justify play. Even primary programs are affected by this focus on academic learning. Some primary programs have eliminated recess, and others have limited it to fifteen minutes at the end of the day.

It is paradoxical that though we know more and more about the benefits of play, teachers are challenged to justify play in today's performance-based society. This book was written to counter this situation by providing a basis for implementing a play-based program and providing samples of how this can be accomplished at different levels. Most books on play focus on research and theories of play and are designed for graduate students. Books on curriculum tend to focus on educational pedagogy for undergraduates in terms of content areas such as math or literacy. This book is designed to provide a solid theoretical basis for play *combined with* program implementation for different developmental levels.

■ The Development of This Book: Play as Pedagogy

Play has always been my passion—from the time I played as a child to the time I played with my son. For me, to play is to be alive. My passion for play accompanied me into the classroom. As a classroom teacher, I implemented a play-based program. It seemed logical that if children naturally play and learn through their play, then we should use play as a teaching mechanism. Like other teacher researchers, I watched for signs of success or failure. The success of my students year after year strengthened my resolve to place play at the core of my program. Teacher educators, reporters, and the innumerable student teachers who came through my door assured me that what I was doing was both beneficial and appropriate. Still, I defended my use of play to parents and some administrators. It was difficult to find empirical support. As a classroom teacher, I could find books on play, books on curriculum, and books on models. It was impossible to find one guide for understanding play *and* developing classroom activities. I gathered materials by grabbing a handout at workshops or an article in a journal, and I developed my own rationale for play.

My interest in how children learn led me out of the classroom and into a doctoral program where I focused on how young children make sense of the world. Studying with Cosby Rogers and Janet Sawyers strengthened my view of the important role of play in learning and creativity. Primarily influenced by Piaget, Kami, Kohlberg and DeVries, and Fostnot, the work of Vygotsky, Bruner, Gardner, Vivian Paley, and Tharp and Gallimore also added to my knowledge base. Travels to the schools of Reggio Emilia, in Italy, introduced me to a program that truly valued play as a legitimate activity. Teachers and parents delight in the child's play and discovery. Everything I read and studied brought me back to play. If children learn through play, then it seems logical to use play as pedagogy.

If play is pedagogy, then play that dominates each age level should be used to guide curriculum development. That is, if very young children are exploring the world through practice play, then encouraging practice play should be the goal of programs for infants and toddlers. In the same way, if pretense dominates the preschool and kindergarten years, then dramatic and sociodramatic play should be a major part of the curriculum. If the dominant play of primary age children involves games with rules, then these should be used to inform the curriculum. This seems logical and fully justified, yet there are no textbooks that use this approach to inform program development. This book fills that void.

■ Organization of the Text

The text is organized around the premise that play is pedagogy. It provides a view of play that includes all ages, birth to age eight, and separates information in terms of age and developmental levels. This separation is designed to foster understanding of the holistic nature of play at each developmental level.

Chapter 1 considers the value of play, the definition of play, and the multiple dimension of play for *all* children. This chapter sets the stage for considering play and its multiple dimensions as a source of curriculum. Chapter 2 looks at the history of play scholarship. This is similar to a walk through the history of early childhood education, with play as the subject of investigation. Knowing the history of the study of play provides a foundation for implementing a play-based program. Chapter 3 looks at the benefits of play in terms of the physical, social, cognitive, and emotional domains of development. These three chapters provide a solid core of knowledge.

Pedagogy is the focus of Chapters 4 through 7. These chapters are divided into commonly accepted age ranges, birth to age two, preschoolers, kindergarten, and primary age. Chapter 4 is devoted to establishing a play-based program for infants and toddlers. Chapter 5 focuses on program development for preschoolers. Chapter 6 focuses solely on kindergarten and includes tips for setting up the first day of school. Chapter 7 is designed for primary age children and includes information on specific content areas.

Chapters 8 and 9 look specifically at two areas, inclusion and outdoor play. Chapter 8 contains information to facilitate inclusion at the infant-toddler, preschool, and primary levels. Outdoor play is the focus of Chapter 9. Information on play, playgrounds, and safety are available for each age level.

Chapter 10 is devoted to current issues, trends, and research. Major areas considered are technology, media, violence, and toys. Professionalism through play advocacy is also examined.

■ Features of This Book

Each chapter has the following features.

Chapter Overview

The chapter overview provides a brief synopsis of the main features of each chapter. This is located at the beginning of each chapter along with a quote selected to inspire, inform, and set the tone of the chapter. The overview prepares the reader for the content in the chapter.

Objectives

Chapter objectives are presented after the overview. Objectives or aims can be included in the class syllabi and keyed to performance objectives. The instructor's manual includes these components.

PlayScape

A brief vignette opens each chapter to bring the material to life for the student. The vignettes are miniature case studies which are followed by a discussion at the beginning of the chapter and are addressed in the PlayScape Reflection at the end of the chapter.

Play Provocation

The provocation or motivation to play is addressed at the beginning of each chapter in response to the PlayScape. This connects the reader to the case study and the new material in the text.

PlayScape Reflections

At the end of the chapter, reflections address the concerns raised in the PlayScape at the beginning of the chapter, in terms of information found in the chapter.

Summary

Points raised in the objectives are embedded in the summary which comes at the end of each chapter. This reinforces and confirms the students' understanding of the material.

Key Terms

Terms that necessary for understanding content are boldfaced and listed at the end of the chapter for review. They are defined in the comprehensive glossary at the rear of the book.

Helpful Web Sites and Technology Resources

Relevant Web sites and helpful computer programs are included for each chapter.

Activities

There are several types of activities at the very end of each chapter.

1. **InClass Lab**

   Activities based on cooperative learning are available that require active participation.

2. **Research and Inquiry**

   Activities that foster research and inquiry skills are designed for each chapter. This is especially beneficial for students who are interested in moving beyond the textbook.

3. **Service Learning**

   Experiences that extend learning through service in the field are included at the end of each chapter. Interaction with schools and community agencies is an especially important part of this experience.

4. **Family Connections**

   Activities that build relationships with families are included. These connect students with families.

5. **Play Advocacy**

   Advocacy activities begin with awareness activities (Chapter 1) and progress to action (Chapter 10). Activities range from group presentations to community activities.

■ How to Use This Book

The text includes comprehensive information on play and the implementation of a play-based curriculum. Chapters 1 and 2 provide an overview of play and Chapter 3 delves into the benefits of play for human growth and development. Chapters 4 through 7 provide a basis for setting up programs in infant-toddler centers, preschool classrooms, and primary grades. Chapter 8 is designed to ensure that children with special needs are included. Outdoor play is covered in Chapter 9. Chapter 10 brings it all together to prepare students to teach infants and toddlers, preschoolers, and primary age children. There is a special section on children with special needs. Materials for instructors are listed below.

Instructor's Manual

The instructor's manual includes activities and support materials for each chapter. A special feature of this manual is the inclusion of a generic syllabus that can be used as a guide for structuring the class. Materials for transparencies and case studies are also included.

Test Bank

A computerized bank of questions is available for use with the text.

Online Companion™

The Online Companion™ to accompany *Supporting Play: Birth Through Age Eight* is your link to early childhood education on the Internet. The Online Companion™ contains many features to help focus your understanding of supporting play:

◆ Frequently Asked Questions (FAQ's)
◆ Web Links
◆ Power Point Slides
◆ Case Studies
◆ Reading Lists
◆ Resources for Toys and Materials

You can find the Online Companion™ at www.earlychilded.delmar.com

■ Total Learning Package

The textbook and supporting Internet materials provide a powerful tool for the student, teacher, professional, or parent. This book is unique in that it provides a play-based approach for infancy through primary school. Those who use this text and supporting materials will have a basis for understanding and developing a play program for young children, birth to age eight.

■ About the Author

Dr. Dorothy Louise Justus Sluss is Associate Professor of Early Childhood Education at Clemson University. She started a career in early childhood education over 25 years ago. The first part of her career was spent in public schools and the second part in higher education. As a public school classroom teacher, she taught kindergarten, primary grades, and started a program for four-year-olds in public schools. She was elected vice-president of the Virginia Association for the Education of Young Children and served in numerous organizations as an advocate for young children from the classroom.

The second half of her career was spent in higher education. She served as Program Coordinator of the undergraduate and graduate Early Childhood Education program at East Tennessee State University, Director of Project TIES (Towards Inclusion in Early Childhood), and started the Mountain View Elementary Professional Development School. She is past president of the Association for the Study of Play (TASP) and the current editor of the TASP Newsletter. She initiated and has chaired the research forum for the NAEYC Play, Practice and Policy Interest Group at NAEYC for the past five years.

Dr. Sluss recently joined the Faculty of Education in the Eugene T. Moore School of Education at Clemson University where she serves as Coordinator of the Early Childhood Education program. She is also a member of the board of the South Carolina Association for the Education of Young Children and continues to serve as an advocate for young children. She has developed undergraduate programs in Early Childhood Education that have received NAEYC approval and has written numerous book chapters and articles that have been published in *Childhood Education*, *Young Children*, *Journal of Research in Early Childhood Education*, *The Allen Review*, and the *Journal of the National Association of Early Childhood Teacher Educators*.

Acknowledgments

This book is a result of many years of working with young children and their families. Like all good ideas, it took a great deal of support for this book to become reality. Special appreciation is extended to Bruce Shewin who provided support, knowledge, and, above all, patience. Thanks to Lindsey P., Ivy Ip, and the wonderful people at Delmar who played a role in making this book a reality.

My play studies have brought me into contact with some very special people. Special thanks to Dr. Cosby Rogers, who inspired and mentored my scholarly study of play, and to Drs. Janet Sawyers, Vickie Fu, and Andrew Stremmel, who always encouraged, enriched, and extended my quest for knowledge. Dr. Rebecca Isbell played a special role in facilitating my study of play, and Dr. Laurelle Phillips challenged me to know even more about block play than I believed possible. A special note of appreciation to the ETSU Child Study Center, Beverly Dugger, Connie Rogers, Lynn Lodien, Su Sorenson, Mary Mryon, and Miss Penny who embraced and supported my study of play at the ETSU Child Study Center; and especially to Professor E. Herbert Thompson for reminding me of the power of writing;

Special appreciation is extended to Drs. Jerome and Dorothy Singer and Harvey Bellin for sharing their new project at Yale (in Chapter 5); to Dr. Pradnya Patet with Britta Pells at Arizona State for their contributions on environmental design; and to Dr. Paul Pritchard for his essay on play in the primary school; to Dr. Samule Meisels, president of the Erikson Institute, who developed the Ounce scale and approved its inclusion in Chapter 4; and to Robert Fulghum for reprinting his poem, *All I Really Need to Know, I Learned in Kindergarten.*

Appreciation is expressed to the faculty, staff, and students of upstate South Carolina and especially to Clemson Elementary School, Code Elementary School, West End Elementary School, and Ravenel Elementary Schools. These exceptional schools graciously allowed me to share their excellence with others. A very special note of thanks to all my colleagues at Clemson who have supported and encouraged me throughout this process.

The author would like to thank the following reviewers, enlisted by Thomson Delmar Learning, for providing helpful suggestions and constructive criticism:

Jennifer Aldrich, Ed.D.
Central Missouri State University
Warrensburg, MO

Rhonda Clements, Ed.D.
Hofstra University
Hempstead, NY

Sue Grossman, Ph.D.
Eastern Michigan University
Ypsilanti, MI

Joan Isenberg, Ed.D.
George Mason University
Fairfax, VA

Jennifer Johnson, M.Ed.
Vance-Granville Community College
Henderson, NC

Cosby Rogers, Ph.D.
Virginia Tech (emerita)
Blacksburg, VA

John Sutterby, MA
University of Texas - Brownsville
Brownsville, TX

Cheryl Van Hook, PhD
Ohio University
Athens, OH

Dorothy Louise Justus Sluss

Valuing Play

*I believe that play is as fundamental
a human disposition as loving and working.*

—David Elkind, 2003

Chapter Overview

The value of play will be the focus of this chapter. *Play* will be defined from multiple perspectives. Play will also be examined among diverse groups including children with special needs and children from a variety of cultural perspectives.

Objectives

After reading this chapter you should be able to:

- ◆ Appreciate the value of play for young children.
- ◆ Identify the defining characteristics of play.
- ◆ Differentiate between play and exploration.
- ◆ Recognize how play differs among children from different cultural groups.
- ◆ Describe two ways to classify observable play behaviors.
- ◆ Explain the influence of context on play.
- ◆ Identify current obstacles to play in the United States.
- ◆ Discuss ways to support play in the classroom.

> ## PlayScape
>
> *Felicia carefully climbed the steps to the slide. When she got to the top, she slid down while laughing loudly. When she reached the bottom, she ran to the steps, climbed up the steps again, and slid down the slide again. She did this until her father intervened saying, "Felicia, it's time to go, baby." Felicia ran to the top of the steps and shouted, "Watch me go down sideways!" She went down one more time and begged to do it again.*
>
> ## Play Provocation
>
> Felicia's behavior is familiar to many adults who remember playing until exhausted or watching others do so. Though children need little provocation or motivation to play, the slide served as a motivator for Felicia's play. Her play is further supported by her father who placed her in a context designed to stimulate play. Felicia's play is typical of play behaviors exhibited by young children who live in areas that have accessible playgrounds and who have parents or other adults who will take them to these sites. Adults who observe children's play frequently witness these paradoxical behaviors during play. Children are so tired that they cannot stand, but they cannot stop playing and laughing. This pleasure, this joy, is a part of the essence of play for young children. But is this valuable?

■ Value of Play in America

As teachers of young children, we need to resist the pressures to transform play into work—into academic instruction.

—David Elkind, 2003

Understanding the role of play in the life of a child requires knowledge of play itself. The United States has a love/hate relationship with play that has its roots in the founding of this country. "For a culture built as ours is, on the Protestant ethic of work and achievement, play presents a problem" (Bronfenbrenner, 1979). We distinguish play from nonplay or work and value work more than play. This has been a concern for more than two decades. David Elkind, a well-known psychologist, first expressed his concern about this valuation of work over play in *The Hurried Child* in 1981. He noted that American children are being rushed through childhood with little time to play. He again voiced concern in 1987 in *Miseducation* when

All children play.

he stated that children do not have time for the journey through childhood. Play is not scheduled in the child's daily Palm Pilot. More recently, he expressed both his concern that children be allowed to play and also his hope that American society will allow children to play for the sake of play itself—for the joy of play (Elkind, 2003). His admonition to parents and teachers to value play for the sake of play is as important today as it was when it was first delivered in 1981.

The proliferation of play literature in the popular press and in the academic world reflects an interest in play by scholars, advocates, educators, and parents (Kirn & Cole, 2001). This book serves to extend this message by providing support for play in early education.

■ Value of Play in a Global Society

> *Play is necessary to affirm our lives.*
>
> —*Joseph Levy, 1978*

Children throughout the world play. Play may look different in other cultures, but all children play (Edwards, 2000; Sutton-Smith, 1997). Children in Norway play in the snow, children in Italy play on the piazza, and children in Japan play with kites on Kodomo Day (Children's Day). Furthermore, children in Norway, Italy, and Japan play with the people who are closest to them. They play with the sounds they can make with their mouths and with the instruments in their environments. All children in the world typically enjoy playing with water, sand, mud, and sticks or bones—whatever nature provides them in their particular region of the world (Rogers, 2003).

Play can be found in all cultures with the exception of the k!ung tribe in Africa. One example of play in another African tribe was reported by David Lancy (1996). In contrast with the nonplayers, he found that young children in Kpelle, Africa, even have a special place set aside for play. They play on this **mother-ground** while adults work. When they are older, children are required to work but often the lines blur between work and play. For additional information, see Lancy's (1996), *Playing on the Mother-Ground*.

In their research of cross-cultural play, Whiting and Edwards (1988) found that children spend 80% of their time in play or social interaction. Recently, Edwards (2000) reanalyzed the data from both the original 1950s study, *Six Cultures: Studies of Child Rearing* by B.B. Whiting (1963) and from follow-up studies (Whiting & Edwards, 1988). Her findings support hypotheses developed by Sutton-Smith (1998) when he examined the original data:

> First, cultural norms determine whether the play will be stimulated or whether it will be neglected (depending on whether adults consider it a good thing or a waste of children's time). Second, norms determine whether parent intervention will serve to conservatively preserve tradition or instead to instigate and foster independence and autonomy in girls and boys. Third, economic and historical conditions are critical resources for both physical and intellectual stimulation for play. (Edwards, 2000, pp. 321–322)

Based on these findings, play appears to be universal. For children throughout the world in both nonindustrialized and industrialized countries, play is a natural part of life.

Play only diminishes when social and cultural factors negatively impact it. In her book, *The Genius of Play: Celebrating the Spirit of Childhood,* Sally Jenkinson (2001) sounded the same alarm for England that David Elkind sounded for the United States. Jenkinson notes that there is a genius in play. She stated that, "The loss of childhood is part of the insidious penetration of the media and its accompanying commercial markets, and is further complicated by the fact that in today's world there is little opportunity for children to play without adult supervision" (p. 6). This sounds very similar to concerns verbalized by Elkind. She is not the only one who is concerned. In an article in the *Times Educational Supplement* in 2002, reporter Stephanie Northern discussed at length the effects of social and cultural factors on children's play. It is interesting that some of the same concerns are arising in England because that country has a national playground program and people use the word *play* frequently when talking about children.

In terms of the state of play in the world, children throughout the world play, and they play in ways that are multidimensional and occur in a variety of contextual settings. Those who are charged with caring for children must be even more careful and sensitive in recognizing and valuing the many faces of play.

■ Distinguishing Animal and Human Play

Play is a phenomenon found not only in humans but also in animals throughout the world. Children and young animals both play. Robert Fagen, a recognized scholar of animal play, noted that ". . . play occurs in only a small minority of the Earth's million or more species. Animal play is easy to recognize. Specific movement qualities and signal patterns characterize the familiar play behavior of cats, dogs, and human children as well as the play of other animals. Mammals and birds, and perhaps a few fishes and reptiles, are the only kinds of animals known to play" (Fagen, 1995). Play occurs among animals and humans who have higher levels of intelligence than other life forms. Some scholars have examined commonalities between animal and human play. Gregory Bateson's (1972) study of otter play informed research on signals that humans use during play. A problem arises when animal play and human play are included in the same category because animals do not have higher level thinking skills. Though there are some similarities, it is important not to overgeneralize when discussing animal and children's play.

Scholars of animal play generally look at play as adaptive behavior necessary for survival whereas scholars of human play see play as serving multiple purposes. Though it is tempting to include the great apes of Cameroon in the study of play, it is important to acknowledge that human play is unique. Humans bring ". . . elements into the situation that were not there before the play began" (Bronfenbrenner, 1979). These elements include toys, rules, and the products of the mind. Those who are more interested in animal play may want to read *Readings in Animal Cognition* by Bekoff and Jamison (1996).

■ Motivation to Play

Play appears to be a natural part of a young child's life. Studies of why children play look at young children and their play. Why, then, do some children fail to play? In a study of 26 convicted murderers in which over 90% had abnormal play patterns as children, none of the participants in the study recalled spontaneous play. Dr. Stuart Brown (1995) who conducted this study also found those who had well developed cognitive processing skills had engaged in a great deal of spontaneous play. Correlation does not mean causation, but does suggest some interesting patterns. When children imitate others, they safely re-create what has already been accomplished. Play requires risk taking and involves joy. This causes one to wonder if it is the inability to take risks or the lack of joy that results in wasted lives. This line of thought leads to the conclusion that play provides a safe place for risk taking and results in flexibility and reciprocity, traits that are necessary for success personally and professionally. Different aspects of human behavior may be better understood by a more thorough knowledge of play and the human motivation to play.

■ Defining Play

In some ways, "play" is a clown in the realm of psychological phenomena. It has eluded precise formulation, and at times seems to be playing hide-and-seek with us. We respond by either dismissing it as an unimportant prankster, or by trying harder to find it.
—*Brian Vandenberg, 1982*

"What is play?" seems to be a simple question. It does not, however, have an equally simple answer. Everyone recognizes play when they see it. Listen to a caregiver's voice when he says, "Stop playing and pay attention." "Stop playing and eat your dinner." "Stop playing and listen to the story." Yet *play* is difficult to define and some scholars even doubt our ability to define *play* (Bergen, 1988; Schlosberg, 1947). One scholar of play stated that "No behavioral concept has proved more ill-defined, elusive, controversial, and unfashionable" (Wilson, 1975). Others believe we can and must define *play*. Klugman (1995) believes that a definition of *play* will advance the field and should fit within the parameters listed below (p. 196).

- ◆ It applies to children from birth through eight.
- ◆ It is explicit enough to speak clearly to knowledgeable practitioners, to those in the field who are not yet students of play, and others outside of the field.
- ◆ It clearly describes play in terms of its different observable forms, functions, and values.
- ◆ It allows the field to speak in one strong voice about the forms, functions, and importance of play.
- ◆ It recognizes the importance of different forms of play for different cultural groups.

One of the first definitions of *play* was provided by the founder of kindergarten, Friedrich Froebel. He stated that, "Play is the highest expression of human development in childhood for it alone is the free expression of what is in a child's soul" (1887). Since Froebel's definition, the literature has been replete with definitions of *play*. Merriam-Webster's Collegiate Dictionary (2003) lists over 50 definitions of *play*. The research world adds even greater volume. Definitions encompass views that range from those put forth by children to those developed by scholars for research purposes. A sample of the definitions that have been developed are included in Figure 1–1.

FIGURE 1–1   Definitions of Play

Scholar	Definition
Froebel	"Play is the purest, most spiritual activity of man at this stage, and at the same time, typical of human life as a whole—of the inner hidden natural life in man and all things" (1887, p. 55).
Freud	"Children repeat everything that has made a great impression on them in real life, and that in so doing, they recreate the strength of the impressions and . . . make themselves masters of the situation" (1961, p. 11).
Erikson	"The growing child's play . . . is the training ground for the experience of a leeway of imaginative choices within an existence governed and guided by roles and visions" (1977, p. 78).
Vygotsky	"Play creates the zone of proximal development. In play a child always behaves beyond his average age, above his daily behavior; in play it is as though he were a head taller than himself" (1978, p. 102).
Piaget	"In every act of intelligence is an equilibrium between assimilation and accommodation, while imitation is a continuation of accommodation for its own sake, it may be said conversely that play is essentially assimilation, or the primacy of assimilation over accommodation" (1962a, p. 87).
Sutton-Smith	"The definitions of play given by child players themselves generally center on having fun, being outdoors, being with friends, choosing freely, not working, pretending, enacting fantasy, drama, and playing games. There is little or no emphasis on the kind of growth that adults have in mind with their progress rhetoric" (1997, p. 49).
Caplan and Caplan	"The highest form of research is essentially play" (1973, p. 129–130).
Bredekamp and Copple	"Play enables children to progress along the developmental sequence from the sensorimotor intelligence of infancy to preoperational thought in the preschool years to the concrete operational thinking exhibited by primary children . . . in addition to its role in cognitive development, play also serves important functions in children's physical, emotional, and social development. . . . Therefore, child-initiated, child-directed, teacher-supported play is an essential component of developmentally appropriate practice" (1997, p. 3).
Klugman	"Play is a major interactive process through which children learn about themselves, their environment, the other people in that environment, and the interrelationships among all of these. Play is intrinsic, self-selected, active, mind involving, and a focus for personal powers. It is intriguing and captivating and frequently involves practice of needed mental and /or physical skills. Play engages and fulfills the player. Authentic play involves choice on the part of the player and can be self-perpetuating. Play takes a variety of forms. Some of these are exploratory, functional, constructive, symbolic, and games with rules" (1995, p. 196).
Ablon	"A free-ranging voluntary activity that occurs within certain time and place limits, according to accepted rules. Play is accompanied by feelings of tension and joy and an awareness that it differs from ordinary life" (2001, p. 357).

The basis for the most respected and used definition of *play* was based on the work of John Huizinga (1955) and further developed by Rubin, Fein, and Vandenberg (1983). They viewed play as a behavioral disposition, as observable behaviors, and as context. Rubin, Fein, and Vandenberg included six factors in the disposition of play. These factors have been modified and are routinely accepted as the characteristics of play (Fromberg, 2002; Klein, Wirth, & Linas, 2003). Though few scholars include observable behaviors and contexts in their definition of *play* or in the characteristics of play, these factors were included in the definition developed by Rubin, Fein, and Vandenberg (1983) and will be included in the definition of *play* used in this book. Play is a ". . . behavioral disposition that occurs in describable and reproducible contexts and is manifest in a variety of observable behaviors" (p. 698). Though *disposition* is used in the definition, the term *characteristic* is now commonly found in the literature and will be used here for the purpose of clarity.

■ Characteristics of Play

1. Play Is Voluntary

Play is intrinsically motivated. Children play because they want to play. Adults can assist and support play, but the motivation comes from within the child. Adults cannot make children play. It is the child who needs and chooses to play. Early educators frequently hear children say, "Make her play with me." Teachers know, however, that you cannot make children play. The urge to play comes from within the child.

2. Play Requires Active Involvement

Play is meaningful and requires the active engagement of the child. Children who are sitting on the periphery of the house play area are not playing, they are watching. Only the children involved are playing. The children are actively involved and totally absorbed in the play. Children who watch play from afar may be trying to join the group. Special attention should be paid to older preschoolers and primary-age children who watch but never participate. Are they choosing not to play or are there other reasons? Sensitive, responsive teachers will seek answers.

3. Play Is Symbolic

Play involves symbolism or pretend play. It is nonliteral and carried out "as if" the activity were real. Children who use chairs to pretend they are riding on a bus are using the chairs as symbols (pivots). The child who

Play requires active involvement.

jumps in a box held by two children and declares she is in the boat is using social pretend play.

4. Play Is Free of External Rules

The rules of play are established by the children. They determine how the play will occur, who will play, what they will say and how they will say it. They determine the acceptable and unacceptable behaviors and direct how the script will flow (Fein, 1981). The child is at once the actor and director.

5. Play Focuses on Action Rather than Outcomes

The process is more important than the product. This is what distinguishes play from work. Play is episodic. This allows play to change at a moment's notice as children choose different goals and directions. Improvisation occurs as the children move from playing hospital to playing fire department. In play, it is the action that is important (Landreth, 1993).

6. Play Is Pleasurable

Play produces a positive affect. It is dominated by the players. They ask "What can I do with this object?" rather than "What will the object do?" (Rubin, Fein, & Vandenberg, 1983). They have the power to make the decisions. They are in control. Children may laugh, smile, or scream in delight as they show their enjoyment. They may also appear very serious but have

Play and exploration dominate the first two years of the child's life.

a very contented look on their face. Children delight in play. Freud (1959) and Piaget (1962a) both recognized the pleasure in play. Some scholars, however, debate the inclusion of pleasure because some play is not pleasurable. Sutton-Smith calls this "cruel play" (1982). For example, when children play games like One Potato, Two Potato or Knuckles, a game played in the border areas between Mexico and the United States, they will play even when their hands are stinging. The joy of the play compels them to play. For the young child, play is pleasurable and should be included when defining *play*.

■ Play or Exploration

Play and **exploration** are often viewed as interchangeable. They are, however, distinctly different. Exploration occurs before play. Exploration has been defined as what occurs when the child is exposed to a novel object and tries to figure it out. She asks, "What can this object do?" During play she asks, "What can I do with it?" (Pelligrini & Boyd, 1993, p. 108).

Exploration is the dominant activity during the first two years. The infant spends most of her time engaged in exploration. The toddler spends about half of her time in exploration whereas the preschooler spends much of her time in pretend. As the child grows and develops, exploration decreases and play increases. When a child explores, mental structures are adapted as the child's mind creates neurological pathways to accommodate new information. Play, however, allows the child to fit reality into existing structures. As practice play occurs over and over during the first two years of life, neural pathways are strengthened. In other words, during exploration children collect data, and during play they mess around with it. Hughes and Hutt (1979) identified three major areas of differences between play and exploration.

Play	Exploration
Positive affect	Neutral affect (cautious)
Creative combinations/ improvisational	Stereotypical behaviors
Casual demeanor, heart rate is variable	Intense, heart rate is steady, and concentration evident

■ Play or Playfulness?

Play has been defined as a behavioral disposition that occurs within a context that manifests itself as observable behaviors. As discussed earlier, play includes actions or behaviors that can be recognized and identified. For example, we can observe a child playing grocery store and laughing gleefully. Characteristics may include positive affect or intrinsic motivation; the context is a familiar shopping experience; and the observable behavior is pretend or symbolic play in a cooperative group setting or sociodramatic play. This is play.

Playfulness is not the same as play. Playfulness does not include observable behaviors. Playfulness is best described as a personality trait or internal disposition (Barnett, 1990; Liberman, 1965; Rogers, Impara, Frary, Harris, Meeks, Semanic-Lauth, & Reynolds, 1998). Components of playfulness include spontaneity, openness, communication, curiosity, emotional expressiveness, joyfulness, and humor. These traits may manifest themselves through behaviors that are culturally specific. For example, in one study of playfulness among Japanese children and American children, American children were found to be much more playful on a 31-item instrument (Rogers, Impara, Frary, Harris, Meeks, Semanic-Lauth, & Reynolds, 1998). The reason may be explained by differences between the two cultures (Tobin, Wu, & Davidson, 1989).

Einstein serves as an example of an individual who was both playful and engaged in play. When Einstein was eight, his uncle showed him a compass with a needle that always pointed north. His play with the compass stimulated a fascination with unseen forces that lasted a lifetime. He was equally playful. Eric Erikson called him the "victorious child" because he never stopped looking at the world through the eyes of a child (Rogers & Sluss, 1999).

■ Observable Behaviors

Everything a child is, does, and becomes may at one time or another
be demonstrated through play.
—*Gary Landreth and Linda Homeyer, 1998*

Behaviors that can be observed during play are *not* the same as the characteristics. Observable behaviors include those that can be observed, described, and classified. Today play taxonomies reflect cognitive and social domains as well as language, motion, and materials. Two taxonomies that are now considered classics were developed by Mildred Parten (1932) and Jean Piaget (1962a). Parten's study of social patterns was conducted on playgrounds and continues to be used in research and practice. Piaget's stages of play reflect his stages of intelligence. Though Piaget's research was conducted on his own children, research has supported his findings in both European-based and other cultural groups (Hale-Benson, 1986; Kagan, 1977; Shore, 1997). First, we begin with Piaget.

Cognitive Development

Play is a powerful form of activity that fosters the social life and
constructive activity of the child.
—*Jean Piaget, 1980*

In his research, Piaget (1962b) described three stages of play behaviors. He found that play becomes more complex with age and he categorized play in three major stages that include practice play, symbolic play, and games with rules. These stages are described in detail in this section.

Stage I. Practice play (birth to age two)

Play that occurs during the first two years of life is called **practice play** or **sensorimotor** (also called **functional play** by Smilansky, 1968). The two-year-old drops a shoe in the bathtub, watches the splash, and returns to put another in the tub of water. She is engaging in practice play. Practice play involves the ". . . pleasurable repetition of skills that have already been mastered; skipping pebbles, tying and untying shoes, riding a bike" (Rogers & Sawyers, 1988). The child engages in practice play for sheer delight and the pleasure of having an activity under control. Piaget used an example that he collected during observations of his child:

> At 2:8 (2) She filled a pail with sand, overturned it, demolished the
> sand-pie with her spade and began again, and she did this for more

than an hour. . . . These are experiments to see the results. (Piaget, 1962a, p. 115)

Two-year-olds generally delight in practice play. It may look different with different objects and in different cultures, but most two-year-olds enjoy repetitive play. Watch the child who can easily step up one stair as she begins to step up and down for no apparent reason. The child laughs as she steps up and down. Doing so meets the criteria of play. The child is not accommodating or learning new materials. The child knows how to step. The activity is under her control and is pleasurable. This fits the definition of practice play. Piaget described three levels of practice play: mere practice play, fortuitous combinations, and intentional combinations. *Though practice play dominates the first 18 months of life, it occurs throughout the life span.*

A. Mere practice play. **Mere practice play** occurs when the child is just repeating an act for pleasure, and it may involve physical and mental activities. For example, the toddler who pulls the paper towels from the rack does so just to watch them fall. She does not care about the number that have fallen, just the process of watching them fall. This is mere practice play.

B. Fortuitous combinations. The second level of practice play is called **fortuitous combinations**. The child engages in mere practice play and in doing so discovers a new way of putting activities together. Old schemata are used in new creations. Piaget described a behavior that is still observed in classes today:

> At 4:2 Y. began by emptying a box of bricks onto the floor and putting them back again. Then he amused himself by pushing one brick against another, thus moving as many as possible at once. Then he put one on top of the other and pushed them all. (1962a, p. 116)

Anyone who has watched children play with blocks has observed this behavior. Children start out by practicing and then figure out a more interesting way to play. Knocking down blocks after creating a structure also falls under this heading. Watch children when the adult says, "Clean-up time!" They really develop very interesting strategies as they deconstruct the block structure.

C. Intentional combinations. The third level of practice play is called **intentional combinations**. This is the most complex and occurs when new behaviors are deliberately combined. When combinations occur, the play will follow one of three directions: (1) children will add symbolism

Constructive play involves both functional play and symbolic play.

and pretend will occur, (2) social interactions will lead to games with rules, or (3) real adaptation occurs and play ceases. A child who is placing blocks one on top of another moves from practice play to symbolic play when she announces, "Now this is the wall. Humpty Dumpty can sit on my wall." The child has engaged in an intentional combination and moves into symbolic or social pretend play.

D. Constructive play. Constructive play is included in Piaget's taxonomy by some scholars (Rubin, Fein, & Vandenberg, 1983). Play behaviors described by Smilansky (1968) as constructive play were viewed by Piaget (1962a) as an intentional combination and identified as constructive practice play, not a separate level of play.

Constructive play occurs when children use materials to create or construct something. Materials used for construction include such items as blocks, paint, clay, or Play-Doh.® Preschool and kindergarten children spend more than half their time in constructive play. Constructive play moves from simple to complex. Different levels of constructive play have been created for block play and art work.

Smilansky's other observable play behaviors, functional play, dramatic play, and games with rules, are similar to Piaget's stages. Though pure Piagetians disagree with the use of constructive play as a separate category, Smilansky's view of constructive play has been generally accepted in the research literature as a level of play (Christie & Johnsen, 1987). Throughout the rest of the book, the stages of cognitive play will include constructive play as a separate category in the stages of play.

Stage II. Symbolic play (two to seven)

Symbolic play occurs when a child uses an object to stand for another during pretend play. Rogers and Sawyers (1988) describe it this way:

> . . . symbolic play, in which the *signifier* is separated from the *signified*. **Symbolic play** marks the beginning of representational thought through the use of substitute objects or actions. (1988, p. 17)

The signifier is the symbol or substitute object that evokes that which is symbolized. When a child picks up a block and pretends to call mom, the block is the signifier because it is a symbol that is substituted for a telephone—the signified. Howes (1992) has found that "social pretend play is salient in the formation of both social interaction skills and friendships from the toddler period into middle childhood, but that there are changes in both the forms and the functions of social pretend play across these periods" (p. 3). Like practice play, symbolic play may appear different for distinct ethnic groups and cultures.

Levels of symbolic play (Piaget, 1962a).   Piaget's view of symbolic play is similar to what Smilansky (1990) called dramatic play, Vygotsky (1978) called pretend, and Pelligrini and Boyd (1993) refer to as fantasy. Piaget's study of symbolism is still respected and serves as the basis for a great deal of research.

Level I. (birth to age two)   Though sensorimotor play dominates the first two years, children begin to engage in symbolic play somewhere between two and three. Symbolic play begins with ". . . projection of symbolic schemas on to new objects" (Piaget, 1962a, p. 121). When young children first begin to pretend that they are sleeping or eating when they know that they are not, symbolism is developing. The child will laugh as she pretends to sleep and will delight in the adult's response.

Level II. (two to seven)   The second level of symbolic play occurs "with simple identification of one object with another" (Piaget, 1962a, p. 123). During the early part of Level II, children benefit from props that reflect reality. Miniature phones, school buses, and dolls stimulate symbolic play or pretend for two- and three-year-olds.

Between the ages of three and four, children begin to engage in a closer approximation of reality. Props are an important part of play. As children increase their ability to symbolize, props that are more open-ended stimulate more pretense as children attempt to make them resemble their real-life counterparts. During this time, a box can become a car, a bus, or a rocket ship. The materials serve as a scaffold for their mental construction. Whereas the two-year-old's play is enhanced by a replicate cell phone, the four-year-old can create a closer approximation to reality with a box. A child might spend time trying to paint it or add materials to make it appear more realistic, but she has a clear idea of what she is doing. Many adults have been surprised to hear a child say, "The wing on the airplane goes here" during play with blocks that seem to look alike. Though the adult does not see what the child is constructing mentally, the child has an idea of what the plane should look like and that is what she is determined to re-create.

Pretend play provides a conduit for bringing home experiences to school. Children assume a familiar role such as the mom or dad in their play in the house area. When children from other cultures or ethnic groups join the classroom, play is enriched and expanded. Karen Evans (2001) shared a story about the lu Mien children who entered her class as a group. During the play center, they built a shrine that looked like one that they had in their home. Because there were several lu Mien children

Cognitive development occurs when children use symbolism to imitate reality.

in the class, they felt comfortable bringing the familiar into the unfamiliar setting of school. Sensitive teachers can extend these experiences for young children.

Piaget further differentiated the second level of symbolic play as (a) orderliness, (b) exact imitation of reality, and (c) collective symbolism with differentiation and complementary adjustment of roles. Again, sensitivity to other cultures is needed. As children attempt to re-create reality, children who have unique social cultural histories may find adjustment difficult. Teachers who are sensitive to these differences can facilitate the child's transition into the group play setting.

(a) *Orderliness* refers to the orderly placement of materials during play, for example, when the child places the spoon on the place mat in its "proper" place. Order provides homeless children with a sense of security.

(b) *Exact imitation of reality* refers to play that imitates life. A child who has attended a family dinner that included caviar may want to pretend that she is eating caviar a certain way. She wants to re-create reality through her own lens. Her playmate may not understand her reality and the change may create a different situation. In the same way, children who have observed videos or explicit sexual activities may attempt to imitate their reality. Teachers must be sensitive yet intervene appropriately when play turns violent or aggressive.

(c) *Collective symbolism with differentiation and complementary adjustment of roles* occurs when children agree to assume different roles. They may borrow from reality as they adjust and change the roles. This may occur at any time, but generally happens at the end of the year in a kindergarten class. After a year of playing in different ways, kindergarten children may decide to play bus and act out driving for a field trip. They will assign roles such as the bus driver or the teacher. Improvisation occurs quickly as children switch roles and change scenes. Maintaining the play theme is important and children who cannot do so may find themselves excluded from the play.

Stage III. Games with rules (seven to eleven or twelve)

Piaget viewed this as more developed and complex. When children move into the concrete operational stage of development, they are more interested in **games with rules**. The roles are clearly defined, the rules are clear-cut, and reality is imitated closely. Running games, board games, cards, or computer games are more interesting and exciting for this age group. Second and third graders begin developing their interest in games and this interest can be used to foster instruction. The utility of the approach for primary school will be revisited in Chapter 7.

Piaget's stages have formed the basis for a great deal of play research. Figure 1–2 illustrates how Piaget's stages can be used to provide a record of the child's play.

Social Development

Observable behaviors that reflect social development were first identified by Mildred Parten. In a classic study, Parten (1932) described social play behaviors of children during outdoor play. She found that social play becomes more complex with age. She classified social play in six categories: unoccupied behavior, onlooker behavior, solitary play, parallel play, associative play, and cooperative play. The first two are nonplay and the last three involve more complex social participation. These behaviors

FIGURE 1–2 Piagetian Play Scale

Observations	1st Observation	2nd Observation	3rd Observation
Practice play Repeats the same play over and over			
Symbolic play: Constructive Creates something			
Symbolic play: Dramatic Pretends			
Symbolic play: Sociodramatic Pretends with a group			
Games with rules Plays games			

Narrative _____

_____

_____

Source: Adapted from Piaget (1962a) and Smilansky (1968).

were originally viewed as developmental but are now viewed by some as descriptions of different play styles (Isenberg & Jalongo, 2001). These stages may look different for other cultures. Watching children at play with their peers who are members of their culture may provide information about social interactions that occur during play.

Unoccupied behavior

In **unoccupied behavior,** the child does not play nor does the child seem to have a goal. The child will play with her body, stand around, or walk about aimlessly. Some parents are concerned when their children display this behavior, but this is not unusual for young children. Nor is this behavior a concern when observed in older children infrequently. If this behavior occurs on a regular basis, adults must investigate to discover the cause of unoccupied behavior.

Onlooker behavior

Onlooker behavior occurs when the child watches, asks questions, and talks to other children that she is observing, but fails to enter play. She uses the skills of a reporter—she observes but does not become involved. This stage allows the child to choose the activity and may easily move to another level as she becomes more comfortable. Children from other ethic or cultural groups may feel more comfortable watching prior to entering play.

Solitary play

The child plays alone and independently during **solitary play**. She may be close to others but is not aware of their activity. Solitary play dominates the first two years of life as children become fascinated and engaged with toys. Older children may also use solitary play as a method of finding solitude or for the enjoyment of playing alone. Watch an eight-year-old play with small building blocks alone. Her play may be very complex, but she may be seeking privacy and the freedom of choosing her own direction during play. We really cannot know. Though her behaviors are observable, her thoughts are not. She plays alone without referencing others. Recent studies indicate that this may reflect a higher level of play than cooperative play (Frost, Wortham, & Reifel, 2001).

Parallel play

When the child is involved in **parallel play,** the child plays alongside other children but does not engage them in conversation. The child may choose similar toys, but will not engage the other children who are in the area. This play is typical of preschoolers and may serve as a precursor for group play. It is interesting to watch this sort of play as the child may mirror what the other child does, yet never say a word.

These children are engaged in associative play.

Associative play

During **associative play,** the child will play with other children. Conversation will occur as materials are borrowed or loaned. Though they may be playing with blocks, there is no attempt to form a group structure. They are content to work on their own creations. They may be in the house area, but they have their own script. This sets the stage for cooperative play.

Cooperative play

Cooperative play occurs when the child plays in a group that has shared goals. This involves complex social organization that may include negotiation, division of labor, differentiated role taking, and organization of play themes. This usually results in very sophisticated play and is often evident in kindergarten and primary grades. Originally viewed as the highest level of play, this may allow children who are less mature to follow the leadership of others mindlessly. This role in a group may require less maturity than self-selected solitary or associative play.

Looking at children at play provides a source of information about children that may aid in developing a profile of the child. A chart useful for recording social interactions during play is included in Figure 1–3.

FIGURE 1–3   Social Play

Observations	1st Observation	2nd Observation	3rd Observation
Unoccupied behavior Not involved in play, wanders around room.			
Onlooker behavior Observing but just watching, not playing.			
Solitary play Plays alone.			
Parallel play Plays beside other children.			
Associative play Plays with other children.			
Cooperative play Plays together as a group.			
Other			

Narrative _____

_____

_____

Source: Adapted from Parten (1932).

■ Contexts of Play

The characteristics of play and observable behaviors associated with play are affected by **context**. That is, factors such as culture, gender, and age affect what children do during play. "The context is conceptualized as a transaction between children and their environments" (Pelligrini & Boyd, 1993). Bronfenbrenner's (2000) ecological model provides a systematic approach for organizing the framework (Pelligrini & Boyd, 1993). The ecological system includes the microsystem, macrosystem, exosystem, mesosystem, and chronosystem. These are explained in terms of the impact on the play of infants, preschoolers, and primary-age children.

Microsystem

Microsystems are systems that surround the individual and are embedded in the macrosystem and exosystem. Factors that impact the child's play include the family, school, after-school programs, neighborhood, and other community events. For example, infants primarily engage in play and exploration for the first two years of their life. Factors in the microsystem that affect infant play include the relationship between the parent(s) and child, the early educator and child, church groups, and neighborhood. Infant play will be impacted by adults who care for them. Preschoolers will also be affected by adults. Toys and materials for play will also impact their pretend play. Primary-age children are influenced by peers, adults, parents, and the neighborhood. At this age, peers have a great influence and can impact their play both indoors and outdoors. Friends influence whether the child chooses to play computer games or outdoor rough-and-tumble play. Generally, many of the factors that alter play are in the microsystem.

Macrosystem

The **macrosystem** is composed of the larger systems of attitudes and ideology of the culture. This includes traditions, beliefs, and values. For example, Americans view the use of plastic shopping bags differently from their counterparts in Europe. In America, shoppers purchase their groceries and assume that the market will supply the container or bag to carry their purchases home. In many European countries, it is assumed that shoppers supply the shopping bag for their purchases. Culture and tradition also impact play. For example, attachment patterns that affect play are different in cultures throughout the world. Some cultures spend a lot of time holding babies, some do not. Some cultures have traditions that encourage children to explore and play independently while others value the child staying close to the adult. These values impact play.

Some children in America are socialized to view a police officer as someone who can help and assist them in a time of need. Children who have grown up in a repressive society may hide when a police officer visits the school and may not want to participate in play activities that involve role-playing a police officer. Children who live in the United States are exposed to media violence and have access to war toys. In some Scandinavian countries, media violence is limited and war toys are banned. The attitudes of the group toward violence shapes the children's play.

Exosystem

The **exosystem** includes systems over which one has minimal control. These include policies established by local governments as well as socioeconomic factors. For example, when a school board makes policies that eradicate recess in a system, it affects play. In the same way, children's socioeconomic status impacts their play. Children who have access to toys can play in ways that are different from those who have limited access. The availability of funds impacts the number of toys, museum visits, and trips, and this affects play.

Mesosystem

The **mesosystem** involves interactions between two systems. A child who is forced to leave home due to a government decision or natural disaster may be forced to relocate to a new area. The child may not be able to speak the language in the new preschool. The interactions of these factors modify play.

Chronosystem

The **chronosystem** is the impact of sociocultural factors on the individual child over time. For example, what is the effect of the computer on play at ages four and eight? Looking at changes over time provides additional insight.

■ Adult Interaction

Adults can assume an important role in facilitating play when they understand the importance of contextual factors. Children of Africa, India, or Japan may display play behaviors that reflect their values and beliefs and are very acceptable in the microsystem of the home. They may or may not be as acceptable in a mainstream preschool setting. Understanding play in different cultures requires knowledge of how play occurs in the child's native culture. In the same way, children who have an Asian background may display different observable behaviors during play. Cultural influences affect play behaviors. See Tobin, Wu, and Davidson (1989) for additional information. Early educators who understand the impact of context on observable behaviors are more capable of facilitating play in classrooms with diverse populations.

Some adult behaviors encourage or facilitate play, while others interrupt or stop play. Some elements that support play in most cultures include:

1. a healthy, safe play place
2. schedules that ensure that basic physiological needs are met
3. an array of familiar peers, materials, or other culturally relevant materials
4. adult behaviors that support but do not disrupt play
5. an agreement between the adult and child that play can occur. Signals are often used to indicate that this is a psychologically safe play place.

Specific behaviors that can extend play for children in the United States have been suggested by Klein, Wirth, and Linas (2003, pp. 40–41).

1. Focus on the process (rather than the goal) of play. Ask exploratory questions that help extend the child's play.

2. Elaborate and build on children's play or interests. Make comments, offer new and varied materials.

3. Reflect the emotions children express in their play and actions. This labels and validates children's feelings.

4. Define the problem. Help children learn negotiation skills. Encourage them to think about alternatives.

5. Provide varied materials to encourage exploration and play.

6. Provide open ended materials for play.

■ Play Issues and Trends

Play is a child's life and the means by which he comes to understand the world he lives in.

—*Susan Isaacs, 1933*

Play is valued differently in diverse cultures by groups and subgroups. Play for middle-class Americans is viewed favorably. Many middle-class parents view play as an educational activity and spend a great deal of money on educational toys. For working-class parents, play may be viewed as frivolous. Parents who are struggling to survive may not have the time or energy to encourage play. The views of citizens of other countries are also modified by sociocultural factors. For example, countries in Scandinavia are very committed to play and have extensive playgrounds. At the same time, citizens of Prague and Moscow are trying to rebuild their national economy and infrastructure. Another example can be found in southern Europe. Play permeates the schools of Reggio Emilia, Italy. The schools of Reggio Emilia, Italy, have been recognized for their excellent programs for infants and young children (New, 2003). They are very committed to understanding the child's language for learning. At the same time, children in countries experiencing armed conflict may have little opportunity to play. Understanding that children of parents from different cultures may have different perspectives is imperative for creating a play-based program.

Children with Special Needs

Play is recognized as equally important for children with disabilities or delays (Cook, Tessier, & Klein, 2000). Programs have been developed that encourage play among children with special needs (Bricker & Woods Cripe, 1992). A play-based assessment approach has been developed that can be used with all children. The Council for Exceptional Children/Division of Early Childhood (CEC/DEC) and the National Association for the Education of Young Children (NAEYC) have collaborated to develop guidelines that will benefit all children (Wolery & Bredekamp, 1994). This movement has affected classroom play and the results will be explored further in Chapter 8.

Technology

Advances in technology have changed play in some preschool and primary classrooms. The changes range from very positive to less than positive. For example, in some classrooms, children sit with a friend and interact with the most current video program, stop and surf the Web for an answer to a question, and then return to the video program. They create books and reports with available technology and communicate with other children around the globe. At the other end of the spectrum, some classrooms have computer programs about blocks, but no blocks. There are numerous concerns about the effect of technology on play and these are discussed further in Chapter 10.

Obstacles to Play

The value of play in the lives of young children has been recognized by global organizations. The United Nations Convention on the Rights of the Child (1989) recognized play as a necessary part of the human existence. Children throughout the world play in different languages and in different ways, but they all play. Concern that the child's right to play was at risk was expressed on an international level by the International Association for the Child's Right to Play over a decade ago (Guddemi & Jambor, 1992). Unfortunately, this situation has changed little. Today, four obstacles to play include:

1. Poverty and violence

Poor children who are working to sustain their own life and families do not have time or energy to play. Poverty anywhere leads to a need for life-sustaining activities such as planting or child care rather than play. Random acts of violence in inner-city and suburban neighborhoods create unsafe situations for children. Streets are quiet when children are neither seen nor heard.

2. *Changing cultural values*

Underdeveloped and highly industrialized countries both value work and view play as frivolous. Children in many underdeveloped countries are often expected to work, not play. In the same way, children in highly industrialized countries are often expected to take lessons and attend activities that will better prepare them to contribute to society and the marketplace. Young preschoolers who regularly participate in the beauty contest circuit may not have opportunities to play.

The media has also changed children's play. Typically, children in America spend over 35 hours a week in front of a television, movie, video game, or computer screen (Levin, 2003). When visiting with a group of teachers from Brazil, the author inquired about the level of play in their country, thinking that they might be spared from the intrusion of television. Their response was surprising. They expressed the same concerns as teachers and parents in America. They said that children are in school all day and in front of the television or playing video games after school. They thought children in rural villages might play more than children in urban settings. The answer was so similar to one given to the author by a group of teachers in the United States that it seemed surreal.

3. *Inadequate space*

Places for play are disappearing in some neighborhoods. It is not just lack of space but also the quality of the space that creates concern. Countries that have playground regulations that set standards for healthy, safe playgrounds include the United States, Canada, Scandinavia, Germany, Netherlands, United Kingdom, Australia, and New Zealand; Singapore, Hong Kong, and Malaysia have begun efforts to regulate playgrounds (Christiansen, 1997).

Using a report rating scale, The National Program for Playground Safety rated playgrounds in the United States as a "C." More than 200,000 injuries occur each year on playgrounds (Tinsworth & McDonald, 2001). For information on the rating of individual states, see the Web site for the National Program for Playground Safety that is listed at the end of the chapter.

4. *Overemphasis on academics*

Some schools have deleted recess from their curriculum. Fewer kindergarten classrooms are set up for play, and too many look like first-grade classrooms. Parents have responded by petitioning and advocating for recess in their local school systems. These grassroot efforts are attempting to change the current setting, but much more support is needed. Organizations like the International Play Association for the Child's Right to Play, The Association for the Study of Play, The National Association for the Education of Young Children and their interest group, Play, Policy, and Practice, are professional groups that are trying to make a difference in the quality and quantity of play in the lives of young children.

■ Support for Play

Mankind owes the child the best it has to give.
—United Nations Declaration on the Rights of the Child, 1959
Marcy Guddemi and Tom Jambor, 1990

Support for play can be found in Article 31 of The Convention of the Rights of the Child that was ratified by the General Assembly of the United Nations on November 20, 1989. It states:

1. Parties shall recognize the right of the child to rest and leisure, to engage in play and recreational activities appropriate to the age of the child, and to participate freely in cultural life and the arts.

2. Parties shall respect and promote the right of the child to participate fully in cultural and artistic life and shall encourage the provision of appropriate and equal opportunities for cultural, artistic, recreational, and leisure activity.

In the United States, Article 31 is supported by the National Association for the Education of Young Children (NAEYC). This is the largest organization of child care providers and educators in the United States. With over 120,000 members, it continues to grow and function as an advocate for children. At the date of publication, Article 31 has not been ratified.

■ Play Research

Perhaps the most powerful support for play can be found in research. Studies of play generally fall into two categories. One view is that play is progress and contributes to development. Those who advocate this perspective believe that play is necessary for human growth and development (Piaget, 1962b; Scales, Almy, Nicolopoulou, & Ervin-Tripp, 1991;

Vygotsky, 1978). Another perspective recommends the study of play as a holistic process. Those who hold this view believe that play is valuable in and of itself (Erikson, 1940). They believe that play creates "a model situation in which aspects of the past are relived, the present represented and renewed, and the future anticipated" (Erikson, 1977). Those who hold this view advocate a view of play that sees play as a unifying process that unites the mind, body, and spirit (Levy, 1978).

The idea of using play to facilitate learning originated with Froebel (1887) and is still used as a way to facilitate development in the preschool years (Trawick-Smith, 1994; Van Hoorn, Nourot, Scales, & Alward, 1993). This text uses a similar vein of thought and considers play as beneficial for progress. Play will be examined as innate and holistic; beneficial for growth, development, and society; and as a stimulus for learning in early education. Heeding the advice of Sutton-Smith (1998) and Elkind (2003), a special effort will be made to not romanticize play or view it as the perfect answer for all educational woes. Rather, early education has room for both planned and unplanned play. If children learn best through play that dominates their age and level, adults should use this as a tool for learning. Play and inquiry-based learning would certainly make a better combination than worksheet skill and drill overkill. The goal of this text is to encourage a view of play that views play as a medium for learning and embraces play as a natural activity that enhances the child's quality of life. Classrooms have room for both and children need time to engage in both structured and unstructured play.

■ PlayScape Reflections

The vignette at the beginning of the chapter depicts a child joyfully sliding while an adult watches. The slide serves as the provocation. After reading this chapter, you may realize that children, like other animals that are intelligent, play. It is apparent that children have an almost innate need to play. The look of joy on the child's face reflects the characteristics of play that include pleasure. Observable behaviors suggest that she is engaged in solitary play while an adult serves as a monitor or guide within a microcosmic setting. Equally interesting is the support for play evident in this scenario, which suggests that factors in the ecosystem are working together to support play. The community supports play by providing a place to play and the family supports play by providing time to supervise play and ensure safety. The value placed on play is evident in the child's expression.

■ Summary

An overview of play was provided in this chapter and sets the stage for the study of play in classrooms. Two major influences inform the study of play. One is the study of play as progress. Play contributes to and fosters human growth and development. The second influence views play as valuable in and of itself. Both views are equally worthwhile and valuable. Play was defined in terms of dispositions, context, and observable behaviors. Dispositions or characteristics of play include 1) voluntary, 2) requires active involvement, 3) symbolic, 4) free of external rules, 5) focuses on action rather than outcomes, and 6) pleasurable. The context for play includes the microsystem, macrosystem, exosystem, mesosystem, and chronosystem. Observable behaviors include play in the cognitive domain and social domain. Knowledge of attributes of exploration, play, and playfulness can enhance the educator's ability to cultivate a climate for play. Play occurs throughout the world and reflects the unique characteristics of individual cultures. Though obstacles to play exist, advocacy groups can overcome these barriers. Advocacy efforts can be enhanced through the use of this book.

■ Key Terms

Associative play
Chronosystem
Constructive play
Context
Cooperative play
Exosystem
Exploration
Fortuitous combinations

Functional play
Games with rules
Intentional combinations
Macrosystem
Mere practice play
Mesosystem
Microsystem
Mother-ground

Onlooker behavior
Parallel play
Playfulness
Practice play
Sensorimotor play
Solitary play
Symbolic play
Unoccupied behavior

■ Helpful Web Sites and Technology Resources

◆ **International Play Association (IPA/USA)**
   http://www.ipa.org   The International Play Association is an international group that is committed to protecting the child's right to play. A branch is active in the United States and can be found on this Web site. They have a very active advocacy movement for recess for all children.

◆ **National Association for the Education of Young Children (NAEYC)**
   http://www.naeyc.org   The National Association for the Education of Young Children is the largest group of early childhood educators in the

world. The Web site has links to several valuable sites. Conferences and state affiliates are located on this site. This site includes information for joining the organization and receiving the journal, *Young Children*.

◆ **National Lekotek Center**
http://www.lekotek.org   National Lekotek Center makes play accessible to children with disabilities. Play and learning centers for children and families are located throughout the country.

◆ **United Nations Interagency Children's Emergency Fund (UNICEF)**
http://www.unicef.org   UNICEF is an organization designed to support and improve the quality of health and life for children throughout the world. As part of the United Nations, it serves children throughout the world.

■ Activities

1. **InClass Lab**

   A. Create a cartoon that depicts either play or exploration. How can you tell that it is play? How can you distinguish exploration? How you can use your knowledge of both to encourage play?

   B. Two children who have Russian ancestry entered the kindergarten classroom. Mary, the kindergarten teacher observed their play. She noticed that they played with each other, played in the home area, and did not interact with other children. Based on your knowledge of contexts, which systemic factors are affecting their play? Explain your answer.
      1. Microsystem
      2. Macrosystem
      3. Exosystem
      4. Mesosystem
      5. Chronosystem

2. **Research and Inquiry**

   A. Write down your favorite memory of play. Ask an older relative or neighbor to recall her favorite play experience. How are these alike? How are they different? Talk to others who have also compared their play with those of their grandparents. Are there are any similar trends?

   B. Observe a group of preschool children in a child care center or school for an hour. Write down everything that you observe. Now observe a group of children in an informal setting such as a park.

Again write down everything that you see. What behaviors were similar? What behaviors were different?

C. Visit a center for two hours. What are the adults doing to support play in this environment? What factors in the microsystem, macrosystem, mesosystem, exosystem, and chronosystem affect play?

D. Interview at least two parents of young children from another culture. What similarities do they see between their play and their child's play. What differences do they see?

3. Service Learning

A. Volunteer in a preschool for two hours. Be sure to follow center policy in terms of parking, dress, and interactions with the children. After the visit, write down as much as you can remember about the play that occurred in the classroom. Did you see support for play? Did you see children play? If so, describe their play. Which children engaged in the most play? Which children did not play? How do you distinguish play from nonplay? Does this fit with what you have read in this textbook and other sources?

B. Find a center that needs assistance repairing materials in the center. Volunteer to assist in repairing the materials and toys.

C. Volunteer to assist in a local park or playground on Saturday morning. Investigate the role of playground monitors in England. Would this be feasible in America? Why or why not?

D. Locate local museums and public resources that encourage play. Offer to support their facility through a service learning project. Some groups create special displays in children's museums.

4. Family Connections

A. Ask a preschool teacher to distribute Figure 1–4 to parents in her class. Ask them to chart how much time their children have for play during one week. The teacher can hold a meeting with parents to discuss the results of their survey and their concerns about their children. Some classes may want to develop a research project. Other classes may want to plan a meeting to discuss television alternatives such as Family Game Night.

5. Play Advocacy

A. Find out about play advocacy groups in your state. Are there recess advocates? Are there parent groups? Who are the play advocates in your state and local region?

FIGURE 1–4   Play Activities Table

Child's name	Play time indoors or outdoors	Time spent in other activities such as television or videos
Monday		
Tuesday		
Wednesday		
Thursday		
Friday		
Sunday		
Total		

How much time does your child have to play? _____

How much time does your child spend in other activities? _____

B. Distribute this poem to local centers and libraries. Though no source is generally attributed to the poem, a version has been distributed at numerous museums such as the St. Louis Children's Museum. This poem has been altered by this author to remove a negative sentence about reading books.

> I tried to teach my child with words,
> They passed her by often unheard.
> I tried to teach my child with flashcards,
> She looked as though I was marred.
> I tried to teach my child with worksheets,
> She yawned and left them incomplete.
> Despairingly, I turned aside;
> "How shall I teach this child?" I cried.
> Into my hand she put the key,
> "Come," she said, "Play with me."
>
> —Anonymous
> Modified by Dorothy Sluss.

■ References

Ablon, S. (2001). Continuities of tongues: A developmental perspective on the role of play in child and adult psychoanalytic process. *Journal of Clinical Psychoanalysis, 10* (3–4), 345–365.

Barnett, L. (1990). Playfulness: Definition, design, and measurement. *Play & Culture, 3,* 319–336.

Bateson, G. (1972). *Steps to an ecology of mind.* New York: Ballantine.

Bekoff, M., & Jamison, D. (Eds.). (1996). *Readings in animal cognition.* Cambridge, MA: MIT Press.

Bergen, D. (Ed.) (1988). *Play as a medium for learning and development: A handbook for theory and practice.* Portsmouth, NH: Heinemann.

Bredekamp, S., & Copple, C. (1997). *Developmentally appropriate practice in early childhood programs.* Washington, DC: National Association for the Education of Young Children.

Bricker, D., & Woods Cripe, J. (1992). *An activity-based approach to early intervention.* Baltimore, MD: Brooks.

Bronfenbrenner, U. (1979). Foreword. In P. Chance (Ed.), *Learning through play.* New York: Gardner.

Bronfenbrenner, U. (2000). Ecological theory. In A. Kazdin (Ed.), *Encyclopedia of psychology* (pp. 129–133). Washington, DC: American Psychology Association and Oxford University Press.

Brown, S. (1995). Through the lens of play. *ReVision: A Journal of Consciousness and Transformation* (USA), *17* (4), 4–8.

Caplan, F., & Caplan, T. (1973). *The power of play.* New York: Anchor Press/Doubleday.

Christiansen, M. (1997). International perspectives of playground safety. *Parks and Recreation, 32* (4), 100–101.

Christie, J., & Johnsen, P. (1987). Reconceptualizing constructive play: A review of the empirical literature. *Merrill-Palmer Quarterly, 33* (4), 439–452.

Cook, R., Tessier, A., & Klein, M. (2000). *Adapting early childhood curricula for children in inclusive settings.* (5th ed.), Columbus, OH: Merrill.

Edwards, C. (2000). Children's play in cross-cultural perspective: A new look at the Six Cultures study. *Cross-Cultural Research, The Journal of Comparative Social Science, 34* (4), 318–338.

Elkind, D. (1981). *The hurried child: Growing up too fast too soon.* Reading, MA: Addison-Wesley.

Elkind, D. (1987). *Miseducation: Preschoolers at risk.* New York: Alfred Knopf.

Elkind, D. (2003). Thanks for the memory: The lasting value of true play. *Young Children, 58* (3), 46–52.

Erikson, E. (1940). Studies and interpretation of play. Part I: Clinical observations of play disruption in young children. *Genetic Psychology Monograph, 22,* 557–671.

Erikson, E. (1977). *Toys and reason.* New York: Norton.

Evans, K. (2001). Holding on to many threads: Emergent literacy in a classroom of lu Mien children. In E. Jones, K. Evans, & K. Rencken, *The lively kindergarten: Emergent curriculum in action,* (pp. 59–76). Washington, DC: NAEYC.

Fagen, R. M. (1995). Animal play, games of angels, biology, and Brian. In A. D. Pelligrini (Ed.), *The future of play theory*, (pp. 23–44). Albany: SUNY Press.

Fein, G. (1981). Pretend play in childhood: An integrative review. *Child Development, 52,* 1095–1118.

Freud, S. (1959). Creative writers and daydreaming. In J. Strackey (Ed.), *The standard edition of the complete psychological works of Sigmund Freud* (Vol. IX). London: Hogarth. (Originally published in 1908).

Freud, S. (1961). *Beyond the pleasure principle.* New York: Norton. (Originally published in 1920).

Froebel, F. (1887). *The education of man.* New York: Appleton.

Fromberg, D. (2002). *Play and meaning in early childhood education.* Boston: Allyn and Bacon.

Frost, J., Wortham, S., & Reifel, S. (2001). *Play and child development.* Upper Saddle River, NJ: Merrill/Prentice Hall.

Guddemi, M., & Jambor, T. (1992). *A right to play: Proceedings of the American Affiliate of the International Association for the Child's Right to Play.* Little Rock, AK: Southern Early Childhood Association.

Hale-Benson, J. E. (1986). *Black children: Their roots, culture, and learning styles.* Baltimore: Johns Hopkins University Press.

Howes, C. (1992). *The collaborative construction of pretend play: Social pretend play functions.* Albany: SUNY Press.

Hughes, M., & Hutt, C. (1979). Heart-rate correlates of childhood activities: Play exploration, problem solving and day dreaming. *Biological Psychology, 8,* 253–263.

Huizinga, J. (1955). *Homo Ludens: A study of the play element in culture.* Boston: Beacon Press.

Isaacs, S. (1933). *Social development in young children.* Oxford: Harcourt, Brace.

Isenberg, J. & Jalongo, M. (2001). *Creative expression and play in early childhood.* Columbus, OH: Merrill.

Jenkinson, S. (2001). *The genius of play: Celebrating the spirit of childhood.* Gloucester, UK: Hawthorn Press.

Kagan, J. (1977). The uses of cross-cultural research in early development. In P. H. Leiderman, S. R. Tulkin, & A. Rosenfeld (Eds.), *Culture and infancy: Variation in the human experience*, (pp. 271–286). New York: Academic Press.

Kirn, W., & Cole, W. (2001, April 22). What ever happened to play? *Time*, 56–58.

Klein, T., Wirth, D., & Linas, K. (2003). Play: Children's context for development. *Young Children, 58,* 38–46.

Klugman, E. (1995). *Play, policy, & practice.* St. Paul: Redleaf.

Lancy, D. (1996). *Playing on the mother-ground.* New York: Guilford.

Landreth, G. L. (1993). Self-expressive communication. In C. E. Schaefer (Ed.), *The therapeutic power of play*, (pp. 41–63). Northvale, NJ: Jason Aronson.

Landreth, G., & Homeyer, L. (1998). Play as the language of children's feelings. In D. P. Frongberg and D. M. Bergen (Eds.), *Play from birth to twelve and beyond: Contexts, perspectives, and meanings.* (pp. 193–198). New York: Garland.

Levin, D. (2003). *Teaching young children in violent times.* Washington, DC: National Association for the Education of Young Children.

Levy, J. (1978). *Play behavior.* New York: Wiley.

Liberman, J. (1965). Playfulness and divergent thinking: An investigation of their relationship at the kindergarten level. *Journal of Creative Behavior, 1,* 391–397.

Merriam-Webster's Collegiate Dictionary, Eleventh Edition. (2003). Springfield, MA: Author.

New, R. (2003). Reggio Emila: New ways to think about schooling. *Educational Leadership, 60* (7), 34–39.

Northern, S. (2002, March 15). Let us play. *Times Educational Supplement*, I 4472, *14* (2).

Parten, M. (1932). Social participation among preschool children. *Journal of Abnormal Psychology, 27,* 243–269.

Pelligrini, A. D., & Boyd, B. (1993). The role of play in early childhood development and education: Issues in definition and function. In B. Spodek (Ed.), *Handbook of research on the education of young children* (pp. 105–121). New York: Macmillan.

Piaget, J. (1962a). The stages of the intellectual development of the child. In S. Harrison & J. McDermott (Eds.), *Childhood psychopathology* (167–176). New York: International Universities Press.

Piaget, J. (1962b). *Play, dreams, and imitation in childhood.* New York: Norton. (Originally published in 1951).

Piaget, J. (1980). Foreword. In C. Kamii and R. DeVries, *Group games in early education.* Washington, DC: National Association for the Education of Young Children.

Rogers, C. (2003). Personal communication to Dorothy Sluss, October.

Rogers, C. S., Impara, J. C., Frary, R. B., Harris, T., Meeks, A., Semantic-Lauth, S., & Reynolds, M. R. (1998). Measuring playfulness: Development of the Child Behaviors Inventory of playfulness. In M. Duncan, G. Chick, & A. Aycock (Eds.), S. Reifel (Series Ed.), *Play and culture studies: Vol. 1 Diversions and divergences in fields of play* (pp. 151–168). Greenwich, CT: Ablex.

Rogers, C. S., Impara, J. C., Frary, R. B., Harris, T., Meeks, A., Semanic-Lauth, S., & Reynolds, M. R. (1999). *Measuring playfulness: Development of the Child Behaviors Inventory of playfulness.* Presentation at The Association for the Study of Play Annual Conference, Santa Fe, NM.

Rogers, C. S., & Sawyers, J. K. (1988). *Play in the lives of children.* Washington, DC: National Association for the Education of Young Children.

Rogers, C. S., & Sluss, D. J. (1999). Revisiting Erikson's views on Einstein's play and inventiveness. In S. Reifel (Series Ed.), *Play and culture studies: Vol. 2 Play contents revisited* (pp. 3–24). Greenwich, CT: Ablex.

Rubin, K. H., Fein, G., & Vandenberg, B. (1983). Play. In E. M. Hetherington (Ed.), P. H. Mussen (Series Ed.), *Handbook of child psychology: Vol.4, Socialization, personality, and social development* (pp. 693–774). New York: Wiley.

Scales, B., Almy, M., Nicolopoulou, A., & Ervin-Tripp, S. (1991). *Play and the social context of development in early care and education.* New York: Teachers College Press, Columbia University.

Schlosberg, H. (1947). The concept of play. *Psychological Review, 54,* 229–231.

Shore, R. (1997). *Rethinking the brain: New insights into early development.* New York: Families and Work Institute.

Smilansky, S. (1968). *The effects of sociodramatic play on disadvantaged preschool children.* New York: Wiley.

Smilansky, S. (1990). Sociodramatic play: Its relevance to behavior and achievement in school. In E. Klugman and S. Smilansky (Eds.), *Children's Play and Learning: Perspectives and Policy Implications.* NY: Teachers College Press, Columbia University.

Sutton-Smith, B. (1982). Play theory and the cruel play of the nineteenth century. In F. E. Manning (Ed.), *The world of play.* West Point, NY: Leisure Press.

Sutton-Smith, B. (1997). *The ambiguity of play.* Cambridge, MA: Harvard University Press.

Sutton-Smith, B. (January 1998). *How do children play with toys anyway?* Unpublished address to the Culture of Toys Conference, Emory University, Atlanta, GA.

Tinsworth, D. and McDonald, J. (April 2001). *Special study: Injuries and deaths associated with children's playground equipment.* Washington, DC: U. S. Consumer Product Safety Commission.

Tobin, J., Wu, D., & Davidson, D. (1989). *Preschool in three cultures: Japan, China, and the United States.* New Haven, CT: Yale University Press.

Trawick-Smith, J. (1994). *Interactions in the classroom: Facilitating play in the early years.* New York: Merrill.

Vandenberg, B. (1982). Play: A concept in need of a definition. In D. J. Pepler & K. H. Rubin (Eds.), *The play of children: Current theory and research* (pp. 15–21). Basel, Switzerland: Karger AG.

Van Hoorn, J. Nourot, P., Scales, B., & Alward, K. (1993). *Play at the center of the curriculum.* New York: Merrill.

Vygotsky, L. (1978). *Mind in society: The development of higher psychological processes.* Cambridge, MA: Harvard University Press.

Whiting, B. B. (Ed.) (1963). *Six cultures: Studies of child rearing.* New York: Wiley.

Whiting, B., & Edwards, C. P. (1988). *Children of different worlds: The formation of social behavior.* Cambridge, MA: Harvard University Press.

Wilson, E. O. (1975). *Sociobiology.* Cambridge: MA: Belknap.

Wolery, M., & Bredekamp, S. (1994). Developmentally appropriate practices and young children with disabilities: Contextual issues in the discussion. *Journal of Early Intervention, 18* (4), 331–341.

CHAPTER 2

Classical and Current Theories of Play

You are troubled at seeing him spend his early years in doing nothing. What! Is it nothing to be happy? Is it nothing to skip, to play, to run around all day long? Never in his life will he be so busy as now.

—Jean-Jacques Rousseau, 1762

Chapter Overview

Over two thousand years ago, play was recognized as a valuable part of childhood. Since its first acknowledgement, play has been examined by a multitude of scholars and researchers who have explored the underlying need of animals and humans to play. Classical theories of play have provided a foundation for modern theories of play. Today, some postmodern scholars even question the study of play. Studying the history of play provides a foundation for understanding play in today's classroom.

Objectives

After reading this chapter you should be able to:

- ◆ Understand the early foundations of play research.
- ◆ Describe the classical theories of play.
- ◆ Recognize the influence of classical theories on today's scholarship.
- ◆ Describe the modern theories of play.
- ◆ Compare and contrast classical and current theories of play.
- ◆ Recognize major play scholars and their contributions to the field.

37

PlayScape

Today was a long day. One of her coworkers didn't show up for work on the early shift and Juanita had to work the main counter. In addition, her car wouldn't start and she had to get someone to bring her home. Thank goodness, they did not mind going by the Head Start center to pick up Roberto, her youngest. Now she could have some time together with Roberto before the older children came home from school . . .

Roberto walked across the floor, jumped upon the couch, and began to tumble. Juanita saw him as he tumbled off the couch and onto the floor. "Roberto, where do you get so much energy? You never run down. Let's go outside for awhile." As Juanita walked to the playground with Roberto, she thought about how much he was like his older brothers. He loved to swing, to slide, and to run. She always enjoyed these times when she could watch him play. She had only been outside for a short while when the bus stopped and the eight-year-old twins ran from the bus, "Roberto, let's play!" As much as she cherished her time with Roberto, she knew that he also needed time with his brothers. They would run, jump, and maybe, even play-fight. Then they would be ready to work on their homework and go to bed. But first, they needed to play.

Play Provocation

Why do children play? What is their provocation to play? Do they even need a provocation to play? In this playscape, the couch served as the child's provocation to jump and the playground served as an impetus for running and chasing. But why do children engage in this type of behavior? Has play always been a part of a child's life? Examining past studies of play can help us understand the child's need to play.

■ Early Influences

Nature wants children to be children before they are men. If we deliberately depart from this order we shall get premature fruits which are neither ripe nor well flavored and which soon decay. We shall have youthful sages and grown up children. Childhood has ways of seeing, thinking, and feeling peculiar to itself; nothing can be more foolish than to seek to substitute our ways for them. I should as soon expect a child of ten to be five feet in height as to be possessed of judgement. (pp. 38, 39)

—Jean-Jacques Rousseau, 1762

Many different cultures around the world have been aware of the role of play in the lives of young children, but the role of play was first acknowledged in print more than 2,000 years ago. Plato (427–347 BC) was one of the first philosophers to discuss play. He stated, ". . . the future builder must play at building . . . and those who have the care of their education should provide them when young with mimic tools" (Lascarides & Hinitz, 2002, p. 10). Though little is known about how children played prior to and in the early Greek civilization, Plato believed that understanding play was critical for understanding the human's role in the world. He even discussed the child's "play leap" that occurs when children jump, skip, and dance (Jenkinson, 2001). This initial recognition of play as a valuable part of the human experience provided the first step in laying the foundation for the study of play (Spariousu, 1989). It is a loss that we have little historical information about how children played in other cultures throughout the world. Because we only have written sources, we will review what has been recorded about play. An overview of early play studies is available in Figure 2–1.

Historically, children throughout Europe were viewed as miniature adults who should work alongside their parents. Their lives were harsh and they had to carve out play on their own. With the onset of the Renaissance, children and play were viewed differently. One philosopher who studied human cognition was the Czech Johann Comenius. His views changed perceptions of how children develop their knowledge of the world.

Comenius

One of the most influential philosophers in education also influenced the study of play. From his home in the former Czech republic, Johann Amos Comenius (1592–1670) wrote about his belief that humans were born craving knowledge and goodness. Rather than beating information into

FIGURE 2–1 History of Early Play Studies

Early Scholars	Contribution to Study of Play
Johann Amos Comenius	Children are innately curious and different materials should be used to encourage their creativity.
John Locke	Children are a blank slate and can learn through play when adults use toys to teach concepts.
Jean-Jacques Rousseau	Children are innately good and nature is a primary force in learning.
Johann Heinrich Pestalozzi	Children should be free to explore and they learn through action (learn by doing).
Friedrich Froebel	Children learn through play.

the child's head, he believed that learning should align with how children acquire knowledge. Comenius believed that curiosity should be encouraged and that children were the future of society. The familiar adage, "children are the future" may sound trite and familiar now, but it was a major departure from the commonly held view of the child at that time. He stated that children under five should be allowed to play freely and noted that, "They are delighted to construct little houses, and to erect walls of clay, chips, wood, or stone, thus displaying an architectural genius" (1896). Because he believed that children learn differently and should be encouraged, not threatened, he wrote the first children's book, *Orbis Sensualium Pictus* (The World Illustrated, 1658/1968). His view of the child as innately curious laid the foundation for those who view play as beneficial.

Locke

I know of a person of great quality . . . who by pasting on 6 vowels (for in our language y *is one) on the 6 sides of a die and remaining 18 consonants on the sides of the 3 other dice, has made this a play for his children that he shall win who at one cast throws most words on these 4 dice.*

—John Locke, 1692/1884

John Locke (1632–1704), an Englishman who was exiled in Europe for several years, has been credited with viewing children as basically a blank slate or tabula rasa on which knowledge is written. In his book, *Some Thoughts Concerning Education*, Locke (1692) stated that his view of play was important for the development, of not only mental processes, but also the child's health and spirit. Though he did not view play as a medium for learning, he believed play was a positive force for overall health. Locke's work is notable because he was the first to talk about the interaction between adults and children during play with toys. In terms of play, Locke contributes to our knowledge of play by being one of the first to recognize the importance of adults and toys in the child's learning process.

Rousseau

In contrast, Jean-Jacques Rousseau (1712–1778), a Swiss who lived in France, believed that humans were born innately good. His view of the child as the noble savage fostered the theory that nature is responsible for development and influenced not only scholars in France but also in other European countries. His book *Emile* (1762) focused on facilitating the

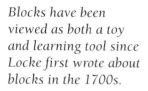

Blocks have been viewed as both a toy and learning tool since Locke first wrote about blocks in the 1700s.

development of emotions rather than instruction. Encouraging children to learn through actions was consistent with his view of how children develop. He believed that they would naturally grow and seek knowledge if not deterred by society. Throughout his writings, he championed the benefits of play and cautioned against pushing children into adulthood too quickly. Rousseau believed the child's interaction with the outdoors and nature was critical for the child's development.

Rousseau's view of play provided a basis for viewing the child and the child's interactions with nature as a natural way of learning. He was the first to recognize different levels of child development and provided the foundation for the stages of play. Rousseau's concern about the loss of innocence in the eighteenth century is still heard in today's highly technological society.

Pestalozzi

Johann Heinrich Pestalozzi (1746–1827), an Italian, also influenced play scholarship. He believed that children should be free to explore and draw their own conclusions. Those who ascribe to free play share his belief. Pestalozzi's view of the goodness of human beings went well beyond those expressed by Rousseau. Pestalozzi's work is most notable because he was the first to discuss action as a way of learning. Rousseau provided the philosophy for the curriculum that Pestalozzi turned into a school. He is credited with being one of the first to move from theory to action. Whereas Rousseau and Locke wrote about their ideas, Pestalozzi developed theory-based practice. In 1801, he published *How Gertrude Teaches Her Children* which describes his views of educating young children.

Froebel

A child who plays and works thoroughly, with perseverance, until physical fatigue forbids, will surely be a thorough, determined person, capable of self-sacrifice.

—*Friedrich Froebel, 1887/1902*

Friedrich Froebel (1782–1852) was a German who was influenced by Rousseau and Pestalozzi. Both Rousseau and Pestalozzi believed in the effectiveness of a permissive school atmosphere and interaction with the natural world. Froebel built on Pestalozzi's work and developed a more complex philosophy of education for young children. Froebel's educational pedagogy was based on four basic ideas: free self-expression, creativity, social participation, and motor expression. His *gifts* were recognized as among the first hands-on teaching materials.

For Froebel, play was viewed as the way children learn. In his book, *The Education of Man* (1826/1902), he stated that:

> The mind grows by self revelation. In play the child ascertains what he can do, discovers his possibilities of will and thought by exerting his power spontaneously. In work he follows a task prescribed for him by another, and doesn't reveal his own proclivities and inclinations; but another's. In play he reveals his own original power. (p. 233)

Froebel is perhaps the individual most responsible for the idea of nurturing play. He also moved the study of play from a discussion of ideas to a curriculum that could be transmitted to other cultures. Many of his students took his kindergarten curriculum to America. Though few are aware of the history, his book influenced the use of music and fingerplays in kindergarten. Many who sing the song "Pat-a-Cake" are unaware that Froebel (1895) recommended this song in the 1800s.

The concept of play as curriculum was initiated by Froebel when he connected play and education. Froebel believed that the object lesson could be extended by specific objects. He called these "gifts" because they would lead to discovery and new insights. He also discussed occupations for the child. The major difference between gifts and occupations is that the gifts were intended to foster the child's knowledge of the world. Occupations, in contrast, were designed to foster skills. The occupations recommended by Froebel (1895) included:

- ◆ **solids:** Plastic clay, cardboard work, and wood-carving
- ◆ **surfaces:** Paper-folding, paper-cutting, parquetry, and painting
- ◆ **lines:** Interlacing, intertwining, weaving, thread games, embroidery, and drawing
- ◆ **points:** Stringing beads and buttons; perforating
- ◆ **reconstruction:** Reconstruct the surface and solid synthetically from the point. It consists of softened peas or wax pellets and sharpened sticks or straws. (p. 287)

Today, his gifts (see Figure 2–2) would be called toys and his occupations, constructive play or crafts.

Classical Theories of Play

As the study of play progressed, western theorists attempted to understand the role of play using a more scientific approach. Influenced by Charles Darwin's work, they looked at play in terms of biological and physiological functions. Four theories reflect this influence: (1) surplus energy theory of play, (2) relaxation and recreation theories of play, (3) practice (or pre-exercise) theory of play, and (4) recapitulation theory of play. For a more in-depth treatment of these theories, see Rubin, Fein, and Vandenberg (1983).

Surplus Energy Theory of Play

This theory is based on the notion that children play because they have too much energy and play will rid them of the excess. Friedrich von Schiller (1892/1954), a German play scholar, was the first to put forth this idea. He included animals and young humans in his theory. He believed that both animals and humans have a certain amount of energy necessary for survival. Since the young of both are cared for by others, they have excess energy. Thus, kittens, puppies, and children play to use up their extra energy. Schiller viewed play as the opposite of work and believed that play provided an outlet for creativity.

Schiller's theory was further supported by Herbert Spencer (1873), a British philosopher who was the first to identify this as the "surplus energy" theory (Rubin, Fein, & Vandenberg, 1983). In an advancing civilization, we do not have to hunt or fish for our food. Since basic survival skills have been met, children have surplus energy. This energy can be used for creative activities. For both Schiller and Spencer, play was an

FIGURE 2–2 Froebel's Gifts

1ˢᵗ Gift: Solids (Ball on String)

Six soft, round spheres with strings that the child can manipulate. These are generally made of different-colored worsted wool and measure about an inch and a half. The round balls can be manipulated by the child, rolled along a surface, or tossed into the air. This shape reflects the round spheres that occur in nature and expresses the idea of individuality—that "we are here" (1895, p. 285).

2ⁿᵈ Gift: Shapes

In contrast with the softness of the first gift, the second gift is hard. Wooden spheres, cubes, and cylinders can be manipulated to demonstrate different properties. These can be manipulated and moved through the air. This expresses the concept of personality.

3ʳᵈ Gift: Number

The third gift consists of eight cubes (1-by-1 inch) that can be put together to form a 2-inch cube ($2 \times 2 \times 2$). This is designed to stimulate self-selected or solitary play.

4ᵗʰ Gift: Extent

The fourth gift expands the notion of the third gift to rectangles. It consists of eight rectangle-shaped blocks ($2 \times 1 \times \frac{1}{2}$) that form a 2-inch cube. This is designed to encourage obedience because it says to the child, "Study us" (p. 286).

5ᵗʰ Gift: Symmetry

A combination of rectangles, squares, half shapes, and quartered shapes, form a 3-inch cube ($3 \times 3 \times 3$). This gift is designed to stimulate an interest in unity and beauty.

6ᵗʰ Gift: Proportion

Twenty-seven brick-shaped blocks, three bisected longitudinally and six bisected transversely, forming a 3-inch cube. Obedience is the goal of this gift as the child controls and manipulates the blocks.

7ᵗʰ Gift: Surfaces

Squares and equilateral triangles that can be used to create designs.

8ᵗʰ Gift: Lines and Circular

The gift of lines is found in straight sticks of various lengths that reflect multiples of the third gift, a 1-inch cube.

Rings reflect knowledge of circular entities. Wooden, metal, or paper rings of various sizes; whole circles, half circles, and quadrants are included.

9ᵗʰ Gift: Points

The ninth gift consists of points such as beans, lentils, or other seeds, leaves, pebbles, pieces of cardboard paper, etc. The child has progressed from the solid to the point. This last gift enables the child to represent the surface and solid with points.

10ᵗʰ Gift: Reconstruction

The child can reconstruct the set of gifts from the solid to the point using sticks and a material for holding them together. See Froebel (1885) for additional details.

---

instinctive behavior that occurred when little energy was required for survival. This view of play appealed to the audience of 1800s.

Criticisms

There are three reasons why scholars no longer recognize the surplus energy theory as a viable theory. First, no research exists to support these claims. This theory was based on the premise that children play until exhausted and then quit, but we all know children who appear to be exhausted and then perk up when they notice something novel. Children in refugee camps have little surplus energy, yet they continue to play. Third, it is not supported by Darwinian knowledge. If all members of a species were engaged in nonproductive activities, the species would disappear. This also places animals and children in one category and this might not be justifiable. Finally, the logic itself does not support the argument. If a young puppy or a young child runs to catch something that is thrown, it can be classified as work or play. If it is work, they are using energy. If it is play, they are ridding themselves of energy. So, the reason for play would also be a reason for work. For many contemporary researchers, this argument is circular and unreasonable (Rubin, Fein, & Vandenberg, 1983).

Current view

Though this theory was developed in the early eighteenth century, remnants of it are alive and well. Those who subscribe to this theory may not be aware that they reflect a surplus energy theory of play. Many adults believe that play allows children to release energy or blow off steam. For example, many parents say, "Go outside and play" and some teachers bemoan the fact that poor weather keeps them inside again. These adults will talk about the child's need to run and get rid of their extra energy—though they have probably never read the surplus energy theory of play!

Relaxation and Recreation Theories of Play

The relaxation and recreation theory was based on the belief that play is necessary to re-energize human cognition. This is the exact opposite of surplus energy theory and originated in Germany in the work of Moritz Lazarus in 1883 (Rubin, Fein, & Vandenberg, 1983). He believed that labor exhausts individuals and they need to play or engage in recreation for leisure or rejuvenation purposes. His work was extended by G. T. W. Patrick in 1916 (Rubin, et al, 1983). Patrick believed that modern occupations that require mental work drain individuals of their energy. He subscribed to the idea that engaging in rigorous recreation restored balance. Hunting, fishing, and other activities necessary for survival in preindustrial society were viewed as the anecdote for fatigue.

Criticisms

There are several reasons why critics dismiss the relaxation/recreation theory. First, if mental work is draining, why do those who engage in physical labor also play? This does not seem rational. Second, there is little research to support this theory.

Current view

This theory has not been substantiated by evidence but tends to have some supporters. Some businesses hold weekend outings that provide employees with an opportunity to engage in more active outdoor activities. The reason this is a sound business practice has little to do with survival versus nonsurvival activities, yet some participants will talk about getting back to nature. They may not subscribe to the theory, but their rationalization is the same.

Practice (or Pre-Exercise) Theory of Play

Practice theory is based on the belief that children's play "serves an adaptive purpose" (Rubin, Fein, & Vandenberg, 1983, p. 696). Groos (1901) believed that children's play provides them with an opportunity to practice adult activities. Groos also thought that children's play changed as they developed and he distinguished different stages of development. While Piaget built on the concept of different developmental levels, he argues against Groos's work in his book, *Play, Dreams and Imitation in Childhood* (1962).

Criticisms

One obvious flaw of Groos's theory is that children may not be able to practice activities for adulthood because they cannot see into the future. Adults who are now using computers in offices may never have seen a computer as a child. Children today are playing with computers but may experience technology as adults that we cannot even imagine today. If play served the function of preparing children to assume certain roles in the future, children would need to be clairvoyant or psychic.

Current view

The idea that play predisposes children to serve in specific roles as adults has a certain amount of appeal even today. This is the rationale used when parents buy four-year-olds golf clubs, fishing lines, or enroll them in tee-ball. The adult may believe that if children engage in certain kinds of play, they will be better prepared to assume this role as an adult. This thinking has consequences that are sometimes tragic. For example, parents who want their children to be prepared to drive a car or motorcycle will sometimes purchase equipment for very young children hoping that they will be able to play with these machines and develop the necessary skills. The problem is very obvious. Some of these children sustain terminal or critical injuries that prevent them from engaging in these activities as adults.

During play, children practice basic components that are later adapted to available technology. Perhaps "flexibility" is the most important thing they practice. Some modern play scholars may not subscribe to the entire theory but still recognize the role of play in preparing children for their role as an adult in today's society (Bruner, Jolly, & Sylva, 1976).

Recapitulation Theory of Play

The most controversial theory is the recapitulation theory of play based on Darwinian theory. It views children as the link between animals and adult human beings. G. Stanley Hall (1916) is generally credited with this theory, though Luther Gulick (1908) made some contributions that are now better recognized due to publicity by the YMCA and Camp Fire Girls. Hall's work has come under a great deal of scrutiny due to Hall's belief in racial recapitulation. His view was criticized by the scientific community when it was published at the turn of the twentieth century. Today his theory is viewed as not only erroneous, but also harmful due to the racist nature of his views. Because Hall believed that children were the missing link, he believed that the entire history of the entire human race could be observed in the child's developing play. He recognized different stages of animal/human development: (1) animal stage (climbing and swinging), (2) savage (hunting, tag), (3) nomad stage (keeping pets), (4) agricultural or patriarchal stage (dolls or sand play), and (5) tribal stage (team games) (Hall, 1916). Though the basis of this theory is ludicrous, two of his ideas have influenced play scholarship and practice. First, the idea that play occurs in hierarchical stages has influenced play research. Second, the notion that children need to play outdoors influenced the study of outdoor play (Hall, 1965). Many recognize Hall as the founder of the American playground movement.

Criticisms

The criticisms are all too apparent. There is no evidence to support this theory. All children do not go through all stages. If the evolutionary process is occurring in this way and characteristics of different cultures could be transmitted, then modern society would be reflected in these stages.

Current view

When discussing the recapitulation theory, it seems odious to many to even consider this possibility or to even discuss this theory. There are, however, remnants of this theory in some of the comments made by parents. For example, some refer to their children as "wild" when they run around the house. Few believe, however, that their children are re-creating civilization!

Classical theories of play are no longer viewed as valid but serve as a basis for current and future study of play. An overview of classical theories is available in Figure 2–3.

FIGURE 2–3 Classical Theories of Play

Theories (Originator)	Purpose of Play	Outcomes
1. Surplus Energy Theory (Schiller, 1954)	Release surplus energy from the body	Physical development
2. Relaxation and Recreation Theories (G. Patrick, 1916)	Regenerate energy used at work	Physical development
3. Practice Theory (K. Groos, 1901)	Develop skills necessary for functioning as an adult	Physical, cognitive development
4. Recapitulation Theory (G. Stanley Hall, 1916)	Eliminate ancient instincts by reliving evolutionary history of the human species.	Physical development

■ Influential Contributions

Research studies that affected play scholarship at the beginning of the twentieth century are included in this section. Though these studies shaped the study of play, these were not theories of play, but rather, research studies.

Child Study Movement

The **Child Study Movement** grew out of the work of Darwin and other scientists of the nineteenth century. Those who were involved in this movement disagreed with the Froebelian movement and ultimately established their own way of studying children based on the scientific method. One of the most influential scholars involved in this movement was G. Stanley Hall who was a student of both Wilhelm Max Wundt and William James. Wundt was a well known German experimental psychologist and William James, an American, was known for his behaviorist views. Part of Hall's influence stems from the fact that he was awarded the first doctoral degree in psychology in America.

G. Stanley Hall

G. Stanley Hall (1844–1924), who was mentioned in the section on recapitulation theory, had a great impact on child development studies through both his own work and the work of his students (Hall, 1965). He wanted to study children using more scientific methods. By using more scientific methods, G. Stanley Hall began to classify observable play behaviors. Many of these observational studies continue to influence play studies today.

Patty Smith Hill

One of Hall's students, Patty Smith Hill (1868–1946) has had a tremendous influence not just on research, but also on practice. Hill began her career in Louisville, Kentucky. She initially used Froebel's methods for teaching kindergarten (Hill, 1941). After studying with G. Stanley Hall one summer, she began a movement to use free play in her kindergarten class. This was the precursor for developmentally appropriate practice. She is also credited with starting the International Kindergarten Union in 1909. Today this group is known as the Association for Childhood Education International (ACEI). Patty Smith Hill is also credited with developing large hollow blocks and the song, "Happy Birthday to You." Her influence on play as a freely chosen and unstructured activity remains one of her greatest contributions to the study of play and implementation of play as early childhood curriculum.

Caroline Pratt

Caroline Pratt was equally influenced by the ideas of Friedrich Froebel. Like Patty Hill, Caroline Pratt also disagreed with Froebel. She believed in free play and used Froebel's materials in unstructured ways. She believed that children could use open-ended materials to represent their world. Pratt is partially responsible for the use of blocks in preschools today. Caroline Pratt developed unit blocks in her "Play school." Pratt's unit blocks are bigger than Froebel blocks, typically measuring about 5½ inches long by 2¾ inches wide by 1⅜ inches in height. John Dewey had previously encouraged the use of Froebel blocks for building and praised Pratt's work with blocks. The blocks created by Pratt are still used as a basic component of high quality preschool and kindergarten classrooms today. Though she died in poverty, she did not seek a patent on unit

Children today still enjoy Pratt's unit blocks.   (Courtesy of West End Elementary, Easley, SC.)

blocks because she wanted all kindergarten teachers and children to have equal access to the materials.

Harriet M. Johnson

Harriet M. Johnson (1867–1934) was the cofounder of the Bank Street College of Education Nursery School at Columbia College in New York City. She is highly regarded for her block play scholarship. Her book on block play, *The Block Book*, has recently been updated and republished (1934/1984). It is still used by many classroom teachers as a guide for block play. Her scale for evaluating block play is equally beneficial. She also contributed to the outdoor playground movement. Her focus on studying physical, social, emotional, and cognitive development continues to influence how we examine play behaviors.

John Dewey

In play the activity is its own end, instead of its having an ulterior result.

—John Dewey, 1913

Though not generally included in play studies, Dewey is included because he has contributed to play in educational settings. John Dewey (1859–1952) is most known for his work in education, but he had a major impact on play in classroom settings. He believed that play involved "activities performed which are enjoyable, performed for their own sake, and with no end result in mind" (Dewey, 1913, p. 725). His work on reforming educational theory and practice placed action at the center of the classroom. Since play involved action, play should be the center of the classroom. Dewey tried out his ideas in the first experimental Laboratory School at the University of Chicago in 1896. Educating children in a democratic classroom was a major emphasis and he believed this was necessary for the survival of democracy.

For Dewey, the value of play was the child's ability to learn through freely chosen play in a democratic classroom. This led him to revere active learning. "The child does not get hold of any idea until he has *done* it. He acts the idea out before he takes it in" (Dewey, 1896/1972, pp. 195–196). Dewey did not see a distinction between work and play, but rather believed the intersection resulted in learning. He stated, "Play and industry are by no means antithetical to one another as is often assumed" (Lascarides & Hinitz, 2002, p. 222). Dewey's ideas on play have most influenced public schools. The concept of hands-on learning, the project approach, and cooperative groups have had a tremendous influence on public school curriculum. Dewey's scholarship supplied the rationale for play in the primary school curriculum.

Social Interaction Research

Herbert Mead

Herbert Mead studied sociodramatic play and found that it promotes the development of self (1934). He believed that play and games formed a two-step process that precede the formation of self-concept. Children who engage in social interaction through sociodramatic play have opportunities to role-play different roles such as parent, police officer, or teacher. Games provide opportunities to monitor and control behavior in terms of the expectations of others. Mead's study served as a basis for studies that examine the consequences of social interactions during play.

Mildren Parten

Mildren Parten (1932), who was also discussed in Chapter 1, built on this work by looking at social interactions during other kinds of play. Her classical study continues to guide observations of social development and influence research today. Parten observed preschoolers, ages two to five, during play and found that children tend to play differently as they mature. Parten provided a framework for social interaction during play that continues to impact play scholarship today.

■ Modern Theories of Play

The dawning of the twentieth century brought not only studies of play, but also additional theories of play alongside theories of human growth and development. Some of the most influential theories of play were developed by Freud, Erikson, Piaget, and Vygotsky, though none of them focused exclusively on play. Modern theories differ from classical theories in one major area. Classical theories all looked at play through a biological lens and viewed physical development as a major outcome. Modern theories examined play for other benefits. Freud, Erikson, and Vygotsky all shared a belief that play allows children to engage in wish fulfillment and pretense and these lead to social, emotional, and cognitive development. More recently, theories of cognitive adaptation, arousal modulation, and communication have influenced the field. Postmodern theories will be presented after modern theories. An overview of both modern and postmodern theories of play is available in Figure 2–4.

Psychoanalytical Theory

The psychoanalytical view of play was developed by Freud and extended by Erikson. From this perspective, play benefits social and emotional

FIGURE 2–4 Overview of Modern and Postmodern Theories

Theory	Play scholar	View of play
Psychoanalytic	Freud (1959)	Play is pleasurable.
	Erikson (1950)	Play is pleasurable and play is cathartic. (It allows children to gain mastery over a situation.)
Cognitive Developmental (Cognitive constructivist)	Piaget (1962)	Play is a way to construct knowledge and is a reflection of intelligence.
Sociocultural (Social constructivist)	Vygotsky (1967,1932/1978)	Play is a way to construct knowledge during social interactions with the world and is a source of cognitive development.
Arousal Modulation Theory	Berlyne (1969) Ellis (1973) Fein (1981) Shultz (1979)	Play occurs as a result of biological adaptation.
Communication Theory	Bateson (1955/1976) Garvey (1977) Corsaro (1986) Farver (1992)	Play is necessary for communication purposes.
Cognitive Adaptation (Symbolic constructivist) Theory of mind	Bruner (1983) Lillard (1998)	Play encourages flexibility and creativity thereby serving as a medium for cognitive adaptation.
Deconstructivist	Cannella (1997)	Play does not occur in stages and play may not be viewed as a positive experience for members of some cultural groups.
Interdisciplinary Approach	Sutton-Smith (1997)	Play has multiple dimensions and scholars must also consider all types of play in research studies.

development. Their work has influenced research play studies throughout the twentieth century and continues to influence play therapy.

Freud

The opposite of play is not what is serious, but what is real . . .
—*Sigmund Freud, 1959*

Sigmund Freud (1856–1939), an Austrian physician and neurologist, founded psychoanalysis. Though he did not develop a full-blown theory of play, his writings reflect his view of the importance of play. Unlike early play scholars, he did not focus on the benefits of play for physical development. Rather, he considered the cathartic benefits of play in terms of social and emotional development.

Play, like a dream, provides wish fulfillment for the child. During play, the child fulfills his wishes by creating and controlling the environment. Wish fulfillment brings pleasure as the child creates a pretend dog that does not bite. The child is motivated to seek pleasure and avoid pain. Freud (1959) viewed the **pleasure principle** as the primary motivation for play.

Freud believed that play was cathartic because children control situations that are normally beyond their control. For example, the child who is angry because her mother insists that she stay indoors may create a play situation in which her dolls go outdoors or travel to the stars. In this play, she transforms her reality. She controls the situation (Ablon, 2001). Play allows children to create a safe situation in an unsafe world. In fact, the basis for displacement is evident during play. Watch the young child who has been scolded by her parent. As she plays with toys, she might, in turn, scold the toys. The child regains control over the situation. Some preschool teachers have watched in horror as young children physically hit a doll or stuffed animal as they tell the object of their fury by saying, "You'll get more if you keep crying." Though this play may appear to be very violent, it may be beneficial for the child who can release anger in a make-believe world. Adults who believe this behavior is symptomatic of the child's experience will alert social services and inform them of their observations and possible abuse. This is the basis of Freud's work. One caveat is that the adult can never read the mind of the child and though psychoanalysis seems to be logical, trying to understand unconscious motives and emotions is always risky business and best left in the hands of trained psychologists.

Erikson

The psychological purpose of play is to enable the individual to organize and master his/her own existence. Play cannot do this in isolation. There is an essential social quality to much if not all of play.
—Eric Erikson, 1977

Eric Erikson (1902–1994) studied with Freud and subscribed to a psychoanalytical view of play similar to that espoused by Freud. They differed in the area of Erikson's explanation of unconscious motivation in terms of psychosocial—not psychosexual—forces. For Erikson, play was an expressive behavior that led to social and emotional development through mastery of psychosocial crises.

Erikson (2000) recognized three major purposes of play: (1) play as ego mastery for emotional development, (2) play as social, and (3) play as a lifelong phenomenon. Play as **ego mastery** serves as catharsis. Play serves as a place where emotions can be "played out" and anxiety reduced. Erikson believed that children could master reality by planning and experimenting with ". . . model situations in which aspects of the past are re-lived, the present represented and reviewed, and the future anticipated" (Erikson, 1977, p. 44). His view of play as beneficial for emotional development set the stage for play therapy.

Play with toys occurs in what Erikson called the microsphere. (Courtesy of Stacy Burr.)

Types of play. For Erikson, play serves as a social force that fosters the development of the child's ego and leads to a sense of identity. As the social world expands, the child engages in increasingly complex social play that occurs through three broad levels of development. The first level of play, according to Erikson, is **autocosmic play.** This occurs in the first year of life when the child explores, experiences, and investigates his own body as he discovers he is separate from other people. During this time, the infants' and adults' bodies are the sources of sensation and interaction. The child engages in a lot of repetitive play—shaking hands, feet, and pulling hair.

As the child's world expands, objects and toys are incorporated in the **microsphere.** In this sphere, toys are used in two ways: first, as props for acting out their emotions, and second, as tools to discover the limits of rules established by caregivers. In this sphere, children gain mastery over their world as they gain mastery over their toys. Solitary play is the primary social mode of play and pleasure is derived from managing and manipulating toys.

When the child enters the social realm, he enters the **macrosphere,** which involves interactions with others beyond the primary caregiver. Children develop a shared view of the world as they engage in sociodramatic play and games.

Erikson viewed play as a lifelong phenomenon. The three stages of play were hierarchical in nature but could be experienced again and again after other stages. For example, even after adults have engaged in play in the macrosphere, they may still continue to play with adult toys such as boats and cars. In this way, stress is reduced. Rather than engage in an unacceptable behavior, they find an activity that is acceptable. Erikson believed that play reduces anxiety by giving the individual control over the world and providing an acceptable venue for release. Though Erikson's view of play is used primarily by play therapists, his work has influenced play scholarship. His contributions to play and play therapy are evident in the printing of the fiftieth edition of his classic, *Childhood and Society* (2000).

Cognitive Developmental Theory

Cognitive developmental theory considers play as an avenue for intellectual growth and development. Piaget has been the most influential theorist in this area. Because he believed that children construct knowledge through interactions with the world, this view is frequently referred to as **cognitive constructivism** (Fosnot, 1996). This approach serves as a foundation for many current preschool programs and will be further explored later in the text.

Piaget

> In every act of intelligence is an equilibrium between assimilation and accommodation, and while imitation is a continuation of accommodation for its own sake, it may be conversely said that play is essentially assimilation, or the primacy of assimilation over accommodation.
>
> —Jean Piaget, 1962

Jean Piaget (1896–1980) was a Swiss scholar who was well known for his theories of cognitive development. He was equally well known for his contributions to play theory. As a genetic epistemologist, he initially set out to understand the development of intelligence in the young child. His quest brought him to the study of the young child's play. Though some of his methods focus on a single cultural group and have come under criticism, his book, *Play, Dreams, and Imitation in Childhood* (1962), remains a classic.

Piaget believed that adaptation is necessary for survival. Development occurs when children adapt to their world through systematic changes in mental structures. Play is a necessary element of development. Intellectual adaptation results from the combined opposition of two invariant processes, accommodation and assimilation. **Accommodation** occurs when the child adjusts his schema or mental structures to accept new knowledge. Accommodation is the action of the environment on the child (Piaget, 1962). The child transforms schemata to fit the demands of the environment. When children imitate reality, accommodation occurs. For example, the child may watch someone turn off the television. This information is accommodated in a newly created mental structure. The child may then imitate the adult and attempt to turn off the television. The child is adapting to the world.

Assimilation occurs when the individual fits information into existing mental structures. Assimilation is the action of the child on the environment. The child transforms the environment to meet his needs. The young child who just learned to turn off the television now has a mental structure for doing so. He imitated reality. Now if the child begins to turn off the radio also, the activity may turn into play. Assimilation occurs when the child modifies reality to meet his needs. He subordinates or modifies reality to fit his world. As the child practices turning off the television, radio, or other items, he is modifying reality to fit his view of the world. The child moves from imitation to play—from accommodation to assimilation—as he engages in practice play for the sheer joy of turning the television set off and on. Adults may not be as excited when the child begins this new play. The child, however, has increased his knowledge of the world through adaptation and play is a major factor in his development. Both accommodation and assimilation are necessary for intellectual development. Play reflects cognitive growth and serves as a vehicle for learning.

According to Piaget, play represents disequilibrium, or an imbalance in which assimilation dominates accommodation. Young children practice new behaviors through play. Watch the toddler who throws food from his high chair. The first time the food hits the floor, he is developing new mental structures for throwing food on the floor. He is accommodating. After he throws it several times, he has practiced and experienced assimilation as he strengthens his schema for objects (food) moving through space. The child will move between accommodation and assimilation as he discovers how to throw food and then realizes different strategies for throwing. The child will engage in this behavior for as long as the adult will allow, all the while practicing, playing, and learning. The initial learning that started as adaptation soon turned into play.

Piaget believed that play facilitates and follows development. He thought the child's intellectual level was reflected in play. It is no surprise then that Piaget's stages of play mirror his stages of intellectual development. His three stages of intellectual development align with three stages of play. The first stage, sensorimotor development, occurs during the first two years of life and practice or functional play occurs during this time. The second stage of intellectual development is the pre-operational stage and this corresponds with the beginnings of pretend and symbolism that is observed in symbolic or dramatic play. The third stage of cognitive development is concrete operations and the last stage is formal operations. During these two stages, logical thinking begins and becomes stabilized. **Games with rules** begin during the concrete operations stage and become more sophisticated during the formal operations stage. Refer to Chapter 1 for a review.

Though Piaget found these stages to be invariant and sequential in the population he examined, research has supported that children in different cultures also experience these same stages. Differences were found, however, in the influence of social norms and culture. Understanding how children develop in different cultures will add to the knowledge of how children develop their knowledge of the world.

Sociocultural Theory

Sociocultural theory considers the social, cultural, and historical factors that influence cognitive development during social interactions. Based on the work of Russian psychologist Vygotsky, this approach suggests that children construct knowledge through interactions with society and culture and is usually referred to as sociocultural theory, but some also view this as a social constructivist approach. (Fosnot, 1996).

Vygotsky

> *A child's greatest self-control occurs in play.*
> —*Lev Semenovich Vygotsky, 1978*

Piaget and Vygotsky began life the same year and both were constructivists, but they differed greatly in their views of cognitive development and play. Lev Semenovich Vygotsky (1896–1934) was a Russian psychologist who also developed a theory of cognitive development. He believed that social-cultural and historical forces affect the child and that children learn during social interactions with an adult or more capable peer. For Vygotsky (1978), learning occurs in the zone of proximal development (ZOPD). He defined the ZOPD as the distance between the point of being capable of doing something with the assistance of others to the point of being capable of accomplishing the task alone. When the child who can ride a toy (pivot) with help from his parent moves to a point where he can ride the toy without assistance, the child has moved through the zone. The child developed as he moved through the zone of proximal development. Adults who provide support and guidance can create a scaffold for the child and move him to a higher level of cognitive development.

For Vygotsky, the zone of proximal development is created during play. During play, "The child always behaves beyond his average age, above his daily behavior; in play it is as though he were a head taller than himself" (Vygotsky, 1978, p. 102). In contrast with Piaget, who believed play follows development, Vygotsky believed that development occurs during play because play creates the zone of proximal development. Vygotsky believed that play has two unique purposes. The first involves pretending that happens ". . . when the child begins to experience unrealizable tendencies" (p. 93). Vygotsky believed that play begins simultaneously with fantasy. When the toddler realizes he cannot engage in activities around him, he creates his own reality through fantasy or pretend. The child who wants to drive the car but is kept from doing so will pretend to drive. The child creates his own reality through play.

This behavior predisposes the child to abstraction. When the child pretends the stick is a horse, he engages in abstract thought. Vygotsky noted that, "The child sees one thing but acts differently in relation to what he sees. Thus, a condition is reached in which the child begins to act independently of what he sees" (1978, p. 97). This capacity is necessary for instruction.

The second purpose emanates from the first and involves rules. Much representational play is rule-bound—either implicitly or explicitly. When children play they will engage in specific behavior according to their own view of how the role they have assumed works. Watch a child playing in a house area. It may look like free play unfettered by rules. Closer observation may reveal a different story. If the adult tries to enter the play as the mommy, the child may cry out, "No, I'm the mommy, you can be the daddy." Some will even become upset that the daddy is not male. The child has created their own world complete with rules of behavior and no one can enter this world of pretend unless beckoned under specific conditions. To do so may end the play. More than one student teacher has watched in shock as attempts to extend play end in the children dispersing and moving to another area. It is critically important that adults enter play to scaffold and support, not extinguish.

For Vygotsky, play contributes to the development of language, memory, reasoning, and social skills. His view of play as beneficial for the development of higher level thinking and social development provides a different way of thinking about play. Rather than focus on the individual child, Vygotsky paved the way for studies of the context and interactions among children. Additional information on his view of play is available in *Mind in Society* (1932/1978).

Arousal Modulation Theory

The Arousal Modulation Theory views play as a behavior that occurs as a result of biological adaptation. Berlyne (1969) was the first to propose a view of play based on a behavior learning theory. He believed that the central nervous system tries to remain in a certain state of arousal. If there is too little stimulation, the child will engage in stimulus-seeking behavior or play. If too much stimulation is present, play will cease. Other scholars who have refined this theory include Ellis (1973), Fein (1981), and Shultz (1979). They believe this theory has implications for understanding and facilitating play. This theory explains why children roam from one activity to another. They are in search of additional stimulation. Watch children at play. After they engage in an activity for a while, they switch to a different activity or modify the activity. Children running though sprinklers will begin by running through in a rather rote way. After two or three trips, they will change how they are running and may even engage in risky behavior that leads to an injury. On the other hand, when some children are overly stimulated by too much noise or interaction, play will gradually diminish. The children seem to have a built-in moderator that causes them to seek novel or stimulating experiences when the play is dull and to close down when the play is overwhelming.

Communication Theory

Even young animals have ways to communicate that play is occurring. Communication theory views play as necessary for communication purposes. That is, specific communication occurs during play that communicates messages that do not occur outside of play. Bateson (1955), Garvey (1977), Corsaro (1986), and Farver (1992) have contributed to this field of knowledge and are discussed in this section.

Gregory Bateson

Gregory Bateson (1955/1972) developed a theory based on his anthropological study of otter play. He believed that children create a context for play when they exchange metacommunicative signals or text that conveys the message that play is occurring. Everyone involved in the play must understand the message. When children say, "This is play," they signal to others that play is occurring—that what we are doing is not real—but is pretend and fun. This communication signals the other child when play begins and when play ends (Bateson, 1956).

Bateson called the shift from reality to pretend a **play frame.** Children enter and exit play frames by signaling to their play partner that play is beginning and play is ending. The child who does not receive or understand the signal may disrupt the play, and this is when the children will yell, "We're not playing now." Bateson's study of text and context provides a foundation for current studies of communication and metacommunication during play.

Catherine Garvey

Garvey (1977) extended Bateson's findings through her research on pretend play. She studied the child's use of language during play and developed a framework for understanding the complexity involved in the child's language. Garvey noted that a lot of the child's communication involves creating, clarifying, maintaining, and negotiating pretend play.

William Corsaro

Corsaro (1986) built on Garvey's work and found that children use particular communicative strategies to share their intentions with their play partner. He recognized developmental differences in the use of communication during play. Cosaro's framework for understanding the complexity of the child's language during play is currently used in research studies that involve children who speak English as a second language.

Jo Ann Farver

Farver extended Corsaro's research by examining how Mexican children communicate their messages to each other during play (Farver, 1992). Her study found that Mexican children use communication strategies very similar to participants in previous studies. She found they use more basic communication (describe actions) and less complex communication (tags). This area of study has potential for understanding how to facilitate play among children of diverse cultures.

Cognitive Adaptation Theory

More recent studies have focused on play as necessary for cognitive adaptation. This builds on the research of Piaget. It differs in that the focus is on the child's construction of knowledge through symbols. This is called **symbolic constructivism** (Fosnot, 1996). The section begins with the work of Jerome Bruner followed by Leslie's theory of mind and current brain-based research.

Jerome Bruner

> *Unless we bear in mind that play is a source of pleasure, we are really missing the point of what it is all about.*
>
> —Jerome Bruner, 1983

Jerome Bruner (1972) viewed play as a medium for cognitive adaptation. During social play the young child can explore or try on different roles. Social and cooperative play provide a venue for developing problem-solving skills and encouraging creativity. Bruner was especially interested in play as a way immature or novice learners could safely explore their world as they prepare to assume adult roles. Bruner's early work tends to support the early practice theory of play developed by Groos. More recently, Bruner (1990) has focused on the role of narrative for development. He views children as "meaning makers" who are trying to understand their world.

Theory of Mind

Leslie (1987) was the first to link play and theory of mind. **Theory of mind** is used to describe a condition in which the child understands that he has an internal mental state and others have internal structures also (Lillard, 1998). This occurs when the child realizes that his view is different from the view of others. This is generally most noticeable when children realize that their view of Santa Claus or other fictional characters may be different from that of others. The link to play involves social pretend play and the mental representations that occur during play. This theory may provide additional information about how children view the world both in and outside the realm of play, and this will add to our understanding of what is going on when the child plays.

■ Postmodern Theories

Postmodern theorists use critical theory to inform their research. Critical theorists believe that the individual's perspective affects their view of the situation and knowledge construction.

Gail Cannella

Cannella also suggests a different method of viewing play. She is especially concerned that in America, play is viewed through a middle-class, European lens. "Applying the notion of play to all peoples in all contexts denies the multiple value structures, knowledge, and views of the world which are created by people in diverse contexts" (Cannella, 1997, p. 128).

She has three major criticisms. The first involves Piaget's stages of development. These appear to be too rigid and do not reflect the realities of children in different cultures. She suggests that these stages are not separate and linear. For example, some children may play games when they are very young, and in early Europe, people of all ages engage in all kinds of play. Her second concern involves the view of play as object driven. For example, African American children may use more verbal than object play. Her third concern involves the use of "appropriate" and "inappropriate" to describe practices. She believes this does not provide an inclusive environment for discussion and leads to the view that one approach is the only correct approach. This perspective challenges past theories but fails to provide alternative ways to consider these issues. This theory benefits play scholarship because it challenges standard belief systems and creates questions for debate and discussion.

Brian Sutton-Smith

Sutton-Smith emphasized the interdisciplinary nature of play. In his pivotal paper in 1966, he pointed out a contradiction in Piaget's theory of play. If play reflects a stage of intelligence then it cannot also contribute to the development of intelligence. In Piaget's terms, if play is almost pure assimilation then it is strengthening the neurological connections, not creating new knowledge. Therefore, intelligence would not be developed through play. In over 300 publications, Sutton-Smith's view of play is that it is ambiguous, difficult to define, and more difficult to capture. He warns us against over-romanticizing play according to middle-class values. He further argues that a great deal of play is not pleasant nor does it lead to more positive outcomes for children (1997). For additional reading, see *The Ambiguity of Play* (1997) in which he explains the rhetorics of play.

An overview of modern, current, and postmodern theories shows a steady progression from the first psychoanalytical theories to current theories. Theory-based play scholarship provides a solid basis for current and future inquiry.

■ Current Influential Contributions

The influence of the most recent research cannot be overlooked. Significant scholars who have contributed to play scholarship in the last part of the twentieth century include: Greta Fein (1981) who has added to the knowledge of symbolic play; Inge Bretherton (1984) who has also contributed significantly to the study of symbolic play; and Jerome Singer (1973) who conducted research in the area of imagination and pretend. Other well-known researchers include Anthony Pelligrini (1988), who investigated the benefits of rough-and-tumble play on the playground for social development and examined the relationship between literacy and play; and Kenneth Rubin and Brian Vandenberg, who co-authored with Greta Fein one of the most important articles on play (1983). These are just a few of the scholars who have been conducting research on play. The impact of brain-based research on play is yet to be realized and is discussed in the next section.

Brain-based Research

In the past 20 years, research on the brain received attention from both the academic and public realm. In 1996, a conference, *Rethinking the Brain*, was held to discuss the implications of brain research (Shore, 1997). As a result of the conference, Rob Reiner, Michele Singer Reiner, and Ellen Gilbert developed a public awareness campaign entitled, "I Am Your Child" to communicate the importance of the first three years of life. Free videos were distributed to teachers at the NAEYC conference in Toronto, Canada, and others were sold at a reduced cost to ensure that early educators could access the information. Publication of the proceedings of the conference, *Rethinking the Brain* by the Families and Work Institute (Shore, 1997) and a special edition of *Newsweek* on "Your Child" ensured public awareness of new research findings on the brain. This affected play studies by publicizing brain research. Shore (1997) described the findings in this way:

> At birth, the human brain is in a remarkably unfinished state. Most of its 100 billion neurons are not yet connected in networks. Forming and reinforcing these connections are the key tasks of early brain development. Connections among neurons are formed as the growing child experiences the surrounding world and forms attachments to parents, family members, and other caregivers. In the first decade of life, a child's brain forms trillions of connections or synapses. Axons hook up with dendrites, and chemicals called neurotransmitters facilitate the passage of impulses across the resulting synapses. Each individual neuron may be connected to as many as 15,000 other neurons, forming a network of neural pathways that is immensely complex. This elaborate network is sometimes referred to as the brain's "wiring" or "circuitry." In the early years, children's brains form twice as many synapses as they will eventually need. If these synapses are used repeatedly in a child's day-to-day life, they are reinforced and become part of the brain's permanent circuitry. It they are not used repeatedly, or often enough, they are eliminated. In this way, experience plays a crucial role in "wiring" a young child's brain. (p. 17)

Scholars of brain research note that infants arrive ready for interaction and what happens to them makes a difference. The National Research Council Institute of Medicine released a list of four major themes based on their analysis of research on the central nervous system (Shornkoff & Phillips, 2000). They found that

- All children are born wired for feelings and ready to learn.
- Early environments matter and nurturing relationships are essential.
- Society is changing and the needs of young children are not being addressed.
- Interactions among early childhood science, policy, and practice are problematic and demand dramatic rethinking.

These findings confirm many research studies conducted prior to the latest advancements in neurology and imaging that make these insights available. For example, many of the findings by Bowlby in the 1950s have been confirmed (Bowlby, 1988). Attachment is important for developing both emotionally and mentally. The value of adult/child interaction as the child explores his world was discussed first by Piaget (1965). These findings have implications for play. Play that occurs between the parent(s) and child or teacher and child contribute to cognitive development.

Marketers also recognized the implications and used this concept to market videotapes, books, and toys. For example, listening to music by Mozart was associated with increased activity in the brain. Many companies sponsored the purchase of hundreds of cassette tapes, *Mozart for Babies*, that could be sent home with newborns. Providing free music for newborns is a wonderful gesture but it may not accomplish the goal of increased IQ. Gains obtained from music and movement occur during loving interactions with adults. Adults may cradle infants as they listen to a favorite song or dance around the room. This is play. When the adult who does not enjoy classical music plays it only for some intended increase in intelligence, the benefit to the child may be less than if the adult played music he or she enjoyed. The effect of music alone is diminished by the lack of interaction from the adult. The impact of brain research is also evident in books. Titles that promote brain growth have replaced previous volumes that promoted play with babies (Silberg, 2000).

Research findings that have resulted from neurological studies confirm a great deal of past research. Children need stable relationships with adults who care for them. A consequence of the "brain-based research" is that toys and materials designed for children have changed the word *play* to "brain based" in their advertisements. This is a concern in terms of unrealistic expectations. As discussed earlier, the parent who turns on the tape and leaves the room because he or she does not enjoy the music is not facilitating development. Early educators and parents must be informed of current research and be wary of child products that tout "brain-based research" as a basis of validity. The products may be effective for other reasons, but it sets an unwise precedent to use materials for stimulating the brain. Knowledge of the brain and the central nervous system that is gained from imaging and neurological studies will continue to add to what we know about children and play.

■ Play Assessment

The history of play assessment parallels that of play itself. Though there is some evidence to suggest that adults have always observed play throughout civilization, written records of documented assessment began as observations or journals of children's play. In the nineteenth century, Froebel observed mothers and children at play and wrote, *Mutter Und Kose-Lieder* (1895). This was followed by the development of Darwin's techniques of observation used to observe his son and recorded in *A Biographical Sketch of an Infant* (1971). Montessori used similar observation techniques when she created detailed observations that served as an impetus for developing her materials and methods. This technique also influenced the Child Study Movement that was discussed earlier in this chapter.

The scientific movement of the early 1920s and 1930s contributed to the development of many taxonomies and scales for evaluating play. Piaget's observations of play were pervasive in his *Play, Dreams, and Imitation in Childhood* (1962) and provided the partial basis for the Piaget-Parten Play Observation Scale (POS) that was later developed by Kenneth Rubin (1985). The Rubin POS scale has been used for a great deal of play research and incorporates the research of Piaget and Parten.

Play assessment at the beginning of the twenty-first century is both similar to and different from its predecessors. Observations of play are still the primary source of information but digital equipment is enabling scholars and teachers alike to observe and capture the very essence of play through video and photographic documentation. Observations, pictorial representations, and informed reflections provide powerful documentation of play.

■ Current and Future Trends/Issues

Few scholars at the beginning of the century could have imagined the state of play today. When Harriet Johnson took children to the roof of the Bank Street Nursery School, little did she imagine the safety and liability issues that today's early educators encounter on a daily basis. On the other hand, could Caroline Pratt dare imagine that her blocks would be as enjoyable at the end of the century? Though it is always risky to predict what issues and trends will impact play in the future, some issues that are currently affecting play and may continue to influence play in the future are discussed in the following section.

Multiculturalism

Play theories have typically looked at play through a specific lens in an attempt to understand and make sense of it. As we move into this new century, we are challenged to use a more culturally inclusive approach. Shirley Brice Heath (1997) suggests we reexamine the use of developmental stages and reconsider development from a more holistic perspective. The cultural influences on play at different ages may need to be developed to include different ethnic and cultural groups. More studies

How will our global village affect play in the future?

are needed that look at characteristics of play in different cultures. Does play transmit culture and tradition and, if so, in what ways?

Inclusion

Play theories generally focus on the behavior of typically developing children. With the passage of special education legislation, children with special needs have been included in classrooms and studies of play among children who have disabilities or delays have grown throughout the past decade. Due to the nature of the population, play theories are generally disability specific. For example, play among children without sight may be the focus of one research study while another looks at play among children with hearing impairments. It is more difficult to generalize in this situation. Future studies may provide information that will foster our knowledge of how individual children who have specific disabilities develop their own play styles.

Globalism

Theories that have influenced play studies in America have also influenced play studies throughout the industrialized world. Many groups of scholars are studying play around the world. For example, Brian Sutton-Smith of the United States and Peter K. Smith of England studied the reality of play as a rough-and-tumble activity that is not always neat and clean. Rough-and-tumble play occurs in America and in England and, most likely, around the world. Cumulative knowledge built on multiple perspectives must be a goal. As the Internet continues to bring continents closer together, it will be interesting to observe how it will influence our study of play.

Future Issues

The future study of play is both promising and menacing for play scholars. During the past two centuries and especially within the past 20 years, a vast amount of knowledge about play has been accumulated. This provides a solid foundation from which to begin construction—or deconstruction. Major concerns for the future include:

◆ the need for better research methods for studying play among culturally diverse groups and subgroups

◆ understanding how culture is transmitted through play

◆ unpacking the findings from research in a way that values the whole child rather than focusing on one aspect of the findings

How these issues are addressed will affect the future of play theory. Play is being examined critically from both within and outside the scientific community and this will increase the knowledge base.

PlayScape Reflections

In the PlayScape at the beginning of the chapter, Juanita recognized her children's need to play. She valued her time with her youngest son and viewed play as a medium for enhancing social development. Goncu's (1999) research on sociocultural perspectives may provide an explanation of the interactions between Juanita and her children. According to sociocultural theory, more knowledgeable adults scaffold and support the child as they acquire skills and knowledge of the world. For example, when Roberto is playing, he might discover ants. When Juanita takes time to talk to him about the ants, and suggests they get a book from the library, Roberto is learning about his world. Not only is he benefiting socially and physically, he is also benefiting cognitively. In the same way, Juanita recognizes the needs of her eight-year-olds to play. She understands their need for unstructured play prior to beginning homework. Though Juanita may not understand the research base of play research, she is aware of the benefits of play on a day-to-day basis. Adults who support play facilitate children's opportunities to play.

■ Summary

This chapter was designed to provide an overview of classical, modern, and postmodern theories of play. The aim of the chapter is to place the study of play within the broader historical and cultural context. This provides a knowledge base from which to begin the study of play. Both animal and human play were considered in the initial discussion. Both share some characteristics, but the play of young children is very different from that of animals. Human play has been acknowledged for more than 2,000 years. One of the first to record his view of play was Plato. Like other areas of psychology, play research was influenced by European perspectives. Early scholars included Locke, Rousseau, Pestalozzi, and Froebel. Froebel had the most influence on the study of play and many of his ideas are still evident today. Classical theories of play were influenced by science and project a biological, scientific view of the world. These are traditionally classified in four different categories: (1) surplus energy theory of play, (2) relaxation and recreation theories of play, (3) practice (or pre-exercise) theory of play, and (4) recapitulation theory of play. Major theories of play in the twentieth century were produced by scholars who were attempting to understand human behavior. Freud and Erikson were two psychoanalysts who recognized the value of play for social and emotional development. Piaget and Vygotsky both investigated play and had a major influence on the study of play. Piaget believed that development led play and, in contrast, Vygotsky believed that play led development. Additional theories of play in the last half of the twentieth century include arousal modulation theory, communication theory, cognitive adaptation theory, theory of mind, and postmodern theories. Moving into the twenty-first century, the challenge is to include multiple perspectives in research that embrace all children from all ethic and cultural groups.

■ Key Terms

Accommodation
Assimilation
Autocosmic play
Child Study Movement
Cognitive constructivism
Ego mastery

Games with rules
Macrosphere
Microsphere
Play frame
Pleasure principle
Sensorimotor play

Sociocultural theory
Symbolic constructivism
Symbolic play
Theory of mind

■ Helpful Web Sites and Technology Resources

◆ **Froebel**
http://www.froebel.com   Specializes in Froebelian education.
http://www.froebelgifts.com   Accurate information about Froebel's gifts.

◆ **Piaget**
http://www.piaget.org   Official site of the Jean Piaget Society. Dedicated to continuing his research.

◆ **Pratt**
http://www.cityandcountry.org   School originally started by Caroline Pratt.

◆ **Vygotsky**
http://marxists.org   Official site of the Vygotsky archives. Recently translated articles and a photo gallery are included on this site.

■ Activities

1. **InClass Lab**

   A. Work in small groups to create a timeline of play scholarship. Display the timeline on the wall. When did most of the play research occur? What factors affected play research?

   B. Jeri was a four-year-old boy in preschool who played with blocks frequently. One day he started building a square with the blocks, and then he placed a long block perpendicular to the creation. Suddenly, he shouted, "Hey, I'm on the *Titanic* and it's sinking and I'm walking the plank." Consider how different theories explain this play.

   C. Consider your own experiences. Make a list of materials that you own that could be considered reflective of Erikson's microsphere. Compare your lists. Do you agree or disagree with Erikson's view of play stages and, if so, why?

2. **Research and Inquiry**

   A. Select an underrepresented group in the United States and investigate its play history. For example, what do we know about how native Americans played? How did social and cultural issues shape their play? What do we know about their play today? Share your findings in class.

   B. Examine all the play theories. Do any of these fit with your view of play? Why or why not? Can you document and justify your answer?

   C. Visit a playground filled with children for an hour. Do your observations support your selected theory?

   D. Many research studies were conducted using homogenous populations. Discuss how the results of these studies influence play theory.

   E. Ask an early educator to discuss his or her theory of play. Compare his or her views with the play theories in the text. Repeat this question with two other teachers. What theories do they most closely reflect? Were you surprised?

F. Select an area of interest that involves children's play—i.e, toys, dolls, games, etc., and investigate the history of the topic. What historical factors influenced the development of the topic?

3. Service Learning

A. Volunteer to develop brochures or a Web site to assist a local center or school in maintaining a record of its history.

B. Investigate the history of preschool and primary education within different cultural groups within your community. For example, did the African-American, French, or Hispanic community develop a preschool or primary school in the area? Did other groups influence preschool or primary school? What do we know about the history of underrepresented groups in society? How can you contribute to the knowledge base?

4. Family Connections

A. Think about your own personal play history. What do you know about your family's play styles? Spend some time interviewing family members to understand your own history. Then share Figure 2–5 with parents in your class at a class meeting with family members. Ask them if they want to bring this to the next family night and share their play history.

FIGURE 2–5   Play Memories

Play Memories

Dear Parents,

   Please help your child complete this form. As you help your child, you may learn more about how you played and how your child is playing today.

Child's name _____ Date _____

My grandparents played

My grandparents' favorite games were

My parent(s)' favorite play included

My parent(s)' favorite games were

I played

My favorite games are

---

5. Play Advocacy

Play advocacy can take on many forms, moving from awareness to action. In the first chapter, distribution of a light-hearted poem that touts the importance of play was recommended. As we move through the book, advocacy efforts will increase as your knowledge of play grows.

A. Offer to present a slide show documenting the benefits of play to a local parent's group.

B. Find out the name of your local, state, and national representatives.

C. Join a local, state, or national professional organization committed to ensuring children's play such as National Association for the Education of Young Children (NAEYC), Association for Childhood Education International (ACEI), International Play Association/USA (IPA), or American Association for the Child's Right to Play. If you don't have a local chapter, start one.

■ References

Ablon, S. (2001). Continuities of tongues: A developmental perspective on the role of play in child and adult psychoanalytic process. *Journal of Clinical Psychoanalysis, 10* (3–4), 345–365.

Bateson, G. (1956). The message is "This is play." In B. Schaffner's (Ed.) *Group processes* (pp. 145–151). New York: Josiah Macy.

Bateson, G. A. (1955/1976). A theory of play and fantasy. In J. S. Bruner, A. Jolly, & K. Sylva (Eds.). *Play: Its role in development and evolution* (pp. 119–129). New York: Basic Books.

Berlyne, D. E. (1969). Laughter, humor, and play. In G. Lindzey & E. Aronson (Eds.) *The handbook of social psychology.* (Vol. 3.) Reading: MA: Addison-Wesley.

Bowlby, J. (1988). *A secure base: Parent-child attachment and healthy human development.* New York: Basic Books.

Bretherton, I. (1984). *Symbolic play: The development of social understanding.* New York: Academic Press.

Bruner, J. S. (1972).The nature and uses of immaturity. *American Psychologist, 27,* 686–708.

Bruner, J. S. (1983). Play, thought, and language. *Peabody Journal of Education, 60* (3), 60–69.

Bruner, J. S. (1990). *Acts of meaning.* Cambridge, MA: Harvard University Press.

Bruner, J. S., Jolly, A., & Sylva, K. (Eds.). (1976). *Play: Its role in development and evolution.* New York: Basic Books.

Cannella, G. (1997). *Deconstructing early childhood education: Social justice and revolution.* New York: Peter Lang.

Comenius, J. A. (1896). *School of infancy.* Boston: Heath.

Comenius, J. A. (1968). *Orbis sensualium pictus.* First English edition, Introduction by J. E. Sadler. Oxford University Press: London. Originally published in 1658.

Corsaro, W. A. (1986). Discourse processes within peer culture: From a constructivist to an interpretative approach to childhood socialization. In P. Adler (Ed.), *Sociological studies of child development* (p. ???). New York: JAI.

Darwin, C. (1971). *A biological sketch of an infant.* Philadelphia: Lippincott.

Dewey, J. (1896). Imagination and expression; and, The psychology of drawing. In *John Dewey: The early works, 1882–1898.* Vol. 5 (pp. 192–201). Carbondale: Southern Illinois University Press. (Originally printed in 1972.)

Dewey, J. (1913). Play. In P. Monroe (Ed.), *A cyclopedia of education* (pp. 725–727). New York: Dutton.

Dewey, J. (1930). *Democracy and education.* New York: Macmillan.

Ellis, M. J. (1973). *Why people play.* Englewood Cliffs, NJ: Prentice-Hall.

Erikson, E. H. (1977). *Toys and reasons.* New York: Norton.

Erikson, E. H. (2000). *Childhood and society.* (3rd Ed.) New York: Norton. (Originally published in 1950.)

Fagen, R. (1981). *Animal play behavior.* New York. Oxford University Press.

Farver, J. (1992). An analysis of young American and Mexican children's play dialogues: Illustrative study #3. In C. Howes, O. Unger, & C. Matheson (Eds.) *The collaborative construction of pretense: Social pretend play functions* (pp. 55–66). Albany: SUNY Press.

Fein, G. (1981). Pretend play in childhood. *Child Development, 52:* 1095–1118.

Fosnot, C. (1996). *Constructivism: Theory, perspectives, and practice.* New York: Teachers College Press, Columbia University.

Freud, S. (1959). Creative writers and daydreaming. In J. Strackey (Ed.), *The standard edition of the complete psychological works of Sigmund Freud* (Vol. IX). London: Hogarth. (Originally published, 1908).

Froebel, F. (1887/1902). *The education of man.* (W.N. Hailmann, Trans.). New York: Appleton. (Originally published in 1826, copyright 1887.)

Froebel, F. (1895). *The songs and music of Freidrich Froebel's mother play (mutter und kose-lieder).* New York: Appleton.

Garvey, C. (1977). *Play.* Cambridge, MA: Harvard University Press.

Goncu, A. (Ed.) (1999). *Children's engagement in the world: Sociocultural perspectives.* Cambridge, UK: Cambridge Press.

Groos, (1901). *The play of man.* New York: Appleton.

Gulick, L. (1908). *Mind and work.* Garden City, NY: Doubleday.

Hall, G. S. (1916). What we owe to the tree-life of our ape-like ancestors. *Pedagogical Seminary, 23*, 94–119.

Hall, G. S. (1965). Life and confessions of a psychologist, selections reprinted in S. Strickland & C. Burgess (Eds.), *Health, growth, and heredity* (pp. 29–39). New York: Teachers College Press, Columbia University.

Heath, S. (1997). Culture: Contested realm in research in children and youth. *Applied Developmental Science, 1* (3), 113–123.

Hill, P. S. (1941/1999). Kindergarten. In K. M. Paciorek & J. H. Munroe (Eds.), *Sources: Notable selections in early childhood education* (2nd ed., pp. 81–90). Guilford, CT: Dushkin/McGraw-Hill.

Jenkinson, S. (2001). *Genius of play: Celebrating the spirit of childhood.* Gloucestershire, UK: Hawthorn.

Johnson, H. (1934/1984). The art of block building. In E. Hirsch (Ed.) *The block book* (pp. 9–26). Washington, DC: National Association for the Education of Young Children.

Lascarides, V. C., & Hinitz, B. F. (2002). *History of early childhood education.* New York: Falmer.

Leslie, A. M. (1987). Pretense and representation: The origins of "theory of mind." *Psychological Review, 94*, 412–426.

Lillard, A. S. (1998). Playing with a theory of mind. In O. N. Saracho & B. Spodek (Eds.), *Multiple perspectives on play in early childhood* (pp. 11–33). Albany: SUNY Press.

Locke, J. (1692/1884). *Some thoughts concerning education.* (R. H. Quick, Ed.) Cambridge: University Press.

Mead H. (1934). *Mind, self, and society from the standpoint of a social behaviorist.* Chicago: University of Chicago Press.

Parten, M. (1932). Social participation among pre-school children. *Journal of Abnormal Psychology, 27*, 243–269.

Patrick, G. T. W. (1916). *The psychology of relaxation.* Boston: Houghton Mifflin.

Pelligrini, A. (1988). Elementary school children's rough-and-tumble play and social competence. *Developmental Psychology, 24*, 802–206.

Pestalozzi, J. H. (1894). *How Gertrude teaches her children.* Translated by Lucy E. Holland and Frances C. Turner. Edited with an introduction by Ebenezer Cooke. London: Swan Sonnenschein. (Originally published in 1801).

Piaget, J. (1962). *Play, dreams, and imitation in childhood.* New York: Norton.

Piaget, J. (1965). *The moral judgement of the child.* New York: Free Press.

Read, J. (1992). A short history of children's building blocks. In P. Gura (Ed.), *Exploring learning: Young children and block play* (pp. 1–12). London: Paul Chapman.

Rogers, C. S., & Sawyers, J. K. (1988). *Play in the lives of children.* Washington, DC: National Association for the Education of Young Children.

Rogers, C., & Sluss, D. (1996). Developmentally appropriate practice in higher education. *Journal of Early Childhood Teacher Education, 17* (1), 4–14.

Rousseau, J. J. (1762/1991). *Émile.* Translated and annotated by Allan Bloom. London: Penguin.

Rubin, K. (1982). Early play theories revisited: Contributions to contemporary research. In D. J. Pepler & K. H. Rubin, (Eds.) *The play of children: Current theory and research* (p. 4–14). Basil, Switzerland: Karger.

Rubin, K. (1985). *The Play Observation Scale. (POS)* (rev.ed.) Available from K. H. Rubin, University of Waterloo, Waterloo, Ontario, N2L 3G1, Canada.

Rubin, K., Fein, G., & Vandenberg, B. (1983). Play. In E. M. Heatherington (Ed.), P. H. Mussen (Series Ed.), *Handbook of child psychology: Vol. 4, Socialization, personality, and social development* (pp. 693–774). New York: Wiley.

Schiller, F. (1954). *On the aesthetic education of man.* New Haven, CT: Yale University Press.

Shore, R. (1997). *Rethinking the brain: New insights into early development.* New York: Families and Work Institute.

Shornkoff, J., & Phillips, D. (2000). *From neurons to neighborhoods: The science of early childhood development.* Washington, DC: National Academy Press.

Shultz, T. R. (1979). Play as arousal modulation. In B. Sutton-Smith (Ed.), *Play and learning* (p. 7–22). New York: Gardner.

Silberg, J. (2000). *Brain games for toddlers and twos.* Beltsville, MD: Gryphon House.

Singer, J. (1973). *The child's world of make-believe: Experimental studies of imaginative play.* New York: Academic Press.

Spariousu, M. (1989). *Dionysus reborn: Play and the aesthetic dimension in modern philosophical and scientific discourse.* Ithaca, NY: Cornell University Press.

Spencer, H. (1873). *Principles of psychology.* (Vol. 2; 3rd ed.) New York: Appleton.

Sutton-Smith, B. (1966). Piaget on play: A critique. *Psychological Review,* 73:104–110.

Sutton-Smith, B. (1997). *The ambiguity of play.* Cambridge, MA: Harvard University Press.

Vygotsky, L. S. (1967). Play and its role in the mental development of the child. *Soviet Psychology, 5* (3), 6–18.

Vygotsky, L. S. (1932/1978). *Mind in society.* Cambridge, MA: Harvard University Press.

CHAPTER 3

Play as Development

It is not an exaggeration to say that play is as basic to your child's total development as good food, cleanliness, and rest.

—*Joanne E. Oppenheim, 1984*

Chapter Overview

The slogan "children learn through play" is often used by educators. This chapter explores the validity of this statement. Beginning with infants, this chapter explores how children develop physically, socially, and cognitively through play.

Objectives

After reading this chapter, you should be able to:

◆ Discuss the progression of play from birth to age eight.

◆ Examine the benefits of play for infants.

◆ Investigate the outcomes of play for preschoolers.

◆ Explore the value of play for primary age children.

◆ Explain the value of interactive play between adults and children.

PlayScape

Lu Chen had just finished her teaching day, picked up the groceries, and walked in the door when she was met by a shoosh and swirl as the twins, Wu Chon and Lu, ran through the house. They both have towels draped around their shoulders and appear to be involved in a pretend game of Superman. Wu Chon came running through and called, "The dragons are coming, the dragons are coming!" Lu Chen's Aunt Nina looked at Wu Chon and said, "Yes, they are and they are on the patio now." Wu Chon and Lu ran outdoors to continue both searching for and fleeing from the dragon. As Lu Chen picked up the mail, she approached her aunt, saying, "Aunt Nina, do they play like this all the time?" Nina, the more experienced one, nodded, "Yes, Lu Chen, when they are not napping or sleeping. They remind me of you when you were a child. They are always busy. As soon as they return from preschool, they play." Lu Chen was delighted to know that her children were in good hands and that they were able to learn through play at school and at home.

Play Provocation

In this scenario, we are unsure of the twins' impetus to play, although being together may explain part of the rationale for their play. The towels serve as a scaffold for the children's pretend play. Once the children have the towels draped around them, they enter the realm of pretend and they control the play. Their play may take them upstairs or downstairs, indoors and outdoors, under the table or around the table. They control the play. But are they learning? Or is this a waste of their time? These are the questions that many parents and teachers face as they deal with play. Is play a good use of their children's time?

■ Play Progression

> *Play is the highest phase of child development—of human development at this period.*
>
> —Freidrich Froebel, 1887

The idea of play as progress is fully developed in this chapter. This concept serves as a basis for examining cognitive, social, and physical development in three broad age ranges: infants and toddlers, preschoolers, and primary age children. It thus provides a starting point for understanding the progression of play and subsequent benefits for human growth and development. Generalizations in this chapter are meant to be just that, generalizations. Children continually progress through increasingly more complex levels of development, but these may not occur in lockstep manner. For example, all typically developing children move from lying in their crib to walking upright. Some will crawl first, some will scoot, but all typically developing, and most atypically developing, children will walk. How this occurs varies in individual children.

■ Infant and Toddler Play

> *The primary ingredient to help young children flourish consists of loving, responsive caregivers, generously committing energy, body-loving, and tuned-in attentiveness to their child's well-being.*
> —*Alice Sterling Honig, 1999*

Infants follow a predictable sequence of growth and development during the first two years. Their physical, cognitive, language, and social development are intertwined in a holistic system. Growth during this period is rapid and follows a general sequence (Santrock, 2003). In the same way, play begins as early as the second month of life and follows a predictable sequence (Bergen, 1998; Brenner & Fogel, 2001; Piaget, 1962), as children engage in object play, symbolic/pretend play, social play, and motor play. *For the first two years of life, children discover the world through play and exploration.* These behaviors are examined in this section through cognitive, social, and physical growth and development.

Cognitive Development

The infant begins with a brain that is very plastic. Positive influences have a stimulating effect on the brain and negative influences decrease the brain's activity. Factors that affect the child's development include nourishment, care, stimulation, and environment. The availability of play activities affects not only development but also the size of the brain (Begley, 1997; Nash, 1997; Shonkoff & Phillips, 2000).

Researchers such as Hughes (1999, p. 64) have found that infants benefit from play in five ways.

◆ It keeps the infant at an optimal level of arousal, so she is neither bored nor overly excited (Power & Park, 1980).

Infants benefit from adult interaction.

◆ It provides the infant with a feeling of control over her environment, thereby fostering self-confidence and promoting intellectual growth (Watson & Ramey, 1972).

◆ It exposes the infant to intense social interaction with her parents and so facilitates the process of parent/infant attachment.

◆ It encourages the infant to explore her surroundings.

◆ It causes the infant to attend more closely to the social aspects of language (Ratner & Bruner, 1978).

Infant/adult interaction

Infants require adult interaction to survive and thrive. The adult/child relationship affects all aspects of development. The most current research on the brain suggests that infants are born with certain neurological pathways that are hardwired and these are strengthened through interactions with others (Shore, 1997). The infant smiles and the adult smiles back; the infant cries and the adult comforts the child; the adult plays "pat-a-cake" and the infant laughs. In this setting, the adult is fostering development because the child feels safe and secure. During the first two years, changes are occurring very quickly, and play that occurs between the adult and child provides opportunities for growth and development (Figure 3–1).

The developmental stages presented in the following section are not intended to reflect an invariant view of development, but to provide general guidelines in terms of what current research tells us about how children grow and develop through play.

FIGURE 3–1 Infant-Toddler Interactions That Impact Play

Research Study	**Implications for Practice**
Title: Maternal mind-mindedness and attachment security as predictors of theory of mind understanding *Authors:* Elizabeth Meinsm, Charles Fernyhough, Rachel Wainwright, Mani Das Gupta, Emma Fradley, and Michelle Tuckey *Child Development* (2002), 73 (12), 1715–1726. *Abstract:* The social relationship between adults and infants was investigated in an attempt to establish a correlation with the child's theory of mind. The study looked at 57 infant/mother pairs and found significant correlation. That is, when mothers talked to six-month-old infants about how they are feeling and what they are doing, those children at four had a more developed understanding that their thinking is different from that of others.	Social interaction between parents, early educators, and infants is very important for later cognitive development. When adults talk to children about what they are doing and how they are feeling, this is absorbed by the infant in a way that is evident at the age of four. Early educators should be well trained so that they can accurately assess and respond to the child's social actions. Games that adults play with children can be used as a way to facilitate these social interactions.

Beginning play

Infants enter the world dependent on their senses and physical ability to develop as human beings. Researchers tell us that some infants play within the second month of birth (Piaget, 1962). Infants can see, hear, taste, touch, and smell from birth. This gives them the ability to grasp, bang, taste, and shake. Their development is directly related to their play and their play is directly related to their development!

As noted earlier, Piaget referred to the first two years of life as the sensorimotor period. Play that occurs during this time reflects the child's level of intellectual growth and is called practice/sensorimotor play. During the first two years of life, functional or practice play dominates. This is not the only kind of play, however. As play develops and becomes more complex, children move from exploration and object play to language and symbolic play.

Piaget discussed six levels of beginning play and these form a framework for conceptualizing the development of play during the first two years. Shore (1997) refers to this as a ". . . **prime time** for optimal development . . . periods during which the brain is particularly efficient at specific types of learning" (p. 39).

1. **Reflexive stage** (birth–one month)

   Reflexes rule this age and infants spend their time watching, observing, and reacting instinctively.

2. **Primary circular reactions** (one–four months)

   Touching becomes important as children begin to develop their ability to cause an effect. They tend to use circular reactions when grasping and reaching.

3. **Secondary circular reactions stage** (four–eight months)

   Reaching and grabbing skills are developing. The joy of causing an effect is evident in laughter. Doing something for the pleasure of doing it evolves at this age.

4. **Coordination of secondary schemes** (eight–twelve months)

   Two factors are influential. The first is trying known actions in new situations. The child can use a previously learned behavior in a novel setting. The second factor is mobility from one scheme to another. The child can move quickly from one action or behavior to another. Pushing and pulling objects and putting materials on their heads are fun for this age.

5. **Tertiary circular reactions** (twelve–eighteen months)

   Children can stand, move, try known actions in new situations, and move from one scheme to another. For example this is when children will put a key in an outlet.

6. **Invention of new means through mental combinations** (eighteen–twenty-four months)

Pretense begins when the child enjoys applying schema to inadequate objects. In other words, the child enjoys pretending that one object is another.

Exploration

During the infant's first year of life, she will spend a lot of time exploring the world through her senses. Looking and listening are most common during this time. As she grows, exploration will become more complex. For the casual observer, it is especially difficult to distinguish between play and exploration in the very young child. Is the child playing or is the child exploring? Infants spend most of their time exploring. They use their senses to find meaning in their world. The toddler splits her time between exploration and practice play. Caruso (1984) even suggests we call it **exploratory play** due to the rapid transitions from exploration to play and back again. By the end of the second year, exploration begins to decrease and pretend begins to increase. Watch some two-year-olds as they explore a roll of toilet tissue. After figuring out how the paper can be pulled around the roll (exploration), they will pull the tissue and laugh in delight as the tissue falls to the floor (practice play), then run through the house with the tissue using it as a flag (pretend). Only the child can know what is intended during imaginary play. During this time the toddler's exploration is both a source of delight and a reason for safety concerns. The child will explore the object (toy, pot or pan, or box) to figure out what it is. After the child is satisfied, she will engage in practice play, over and over. Exploration allows the infant to understand the world through her physical senses, and practice play provides a venue for infants and toddlers to strengthen neurological connections.

Object play

Object play begins when the infant can grasp objects. This usually develops around four months when infants are in the secondary circular reaction stage. Object play becomes more complex as the child grows and develops. The child moves from being conscious of only her body to being conscious of the external world as she develops and progresses through the tertiary circular reactions to the invention of new means through mental combinations (Piaget, 1962). Infants who lack sensory and physical capabilities to fully engage in object play may experience delays in development.

Children who engage in sociodramatic play have moved from object play to the apex of symbolic play.

Young children begin by using one object and then proceed to the use of two or more in increasingly more complex combinations. During early object play, the object directs the infant's attention. Give the six-month-old a rattle and it is the rattle that will direct the child's interaction. Does it make a noise? Does it change when moved? The question that dominates is, "What can this thing do?" As the child matures, the child directs the action on the object. At the end of the first year, when given a pot, the toddler will put things in and take things out of it. A change occurs again by the end of the second year. The child who encounters a pot will, most likely, put it on her head. The child has moved from being guided by the object to guiding the object.

Object play generally elicits different behaviors during functional and indiscriminate play (Rubin, Fein, and Vandenberg, 1983). During **functional play**, the child uses the object for the function that the object was intended in her culture. A drinking cup is used to pretend drinking. A toy cell phone is used as a real cell phone. The child uses the object to imitate reality. **Indiscriminate** or **stereotypical play** occurs when the child uses the object in an indiscriminate way—banging the cup or throwing the cell phone. This type of object play is the kind that results in such outcomes as bread being placed in the DVD player and is frequently a source of both frustration and amusement for young parents and early educators.

Levels of Object Play

Symbolic play

Young children begin to engage in pretend or nonliteral play around their first birthday and becomes more complex during the second year of life. Piaget's initial work on symbolism continues to serve as the foundation for current studies. Three major elements in symbolic play occur during the first two years of life (Bretherton, 1984; Fenson, 1986).

1. decontextualization
2. decentration
3. integration

(1) **Decontextualization.** **Decontextualization** occurs when the child represents objects and actions symbolically with *other* objects and actions. The child's first pretend is decontextuallized. The child may be in the middle of playing with some objects (toys) when she sees a pillow. Though she is playing on the carpet, she may place her head on the pillow as though she is going to sleep. As soon as her head touches the pillow, she will look at adults and smile because she knows it is not real. Sleeping and eating routines tend to lend themselves to the first decontexualized behaviors because they involve daily routines.

(2) **Decentration.** **Decentration** occurs when the child moves from focusing on self to focusing on others. The child will begin to involve others in pretend play around eighteen months. Though symbolism might be noticed around the first birthday, the child focuses on self. At a year the child might be content to pull a blanket over her head. By eighteen months, she wants to put the blanket on her head and the head of the nearest person. She begins to realize that other people are a part of the world also.

(3) **Integration.** Integration involves the combination of several single schemes into a multiple scheme play experience. The child pretends to put the doll in the bed. These behaviors are generally observed around the second birthday. Most of the play involves imitating reality and seems to follow the social conventions for the activity. This indicates that play is governed by rules.

Language Development

Interactions between adults and infants are necessary for the development of communication skills. The basis for language and communication is established during this adult/infant play. Some believe that this is a form of game playing because of the reciprocal nature of the interaction, though some scholars view this not as game playing, but of *mutually reciprocal interactive play*. The adult says "Ooh, you are soooo happy today," and the child tries to move her mouth. The adults says, "Are you ready to look at the bear?" and the infant responds with babbling sounds. This continues until the infant or the adult disengages from the interaction. Was this play or was it social interaction? It was both. As the parent engaged the child, she developed the child's knowledge of turn-taking which is necessary for both play and conversation.

Social Development

> *When parent and infants are playful and enjoy their interactions with one another, infants are more likely later to be securely attached, to enjoy problem-solving tasks, and to be sociable with adults and with peers.*
>
> —Leila Beckwith, 1985

Infants and young children are socialized into their culture by adults and older peers. Adult-child relationships vary among cultures and ethnic groups. Western cultures tend to cultivate independence whereas some eastern cultures tend to foster cooperation (Tobin, Wu, & Davidson, 1989). Awareness of unique characteristics of ethnic and cultural groups represented in group settings is essential in fostering social growth and development for all children (Marshall, 2003). Activities handed down from one generation to the next that are continuously followed by most people are referred to as *traditional play forms* (Cooney & Sha, 1999). Social interactions must always be considered in terms of the individual child and her unique social and cultural traditions and history.

Attachment

Initial relationships are established in the microsphere with adults and may include parent(s), early educators, grandparent(s), sibling(s), and neighbors. The child will form an attachment to one or more adults. Attachment serves as the foundation for social and emotional growth and development. Honig (2002) described **attachment** as ". . . a strong emotional bond between a baby or young child and caring adult who is part of the child's everyday life—the child's attachment figure" (p. 2). A secure attachment forms the basis of the child's sense of self and view of the world. Infants who have a caring, consistent caregiver learn to trust, and this leads to good social and emotional health.

FIGURE 3–2 Infant-Toddler Social Play

Research Study	Implications for Practice
Title: Attention and memory for faces and actions in infancy: the salience of actions over faces in dynamic events *Authors:* Lorraine E. Bahrick, Lakshmi J. Gogate, and Ivonne Ruiz *Child Development* (2002), 73 (15), 1629–1643. *Abstract:* This study tried to determine what infants understand about the events that occur around them. Infants could discriminate and remember faces better when bimodal rather than unimodal stimuli was involved. They preferred faces over scatter plots and bimodal (rhythm, tempo, intensity) movement over stationary faces.	Infants respond to movement and motion more than faces. Early educators who interact with infants, sing songs, and rock may establish familiarity through their actions more quickly than with their faces.

Play can enhance attachment. When adults and infants play, babies develop knowledge of turn-taking and communication signals, and they start to make sense of their world. Opportunities for fostering attachment occur when adults respond to their smile with a smile, when adults sing a comforting song and hold them as they move around the room, or when the adult plays peekaboo. Responsive adults who form an attachment bond with an infant during the first months will notice a difference as the child matures. Around the age of nine to ten months, the child may become anxious if the familiar caregiver or attachment figure is not available. Though this is most intense during the period from nine months to eighteen months, some older children have attachment issues and these will be discussed later in the chapter. Social interactions between adults and infants leads to later cognitive development. See Figure 3–2.

Emotions

Erikson created a life-span perspective of social and emotional growth. During the first two years, he recognized the need for infants to develop trust rather than mistrust. A secure attachment reflects the establishment of a trusting relationship. The development of trust leads to healthy emotions. Emotional growth has frequently been linked to attachment issues. Greenspan and Greenspan (1990, p. 3) identified six levels of emotional growth that lead to good mental health.

1. birth–three months: protection, comfort, and interesting sights and sounds *to feel regulated* and *interested in the world*

2. three–seven months:	wooing and loving overtures to *fall in love*
3. four–ten months:	sensitive, empathetic reading of cues to foster *purposeful communication*
4. nine–eighteen months:	admiring, organized, intentional interactions to foster *a complex sense of self*
5. eighteen–thirty months:	pretend play and functional use of language to foster *emotional ideas*
6. thirty–forty-eight months:	effective limits and use of logic in pretend play and language to foster *emotional thinking*

Peer play

Those who have studied infant-toddler social play with peers believe that the basis of social interaction begins in infancy (Fogel, 2001; Verba, 1994). Very young infants can distinguish happy and sad faces (Rubenstein, Kalakanis, & Langlois, 1999). Many centers place pictures of babies near diaper changing areas and throughout the room to encourage familiarity. Though early studies of infants found that they do not engage in extended peer play prior to the age of two (Piaget, 1962), more recent research has found that young children begin to develop an interest in looking at and playing with other young children around the age of sixteen to twenty months (Howes, 1992). Given the increasing number of infants and toddlers in child care, there is a need for additional study in this area.

Types of social play

Most infant-toddler social play is examined in terms of mother, father, or other adult interaction. For example, Tiffany Field (1979) found that toddlers' interactions with others is influenced by their mothers. Research on types of social play with peers has found that infants move from looking at peers to engaging in behaviors that include give-and-take or run-and-chase. Social pretend play begins around the age of twelve to fifteen months when infants imitate the actions of their peers and follows a steady progression that leads to interactive social pretend play by the age of thirty-one to thirty-six months (Howes, 1992). These early interactions provide a basis for the development of sociodramatic and cooperative play.

Physical Development

The most rapid period of physical growth and development occurs during the first two years. Within a year of birth, the child's weight triples and she can crawl, stand, and walk. Mobility is refined and practiced during the second year of life. Two major factors that impact play during the first two years include the processes of gaining teeth (seven months to three years) and toilet training (fourteen months to two-and-a-half or three years). Both processes can limit the child's comfort level and play.

Infant and toddler movement can be divided into three stages: no mobility, low mobility, and high mobility (Wellhousen, 2002). *No mobility* is a term used to describe infants who cannot propel themselves, have limited mobility, and must be carried by adults. They discover the world by listening, looking, and touching. *Low mobility* infants are those who have limited mobility but can move from one place to another. *High mobility* infants can crawl, cruise, or climb anywhere!

Psychomotor skills

Motor development produces the most obvious changes during the first two years. Infants begin as somewhat immobile and by the end of the second year, any adult can attest to their mobility. Seefeldt and Barbour (1998) described these interactions:

> The baby's early movements are gross body actions, starting with the shoulders but without separate arm, hand, or finger movements. More than a year passes before the baby can make independent finger movements or oppose thumb and forefinger to grasp an object. (p. 429)

Gross motor development involves the large motor muscles and fine motor skills involve the use of smaller muscles. During the first two years, both are developing, but gross motor movement is more dominant. A study that looked at beginning motor skills is described in Figure 3–3.

■ Preschool Play

The importance of play and fantasy are not to be found in their indirect stimulation of cognitive skills and problem solving. Rather, play and fantasy are central features of what it means to be human, and problem-solving skills are a spin-off of the ability to imagine.
—*Brian Vandenberg, 1985*

Young children continue to grow and develop during this period though not as fast as they did during the first two years. Some children are well coordinated and can walk and run at a very early age. Others are very ar-

FIGURE 3–3   Infant-Toddler Motor Play

Research Study	Implications for Practice
Title: What changes in infant walking and why?	Walking is a developmental process that develops with age and experience. Early educators who provide opportunities for children to cruise and move freely are facilitating the child's physical development.
Authors: Karen E. Adolph, Beatrix Vereijken, and Patrick E. Shrout	
Child Development (2003), 74 (23), 475–497.	

Abstract: When nine-month-, seventeen-month-, five- to six-year-olds, and college students were examined in terms of walking, their footprints indicated a steady increase in walking skills. With age, walking became longer, narrower, straighter, and more consistent. The infant's age and duration of walking experience contributed to improvement. The major factor affecting walking skills was experience. This finding suggests that practice is the more important developmental factor for helping infants to conquer their weak muscles and precarious balance.

ticulate and can solve puzzles very easily. Common to all children at this age is play. Berger and Thomson (1996) called the time from two to six the **play years.** Preschoolers are in the middle of their play years. Fantasy and pretend are dominant during this time. Children develop play skills as they move from practice to pretend, from novice to mature play. The two-year-old who wants to throw his food from the table turns into a four-year-old who pretends the sofa is a lion cage. This progression occurs in the physical, social, and cognitive domains through different types of play and varies among different cultures, ethnic groups, and individuals. Early educators who are aware of different levels are sensitive to children and their play.

Cognitive Development

These are the play years.

Imagination means creating images that are not present to the senses. All of us exercise their faculty virtually every day and every night . . . the whole crux of human intelligence hinges on this ability of mind . . . nature has not programmed error into the genetic system and . . . the child's preoccupation with fantasy and imagination is vital to development.

—*Joseph Chilton Pearce, 1997*

Preschool children have thought processes that have not completely matured. Piaget (1952/1974) called this the **preoperational** period. Two characteristics of this age include the attribution of animistic characteristics to inanimate objects and egocentrism. Preschoolers believe they are the center of the universe. Listen to the four-year-old talk to the moon. She believes that the moon follows her from place to place. Preoperational thought signals the beginning of the ability to reconstruct in thought what has been established in behavior. These characteristics impact play which peaks during this time.

Children at this age believe what they see and rely on their senses instead of logic. So, magic is really magic to them. Paley (1981) refers to this in *Walley's Stories* when she writes about the children's discussion of the moon:

On the other hand, when Earl mentioned the man in the moon, the children earnestly examined the issues.

Earl: My cousin says you can wish on the man in the moon. I told my mother and she says it's only pretend.

Wally: He doesn't have a face or a body.

Lisa: Then he can't see. He's not real.

Deane: But how could he get in?

Wally: With a drill.

. . . As long as children are unsure of the boundaries between fantasies and reality, they will invent supernatural beings to protect them. When part of the moon disappears, they like to think of a moon man capable of adjusting to those strange circumstances and they like to talk about their ideas. Whether they do discuss them or not depends as much on the adult reception as on their own verbal ability." (excerpted from pp. 63–65).

Another example in Figure 3–4 supports the notion that adults need to understand how children think.

During the preschool years, changes in cognitive processing occur and are reflected in play. Children move from practice play to symbolic play as they develop their ability to engage in abstract thought. The literature from brain research suggests that the brain reinforces some connections and prunes others as it becomes more focused and specialized. Play allows children to develop symbolic thought necessary for higher-level thinking that involves imagination and creativity. "The concept of 'what might be'—being able to move in perception from the concrete given, or 'what is', to 'what was, what could have been, what one can try for, what might happen,' and, ultimately, to the purest realms of fantasy—is a touchstone of that miracle of human experience, the imagination" (Singer & Singer 1992, p. 108).

FIGURE 3–4 Preschoolers' Thought Processes That Impact Play

Research Study	Implications for Practice
Title: Preschool children's reasoning about ability *Authors:* Gail D. Heyman, Caroline L. Gee, and Jessica W. Giles *Child Development* (2003), 74 (19), 516–534. *Abstract:* This study examined 155 preschoolers (M = 4 years, 10 months) in an attempt to understand children's reasoning about their own mental state and that of others. Findings indicate that preschoolers see relationships between working hard and academic success. They also see relationships between prosocial behavior and academic success. When a group of forty 9- to 10-year-olds (M = 9 years, 10 months) were examined, the patterns tended to diminish with age.	This study provides information that can be used in terms of play. Children believe that being nice makes a difference in terms of academic success, so they probably think that being nice is a casual factor for other positive actions. This also has implications for the use of rewards in the classroom. Preschoolers believe that effort is related to outcomes.

Constructive play

One type of play that occurs during this time is constructive play and occurs when children use materials to create (Forman & Hill, 1984; Isenberg & Jalongo, 2001). They may be creating a representation of an object or they may be just creating. When children play with play dough, build with blocks, or paint a picture, they are engaging in **constructive play.** Constructive play generally leads to an end product. Piaget did not believe that constructive play was play because it is more adaptive to reality. He believed that when children were exploring or constructing, they were creating new mental structures or accommodating the information. Smilansky's (1968) work recognized this as a different type of play and now most scholars include constructive play under the heading of play as a transition stage between practice and symbolic play. Though children engage in constructive play more frequently than any other type of play in the preschool class, constructive play continues to be understudied in the preschool classroom (Sluss & Stremmel, 2004).

When a child plays with blocks, she may begin by building (constructive play). As she looks at it, she adds more blocks to the left and right side (exploration), adds more blocks (practice play), looks again, and then declares, "It's a skyscraper and the monster is coming . . ." (symbolic play). Constructive play occurs as the child moves from exploration, practice play, and then to symbolic play and repeats the cycle again. During constructive play, the child may engage in more constructive and practice play as she carries the blocks around the center. As she develops, constructive play and symbolism become more prevalent.

Symbolism is an important part of dramatic play.

Symbolic play

Symbolic play or pretend occurs when the child uses an object or action to represent another object or idea. The child might use a block to represent an airplane or lay her head down to pretend she is sleeping. Symbolism appears as early as eighteen months and dramatic play begins to develop during the second year of life. It grows more complex as the child matures and reaches a peak at five or six. **Dramatic play** is viewed as an imitation of reality that includes orderliness, exact imitation of reality, and collective symbolism of play roles (Piaget, 1962). Dramatic play enables children to engage in complex pretend requiring symbolic thought. Children (two-to-three-year-olds) initially direct their play toward materials or objects during pretend play. As children mature (four-to-five-year-olds), they include people and assume different roles. This is the most complex pretend play and is called **sociodramatic play.**

Sociodramatic play

A special type of dramatic play occurs among two or more children who communicate verbally and then cooperatively adjust their roles during the play episode (Isbell & Raines, 2003; Isenberg & Jalongo, 2001). Sarah Smilansky (1968) found that children in other parts of the world engage in different kinds of social play. What begins as dramatic play turns into sociodramatic play. She described six characteristics that are typically found in sociodramatic play (Smilansky & Shefatya, 1990). The first four are common to both dramatic and sociodramatic play. The last two occur only during sociodramatic play. They are:

1. *Imitative role-play.* The child undertakes a make-belive role and expresses it in imitative action and/or verbalization.

2. *Make-believe with regard to objects.* Movements or verbal declarations and/or materials or toys that are not replicas of the object itself are substituted for real objects.

3. *Verbal make-believe with regard to action and situations.* Verbal descriptions or declarations are substituted for actions and situations.

4. *Persistence in role-play.* The child continues within a role or play theme for a period of time at least 10 minutes long.

Only found in sociodramatic play:

5. *Interaction.* At least two players interact within the context of a play episode.

6. *Verbal communication.* There is some verbal interaction related to the play episode (p. 24)

Pretend reaches its peak at the end of the kindergarten years.

Superhero play

Superhero play begins in the preschool years. While relatively brief in duration, many adults ban this type of play in their classroom. Superhero play combines pretend play and rough-and-tumble (R&T) play. Some teachers believe that all superhero play is linked to violent themes or aggression. Though aggression and violent themes should never be condoned or permitted, stopping play always carries the risk of diminishing play. The real message becomes "It is only acceptable play when I say it is acceptable," and that may be a message that stops more than play.

Superhero play can be beneficial for children. It combines symbolism with a type of rough-and-tumble play. These are both accepted as beneficial forms of play. Children who don a cape or towel as make-believe cape assume a role that allows them to be strong and powerful. They are developing empathy as they aid the victim of an attack. They develop symbolism when they imagine other villains. Some children will take capes to school to play out their themes. This also encourages group and cooperative play for children who may not have access to playmates at home. The same children who would never engage in sociodramatic play indoors will engage in sociodramatic play on the playground as they negotiate the role of the superhero.

Before ending superhero play, it may be worthwhile to observe the play that is occurring and to decide if it is superhero play, rough-and-tumble play, or war play. Superhero play and R&T play have positive attributes and should be encouraged. On the other hand, war play or violent themes should be approached differently; these are explained in the following section.

War play

Many adults confuse superhero play and war play. As mentioned previously, war play has been banned in some countries in Scandinavia. In contrast, in the United States, it is not only allowed, but promoted through a barrage of toys and media. Even parents who want to prevent their children from exposure have little control over the media and advertising agencies (Carlsson-Paige & Levin, 1990). Early educators face the same issues. Today, many centers have a no-gun rule. Other centers believe that this is a part of popular culture. Teachers at one conference began shouting and almost broke into a fight while debating the merits of guns and war toys in the classrooms. Teachers and parents have very strong views about this topic.

Children have always played with guns or weapons that they observe others using. Teachers who remove guns from the hands of young children are often surprised and frustrated to later watch them put up their finger and make a pretend gun. Even carrots on a plate can turn into a gun. How can we explain this behavior? Can it be explained through Groos's classical theory of practice play (see Chapter 2) that children are preparing for this role when they are adults? Is it the intersection of symbolic play and physical play that makes this appealing? Is it influenced by the power that is associated with guns? It's probably a combination of all these factors. Additional research is needed in this area.

Preschoolers are still in the early stage of pretend and engage in dramatic play rather than sociodramatic play. Their play is very brief, episodic, and improvisational. Many teachers believe that if they are left alone, they will tire of the superhero or gun play and move to another theme. Other teachers ban both superhero and gun play in the classroom. Neither approach is helpful. Guiding play requires sensitive, thoughtful teachers. Approaches for guiding preschool play will be further explored in Chapter 5.

Language Development

Language development during the preschool years occurs at a very rapid rate. Sociocultural influences impact the development of language. In her classic study, Shirley Brice Heath (1983) reminds us of the language differences that children bring to school. Children from lower socioeconomic homes have fewer words in their vocabulary than do those from affluent homes. Play allows children to use words in an informal situation. Play is episodic and language is equally fluid. Play facilitates language development as children play, talk about their play, and tell stories about their play.

Social Development

The social changes that occur from age two to five are remarkable. The child is developing a sense of self that leads to social competence. Preschool children are moving into what Erikson referred to as the "industry versus guilt" stage. They are moving from dependency on their parents to becoming autonomous individuals. Play provides an opportunity for social and emotional growth. Mildred Parten's (1932) classic study includes six levels. Preschoolers generally participate in all levels cited in the research. In the preschool years, onlooker and solitary play still occur but parallel, associative, and cooperative play develop at this time. Parallel play occurs when two children play side by side but do not interact with one another. This is often evident in three-year-olds. Associative play is defined as play between two children that involves interaction. Three- and four-year-olds engage in a great deal of associative play. Cooperative play is generally not evident until the age of four. Cooperative play reflects the most mature level of social interactions. An overview of stages was presented in the Chapter 1.

Peer Play

Peer play during the preschool years usually involves pretend play. Children who engage in high-quality pretense are usually well adjusted. Connolly and Doyle (1984) found that "The amount and complexity of children's fantasy play were significantly correlated with four measures of social competence: teacher rating of social skill; peer popularity; affective role-taking ability; and amount of positive social activity (e.g. expressions of friendship, invitations to play and amount of conversation)" (p. 16). Children who can engage in highly symbolic play are leaders; they not only direct but engage others in their play. One caveat: culture may impact social interactions as described in Figure 3–5.

FIGURE 3–5   Preschool Social Play

Research Study	Implications for Practice
Title: Self in context: autonomy and relatedness in Japanese and U.S. mother-preschooler dyads	Early educators must be aware of the influence of culture on preschoolers. What may appear to be atypical behavior or dependency may actually be a reflection of the child's culture.
Authors: Tracy A. Dennis, Pamela M. Cole, Carolyn Zahn-Waxler, and Ichiro Mizuta	
Child Development (2002), 73 (15), 1803–1817.	
Abstract: This study examined differences and similarities between a sample of 30 Japanese mothers with their preschoolers and a sample of 30 American mothers with their preschoolers. During free play, observable behaviors coded included speech, emotion, and attention. Differences were significant for mothers, but not as much for children. The American mothers placed more emphasis on autonomy and Japanese mothers placed more emphasis on coexistence.	

Physical Development

We are underexercised as a nation. We look instead of play. We ride instead of walk. Our existence deprives us of the minimum of physical activity essential for healthy living.

—John F. Kennedy, 1961

From the age of two through five, children are acquiring amazing dexterity and motor control. Their locomotor skills are also becoming more refined. **Locomotor skills** refer to skills that involve movement. These include running, jumping, hopping, climbing, skipping, rolling, creeping, crawling, stepping up and down, bounding, and galloping. The list is exhaustive. Fine motor skills are developing at a regular pace. Preschoolers enjoy and learn by working puzzles, using brushes, manipulating small blocks, working with modeling clay, zipping and snapping.

Three- and four-year-olds are more capable than toddlers. They can walk and run easily. They can hop, jump, skip, throw a ball, climb stairs, and ride simple tricycles. During this time they are learning how to make whole or part body movements to music as they clap, turn, stamp, and move to music.

Two types of physical play that develop during the preschool years include chase and rough and tumble. Both involve large muscle movement, and although adults would like to restrict them to the playground, they can and do occur at anytime and in any place.

Chase

Chase involves one child running after another. With preschoolers, the chaser may become the chased within a minute with no apparent rationale. They run for a while, rest for a while, and then run some more. Sometimes one child will become angry because the other ceases to chase. It is very sporadic at this age.

Rough and Tumble

Rough-and-tumble play only occupies only about 5% of a preschooler's behavior on the playground (Pelligrini & Boyd, 1993). Because play at this age is so egocentric and short lived, rough-and-tumble play is brief. The next section on primary-age children includes a section on rough-and-tumble play. For an in-depth study that looks at preschool motor development and play in one culture, see Figure 3–6.

As the child develops, she moves into the primary years. With change in capabilities, play changes. Piaget (1965) would argue that this is a reflection of her intelligence and Vygotsky (1978) would disagree and say

FIGURE 3–6   Preschool Motor Play

Research Study	Implications for Practice
Title: Learner and environmental constraints influencing fundamental motor skill development of at-risk Hispanic preschoolers. (Motor Behavior)	Preschoolers who belong to specific cultural groups may be at-risk for not developing basic physical skills that provide a foundation for later physical development and movement. Skill must be used in determining how best to facilitate physical development without alienating them from their culture and within the confines of environmental factors.
Authors: Jacqueline D. Goodway and Richard Suminski *Research Quarterly for Exercise and Sport* (2003), 74 (2), 12–15.	
Abstract: The Center for Disease Control and Prevention has recognized a need for more information about the development of physical activity among the Hispanic children in America.	
Fundamental motor skills (FMS) serve as precursors for later physical development. This study examined a population of Hispanic preschoolers in order to understand and promote physical activity.	

that play is how intelligence develops. Regardless of the theoretical stance, children change with age and so does their play. The next section focuses on play behaviors common in the primary school. As in the previous sections, the discussion will occur in terms of cognitive, social, and physical development.

■ Primary Play

Children in primary grades are generally between six and eight years of age. According to Hughes (1999), there are three major characteristics of development during this time that impact play: (1) a need for order, (2) a need to belong, and (3) a sense of self. In the cognitive domain, the child is developing logical thought and has a *need for order* and structure. Socially, the child wants to be accepted by his peers and has a *need to belong*. Emotionally, the child is in what Erikson described as the industry versus inferiority stage (Erikson, 2000). The child needs to develop confidence and a sense of self-esteem. These traits affect the type of play that occurs in the primary years.

Cognitive Development

Children develop a more organized and logical view of the world during school-age years. Piaget (1962) referred to this as *concrete operational thinking*. Children at this age can generally engage in decentering, reversibility, seriation, and spatial reasoning, and they are beginning to conserve. That is, they are aware that the quantity may be the same though it appears in different forms. They are developing logical thinking skills. They can use specific strategies for remembering information, such as mnemonics. They find games especially enjoyable and this may help explain why school-age children are drawn to computer games.

Symbolic play

Symbolic play or pretend decreases during this time. Piaget (1962) cites three reasons for the ". . . diminution of ludic symbolism with age" (p. 145). First, the child no longer needs the cathartic effects of play. The child finds pleasure and power in different aspects of his life. For example, the child of five who does not like leaving home to go to preschool may pretend that he has an imaginary playmate that he can control. By seven, the child will share his frustrations with his friends and then write a story about "No school today." Second, games of make-believe become games with rules. The child who plays zookeeper at four may be more interested in playing a game of Sorry at seven. The world makes sense and he has a decreased need for creating a make-believe world. The five-year-old who does not understand why he is moving to a new town may engage in pretend play or create an imaginary friend whereas the second grader may tell or write a story about his experience. Symbolism in the primary grades occurs in stories or plays that children write, in dramatic plays, or in the creation of music or art. *Symbolism occurs as creative symbolism and creativity increase.* This change in thinking also changes and alters play. Sociodramatic play becomes storytelling as children act out elaborate scripts with Barbie dolls or miniature cars. Changes in cognitive thinking affect how they learn. Jerome Bruner (1985) noted that "There is evidence that by getting children to play with materials that they must later use in a problem-solving task, one gets superior performance from them in comparison with those children who spend time familiarizing themselves with the materials in various other ways. . . . The players generate more hypotheses and they reject wrong ones more quickly. They seem to become frustrated less and fixated less" (p. 603). Teachers who align their teaching with the child's developmental level will need to include play in the primary curriculum.

Play rituals

Differences between genders become more evident and appear in play rituals. Boys will tend to play games that require some sort of physical interaction before, during, or after the activity. This may be a "high five" or play fighting. Some girls will play games and engage in play rituals. **Play rituals** are defined as activities that instill ". . . cultural values in aesthetically

Rituals are a part of primary play.

satisfying behaviors" (Barnes, 1998, p. 12). Common examples of play rituals include jump rope, cheerleading, and dancing. Children are especially drawn to games like One Potato, Two Potato and games like Rock, Paper, Scissors which is popular in Japan. See Opie and Opie (1959) for additional information on school yard songs and chants. At this age, the increase in logical thinking leads to a need for order that can be found in play rituals. The author spent a year in a Professional Development School observing recess and the differences continue to be as visible as they were 20 years ago. Even though the playground was state-of-the-art, complete with wood climbers and sandboxes, the boys created a football game and the girls found places for jump rope and cheering. Consistent with research, the boys occupied most of the playground space and the girls found a small space for their play.

Language Development

During the school-age years, play affects the child's ability to understand jokes and play with words. Children will try off-color jokes or have humorous meanings for particular words. It is interesting to listen to them discuss words they consider naughty ones. They may even have certain words that are codes that are used among a certain group. In one class, I found that children thought *cat* was a bad word. Yes, they recognized that a cat is an animal, but were just sure that it had a naughty meaning. For about a week, whenever anyone mentioned cat, everyone either snickered or winced, "oooo!" It took a class meeting to discuss that words

FIGURE 3–7   Communication and Impact on Primary Play

Research Study	Implications for Practice
Title: From children's hands to adults' ears: gestures' role in the learning process *Authors:* Susan Goldin-Meadow and Melissa A. Singer *Developmental Psychology* (2003), *39* (12), 509–520. *Abstract:* This study investigated the role of hand gestures in learning. Eight adults provided instruction for 38 third and fourth graders on a math problem. Findings of the study reveal that adults offered more assistance to children whose hand gestures did not match their words. Hence, children who used hand gestures that did not match their words influenced their teacher through their behavior. Gestures with hands extend cognitive processing.	Children who use hand gestures that do not match their verbal expressions tend to elicit more assistance that is varied than children who do not have a mismatch between gestures and words. This raises a research question for play research. Are children who play string games, make origami with their hands, or engage in drama better able to use their hands in communicating their learning? How does this influence adults who are providing assistance?

could have more than one meaning before order was restored. This is not unusual at this age. Research in this area has found that children may also engage in language and hand gestures that do not match. See Figure 3–7 for a full discussion.

Problem solving and creativity

Bruner (1976) wrote about the role of play in developing problem-solving skills. As children try one maneuver after another on the game board, they must revisit and reconsider their moves. Cognitive skills used and developed during a game of Sorry are those skills that useful for problem solving.

Social Development

Social development changes during this time. The young child may play with others but now the child's play will be influenced by peers, the media, advertisements, and other influences in their world. Now their choice of toys may be as influenced by these factors as by their parents.

Games with rules

Games with rules occur among primary-age children. Piaget established two conditions for games with rules, competition and rules. He noted that games with rules are:

> Sensory-motor combinations (races, marbles, ball games, etc.), or intellectual combinations (cards, chess, etc.) in which there is competition between individuals (otherwise rules would be useless) and which are regulated either by a code handed down from earlier generations or by temporary agreement. (Piaget, 1962, p. 144)

Games with rules have an element of competition whereas play does not. Play occurs just for the sake of the play.

Physical Development

Children's skills really begin to emerge during the school years. Gender differences are noticeable between the ages of six and eight as boys gain more height and weight than girls (Frost, Wortham, & Reifel, 2001). Environmental factors influence health, and thus play, during this time. Children who are malnourished or obese will not be able to perform at the same level as their peers. Children who have serious illnesses will also be limited by their physical capabilities. During this time, children will take risks. They may not see the car as they chase a ball, or they may not realize that they will slide into a tree. As children become more mature, they become more aware of risks but may be more influenced by peers. Those who are allowed to play still enjoy recess at this age. See Chapter 9 for a full discussion of recess.

Fine motor

Fine motor skills become more developed during this time. Some children will become especially skilled, and others will continue to develop. For children who are especially coordinated, games with strings and other tasks that require hand-eye coordination will begin to take on a separate role. It is not unusual to watch a budding musician emerge as she realizes that she can reach the octaves much more easily than her friend. Many games are played that develop hand-eye coordination. In some countries such as China and Hungary, the game of marbles is played by both girls and boys (Ulker & Gu, 2004). Today, very few children in the United States play marbles. Rather, they demonstrate their agility through keyboarding or video games.

Gross motor

Gross motor skills become more refined as children develop skills in running, jumping, climbing, and chasing. They ride bicycles, play tee-ball, Little League (age eight), tennis, and other sport activities. Children play games that involve both movement and thought. For example, tag, jump rope, and hide-and-seek all take on different levels of complexity during these years. These involve chase, but they can lead to rough-and-tumble play which may turn into play fighting. For this reason, many schools ban chase games and rough-and-tumble play in an attempt to prevent aggression. (See Figure 3–8 for additional information.) This ban, however, may lead to more aggression. A brief overview is provided below and this topic is revisited in Chapter 9.

FIGURE 3–8 Primary Social Play

Research Study	Implications for Practice
Title: "I got some swords and you're dead!": Violent fantasy, antisocial behavior, friendship, and moral sensibility in young children *Authors:* Judy Dunn and Claire Hughes *Child Development* (2001), 72, 491–505. *Abstract:* Preschoolers who were rated as "hard to manage" were observed two years later and administered a battery of tests. Participation in violent fantasy was a common factor found in all the children in the study. The authors found a relationship between violent fantasy and displays of anger and refusal to help a friend, poor language ability, frequent antisocial behavior, poor communication and coordination of play, more conflict with a friend. Two years later, they showed less empathic moral sensibility. Children's pretend play may serve as an important window for identifying children who display antisocial behavior.	Teachers may need to be more cognizant of the themes that are occurring during pretend play. Children who engage in violent fantasy might also display antisocial behaviors in other areas.

Chase games

Chase games begin in the preschool years, escalate in primary school, and disappear by middle school (Pelligrini & Boyd, 1993). Chase games include threats of kissing, themes from popular culture, traditional hide-and-seek, and any kind of make-believe "contamination."

Rough-and-tumble play

The decrease in symbolic play is accompanied by a simultaneous increase in rough-and-tumble play (R&T). Rough-and-tumble play is defined as play that involves running, chasing, fleeing, and wrestling behaviors. Rough-and-tumble includes ". . . play face, run, chase, flee, wrestle, and open-hand beat" (Pelligrini & Boyd, 1993, p. 115). These can be defined as

play face	wide-smile or exaggerated expression
run	rapid sustained movement from one place to another
chase	one child pursuing another
flee	rapid movement from one spot to another
wrestle	physical contact involving both children in an interactive tussle
open-hand beat	using the open hand for tagging rather than a closed fist

Aggression, on the other hand, usually includes frowning, fixation, hitting, pushing, taking, and grabbing (Blurton Jones, 1972). Children take turns during rough-and-tumble play and it has specific rules that govern

FIGURE 3–9   Primary Motor Play

Research Study	Implications for Practice
Title: Young children's play qualities in same-, other-, and mixed-sex peer groups *Authors:* Richard A. Fabes, Carol Lynn Martin, and Laura D. Hanish *Child Development* (2003), 74 (12) 921–932. *Abstract:* This study investigated how boys and girls interacted with one other on the playground. Contextual factors that impacted their play included the sex of the child, the sex of the play partner, and whether they played in dyads or groups. Findings indicate that when boys played together they were more aggressive and they stayed away from the adults and exhibited more stereotypical behavior. Girls were unlikely to play only with girls. Play among mixed-sex dyads occurred about 25% of the time when dyads were close to adults. The sex of the child and play partners affects children's experiences in peer groups.	Teachers should be aware that they impact play just by being on the playground. Teachers may want to be sure that children have time to engage in mixed-sex play in other settings. It is interesting to note that boys played with exclusive male groups, but that girls did not play with "girls only" groups.

the play. Pelligrini observes that ". . . in R&T children learn to use and practice skills that are important for their social competence. For example, in R&T children alternate roles between the victim and victimizer. Such reciprocal role-taking may be important for children's perspective-taking ability" (1988, p. 15). The difference between R&T and aggression is real. R&T, like chase, is a normal, beneficial activity for primary-age children. It can and should be encouraged while simultaneously discouraging aggression. (See Figure 3–9.)

Bruno Bettelheim (1987) points to the work of K. Groos and Piaget and the function of play in developing motor and cognitive and intellectual abilities.

> Play teaches the child, without his being aware of it, the habits most needed for intellectual growth, such as stick-to-itiveness, which is so important in all learning. Perseverance is easily acquired around enjoyable activities such as chosen play. But if it has not become a habit through what is enjoyable, it is not likely to become one through an endeavor like school work. (p. 36)

Understanding the types of play observed frequently at this age and their progression provides a background for creating and implementing programs that are appropriate for young children. This chapter provides the base for developing programs in Chapters 4, 5, and 6.

> ## *PlayScape Reflections*
>
> Lu Chen, like Jaunita in the previous chapter, values play. She may not know that Wu Chon and Lu are developing their large motor skills when they engage in chase games that involve running and jumping. Or that they are developing social skills as they interact with each other and negotiate their aunt's rules. This also helps them understand and adjust to their culture and society outside their home. But are they learning? Pretend play develops their ability to engage in *abstraction*, which is a critical skill for learning and recognizing the alphabet and numbers. The twins play at school and at home. At school, they will play with English-speaking Americans. Their play will reflect a blend of the play that the other children bring to school. In contrast, at home they will be able to learn games and stories passed along from their Chinese ancestors. The transmission of culture is an important part of their life because they are the first generation in a new land. Lu Chen can enrich their lives by taking them to parks, libraries, social and spiritual activities on the weekend. Wu Chon and Lu will be ready to learn when they enter the public school system. The wise kindergarten teacher will help Lu Chen transition the children into a setting through play. Play can serve as a conduit for transitioning from one culture to another.

■ Summary

Play as beneficial for growth and development formed the core of this chapter. Though children develop holistically through play, this chapter teases it apart for the purpose of examination. The benefits of play are explored for infants and toddlers (birth to age two), preschoolers (three- to-five-year-olds), and primary age children (six- to-eight-year-olds). Their progress is examined in terms of cognitive, social, and physical growth. The progression of play is examined as the child moves from sensory exploration to complex games with rules.

■ Key Terms

Attachment
Chase
Constructive play
Coordination of secondary schemes (eight–twelve months)

Decentration
Decontextualization
Dramatic play
Exploratory play
Fine motor skills

Gross motor skills
Functional (or practice) play
Indiscriminant (or stereotypical) play

Invention of new means through
  mental combinations
  (eighteen–twenty-four months)
Locomotor skills
Object play
Play rituals
Play years

Preoperational thinking
Primary circular reactions
  (one–four months)
Prime time
Reflexive stage
  (birth–one month)
Rough-and-tumble play

Secondary circular reactions
  stage (four–eight months)
Sociodramatic play
Tertiary circular reactions
  (twelve–eighteen months)

■ Helpful Web Sites and Technology Resources

◆ **Fisher Price**
http://www/fisherprice.com   A commercial site that discusses each stage of play and appropriate toys.

■ Activities

1. InClass Lab

A. As a group, create a table depicting the levels of either cognitive, social, language, or physical growth of a child. Make an accompanying table that depicts the development of play in that domain or area. What developmental factors affect play?

B. Observe a small child either in class, at an on-site lab school, or in a video clip. Where is the child developmentally? What kind of play did you observe? Does this fit the information in the textbook?

2. Research and Inquiry

A. Visit a local park. Watch the play of four- and five-year-olds. Now find some older children (six- to eight-year-olds) to observe. Is the play of younger children different from that of the older children? If so, identify the differences. Are the differences evident to casual observers?

B. Visit a local park. Watch the play of one age group. What developmental dimensions were evident? Describe their play. Does it fit with the information in the text?

C. Piaget believed that play followed development, but Vygotsky believed that development followed play. Investigate this issue. Does play precede or follow development?

3. Service Learning

A. Volunteer in a local after-school program. After you leave the center, write a description of the observed play. Did the center encourage play for different ages? If so, how? What games did you observe? Did you see "boys only" or "girls only" groups emerge in play?

B. Find out what play opportunities are available for children who are in local homeless shelters. Work in teams of four students. Each person should create a toy box for one age group. For example, each person will complete a toy box for either infants, toddlers, preschoolers, or primary.

4. Family Connections

Choose one of the following projects:

A. Develop brochures that communicate the stages of play to parents. Place these in local medical officers' and public offices that parents visit.

B. Create posters that depict different types of play (functional, constructive, dramatic, sociodramatic, and games). Place these in local grocery stores or community centers.

5. Play Advocacy

A. Find out what play opportunities are available for children in local homeless shelters and offer to develop additional materials. See 3B above.

B. Ask what play arrangements are available at the local police office. Do they have teddy bears in police cars?

References

Adolph, K., Vereijken, B., & Shrout, P. (2003). What changes in infant walking and why? *Child Development, 74* (23), 475–497.

Bahrick, L. E., Gogate, L. J., & Ruiz, I. (2002). Attention and memory for faces and actions in infancy: the salience of actions over faces in dynamic events. *Child Development, 73* (15), 1629–1643.

Barnes, D. (1998). Play in historical context. In D. Fronberg and D. Bergen (Eds.) *Play from birth to twelve and beyond* (5–13). New York: Garland.

Beckwith, L. (1985). Parent-child interaction and social-emotional development. In C. C. Brown & A.W. Gottfried (Eds.), *Play interactions: The role of toys and parental involvement in children's development* (pp. 152–159). Skillman, NJ: Johnson & Johnson.

Begley, S. (1997, Spring-Summer). How to build a baby's brain. *Newsweek Special Edition*, pp. 28–32.

Bergen, D. (1998). Stages of play development. In D. Bergen (Ed.), *Reading from play as medium for learning and development* (pp. 71–93). Olney, MD: Association for Childhood Education International.

Berger, K. S., & Thompson, R. A. (1996). *The developing person through childhood*. New York: Worth.

Bettelheim, B. (1987). The importance of play. *Atlantic*, pp. 35–46.

Blurton Jones, N., (1972). Categories of child-child interaction. In Blurton Jones (Ed.), *Ethological studies of child behavior* (pp. 97–129). Cambridge, UK: Cambridge University Press.

Bremner, G., & Fogel, A. (2001). *Handbook of infant development*. London: Blackwell.

Bretherton, I. (1984). Representing the social world in symbolic play: Reality and fantasy. In I. Bretherton (Ed.), *Symbolic play: The development of social understanding* (pp. 1–41). New York: Academic.

Bruner, J. (1976). The nature and uses of immaturity. In J. Bruner, A. Jolly, & K.Sylva (Eds.), *Play: Its role in development and evolution* (pp. 28–64). New York: Basic Books.

Bruner, J. (1985). On teaching thinking: An afterthrought. In S. F. Chipman, J. W. Segan, & R. Glasser (Eds.), *Thinking and learning skills* (Vol. 2, pp. 597–608). Hillsdale, NJ: Lawrence Erlbaum Associates.

Cannella, G. (1997). *Deconstructing early childhood education: Social justice and revolution*. New York: Peter Lang.

Carlsson-Paige, N., & Levin, D. (1990). *Who's calling the shots? How to respond effectively to children's fascination with war play and war toys*. Philadelphia, PA: New Society Publishers.

Caruso, D. (1984). Infants' exploratory play. *Young Children, 40* (1), 27–30.

Christie, J., & Johnsen, P. (1987). Reconceptualizing constructive play: A review of the empirical literature. *Merrill-Palmer Quarterly, 33* (4), 439–452.

Conolly, J. A., & Doyle, A. B. (1984). Relation of social fantasy to social competence in preschoolers. *Developmental Psychology, 20,* 797–806.

Cooney, M., & Sha, J. (1999). Play in the day of Qiaoqiao: A Chinese perspective. *Child Study Journal, 29* (2), 97–111.

Dennis, T., Cole, P., Zahn-Waxler, C., & Mizuta, I. (2002). Self in context: autonomy and relatedness in Japanese and U.S. mother-preschooler dyads. *Child Development, 73* (15), 1803–1817.

Dunn J., & Hughes, C. (2001). "I got some swords and you're dead!": Violent fantasy, antisocial behavior, friendship, and moral sensibility in young children. *Child Development, 72,* 491–505.

Erikson, E. (2000). *Childhood and society*. New York: Norton. (Originally published in 1950.)

Fabes, R., Martin, C., & Hanish, L. (2003). Young children's play qualities in same-, other-, and mixed-sex peer groups. *Child Development*, 74 (12), 921–932.

Fenson, L. (1986). The developmental progression of play. In A. Gottfried & C. C. Brown (Eds.), *Play interactions: The contribution of play materials and parental involvement to children's development*. Lexington, MA: Heath.

Field, T. (1979). Infant behaviors directed toward peers and adults in the presence and absence of mother. *Infant Behavior and Development*, 2, 47–54.

Fogel, A. (2001). *Infancy: Infant, family, and society* (4th ed.). Belmont, CA: Wadsworth.

Foreman, G. & Hill, F. (1984). *Constructive play: Applying Piaget in the preschool* (Rev. ed.). Menlo Park, CA: Addison-Wesley.

Froebel, F. (1887). *The education of man*. New York: Appleton.

Frost, J., Wortham, S., & Reifel, S. (2001). *Play and child development*. Upper Saddle River, NJ: Merrill/Prentice Hall.

Goldin-Meadow, S., & Singer, M. (2003). From children's hands to adults' ears: gesture's role in the learning process. *Developmental Psychology*, 39 (12), 509–520.

Goodway, J., & Suminski, R. (2003). Learner and environmental constraints influencing fundamental motor skill development of at-risk hispanic preschoolers. (Motor Behavior) *Research Quarterly for Exercise and Sport*, 74 (2), 12–15.

Greenspan, S., & Greenspan, N. (1990). *The essential partnership: How parents and children can meet the emotional challenges of infancy and childhood*. New York: Penguin.

Heath, S. (1983). *Ways with words: Language, life, and work in communities and classrooms*. Cambridge, UK: Cambridge University Press.

Heyman, G., Gee, C., and Giles, J. (2003). Preschool children's reasoning about ability. *Child Development*, 74 (19), 516–534.

Honig, A. (1999). Quality infant/toddler caregiving. In K. Paciorek and J. Munroe (Eds.), *Sources: Notable selections in Early Childhood Education* (70–76) (2nd ed.) Guilford, CO: McGraw-Hill.

Honig, A. (2002). *Secure relationships: Nurturing infant/toddler attachment in early care settings*. Washington, DC: NAEYC.

Howes, C. (1992). *The collaborative construction of pretend: Social pretend play functions*. Albany: State University of New York Press.

Hughes, F. (1999). *Children, play, and development*. Boston: Allyn and Bacon.

Isbell, R. T., & Raines, S. (2003). *Creativity and the arts with young children*. Clifton Park, NY: Thomson Delmar Learning.

Isenberg, J. & Jalongo, M. (2001). *Creative expression and play in early childhood*. Columbus, OH: Merrill.

Kennedy, J. (1961). Address in New York City at the National Football Foundation and Hall of Fame Banquet. Public Papers of the Presidents of the United States. John F. Kennedy (p. 770). Washington: United States Printing Office.

Marshall, H. (2003). Cultural influences on the development of self-concept: Updating our thinking. In C. Copple (Ed.) *A world of difference: Readings on teaching young children in a diverse society.* Washington, DC: National Association for the Education of Young Children.

Meinsm, E., Fernyhough, C., Wainwright, R., Das Gupta, M., Fradley, E., and Tuckey, M. (2002). Maternal mind-mindedness and attachment security as predictors of theory of mind understanding. *Child Development, 73* (12), 1715–1726.

Nash, J. M. (1997, February). Fertile minds. *Time: Special Report,* pp. 49–56.

Opie, I., & Opie, P. (1959). *The lore and language of schoolchildren.* Oxford, UK: Claredon Press.

Paley, V. (1981). *Wally's stories.* Cambridge, MA: Harvard University.

Parten, M. (1932). Social participation among pre-school children. *Journal of Abnormal Psychology, 27,* 243–269.

Pearce, J. (1997). *The magical child.* New York: Plume.

Pelligrini, A. (1988). Elementary school children's rough-and-tumble play and social competence. *Developmental Psychology, 24,* 802–206.

Pelligrini, A. & Boyd, B. (1993). The role of early childhood development and education: Issues in definition and function. In B. Spodek (Ed.), *Handbook of research in early childhood education.* New York: Macmillian.

Piaget, J. (1962). *Play, dreams, and imitation in childhood.* New York: Norton. (Originally published in 1951.)

Piaget, J. (1974). *The origins of intelligence in children.* New York: Basic Books. (Originally published in 1952.)

Piaget, J. (1965). *The moral judgement of the child.* New York: Free Press.

Power, T. G., & Park, R. D., (1980). Play as a context for early learning: Lab and home analyses. In I. E. Sigel & L. J. Laosa (Eds.), *The family as a learning environment* (pp. 147–178). New York: Plenum.

Ratner, N., & Bruner, J. (1978). Games, social exchange, and the acquisition of language. *Journal of Child Language, 5,* 391–401.

Rogers, C. S., & Sawyers, J. K. (1988). *Play in the lives of children.* Washington, DC: National Association for the Education of Young Children.

Rubenstein, A., Kalakanis, L., & Langlois, J. (1999). Infant preferences for attractive faces: A cognitive explanation. *Developmental Psychology, 35* (3), 848–956.

Rubin, K. H., & Coplan, R. J. (1998). Social and nonsocial play in childhood: An individual differences perspective. In O. N. Saracho & B. Spodek (Eds.), *Multiple perspectives on play in early childhood* (pp. 144–170). Albany: State University of New York Press.

Rubin, K. H., Fein, G., & Vandenberg, B. (1983). Play. In E. M. Hetherington (Ed.). P. H. Mussen (Series Ed.), *Handbook of child psychology: Vol. 4, Socialization, personality, and social development* (pp. 693–774). New York: Wiley.

Santrock, J. (2003). *Children* (7th ed.). Boston: McGraw Hill.

Sawyer, R. K. (1997). *Pretend play as improvisation: Conversation in the preschool classroom*. Mahwah, NJ: Erlbaum.

Seefeldt, C., & Barbour, N. (1998). *Early childhood education: An introduction*. Columbus, OH: Merrill.

Shore, R. (1997). *Rethinking the brain: New insights into early development*. New York: Families and Work Institute.

Shonkoff, J., & Phillips, D. (2000). *From neurons to neighborhoods: The science of early childhood development*. Washington, DC: National Academy Press.

Singer, J., & Singer, D. (1992). *The house of make believe*. Cambridge, MA: Harvard University Press.

Sluss, D., & Stremmel, A. (2004). An investigation of collaborative constructive block play. *Journal of Research in Childhood Education, 18* (4), 293–305.

Smilansky, S. (1968). *The effects of sociodramatic play on disadvantaged preschool children*. New York: Wiley.

Smilansky, S., & Shefatya, L. (1990). *Facilitating play: A medium for promoting cognitive, socio-emotional, and academic development*. Gaithersburg, MD: Psychosocial and Educational Publications.

Tobin, J., Wu, D., & Davidson, D. (1989). *Preschool in three cultures: Japan, China, and the United States*. New Haven, CT: Yale University Press.

Ulker, R., & Gu, W. (2004). *Traditional Play: Chinese and Turkish Examples*, Presentation at The Association for the Study of Play. Atlanta, GA.

Vandenberg, B. (1985). Beyond the ethology of play. In C. C. Brown & A. W. Gottfried (Eds.), *Play interactions* (pp. 3–10). Lexington, MA: Heath.

Verba, M. (1994). The beginnings of collaboration in peer interaction. *Human Development, 37* (3), 125–140.

Vygotsky, L. (1978). *Mind in society: The development of higher psychological processes*. Cambridge, MA: Harvard University Press.

Watson, J. S., & Ramey, C.T. (1972). Reactions to response contingent stimulation in early infancy. *Merrill-Palmer Quarterly, 18*, 219–227.

Wellhousen, K. (2002). *Outdoor play every day: Innovative play concepts for early childhood*. Clifton Park, NY: Thomson Delmar Learning.

Supporting Play in Infant-Toddler Centers

The game is not important to the infant because people play it, but rather people become important to the infant because they play "The Game."

—*J. Watson, 1976*

Chapter Overview

Infants and toddlers learn through play and this serves as the foundation of this chapter. The important role of adults in the lives of very young children will be examined in home and in center settings. Facilitating cognitive, social, emotional, and physical development through play with music, movement, and art will be explored in terms of creating appropriate indoor environment for all very young children. Opportunities for observing and assessing play will also be presented in this chapter.

Objectives

After reading this chapter, you should be able to:

- ◆ Discuss the advantages of a play-based curriculum for infants and toddlers.
- ◆ Recognize the role of the adult in facilitating play.
- ◆ Describe activities that can encourage play.
- ◆ Explain three ways to assess infant-toddler play.

PlayScape

Sonda enrolled Jermaine in the center this morning. She knew that as a two-year-old, he was very bright. He talked before other children and now she really expected him to excel in the infant-toddler center. As she rounded the corner, she heard him laughing. She watched as he quietly placed soft, multicolored blocks side by side. As he placed a soft teddy bear on top of the blocks, he giggled with glee. When he saw her, he came running. "Payed all day!" She looked at him and quizzed, "You played all day?"

Sonda put Jermaine down and turned to the teacher, "Thank you for taking such good care of him. He loves to play."

Play Provocation

Jermaine's provocation to play is a set of blocks. Toddlers use blocks in a functional way. They begin by picking up, carrying around, dumping, and filling before they move into stacking and constructive play. Sonda, like many other parents, was delighted that Jermaine played at the infant-toddler center. Today, some centers have suggested flash cards for toddlers. Others have even added math to schedules for infants! Clearly, there is a misunderstanding about how infants and toddlers learn (Szanton, 2001). Infants and toddlers grow and develop through interactions with adults and more competent others. They construct their understanding of the world as they explore. An aesthetics-based approach including play, music, movement, language, and art creates an appropriate environment for very young children. Programs that emphasize play facilitate growth at an appropriate pace.

■ Play as Curriculum in Infant-Toddler Centers

When infants and toddlers are not sleeping, they are engaged in play and exploration. Programs that meet the needs of this age group must include play and exploration as key components of the curriculum. Infant-toddler programs are by design different from those of preschoolers. The care of infants is different from that of toddlers. Infant caregivers must be aware of stimulating without overstimulating. Programs for toddlers should not be scaled-down preschool programs (Weiser, 1991). Children with disabilities

Play facilitates growth and development.

or delays require more stimulation (Cook, Tessier, & Klein, 2000). Children without delays will require less stimulation. Understanding this balance requires an attitude of *respect, responsiveness, and reciprocity* (Gonzalez-Mena & Eyer, 2001).

Programs that support play and exploration maintain a safe, healthy, caring environment. Essential elements include movement, music, art, toys and materials, language and literacy activities that ensure object play, motor play, social play, and symbolic/pretend play. Developmental characteristics of infants and toddlers should inform the curriculum because at this age developmental domains are so intertwined (Weiser, 1991). Infants need a relatively small space with areas for sleeping, eating, messy activities, and well-defined floor play areas. Toddlers need more space for moving and clearly defined areas for play. The unique characteristics of nonmobile infants (lap babies), mobile infants (cruisers), and highly mobile toddlers (movers) serve as a basis for developing programs and environments that reflect best practices for young children.

■ Creating a Context for Play

Good programs create a context for play by providing love, protection, and a developmentally appropriate pace. Alan Fogel (1998) noted that ". . . a first-century BC Chinese text, *Liji (Record of Rituals)*, states, 'When training is premature, nothing is gained other than a great deal of work'" (Kojima, 1986, p. 44). Programs that are sensitive to the developmental needs of the infant have specific characteristics. Studies of infant-toddler programs have found specific indicators of high-quality care that include (McMullen, 1999, p. 73):

♦ use of developmentally appropriate practice as a philosophy in setting up the environment and developing the curriculum

♦ low adult-to-child ratios and group sizes that are strictly maintained

♦ health and safety recommendations and guidelines that are rigorously followed

♦ staff who are knowledgeable in child development and learning that is specific to the infant and toddler developmental period and who know how to use this knowledge appropriately

♦ administrative policies and workplace conditions that discourage staff turnover and thus encourage consistency of caregiving for babies

Skills are developed through adult/child interactions that occur through play.

◆ staff who demonstrate that strong interpersonal skills and positive communication exist and are facilitated among caregivers, colleagues, parents, and babies

◆ sensitively responsive caregivers who know each baby so well that they can anticipate the babies' needs, read their verbal and nonverbal cues, and consistently respond quickly in a loving and affectionate manner to meet those needs

Children in high-quality centers should (Stonehouse, 1999, p. 155):

◆ feel safe, secure, respected, valued, cared for, happy, encouraged, and reassured

◆ know about themselves, others, the environment, routines, and limits

◆ acquire living skills, including social skills, language skills, physical skills, and a respect for people and things

■ Adult Facilitation

Babies need social interactions with loving adults who talk with them, listen to their babblings, name objects for them, and give them opportunities to explore their worlds.

—Sandra Scarr, 1984

Next to safety, adult interaction is perhaps the most important component in the infant-toddler curriculum. When adults establish a strong relationship with the infant, it results in positive outcomes (Brazetton & Cramer, 1990; Honig, 2002). Infants who do not bond to an attachment figure may be at risk even in their adolescent years (Honig, 2002). For this reason, the child care community is concerned about the high turnover rate in child care centers. Currently over half of the infant-toddler teachers leave each year and over half of all infant-toddler teachers are generally first-year teachers (Szanton, 2001). The effect on consistency and attachment is both regrettable and a cause for alarm.

Consistency is not the only requirement. Adults in infant-toddler centers have a complex role. Not only are they involved as a play partner during floor play, they must watch the children's reactions, and assess how well they are doing. Gonzalez-Mena and Eyer (2001) recommend ten guidelines for meeting this challenge.

1. Involve infants and toddlers in things that concern them.
2. Invest in quality time.

3. Learn each child's unique ways of communicating and teach them yours.

4. Invest time and energy to build a total person.

5. Respect infants and toddlers as worthy people.

6. Be honest about your feelings.

7. Model the behavior you want to teach.

8. Recognize problems as learning opportunities and let infants and toddlers try to solve their own.

9. Build security by teaching trust.

10. Be concerned about the quality of development in each stage.

Also see Figure 4–1 on how to help babies play.

FIGURE 4–1 Helping Babies Play

Birth–four months

In these early months, babies explore their new world with their eyes. Things you can do to help this exploration are:

- Provide bright, moving objects for babies to practice looking at. Mobiles should be interesting from the baby's view. Provide consistency by leaving the objects in their place so the baby begins to recognize familiar objects in the crib at home as well as in out-of-home care settings.

- Move objects close to and away from babies. Also, move your face close to and away from them. This will make a visual impact different from things that stay still. It helps babies judge the relationship between objects and between themselves and objects.

- Hold babies up to your shoulder and move them around to provide a better view.

- Show the baby in a mirror how beautiful and wonderful he is.

- Playfully engage the baby in repetitions of looking, smiling, talking, and laughing. The adult usually starts the game by smiling and talking to gain baby's attention. Experienced caregivers and mothers find that tongue clicking, head shaking, moving quickly toward baby and then stopping, and repeating certain sounds are entertaining to babies. Perform in a clownlike fashion and stop to wait for baby to do his part—laughing, smiling, or moving his arms and legs in excitement. Repeat the clown show several times, each time stopping for baby to have a turn. The show stops when baby starts to look away or show other signs of fatigue, overstimulation, or lack of interest.

Babies explore sound and motion too. Some suggestions for increasing these explorations are:

- Talk to babies in a playful way. Smile and repeat soft sounds. Stop between sounds and watch for them to smile or move in response to your voice. If you get a playful response, repeat the show.

- Sing to the baby. Make up songs just for the baby. Dance with the baby nestled on your shoulder.

- Play with the baby's hands and feet, gently patting and rubbing, making silly, soft sounds to match. "Pedal" the baby's legs for a bike ride, describing where you're going.

Four–eight months

In this stage, infants can use not only eyes and ears but hands and mouth to explore objects. Some ideas for this age group's play are:

- Keep toy safety a primary concern. Provide objects that can be held by small hands but that are not small enough to fit entirely in the mouth. Toys must be washable and made of tough, durable materials. There must be no sharp edges or points that can injure and no small parts that can come off (small wheels or buttons, for example).

- Toys that move or make a sound in response to the baby's actions are best. Look for toys that pop up, turn, honk, rattle, or play music when the baby pushes, punches, hits, or pokes at them.

(continued)

FIGURE 4–1 *(continued)*

- Minimize interruptions to protect babies' exploration of new objects. Watch but don't interrupt when babies are busy exploring. Also prevent other children (especially older ones) from interrupting play. Having duplicates of several toys will help prevent would-be "snatchers" from robbing the explorer.

Babies are also becoming more social and enjoy your efforts to entertain them by:

- playing "This Little Piggy Went to Market" with their toes
- singing special songs while changing their diapers and clothes or cutting nails

Eight–twelve months

Babies now are fully active in exploring their world. Almost all babies crawl or creep; many walk around the room holding on, and some are independently walking. Babies now combine objects and practice dropping, throwing, and squeezing. Some suggestions for fostering their play are:

- Provide objects to put in containers and dump out. Some good containers are plastic bowls, plastic storage boxes, baskets, and shoe boxes. Make sure that items to put in the containers are small enough for small hands but not small enough to fit entirely in the mouth. Good things to put in are small clocks, yarn balls, plastic lids, and rings from stack-a-ring toys.
- Help babies practice sounds by repeating their sounds back—for example, "dada," "oh oh," and by the end of the first year, words like "kitty," "baby," and "doll." Don't limit speech to imitating babies, but extend and expand their words into sentences.
- Read to the baby.
- Provide toys that challenge the infant's skills. Children this age practice pulling, pushing, poking, and punching.
- Be sure toys are in working order. Toys that don't work are just no fun. They can be very frustrating.
- Introduce toys with more than one part. Infants this age especially like things that fit inside something else.
- Stretch baby's arms above her head, asking, "How big is baby? SOOOO Big!" After a while, baby will hold her arms up alone to respond to your question.
- Play pat-a-cake, peekabo, and copycat with the baby.
- Children in this age group enjoy the sensory feeling of moving through space—riding piggyback, swinging in child-seat swings, riding in wagons, and dancing in an adult's arms. They and older babies also enjoy bouncing on an adult's knee to the accompaniment of a song or verse such as "This Is the Way the Baby Rides."

Twelve–eighteen months

Infants in this age group are great experimenters, trying out all their skills this way and that just to see what will happen. The first pretend play occurs in this group when infants begin to act "as if " doing daily activities. They pretend to sleep, eat, or bathe. They then apply these acts to others and later copy others' behaviors as their own. Some suggestions for supporting play for these babies are:

- Provide simple pictures of familiar items (laminated, covered with clear plastic, or put into zip-type plastic bags) for baby to practice naming.
- Read to the baby, talking about the book as you go.
- Provide safe places (indoors and outdoors) for moving, walking, and climbing. Due to the likelihood of many falls, climbing steps should be plastic or covered with carpet. Tunnels and cabinets provide opportunities for going in, out, through, and under.
- Be the receiver of the child's pretend actions. Take a drink from the empty cup, smack your lips, and say, "Ummmmm, good." Let the child comb your hair or pretend to wash your face. Then extend the pretense to another recipient such as a doll. Support the child's language development by narrating the drama as it progresses: "Corey is asleep," or "Oh, I'm going to be clean. I'm getting a bath."
- Provide real-looking toys for daily activities such as eating, bathing, riding, and cleaning. Important toys for pretense at this age are dolls (realistic, representative of a variety of racial/ethic groups) and daddy, mommy, brother, sister, baby) and transportation vehicles (boats, planes, cars, trains).

Source: Excerpted from Janet K. Sawyers and Cosby Rogers, *Helping Young Children Develop Through Play: A Practical Guide for Parent, Caregivers, and Teachers* (Washington, DC: NAEYC, 1988). Used with permission of the authors.

■ Aesthetics-based Approach

An aesthetic approach to infant-toddler care can enrich the life of both the child and early educator. This approach utilizes the arts to create a beautiful, enjoyable environment. Play, music, movement, art, story, and reenactment provide the basis for an aesthetic approach.

Music

Of all the gifts with which individuals are endowed, none emerges earlier than music.

—Howard Gardner, 1995

Infants are born ready for music. Many interactions between parents and infants have a musical quality. When adults talk to babies, their voices have a higher pitch and phrases have distinct contours that are specific to that culture (Custodero, 2003; Papousek, 1996). Speech directed toward infants has a musical quality that may serve as a survival mechanism. Parents intuitively use music with younger children. The musical interactions that occur between adult and child foster the development of the young child as they learn about turn-taking, meaning-making, and belonging (Custodero, 2003).

These ideas are not new. Comenius in the 1600s was the first to advocate the use of music with young children. Froebel valued music and incorporated it into the curriculum in the 1800s. Play, music, and movement are almost impossible to separate. All are intrinsically motivated. Some scholars believe the play that occurs between the mother and child during reciprocal interactions has a musical quality. Like play, music develops social, motor, and, sometimes, object and pretend play as it develops skills listed in Figure 4–2.

FIGURE 4–2 Benefits of Music in Child Care Programs

Music benefits children in a variety of ways:
- children are exposed to the music of their culture and other cultures.
- children develop an appreciation for music.
- communication increases when children are singing and interacting with each other.
- social interaction increases as children sit, stand, and move together as a group.
- language develops as children use rhymes and rhythms.
- motor skills develop as children use their large and small muscles during fingers plays and dances.
- creativity develops as children play instruments, make up their own songs and create dances.
- music provides an integrative activity that develops the whole child.

Early childhood teachers and music

Teachers who are excited about music stimulate this interest in others. Music can play a major part in the curriculum even thought the teacher may not be so inclined. There are numerous recordings that can be used. The teacher's attitude toward music is very important. Too often, teachers have the mistaken belief that anyone not sounding like a major recording star should not sing. Children need interactions with adults who will sing while they diaper, sing during daily routines, and sing in response to the child's needs. Music is developmentally appropriate for infants and toddlers. The infant or toddler who responds to songs is learning both music and language. The teacher's role is to facilitate, not perform.

Stages of development of musicality

The stages of development of musicality are recommended as one way to think about the infant's development in the area of music. These stages include newborn, birth–six months, six–nine months, twelve–eighteen months, and older toddlers (Trevarthen & Malloch, 2003).

Newborn: The newborn is receptive to sounds in the immediate surroundings, including music. Though the benefits of the Mozart Tapes for babies has been overemphasized by the media and marketing agencies, infants are absorbing everything from the environment. When music is too loud or abrasive, infants withdraw. When it is pleasant and melodious, they play. Daily activities can be situated within a framework of music. The teacher's hum, peaceful musical recording, or the sounds of conversation create pleasant sounds for babies.

Birth–six months: Play and music go hand in hand at this age. Beginning with **motherese, parentese,** or **infant-directed speech (IDS),** the child is learning how to be musical. Babies are naturally sociable and intensely aware of the feelings of those around them. The child and teacher play with music as they develop a relationship together. Around the middle of the first year, babies develop the ability to ". . . join in collaborative rhythmic games of toe-pointing, leg-wagging, and arm-waving, accompanied by a variety of calls, crows, and babbles" (Trevarthen & Malloch, 2003, p. 14).

Six–nine months: This is the age when babies develop an awareness of self and others. They enjoy one-on-one play and enjoy performing in a familiar setting. As they develop an awareness of familiar and unfamiliar, they may be timid around strangers.

Twelve–eighteen months: The child begins to enjoy interactive games such as peekaboo. He will move as he listens to music and he likes social interaction such as holding, rocking, swaying, and singing when he is sad or tired. At this age the child begins to enjoy games that involve abrupt movement that coincides with a chant. "Pop Goes the Weasel" is a favorite of this age.

Older toddlers: The toddler will mimic and participate in family and community musical rituals. They are able to chant a singsong speech of repeated tones. Children who are in a musical environment will reflect the music and movement they are exposed to in their culture. For example, children who listen to Caribbean music will be inclined to enjoy and participate in movement and singing when their families and neighbors sing and dance. This is the age when children will bang or hit objects to make a loud, violent noise. At home, pots and pans are a favorite. Centers will want to provide materials that can be used in the same way such as a drum made from an oatmeal container. Children at this age will choose certain favorites songs that they enjoy and ignore others that do not appeal to them. Many adults notice their affinity to a particular commercial on the television. They stop what they are doing, look and perhaps move to the music, and, just as quickly, turn away. As they sing along, they are developing language skills as well as music skills (melody, rhythm, and expressive time).

Songs for infants and toddlers

Early educators must have a repertoire of songs to sing or play in the infant-toddler room. Including songs from all cultures in the classroom will ensure a culturally enriching setting for the young child.

Lullabies: Lullabies are found in every culture (Honig, 1995). These are often sung in a slow, gentle voice. Lullabies are soothing for both the child and adult. They provide a signal that comfort is available and sleep may soon follow. Lullabies have been transmitted orally for many centuries but are now available through books and digital recordings. Some lullabies from other cultures include "Ladino lullay"; "Durme, Durme, Hermozo Hijico" (Sleep, Sleep, My Beautiful Little Son) (Commins, 1967); "All the Pretty Little Horses"; and, of course, "Rock-a-Bye Baby" (Sutterby, Linck, Arrona, Murillo, 2004).

Nursery rhymes: Nursery rhymes have been handed down from one generation to another. Nursery rhymes are simple and easy for the child to remember. One of the most popular is

> Peter, Peter Pumpkin Eater,
> Had a wife and couldn't keep her;
> Put her in a pumpkin shell and
> There he kept her very well.

This poem suggests that the wife is the property of the husband and that he can use whatever force to ensure that she does as he bids. Of course,

FIGURE 4–3   Music Resources

- *Lullabies: A Songbook Companion.* (1997). ESS.A.Y Recordings, CD # 1054.
- *Sweet Dreams.* (1989). Sony, CD #44998.
- *Build Your Baby's Brain 1.* (1998). Sony, CD # 60815. (Excellent music even though the effects on infants are disputed.)

the small infant or young toddler does not understand the social issues involved in this simple rhyme, but they do internalize the words. The use of rhymes that are culturally appropriate is recommended. For example, *Mary Had a Little Jam and Other Silly Rhymes* (Lansky, 2003) is a much better choice. For example, the new version of the old rhyme delivers a much-needed message today.

> Peter, Peter, sugar eater;
> > Always wanted food much sweeter.
> Adding sugar was a blunder.
> > Now he is a toothless wonder (p. 18)

Incorporating rhymes from different cultures is essential in today's classroom. Young children need to hear poems, songs, and rhymes that reflect multiple cultures. (See Figure 4–3.) Music is a powerful force for transmitting culture. When combined with play, it provides a powerful method of transmitting and transforming culture.

Movement

Movement and music are interrelated in humans. Movement begins in the mother's womb. Infants will react to the kinds of music they hear. They become more active with lively music and less active with slower music. Jalongo and Stamp (1997) note that ". . . a baby's behavior is dominated by reflexes—gasping, sucking, startling at a loud noise" (p. 67). Early educators must hold, rock, and cuddle them during this time. It is important to engage the child without overstimulating. Understanding how humans move from being nonmobile infants to highly mobile toddlers will help differentiate activities for each age.

Nonmobile (Lap baby)

Infants are sometimes referred to as "lap babies" so that everyone who cares for them will be aware of their abilities and need to be held. Some sources refer to this as "no mobility." Others use the term "low mobility" because they do have mobility, even though it won't move them across the room during the first month. Children are born with specific reflexes including the Palmar grasp, Moro reflex, Babinski reflex, rooting and sucking, hand-to-mouth reflex, righting reflex, and tonic neck reflex. After birth they develop reciprocal kicking, neck righting, parachute, and Landau reflexes (Gonzales-Mena & Eyer, 2001). When babies begin making motions that are voluntary, not automatic, they will use both gross motor and fine motor movements. Movement need not be taught, but it should be facilitated through interactions that involve observation and support. Movement is restricted in many of the containers designed for infants (such as strollers, walkers, car seats, and infant carriers). Although car seats are required and should be used for safety during travel, the overuse of baby containers separates the child from the parent and restricts movement.

Mobile infants (cruisers and creepers)

During the first two years of life, the child will move progressively from an infant who could be placed on a bed safely to a toddler who is beginning to walk. The progression moves from less to more complex and generally follows the pattern below:

1. raises to a prone position
2. crawling or scooting
3. pulling to sitting

Infants and toddlers develop mobility with the assistance of caring adults.

4. pulling up on furniture

5. standing alone

Current research recommends that adults place children on their backs to sleep to prevent SIDS and choking (American Academy of Pediatrics Task Force on Infant Positioning and SIDS, 2000). Many young parents are reporting that children are not crawling as early or are not crawling at all. Though the data is still anecdotal, this may be related to infants not being placed on their stomachs to sleep. Safety concerns must be given the highest priority, but *teaching* motor skills should be discouraged. Children will progress naturally if supported appropriately.

High mobility (movers)

Approximately 25% of babies climb by the age of fourteen months and over half climb by the age of seventeen months. By their second birthday, almost all children are climbing (Readdick & Park, 1998). Once children begin walking, they must be moved into a different area of the child care center. Nonmovers and movers have different needs. Children who are mobile need an environment that will allow them to walk, jump, hop, and climb. Gates may be needed to limit access in some areas. For example, some centers separate infants and toddlers during infant floor play and toddler center time which may include house, block, movement, or water play centers. They encourage interaction at other times. Gates allow them to control the traffic flow but should be used judiciously.

Music and movement have been discussed separately only for the sake of clarity. Young children combine movement and music when they bounce, sway, shake, nod, tap, gallop, swing, or jump with music. Play and movement are inseparable. From the first pat-a-cake to the tyke bike, motor development occurs at an amazing rate and motor play facilitates this development.

Art

> *Every child is an artist. The problem is how to remain an artist once he grows up.*
>
> —*Pablo Picasso, 1973*

Infants respond to sensory stimulation at birth. Because art involves the senses, art begins at birth. Jalongo and Stamp (1997) point out that infants can taste, see, listen, and respond to touch. Babies are capable of visual tracking or following an object with their eyes within two weeks of birth. Research has established that they prefer patterned over nonpatterned, complex over

FIGURE 4–4 First Patterns

simple, flashing colored lights over white light, moving over stationary, and the human face more than any other object (Jalongo & Stamp, 1997).

The child's appreciation for art begins when they first recognize that two dots at the top and dot at the bottom may be their parent's face (See Figure 4–4.) This generally occurs around the age of three months. As their first recognition of patterns develops, so does their sojourn into art appreciation. Research has found that infants will spend a longer amount of time watching a face deemed attractive (symmetrical) than one that is considered less attractive (Langlois, Roggman, & Rieser-Daner, 1990).

As infants absorb knowledge from the world, they are receptors of art. They tend to enjoy colors that contrast such as black, white, and red, rather than pastels. They do not become producers of art until they are older—although infants are observers of art when they are born.

Developmental stages of art

Adults who expose children to beautiful environments prepare children for an aesthetic approach to life. There has been some concern lately about when and how early to expose children to art. Art involves more than production. For the very young child, the foundation for art develops through experiences with the world. Looking at pictures and patterns, touching different objects, tasting different flavors, and experiencing a variety of materials all form a foundation for art. Toddlers playing in water run from the grass to the sidewalk and back again—all the time experiencing the unique texture of each. This is an art experience.

Newborn–six months: Stimulation should be reasonable. The infant center should not be overstimulating. Unbreakable mirrors, pictures of human faces, other infant faces, and contrasting colors with different shapes are recommended. Infants enjoy different materials and fabrics. Blankets that have different textures sewn together are also enjoyable. Simple paper-plate puppets are enjoyable without being overstimulating.

Infants, six–twelve months: At this age, babies are beginning to develop an awareness of taste and an awareness of cause and effect. Their play reflects a lot of practice. As they explore their world, babies will use food in a variety of ways. This is at once play, science, and art. Many early childhood educators discourage the use of food as art material (Jalongo & Stamp, 1997). This author believes that babies will play with their food with no encouragement from adults; food should be provided for intake only and not for art. This is supported by the guidelines for appropriate practice (Bredekamp, & Copple, 1997). *Inappropriate* practice includes:

> Toddlers are "helped" by teachers to produce a product, follow the adult-made model, or color a coloring book or ditto sheet. Because toddlers are likely to put things in their mouths, adult gives them edible, often tasty, fingerpaints or playdough. (p. 85)

It is preferable to give toddlers real materials that they can manipulate. For example, they can use nontoxic materials such as finger paint or shaving cream. The experience is the goal, not the finished product. Again, a word of caution: pay close attention to the child's interest. Art is still more receptive than expressive at this age.

Toddlers, twelve months–two years: Everything is a multisensory experience to toddlers. They experience sensory materials and engage fully in any activity that interests them. Isbell and Raines (2003) point out that children at this age are in the **scribble stage** of artistic development. The very first marks that young children make are **uncontrolled scribbles** and can be made with markers, crayons, or sticks in the sand. As toddlers develop fine motor skills, they move to **controlled scribbles.** They delight in marking and experimenting with designs. Other materials that are enjoyable include crayons, markers, and large paper for toddlers to explore and manipulate. Watching toddlers discover that they can draw large circles on a white wall creates a dilemma for adults. The thrill of watching a human being discover their power is mediated by the thought of repainting the wall!

Toddlers enjoy natural materials including mud, water, sand, dirt, grass, and plants. Caution is urged because some plants are poisonous. Toddlers also enjoy shredded paper in a dry swimming pool. This provides both a sensory experience and an opportunity to recycle. Different cultures may emphasize certain aspects earlier than others. In some European countries, one-year-olds work with paint and older toddlers enjoy using clay. In the United States, paint has generally been reserved for older two- and three-year-olds. The main focus of art at this age is to expose the child to a beautiful, orderly environment that allows them to fully develop their senses and to provide sensory stimulation through a variety of authentic art experiences.

Story and Reenactment

Infants need to interact with books in a variety of ways. The essential component is the adult who reads to the infant and young child. Children benefit from hearing a variety of books read to them on an ongoing basis and having access to them. The International Reading Association (IRA) and the National Association for the Education of Young Children (NAEYC) prepared a report that outlined guidelines for literacy from birth through the primary years. Recommendations for infant-toddler literacy development reflect the views of both groups and are included below.

> Children need relationships with caring adults who engage in many one-on-one, face-to-face interactions with them to support oral language development and lay the foundation for later literacy learning. Important experiences and teaching behaviors include (IRA/NAEYC, 1998, p. 42) but are not limited to
>
> ◆ talking to babies and toddlers with simple language, frequent eye contact, and responsiveness to children's cues and language attempts
> ◆ frequently playing with, talking to, singing to, and doing fingerplays with very young children
> ◆ sharing cardboard books with babies and frequently reading to toddlers on the adult's lap or together with one or two other children

When children listen to stories, they develop language skills, listening skills, literacy skills, and they develop scripts for play.

■ Play Places and Spaces

High-quality play interactions are encouraged in some centers and discouraged in others. The difference depends on the adult and the context for play that is created. If adults are overly concerned about safety issues, they may stifle the child. Unsafe classrooms are not an option, however. The early educator must create a safe environment that fosters exploration. Some possible guidelines to consider when creating an environment have been referred to as the multi-"S" approach by Lowman and Ruhmann (1998). These include:

◆ Safety and health
◆ Sanitation
◆ Stability and order

- ◆ Scale and comfort
- ◆ Simplicity and convenience
- ◆ Seclusion and choice
- ◆ Stimulation
- ◆ Softness
- ◆ Sensory appealing
- ◆ Soothing and sunny

Safety and health

The younger the child, the more important the safety and health issues. Far West, an organization that provides professional development in the area of infant-toddler care, has guidelines that can be used to do a complete safety check of the room. Guidelines for NAEYC recommend a ratio of one adult for three infants (Bredekamp & Copple, 1997, p. 80). Get on the floor and pretend you are a toddler. Are outlets covered? Remember toddlers want to try different combinations. What is safe, what is not safe? Use a **choke tube** to check small parts of toys. A choke tube is used to check the size of an object. If the object fits inside the choke tube, it is unsafe. If it does not fit inside the tube, it is safe. Be sure to look at all areas.

Sanitation

Sanitation includes ensuring that diapering, toileting, and feeding have sanitary routines. Toys that infants mouth must be sanitized daily with a bleach solution to minimize the transmission of germs.

Stability and order

Children need a stable environment. They need to know that the toy on the shelf will be on the shelf tomorrow. The rotation of materials should happen on a slow basis. Children will become familiar with certain items and may show distress when they are abruptly removed from the environment. Adults also benefit from order and stability in the center.

Scale and comfort

This is important in an infant-toddler room and a toddler room. Adults need rocking chairs in the sleeping area of the infant center, but rocking chairs in the toddler room can create a problem. The younger the child, the smaller the space. Infants need a limited amount of space so they can become familiar with their surroundings. Toddlers need more space and defined boundaries.

Simplicity and convenience

The space needs to be relatively simplistic. Movement patterns should allow free flow and be convenient for the child care providers. Adults who have to step over a 3-foot gate throughout the day will become physically exhausted just from their movement throughout the room. Cushions can be used as barriers and are safer and easier to move.

Seclusion and choice

Since more and more children are spending more of their waking hours in group care, it is essential that they have places where they can be alone and the freedom to make that choice. Do infants have the choice of looking at a black and white spiral or a mirror? Do toddlers have choices? They can't explore their own kitchen cabinets, so how can we create small spaces that they can explore? Toddlers need a safe, secluded space that they can use if they want to be alone. An empty rubber toddler swimming pool or short tunnels can serve this purpose.

Infants need safe places to explore.

Stimulation

Infants should receive a reasonable amount of stimulation—not too much and not too little. It requires keen insight and experience on the part of the early educator to understand this balance and to be able to maintain it. Responsive teachers make good choices for children in terms of how much stimulation is appropriate.

Softness

Creating an environment that is more like home than an institution creates a pleasing environment for young children and adults. Hanging an example of a local fabric brings the culture into the center. For example, some area have beautiful quilts, others have woven blankets or rugs. Bringing in soft items creates a more inviting space for young children.

Sensory appealing

The schools of Reggio Emilia, Italy, which emphasize an aesthetic-based approach with beautiful environments, have helped emphasize the value of an aesthetically pleasing space. Infants and toddlers need to hear classical music, see mirrors and light throughout the room, feel different textures beneath their feet, and crawl into small spaces with mirrors that allow them to explore and experience a sense of security. Adults also enjoy and benefit from beautiful spaces.

Soothing and sunny

The environment should be soothing and sunny. When young children are placed in rooms with red walls and Disney characters on a long-term basis, it may be overstimulating. The room should be light and bright. Too often infant-toddler centers are relegated to the basement. Natural light should flood as much of the center as possible with the exception of the sleeping area. Windows, translucent walls, and mirrors bring light into the center. An aesthetically pleasing environment enhances the pleasure and play of both the child and adult.

■ Designing Environment for Infants

Creating an environment that includes all the elements described in the previous section is a challenge. How do adults design an environment that encourages play? Before beginning the design process, contact the local and state regulatory agencies. Regulations vary from state to state. In some states, licensing requirements are very rigid. In some areas, there are minimum requirements. For example, in some states, two exit areas are required; other states require little more than covering electrical outlets. Meeting the criteria for state and local licensure is not optional. High-quality programs meet not only health and safety requirements, they meet the voluntary NAEYC accreditation requirements. The accreditation process ensures that recommended adult/child ratios are met and that *optimal*, not minimal, standards of care are provided. Knowledge of the state requirements and NAEYC guidelines up front will prevent problems later. Before we consider areas for children, it should be noted that adults have needs also. Early educators who are in centers for long periods need a variety of seating and movement arrangements. A rocking chair in the sleeping or quiet area, a comfortable chair or couch with book baskets nearby, and chairs in the dining area are all appropriate for adults. According to NAEYC guidelines, the infant area should include six basic areas (Bredekamp & Copple, 1997):

- ◆ entrance and exit
- ◆ dining areas
- ◆ diapering areas
- ◆ sleeping areas
- ◆ floor play areas
- ◆ gross motor areas

Entrance and exit

The entrance and exit for parents should provide a safe, orderly environment. The entrance should be inviting to parents and should include some items, such as mirrors, that infants find interesting. A family bulletin board should be available so parents will know what is going on in the center and can communicate with others as needed. Placing the infant's cubbies in the entry way increases efficiency. Clipboards containing information about feeding and toileting should also contain information about play or perceptual changes.

Dining areas

Dining areas should be sanitary and as natural as possible. Some children who have disabilities may need special feeding arrangements. Placing five or six infants in bucket seats at a table is not appropriate, nor is placing four infants in a row in high chairs. The consumption of food should be a nutritious, enjoyable experience. Soft music in the background contributes to the ambience of the eating experience. The word *dining* has been purposefully used instead of the word *feeding*. Adults should look at their environment and consider ways to feed children with respect.

Diapering areas

Diapering areas should be sanitary and close to a source of water. The placement of mirrors and wind chimes create an interesting, familiar environment when they are diapered. This is a time when early educators talk, sing, and play special games with children. Using different songs or games with different children can add to the infant's development of self. For example, if a child has a parent from a unique cultural group, using a song from home will add to the child's comfort level.

Sleeping areas

An area of the center should be set aside for rest, relaxation, and sleep. A rocking chair will allow teachers and parents to comfort the child in a relaxing atmosphere. Mothers who are nursing can enjoy the peacefulness of the area as they nurse their infant. Cribs are for sleeping and should not be cluttered with too many toys. As soon as the child is awake, he should be moved to the floor area (Gerber, 1998).

Floor play areas

The floor is the stage for play with infants. Floor play is encouraged when caregivers engage in the following behaviors:

◆ *Separate the play space from the care giving space.* Cushions can be used to define the area and a soft fabric should cover the floor. This can range from carpet to a blanket or quilt.

◆ *Make sure everything in the play space is touchable.* Everything should be mouthable also.

◆ *Include both fine and gross motor activity.* Floor play provides an opportunity to use beach balls, aluminum pie pans, empty boxes, and soft cloth balls. Putting a mirror on the floor play area increases the child's interest in the play area. An inclined plane and bar on the side of the wall works for both crawlers and cruisers.

◆ *Let children find unique ways to combine toys and materials.* This is the key to good floor play. Observe the children. If they are playing with scarves, let them touch them in a variety of ways. If they are playing with sensory bottles, let them roll, shake them. Let them put the scarves over the bottles if they choose. Floor play is exploration time with objects and materials. During floor play with scarves and sensory bottles, safety must be paramount. Be sure scarves are not used in a way that can create a dangerous situation.

◆ *Put out the right number of toys.* The right amount varies. It is important not to overstimulate the children. They might find one or two sensory bottles interesting and stimulating. Putting five sensory bottles in the center is not appropriate. Too many toys can be confusing. It is better to have toys that can be combined and manipulated.

◆ *Provide the correct balance of choices.* The right amount varies. A good rule of thumb for floor play is to start with two choices per child with a limit of five choices for three children. Observe the children. Is this amount sufficient or do they need more? Young children should not be overwhelmed by choices (Gonzalez-Mena, & Eyer, 2001, p. 69).

Floor play should also include both movement and perception. As soon as the baby begins to move on his own, place the baby flat on his tummy on a quilt with multiple colors that will interest him, and *never leave the infant during floor play*. When the baby tires of looking at the materials on the quilt, place a soft texture ball or stuffed animal about 5 inches in front of him. Watch as he tries to move toward the ball. Be careful not to frustrate him. Adjust the distance as needed. The object of the play is fun. When the baby can reach the object and shake it, he will laugh with a sense of accomplishment.

Gross motor area

A gross motor area is a necessary part of the infant area. Children need spaces that allow them to crawl and cruise safely. A low inclined plane on the floor provides a good place for crawlers. A couch provides a comfortable place for adults and for children who are cruising. A variety of choices including toys for pushing and pulling should reflect the diverse abilities in the group. Daily outings in the fresh air are healthy for infants and caregivers.

■ Designing Environment for Toddlers

The toddler area should include six basic areas with at least five play areas:

◆ entrance and exit
◆ dining area
◆ sleeping and resting area
◆ toileting area
◆ gross motor area
◆ play centers

1. block
2. home center

3. dramatic
4. quiet zone
5. sensory
6. water zone
7. art

Entrance and exit

The entry to the center should be safe and serviceable, aesthetically pleasing, and appropriate to toddlers. Some centers place items that will attract the children's attention when they enter the center. For example, some will place mirrors near the entry, others will place animals. It is important not to clutter the entry way due to fire codes, but it is also important to set the stage for play by providing stimulating materials in a variety of places. The entrance to the toddler area should include a place where children can place their personal belongings. A family board should be available so parents can keep current and communicate with others as needed. Placing the toddler's cubbies near the door increases efficiency and can limit messy feet to one area.

Dining area

The eating area for toddlers should be separate and near the preparation area. All appropriate sanitation measures should be taken in the preparation area. Rules for following hand-washing should be posted so new personnel know the proper procedures. Toddlers should have the opportunity to eat on low tables with their friends and an adult. As soon as they finish, they should be able to leave the table and move to a gross motor or play area.

Sleeping and resting area

Rest time is easier when children have a routine. When the music begins to play and the lights are dimmed, children become accustomed to what happens next, rest time. Toddlers need cots for rest. These can be stacked in one area of the room. Children who sleep on carpet on the floor can become chilled and adults who are not on the floor are unaware of their discomfort. Children should have a stuffed animal, doll, or toy during this time to comfort and entertain them. Classical music or lullabies create a mood for rest.

Toileting area

Toddlers are between diapers and independence. Facilities that have both a place for diapering and child-size commodes encourage toilet learning.

Parents and teachers must be consistent in their practice. The ease of pull-ups is causing some children to stay in training pants longer than in the past. Some centers have even banned them due to their belief that they prolong the process. Adding low, shatterproof mirrors can create an atmosphere that is pleasant and appealing.

Gross motor area

Toddlers need an area for gross motor movement. This can consist of a loft that children enter and exit through a ramp, steps to a window, steps up and down in a corner, or a beach ball. Toddlers need to move and adults must provide safe options.

Toddler play centers

Centers first appear in the toddler room as play areas. What may later become a block center in the three-year-old room begins as an area for playing with different types of blocks. This should not be confused with the kind of center time that occurs in preschool or kindergarten. These areas provide order and assist children in choosing play. Exploration and play are dominant activities and interest areas should stimulate both.

1. Block. The block center should have a variety of blocks on low shelves. Modern materials provide a variety of lightweight, durable materials that include soft foam, cardboard, and plastic. At this age, symbolic play is stimulated by real-life objects, so placing miniature school buses, barns, and people in the center will support play.

2. Home center. Realistic home materials can contribute to the child's developing dramatic play. The use of real pots and pans, real dishes, and clean, empty containers is recommended. A large box placed in the middle of the house area can become a car, a truck, or a boat.

3. Dramatic. Toddlers enjoy dress-up and are especially intrigued by hats. They need realistic props to encourage their play. Real materials like phones or real police hats add to the richness of their play. Safe mirrors increase opportunities to pretend.

4. Quiet zone (object play/toys)(book baskets). Toddlers also need an area where they can sit and work a puzzle, look at a book, or sit in someone's lap. Baskets filled with books are convenient and very accessible for toddlers to pick-up and return. Soft pillows add to this center space. This center provides a good transitioning center for the young toddler who has been accustomed to floor play.

5. Sensory (paint, sand, shredded paper). Perception skills are developing during this time. Helping children differentiate the red and blue fingerpaint facilitates visual perception. When children play with clay,

Toddlers develop their knowledge of the world through exploration.

water, or mud, they are increasing both their cognitive and sensory knowledge of the world. Sand can be used both inside and outdoors. It provides an excellent sensory material for toddlers. Toys that can be used to pour, scoop, and shovel sand extend play.

6. Water zone. Water play can be encouraged by using small pans of water. Safety around water is a concern at this age. Toddlers do not understand the dangers of water. They can drown in a small amount of water and will jump into a pool without understanding the consequences. Dishpans that are no more than 8 inches tall can provide a *safe* source of water for toddlers. To prevent transmission of germs, individual tubs of water are preferable to a large water table.

7. Art. Finger painting is a favorite for this age. Be sure smocks are available so children don't paint new clothes. As discussed at the beginning of the chapter, infants and toddlers do not differentiate between edible and nonedible materials. It is confusing to use food for art, and many cultures find the use of food for art offensive. For these reasons, other choices should be made when considering art materials.

Developing a program that includes all the areas mentioned above requires knowledge, creativity, energy, and enthusiasm. The following section provides an overview of models that can be used to develop an infant-toddler program.

■ Program Models

Components of an aesthetics-based curriculum based on play, art, music, and movement have been presented in this chapter. Other program models are available for those who prefer a different curriculum framework. It would be impossible to present all the available models within the scope of this book, so representative models will be presented briefly. For more information, contact the individual program.

- ◆ Developmental-interaction model (Bank Street College of Education)
- ◆ Cognitive developmental model (High/Scope)
- ◆ Constructivist model (Reggio Emilia)
- ◆ Professional development programs
     Creative Curriculum
     West Ed Program
     Educaring
- ◆ Family child care

Developmental-Interaction

The developmental-interaction approach is known by many as the Bank Street approach. It is based on the philosophy that children construct knowledge through interactions with the world. Although this term is relatively new—it was coined in the seventies—the approach reflects the philosophy of the approach used in the Bank Street schools started in the early part of the twentieth century (Cuffaro, Nager, & Shapiro, 2000). The program for infants and toddlers is called the Family program and is based on the work of Erikson (1950) and Piaget (1965). Mental health and experiential activities are the guiding principles of the program. Infants and toddlers experience a very calm, relaxed atmosphere. The curriculum consists of living the daily schedule with time for playing, eating, resting, and playing outdoors. Transitions are viewed as important times for children. Faculty are committed to minimizing difficult transitions. Their program for "easing in" children new to the center served as a model for the "looping" models used by many programs. Parents commit to staying with the child until they can leave without distress. Activities available for infants and toddlers include art, blocks, sensory experiences, music, movement, and gross motor play and outings. The outings are local excursions that involve two or three children. The Bank Street approach has always used a multiage group setting to reflect a natural social setting. This program is located in New York at Columbia Teachers College. Information is available on their Web site and their address is located at the end of this chapter.

Cognitive Developmental

The cognitive developmental approach is also known as the High/Scope program. The program was initiated as a traditional preschool program and, after the first year of struggling for a philosophy, the program decided to use a program informed by the work of Jean Piaget. This view posits that knowledge is constructed through interactions between children and adults. The child develops knowledge through ". . . personal interaction with ideas, direct experience with physical objects and events, and application of logical thinking to these experiences. The teacher's role is to supply the context for these experiences, to help the child think about them logically, and, through observation, to understand the progress the child is making" (Weikart & Schweinhart, 2000, p. 279). It is worth noting that High/Scope is the only program model that has been validated through longitudinal studies (Weikart & Schweinhart, 2000).

The High/Scope program for infants and toddlers provides a warm and nurturing environment for children under three. Active learning experiences and key experiences are designed for sensory-motor learners. The organization of space and materials, children's daily schedules, caregiving routines, and adult support based on child observation, team planning, and partnerships with parents are consistent with High/Scope's Piagetian perspective. High/Scope is used by many Head Start centers throughout the United States. Those interested in additional information can purchase materials from High/Scope or their training sites in Michigan. Information is available on their Web site, and the address is located at the end of this chapter.

Constructivist

Many Piaget-based programs are also based on a constructivist philosophy. The example used here reflects a social constructivist model found in Italy. The infant-toddler programs of Reggio Emilia have been recognized around the world. They are referred to as *Asili Nido* or safe nests and serve infants from four months through three years. The child sets the schedule throughout the day with a specific time established for lunch only. Most centers include a separate room for sleeping, a floor play area, an area for diapering, a room for gross motor movement, and a place for eating/dining. The infant-toddler centers are beautiful spaces with areas that children can explore intently.

Relationships that develop among adults and infants are the most important part of the curriculum. The foundation for this perspective flows out of the work of Loris Malaguzzi (Gandini & Edwards, 2001). The curriculum is based on the child's needs and desires for the day. Children are valued for their many different ways of knowing the world. Those who are interested in this approach can find additional information in the book, *Bambini: The Italian Approach to Infant/Toddler Care*. The model also provides tours of their sites in Italy and sponsors conferences in the United States. Visit their Web site or the Merrill-Palmer Institute Friends of Reggio Emilia for additional information.

Professional Development

Creative Curriculum

This training approach was developed by Amy Dombro, Laura Colker, and Diane Twister Dodge (1999) and provides a structure for developing programs. Unlike the other program models, it does not have an on-site center nor is it associated with a university. It is designed for use in professional development programs and relies heavily on the publications. Publications are user-friendly and provide good information. Materials designed for parents are especially beneficial. The program designed for infants and toddlers is called *Innovations: The Comprehensive Infant & Toddler Curriculum*. (Miller & Albrecht, 2001). They provide training materials and training opportunities for instructors and students.

The philosophy of *Innovations* is based on the infant-toddler stage of sensorimotor development and encourages play as a primary focus for young infants and toddlers. The program uses Alice Honig's interpretation of Piaget's theories as a guide for daily activities. Honig's (1982) 12 categories include learning tasks that are integrated throughout the day and include (Miller & Albrecht, 2001, p. 96):

1. learning to make groups
2. learning to separate parts from the big group
3. learning to line up objects in a logical order
4. learning time relationships
5. learning about places and how space is organized

6. learning what numbers mean
7. learning to recognize change
8. learning to use body parts together
9. learning to reason
10. use imagination
11. learning language and using books
12. learning social skills

The learning tasks listed above are integrated in daily interactions. Teachers are challenged to know the tasks and discover ways to integrate them throughout the day.

The tasks are divided into six areas of emphasis:

1. separating from parents
2. connecting with school and teacher
3. relating to self and others
4. communicating with parents, teachers, and friends
5. moving around
6. expressing feelings with parents, teachers, and friends

The environment is designed around the concepts of creating the environment, maintaining the environment, and refreshing the environment. Maintaining the environment includes routine safety checks and disinfecting toys. Refreshing the environment requires balancing experienced and novel materials. For additional information, the reader is referred to the book, *Innovations: The Comprehensive Infant & Toddler Curriculum* (Miller & Albrecht, 2001). Teaching Strategies also conducts professional development throughout the United States and information is available on their Web site.

The West Ed Program for Infants and Toddlers Caregivers (PITC)

The West Ed Program is a well-known program designed to foster high-quality infant-toddler care. At West Ed they believe that infant-toddler care is not babysitting, nor is it a miniaturized preschool. They recognize a unique difference built on relationships and emphasize six areas: primary care, small groups, continuity, individualized care, cultural responsiveness, and inclusion of children with special needs. Ron Lally, who directs the center, has been influential in providing training throughout the United States. Training programs are located throughout the country; for additional information, see their Web site for the nearest training site and a list of recommended books and materials.

Educaring

Educaring is an approach developed by Magda Gerber (1998). Resources for Infant Caring (RIC) emphasizes the natural development of the child. This program is concerned about too much stimulation too early and advises adults to respect and respond sensitively to the needs of the infant. Play is a major part of this program and "wants nothing" is a term used to just spend time watching and observing the infant. Advocates of this approach try to use an approach that is aligned with the child's natural growth. For additional information, read Gerber's *Your Self-Confident Baby* (1998).

■ Family Child Care

Toddlers enjoy realistic props.

Family child care centers should utilize many of the guidelines for group care. Play centers should be available to provide a sense of stability and security. Play that occurs in home centers may include materials not typically found in centers. For example, see the photograph of the child who is using a golf club. While play with a variety of real materials is especially rich, it also creates safety concerns. For this reason, there are additional safety precautions that must be taken in home-based programs. A survey must be conducted to ensure safety. Cabinets must have secure fasteners; electrical and water dangers should be considered; and places that create a climbing or falling hazard should be removed or eliminated. All areas that the children access should be safe. Licensed public centers must follow rules and regulations regarding fire codes and safety. Home centers should be equally committed to following all procedures for safety, health, and development. As in other programs, a play-based approach is recommended. Additional information can be attained from any of the resources listed above as well as in the following books:

Secure Relationships: Nurturing Infants/Toddler Attachment in Early Care Settings by Alice Honig (2002)

Infants, Toddlers and Caregivers by Janet Gonzales-Mena and Dianne Widmeyer Eyer (2001)

The Complete Learning Spaces Book for Infants and Toddlers by Rebecca Isbell and Christy Isbell (2003)

Places for Childhoods: Making Quality Happen in the Real World by Jim Greeman (1998)

■ Toys and Materials

A caring relationship that leads to the child's sense of trust is a major focus during the first two years of life. Materials and toys that foster this relationship are valuable. Watch a one-year-old play with a soft, cotton-filled ball. He looks at it, touches it, mouths it, throws it, and waits for someone to return it to him. He is the consummate explorer. Play materials and toys that are appropriate support and scaffold sensorimotor development. Materials or toys with contrasting colors such as yellow and red are appealing to young infants. Though very young children need few toys, by the age of one, some believe that the average child in the United States has approximately 25 toys in his collection. Duplicate toys should be available to toddlers who should not be forced to share. Safety is a concern with children under two years-old in group care. Most centers have a choke tube. A choke tube is used to see if an item is dangerous for young children. Most commercial companies sell choke tubes. If the item fits in the choke tube, it will fit in a young child's throat and should not be used. Some centers make their own tubes out of paper towel rolls. Selecting toys and play materials to match the age and stage of the child will minimize accidents.

Infants

The nonmobile child (birth to six months) benefits from materials that he can see, hear, or touch. Young infants respond to bright colors such as yellow and red and enjoy watching movement. Hanging mobiles that move and emit a gentle song are especially interesting to babies. Be wary of toys that make loud sounds or have rough edges. Safety is always paramount when selecting and using play materials. As the child grows, he explores his world and soon learns that he can cause an action when he acts on a toy. As soon as the child realizes that he can kick or hit and create a sound or movement, the infant will begin to enjoy play materials. The infant does not need a large number of toys. Infants in group care need one or two items that they can bring from home to use exclusively. These can be placed in the infant's cubby to ensure that they are sanitary and the child has complete access to them. The center's collection should be sterilized on a daily basis to ensure good health. Figure 4–5 includes a list of recommended materials.

Infants (seven–twelve months) have some mobility and are beginning to discover their world on their own. They need toys that they can manipulate and explore. During this time, they can sit upright and use their hands. The "pincer" grasp is developing so the child can hold things with one hand and manipulate with the other. They can stick their fingers in

FIGURE 4–5   Play Materials for Infants to Six Months

Basic play materials for young infants:

- unbreakable mirrors that can be attached to a crib, changing table, or other play area
- one or two special items, such as dolls or stuffed animals, that may be brought from home as comfort items for individual children (for hygienic reasons, not to be used by other infants)
- a variety of mobiles/visuals that can be changed and rotated among infants
- a variety of toys that infants can bat or kick, mouth, grasp, and manipulate
- rattles and bells (with a handle or elastic for the wrist or ankle) that make interesting sounds when manipulated

Source: From *The Right Stuff for Children: Birth to 8* (pp. 26, 42, and 81) by M.B. Bronson, Washington, DC: National Association for the Education of Young Children, 1995. Copyright 1995 by the National Association for the Education of Young Children. Reprinted by permission.

small places. (This is why electrical outlets must be covered.) They like to stack things and enjoy kicking and splashing (water play) during bath time! Around the age of nine to ten months, they will begin to distinguish the familiar versus the unfamiliar. One or two soft objects from home can make life better at the center. Items from home should be placed in a cubby and used by that child only. Because they are developing object permanence around eleven months, they enjoy toys such as jack-in-the-box and materials in Figure 4–6.

FIGURE 4–6   Play Materials for Infants—Seven Months through Twelve Months

Basic play materials for older infants:

- large, unbreakable mirror(s) placed so that children can see themselves move
- a few soft, washable dolls and stuffed or other play animals
- a small selection of soft, lightweight blocks
- a variety of grasping toys that require different types of manipulation
- a varied selection of skill-development materials, including nesting and stacking materials, activity boxes, and containers to be filled and emptied
- a variety of small cloth, plastic, or cardboard books for children to handle, and additional books for adults to read
- a few varied bells and rattles that produce interesting sounds when manipulated
- some recorded music, songs, and interesting sounds
- several types of one-piece push toys (cars, animals) for children who can crawl
- a variety of balls, including some with interesting special effects
- a climbing platform for crawlers (no higher than 4 to 6 inches)

Source: From *The Right Stuff for Children: Birth to 8* (pp. 26, 42, and 81) by M.B. Bronson, Washington, DC: National Association for the Education of Young Children, 1995. Copyright 1995 by the National Association for the Education of Young Children. Reprinted by permission.

The one-year-old is usually mobile or in the process of developing mobility. Play materials reflect this change. They climb and carry, push, and dump materials. They will move objects from one place to another. This is especially troublesome to parents when they find the keys have been carried to the trash can! They can participate in painting and other sensory experiences. Toddlers at this stage are beginning to imitate adult behaviors and are especially fascinated by hats and empty boxes. One caveat is that toddlers who play in water should have their own small container. Plastic dishpans are ideal. Group water play in the toddler area has been identified as a source of disease transmission. Keeping children in group care healthy is a goal of programs, so the water table should be washed out with bleach after each use and each child must wash their hands before and after using the table. Additional materials for play are listed in Figure 4–7.

FIGURE 4–7   Play Materials for Young Toddlers

Basic play materials for young toddlers:
- a sturdy, unbreakable full-length mirror
- a few, simple, washable dolls
- a few small wood or sturdy plastic people and animal figures
- simple dress-ups (kept very clean), and a doll bed and carriage that a toddler can fit into
- several lightweight transportation toys (cars, trucks)
- simple sand and water play materials (from about eighteen months onward)
- a beginning set of small, lightweight blocks and simple, press-together bricks
- a variety of 3- to 5-piece puzzles with knobs
- a number of large, colored pop beads or stringing beads (after about eighteen months)
- a variety of specific skill-development materials including shape-sorters, stacking and nesting materials, pop-up and activity boxes, and simple matching materials
- foam/wood/plastic pegboard(s) with large, blunt ended pegs
- a variety of sturdy books for children to handle and additional books for adult to read
- a supply of sturdy paper and large, nontoxic crayons in bright, primary colors
- a beginning set of simple musical instruments (from about fifteen months onward)
- recorded music and a record, CD, or tape player
- a variety of push and pull toys
- several types and sizes of balls
- a few stable ride-on toys with four wheels or casters and no steering mechanism or pedals
- low, soft, climbing platform(s) and tunnel for crawling through.

Source: From *The Right Stuff for Children: Birth to 8* (pp. 26, 42, and 81) by M.B. Bronson, Washington, DC: National Association for the Education of Young Children, 1995. Copyright 1995 by the National Association for the Education of Young Children. Reprinted by permission.

Toddlers

Two-year-olds are beginning to develop independence as they explore their world. They are highly mobile and can walk, run, chase, and climb. They imitate real life through pretend play. Developing fine motor skills allow them to control crayons and markers. Placing a sheet of paper securely on a table with markers nearby encourages developing artistic skills. Materials and toys should be culturally appropriate and reflect the diversity of the classroom. Dolls should represent the racial composition of the population of society, not just the classroom. A safety concern for this age group stems from the child's heightened sense of independence and mobility. Appropriate materials and play are listed in Figure 4–8.

FIGURE 4–8   Materials for Two-year-olds

Basic play materials for older toddlers:

- a full-length, unbreakable mirror
- dolls with simple garments and caretaking accessories
- role-play materials, including a selection of dress-ups; large sturdy doll bed; child-sized stove and refrigerator; simple pots and pans; and a cleaning set
- a variety of wood, plastic, rubber, or vinyl people and animal figures to use with blocks
- vehicles (cars, trucks) to be used with blocks: a few large ride-on trucks (if cost permits)
- sand/water table(s) with containers and simple pretend materials
- a set of unit blocks and other construction materials, such as plastic bricks and large plastic nuts and bolts
- an assortment of fit-in puzzles
- pegboards with large pegs
- large beads for stringing; lacing shoes or cards with large holes; and materials to practice buttoning, snapping, buckling, etc.
- simple matching and sorting materials; graduated nesting, stacking, and ordering materials; simple lock boxes; and sensory materials, such as "feel bags"
- simple lotto games and giant dominoes
- a variety of sturdy books
- a supply of crayons, paints, paintbrushes, markers, clay or dough, scissors, chalkboard, chalk, plain and colored paper, and an adjustable easel
- a standard rhythm instrument set
- recorded music and a record, CD, or tape player
- push toys that support pretend play (vacuum cleaner, baby carriage)
- large ball(s) to kick, throw, or roll
- stable ride-on materials pushed by feet
- a low climbing structure and slide

Source: From *The Right Stuff for Children: Birth to 8* (pp. 26, 42, and 81) by M.B. Bronson, Washington, DC: National Association for the Education of Young Children, 1995. Copyright 1995 by the National Association for the Education of Young Children. Reprinted by permission.

■ Play Assessment

Programs and children in programs are evaluated using different systems. When most people think about assessment, they think about report cards and children. In today's world, assessment has multiple meanings that include program assessment as well as child assessment. Evaluating child development is one dimension of assessment. There are, however, other areas that are evaluated and regulated. Program assessment is very important in today's world of accountability and government funding. Play-based assessment offers a unique perspective for looking at both child growth and development during play as well as program quality.

Play-based Infant-Toddler Assessment

Assessment in infant-toddler centers should reflect the philosophical approach used in the center. Programs using a high-quality approach will use a systematic, ongoing system. The Bank Street program has a systematic approach that is congruent with their approach, High/Scope has a tool, and Innovations has a system for evaluating children. Reggio Emila places less emphasis on individual assessment but uses documentation to capture infant-toddler growth and development in a developmentally appropriate way. It is beyond the scope of this book to cover the many assessment tools designed for children under two. Rather, this section will look specifically at play-based assessment instruments.

Play assessment is routinely used in clinical settings (Schaefer, Gitlin, & Sandgrund, 1991). It is also used in early intervention settings. Few programs assess play. One instrument that has been developed to assess overall infant development that includes play is the Ounce **Scale**, recently developed by Dr. Samuel Meisels, president of the Erikson Institute. A comparison of developmental areas included in the Ounce scale to those in traditional domains is included in Figure 4–9. The program is based on the work-sampling system and provides a venue for parents and early educators to look at the child together in an interactive manner.

Assessment in infant-toddler centers is especially meaningful because this is the time when disabilities or developmental delays should be identified so intervention strategies can begin.

Ounce Scale Assessment System

The Ounce Scale is an observational assessment for evaluating infants' and toddlers' development over a period of three-and-a-half years—from birth. Its purpose is twofold: (1) to provide guidelines and standards for

FIGURE 4–9 Comparison of Areas of Development to Traditional Domains

Traditional Domain	Area of Development	Aspects of Development Covered
Social and Emotional Development	**Personal Connections:** *It's About Trust*—How children show they trust you	1. How children build relationships with familiar adults 2. How children respond to unfamiliar adults
	Feelings About Self: *Learning About Me*—How children express who they are	1. The way children express who they are, their personality, their temperament, the way they are building self-esteem, learning independence 2. How children manage their own behavior, self-regulation 3. Expression of feelings, learning social skills when expressing feelings, needs, and wants
	Relationships With Other Children: *Child to Child*—What children do around other children	1. The way children show awareness of other children, interact with and play with them 2. Recognizing and responding to other children's feelings (empathy)
Language Development	**Understanding and Communication:** *Child Talk*—How children understand and communicate	1. Receptive language—understanding gestures, words, directions, questions, and routines 2. Expressive language—using gestures, words, several words together, conventions of speech, expressing thoughts and ideas 3. Participating in conversations
Cognitive Development	**Exploration and Problem Solving:** *Seek and Solve*—How children explore and figure things out	1. How children attend, pay attention, explore, and understand concepts of color, size, matching, weight, and number 2. Memory, reasoning ability, imagination 3. Making things happen, purposeful activity, expectations of planned results, anticipating consequences, solving problems
Physical Development	**Movement and Coordination:** *Body Basics*—How children move their bodies and use their hands to do things	1. Gross motor—controlling body, moving around, combining movements, playing games 2. Fine motor—reaching, holding, letting go, intentional exploration, eye-hand coordination, creative activities 3. Self-help activities

Source: Used by permission of Dr. Samuel J. Meisels, Ed.D., President, Erikson Institute. The Ounce Scale (2003) is published by Pearson Early Learning, New York.

observing and interpreting young children's growth and behavior, and (2) to provide information that parents and caregivers can use in everyday interactions with their children.

The Ounce Scale has three elements:

1. *The Observation Record* provides a focus for observing and documenting children's everyday behaviors and provides data for making evaluations about development.

2. *The Family Album* provides a structure for parents to learn about and record their child's development as they write down what they see, using photos, telling stories, and responding to observation questions that are the same as the ones in the caregiver's Observation Record.

3. *The Developmental Profile* enables caregivers and other staff to evaluate each child's development and progress over time, comparing their observation data to specific performance standards.

A User's Guide, the Standards for the Developmental Profiles, and Reproducible Masters are also available to assist you in implementing the Ounce Scale.

The Ounce Scale is organized around six major areas of development:

1. **Personal Connections**—*It's About Trust:* How children show that they trust familiar adults

2. **Feelings About Self**—*Learning About Me:* How children express who they are

3. **Relationships With Other Children**—*Child to Child:* What children do around other children

4. **Understanding and Communicating**—*Baby and Toddler Talk:* How children understand and communicate

5. **Exploration and Problem Solving**—*Seek and Solve:* How children explore and figure things out

6. **Movement and Coordination**—*Body Basics:* How children move their bodies and use their hands to do things

The Ounce Scale provides an interactive system of documentation, monitoring, and evaluation of development for Early Head Start programs, early intervention programs, (including children at risk for special needs or those with disabilities), and other home- and center-based infant, toddler, and preschool child care in the community. It provides a meaningful way to evaluate children's accomplishments, areas of difficulty, and approaches to learning. There is guidance for thinking about future goals so that family and caregivers can work together. Families and caregivers using the Ounce Scale learn to observe their children and to use this information to enhance relationships and support development, and document play.

Program Assessment

Program evaluation tends to be controversial (Dickinson, 2003). There is no required national system for evaluating systems and the mandatory systems that exist in states vary from state to state. Infant-toddler centers are evaluated using both voluntary and mandated systems. States have specific mandated requirements for state licensing that vary in level of rigor. Some states also have a system for recognizing high-, medium-, and low-quality centers.

A voluntary system for accreditation is available through the National Association for the Education of Young Children. This system requires a commitment from the center faculty, staff, parents, and community. Centers that complete this process are listed on a national register that can be assessed on-line. Because it is a voluntary program, it is not mandated and is optional.

Infant-Toddler Environmental Rating Scale (ITERS)

Some programs use a program assessment system to determine the quality of their center. One that is well known in the field is the **Infant-Toddler Environmental Rating Scale** (ITERS) (Harms, Cryer, & Clifford, 2003). ITERS is designed to give a quick overview of quality in a center and is respected in the field. Evaluators who use ITERS must have training prior to use; tapes and workshops are available to those who choose to use this method. Areas included in the rating scale include: (Harms, Cryer, & Clifford, 2003, p. 9).

1. space and furnishings
2. personal care routines
3. listening and talking
4. activities
5. interaction
6. program structure
7. parents and staff

ITERS evaluates the *context* for play; it does not evaluate play. Still, it is useful. Assessment is not an *option* for infants and toddlers, it is a necessary part of a play-based program.

> ## *PlayScape Reflections*
>
> Sonda was glad that her two-year-old son, Jermaine was playing all day in a child care center. Some parents, however, need reassurance. Many early educators are familiar with these concerns. Sonda needs to be supported in her positive view of play by understanding how Jermaine learns through play. He is developing his knowledge of spatial relations as he uses the blocks, he is learning how to cooperate with others during play, and he is developing fine motor and perceptual skills. He is beginning to engage in constructive play, which combines practice play and symbolic play. This play develops task-completion skills, concentration skills, and abstraction skills which he will need to be successful in school. The wise teacher is always prepared to discuss the child's right to play by regularly distributing materials that detail the benefits of play for infants and toddlers. The teacher may also want to invite parents to spend a day at school so they can see how these activities occur throughout the day.

■ Summary

Play is the curriculum for infant and toddler centers. The major influence is the adult who must be sensitive, caring, and responsive. An aesthetics-based approach includes play, music, art, movement, and storying for all children. Infant and toddler center play places and spaces must be safe, healthy, sanitary, soft, stable and orderly, comfortable and scaled appropriately, simple and convenient, provide for seclusion and choice, and have sensory appeal.

Major areas in an infant center include entry and exit areas, food preparation and dining areas, diapering areas, sleeping areas, and floor play areas. Major areas in a toddler center should include entry and exit, food preparation and dining areas, sleeping and resting areas, toileting area, and play centers. Infant-toddler play centers should include an emphasis on toys and materials (object play), music and movement (social, symbolic, and motor play), language and literacy (symbolic/pretend), and sensory stimulation (motor and social play). Program models used to organize experiences include the Bank Street model, High/Scope program, Reggio Emilia approach, Creative Curriculum, West Ed Program Educaring, and family home centers. Some centers use an eclectic model that combines elements of different program models. Assessment systems evaluate both the child and the program. Program assessment should reflect the philosophy and the program model and be developmentally appropriate for infants and toddlers. Assessments that facilitate play provide the most natural assessment system.

■ Key Terms

Choke tube	*Infant-Toddler Environmental*	*Ounce Scale*
Controlled scribbles	*Rating Scale (ITERS)*	*Scribble stage*
Infant-directed speech (IDS)	*Motherese or Parentese*	*Uncontrolled scribbles*

■ Helpful Web Sites and Technology Resources

◆ **Bank Street College**
http://www.bankstreet.edu   Bank Street College of Education has an excellent Web site with resources for teachers and parents. Nonprofit agency.

◆ **Culturally and Linguistically Appropriate Services Early Childhood Research Institute**
http://www.clas.uiuc.edu   Nonprofit agency.

◆ **Creative Curriculum**
http://www.teachingstrategies.com   Commercial site with resources for teachers.

◆ **High/Scope**
http://www.highscope.org   High/Scope Web site with resources for teachers and parents. Nonprofit agency.

◆ **Reggio Emilia**
http://zerosei.comune.re.   Home page for the schools of Reggio Emilia. This site can provide links throughout the world. Nonprofit agency.

◆ **West Ed**
http://www.wested.org   West Ed is a program for professional development in the area of infant and toddler training. Nonprofit agency.

◆ **Zero to Three**
http://www.zerotothree.org   Web site designed to provide information and support for families with children three or younger. The available information is impressive and comprehensive with valuable links to other information sources. Nonprofit agency.

■ Activities

1. **InClass Lab**

   A. Develop a table to reflect the progression of mobility from infancy through toddlers.

   B. Draw a room that includes the areas recommended in the chapter. What kind of play is encouraged in each section of the room?

2. **Research and Inquiry**

   A. Visit an infant center for two hours in the morning. Did you see play? Did you see support for play? If so, what type of play did you observe? How does this fit with the information in the text?

   B. Watch an infant play for an hour. Did you see practice play?

   C. Perform an inventory of all items that facilitate play in the center.

   D. What books are available on infant-toddler care in your college library? In your local library? What access do parents in different neighborhoods have to information?

3. **Service Learning**

   A. Volunteer at an NAEYC-accredited center for a day. Now, volunteer at a center that serves low-income infants and toddlers that is not NAEYC-accredited. What differences did you see?

   B. Visit a neonatal center in a local hospital. Volunteer to assist in rocking and holding babies. How is care provided? How does music, movement, or art impact the infant's care?

   C. Visit local pediatric clinics. Do they have toys and books for older infants and toddlers to use while waiting for the doctor? If not, ask if you can provide toys and books that parent can use with their children. Be sure to discuss sterilization procedures that will need to be followed after the toys are placed in the center.

4. **Family Connections**

   A. Create a Web site with links to information about infants and toddlers.

   B. Plan a hands-on workshop on play and toys that you can make.

   C. Create a Web site that lists five things you can do to encourage toddler play. Refer to Figure 4–10.

FIGURE 4–10 Five Things You Can Do to Help Your Toddler Play

- Talk with your child, engage him in conversations, and explain the events that are occurring around him.
- Select toys that encourage creativity such as boxes, hats, and scarves.
- Make time to play every day.
- Make time for outdoor play every day.
- Value your child's play.

5. Play Advocacy

A. What are the state regulations for infant-toddler care?

B. What are national issues affecting infant-toddler care?

C. What are the state and local issues affecting infant-toddler care?

D. Compare the requirements for becoming a profession beautician and infant-toddler child care provider.

E. Volunteer to hand out play brochures with other parent education materials at a local discount store or supermarket.

■ References

American Academy of Pediatrics Task Force on Infant Positioning and SIDS. (2000). Changing concepts of sudden infant death syndrome, *Pediatrics, 105,* 650–656.

Brazelton, T., & Cramer, B. (1990). *The earliest relationship: Parents, infants, and the drama of early attachment.* New York: Addison-Wesley.

Bredekamp, S., & Copple, C. (1997). *Developmentally appropriate practice in early childhood programs.* Washington, DC: National Association for the Education of Young Children.

Bronson, M.B. (1995). *The Right Stuff for Children: Birth to 8.* Washington, DC: National Association for the Education of Young Children.

Commins, D. B. (1967). *Lullabies of the world.* New York: Random House.

Cook, R., Tessier, A., & Klein, M. (2000). *Adapting early childhood curricula for children in inclusive settings.* (5th ed.). Columbus, OH: Merrill.

Cuffaro, H. K., Nager, N., & Shaprio, E. (2000). The developmental-interaction approach at Bank Street College of Education. In J. Roopnarine and J. Johnson (Eds.), *Approaches to Early Childhood Education* (3rd ed.) (pp. 263–276). Upper Saddle River, NJ: Merrill/Prentice Hall.

Custodero, L. (2003). The musical lives of young children: Inviting, seeking, and initiating. *Zero to Three, 23* (1), 4–10.

Dickinson, D. (2003). Are measures of "global quality" sufficient? *Educational Researcher, 32* (4), 27–29.

Dombro, A., Colker, L., & Twister Dodge, D. (1999). *The creative curriculum for infants and toddlers* (rev. ed.). Washington, DC: Teaching Strategies.

Erikson, E. H. (2000). *Childhood and society* (3rd ed.). New York: Norton. (Originally published in 1950.)

Fogel, A. (1998). *Infancy: Infant, family, and society* (2nd ed.). St. Paul, MN: West.

Gandini. L., & Edwards, C. (2001). *Bambini: The Italian approach to infant/toddler care.* New York: Teachers College Press.

Gardner, H. (1995). *Frames of mind: Multiple intelligences.* New York: Basic Books.

Gerber, M. (1998). *Your self-confident baby.* New York: Wiley.

Gonzalez-Mena, J. & Eyer, D.W. (2001). *Infants, toddlers, and caregivers.* Mountain View, CA: Mayfield.

Greeman, J. (1998). *Places for childhoods: Making quality happen in the real world.* Redmond, WA: Child Care Information Exchange.

Harms, T., Cryer, D., & Clifford, R. (2003). *Infant/Toddler Environment Rating Scale (ITERs)* (Rev. ed.). New York: Teachers College.

Honig, A. (1982). Research in review. Infant-mother communication. *Young Children, 37* (3), 52–62.

Honig, A. (1995). Singing with infants and toddlers. *Young Children, 50* (5), 72–78.

Honig, A. (2002). *Secure relationships: Nurturing infants/toddler attachment in early care settings.* Washington, DC: National Association for the Education of Young Children.

International Reading Association (IRA) and the National Association for the Education of Young Children (NAEYC) joint position paper. (1998). Learning to read and write: Developmentally appropriate practices for young children. *Young Children, 53,* 4, 30–46.

Isbell, R. & Isbell, C. (2003). *The complete learning spaces book for infants and toddlers.* Beltsville, MD: Gryphon House.

Isbell, R., & Raines, S. (2003). *Creativity and the arts with young children.* Clifton Park, NY: Thomson Delmar Learning.

Jalongo, M., & Stamp, L. (1997). *The arts in children's lives: Aesthetic education in early childhood.* Boston: Allyn & Bacon.

Kojima, H. (1986). The history of child development in Japan. In H. Azuma & H. Stevenson (Eds.). *Child development and education in Japan.* New York: Academic Press.

Langlois, J. H., Roggman, L. A., & Rieser-Danner, L. A. (1990). Infants' differential social responses to attractive and unattractive faces. *Developmental Psychology, 26,* 153–159.

Lansky, B. (2003). *Mary had a little jam and other silly rhymes*. New York: Scholastic.

Lowman, L., & Ruhmann, L. (1998). Simply sensational spaces: A multi-"s" approach to toddler environments. *Young Children, 53* (3), 11–17.

McMullen, M. B. (1999). Achieving the best practices in infant and toddler care and education. *Young Children, 54*, 69–76.

Miesels, S. (2003). *The Ounce Scale*. New York: Pearson Early Learning.

Miller, K. (1989). *Ages and stages: Developmental descriptions and activities birth through 8 years*. Chelsea, MA: Telshare.

Miller, K., & Albrecht, K. (2001). *Innovations: The comprehensive infant & toddler curriculum*. Beltsville, MD: Gryphon House.

Papousek, M. (1996). Intuitive parenting: A hidden source of musical stimulation in infancy. In I. Delige & J. Sloboda (Eds.), *Musical beginnings: Origins and development of musical competence* (pp. 88–112). New York: Oxford University.

Piaget, J. (1965). *The moral judgement of the child*. New York: Free Press.

Pica, R. (2000). *Experiences in movement with music, activities, and theory* (2nd ed.). Clifton Park, NY: Thomson Delmar Learning.

Picasso, P. (1973). Every child is an artist. The problem is how to remain an artist once he grows up. Recalled upon his death, Apr. 8, 1973. *Columbia Encyclopedia*. Retrieved from Simpson's Contemporary Quotations. Published by Houghton Mifflin.

Readdick, C., & Park, J. (1998). Achieving great heights: The climbing child. *Young Children, 53* (6), 14–19.

Sawyers, J. & Rogers, C. (2003). Helping babies play. *Young Children, 58* (3), 52–54.

Scarr, S. (1984). *Mother care, other care*. New York: Basic Books.

Schaefer, C., Gitlin, K., & Sandgrund, A. (Eds.) (1991). *Play diagnosis and assessment*. New York: Wiley.

Stonehouse, A. (1999). Play: A way of being for babies and toddlers. In E. Dau (Ed.) *Child's play: Revisiting play in early childhood settings*. Baltimore: Paul Brooks.

Sutterby, J., Linck. R., Arrona, A., & Murillo, S. (2004). Games and songs of the border. Presentation at *The Association for the Study of Play Annual Conference*, Atlanta, Georgia.

Szanton, E. (2001). For America's infants and toddlers, are important values threatened by our zeal to "teach"? *Young Children, 56* (1), 15–21.

Trevarthen, C. & Malloch (2003). Musicality and music before three: Human vitality and invention shared with pride. *Zero to Three, 23* (1), 10–18.

Watson, J. (1976). Smiling, cooing, and "The Game." In J. S. Bruner, A. Jolly, and K. Silva (Eds.), *Play: Its role in development and evolution* (p. 275). New York: Basic Books.

Weiser, M. (1991). *Infant/Toddler care and education* (2nd ed.). New York: Merrill.

Weikart, D., & Schweinhart, L. (2000). The High/Scope Curriculum for Early Childhood Care and Education. In J. P. Roopnarine & J. Johnson (Eds.) *Approaches to Early Childhood Education* (3rd ed.). Upper Saddle River, NJ: Merrill/Prentice Hall.

CHAPTER 5

Supporting Play in Preschool Centers

Young children learn the most important things not by being told but by constructing knowledge for themselves in interaction with the physical world and with other children—and the way to do this is by playing.

—Elizabeth Jones and Gretchen Reynolds, 1992

Chapter Overview

Play promotes development and occurs within a classroom context of fun but challenging activities often involving music, movement, and art. Creating environments indoors (blocks, house, manipulatives, and literacy areas), the benefits of toys and adult interactions in center- and family-based settings, and the opportunities for observing and assessing play will be presented in this chapter.

Objectives

After reading this chapter, you should be able to:

- ◆ Discuss the value of play for preschoolers.
- ◆ Describe attributes of an optimal play environment.
- ◆ Compare and contrast two play programs.
- ◆ Describe play documentation and assessment for preschoolers.

PlayScape

Rosalie had just completed a great day at work. She closed a major sale for the company and picked up a $10,000 bonus. This was a great day to be alive. She finished some contracts on her desk, closed her e-mail, and walked to the corporate child care center. She knew the teachers because they had visited her home before she enrolled Juan in the program and she chatted with them every day. She liked the brightness and light that flooded the center and that she could bring Juan with her and they could leave together every afternoon. As she rounded the corner, she heard laughter coming from Juan's classroom. She watched him from the doorway. He was putting some blocks on a large square. Jumping up, he started dancing inside the square and singing, "I'm king, I'm king, I'm king of the wild things!" As she looked at her child, she wondered where he got such notions—king of wild things! She was so impressed with his keen imagination. He was so intelligent. He might grow up to be President. She was so glad she had selected the company center over home child care. She could come by and visit between projects in the office and they could travel together. More than anything, she enjoyed watching him play.

Play Provocation

The provocation to play emerged from the blocks and the story that he had heard earlier in the day. Unaware of the story, his mother assumed that he made up his title. At this age, play takes on an added dimension as children begin to integrate physical, social, and symbolic aspects of play. These are called "the **play years**" because play informs their view of the world and pretend play reaches its peak. During this time children play with words, toys, people, playmates, dogs, and cats, just to name a few. Anything and everything is a game as they explore and play with their world. Supporting play in preschool centers and providing support for teachers who facilitate play will be the focus of this chapter. It is important to note that young three-year-olds may still need special safety considerations.

■ Supporting Preschool Play

All theorists recognize that pretense permits children to become familiar with social role possibilities in their culture, providing important insights into the link between self and wider society.
—Laura E. Berk, 1994

More American children are in preschools than at any other time in this country's history. About 60% of children under five are cared for by someone other than their parents for an average of 30 hours a week (Olson, 2002). As the traditional nursery school changes to become more focused on academic learning, play is at risk in the preschool classroom, yet play is how children learn. One study looked at 100 children in academic-centered preschools and play-based preschools. By the end of the kindergarten year, they found there were no significant differences in academic abilities, and children in the academic environment had less positive attitudes toward school and thought less creatively (Rescorla, Hyson, & Hirsh-Pasek, 1991). This should not be a dichotomy; programs can do both. Research focusing on the child's early learning and healthy development demonstrate that when children are properly supported in their play, play activities can enhance learning (Bergen, 2002, Bodrova & Leong, 2003). Though Elkind (2003) warns us of the danger of this approach lest we lose the essence of play, this can be a win–win situation for academics and play. The use of the dominant type of play to enhance academics has been proposed by others (Pelligrini & Boyd, 1993). Pretense is the dominant play during this age span. The use of pretend play to extend and expand academic learning utilizes the child's natural learning style to help the child make sense of the world.

■ Role of Adults

Teachers play an important role in creating a high-quality play program. "The relationships that children have with adults and other children in their families, child care, and school programs provide the foundation for their success in school" (Pianta & La Paro, 2003, p. 24). These relationships are established throughout the day and especially through play. The teacher who pushes the child in the swing, engages in a tea party, or creates a situation that encourages children to develop a complex play script is facilitating learning and the development of new skills. Teachers who know how to foster high-quality relationships are powerful agents of change. As children move from exploration/instruction to play, the teacher stimulates or bores, facilitates or stifles, builds self-esteem or ridicules—and these interactions make a difference for life.

One avenue for accomplishing this is to ensure that programs are high-quality programs that meet national guidelines. The National Association for the Education of Young Children (NAEYC) has identified characteristics to distinguish high-quality programs for preschoolers; these are listed in Figure 5–1. NAEYC has emphasized the importance of play in

FIGURE 5–1   Components of a High-quality Program

1. Interactions between children and staff provide opportunities to develop an understanding of self and others.

2. The curriculum encourages children to be actively involved in the learning process, to experience a variety of developmentally appropriate activities and materials, and to pursue their own interests in the context of life in the community and the world.

3. Communication with parents is based on the concept that parents are the principal influence on children's lives. Parents are well-informed about, and welcomed as observers and contributors to, the program.

4. The program is staffed by adults who are trained in child development and early education and who recognize and provide for children's needs; the quality and competence of the staff are the most important determinants of the quality of an early childhood program.

5. The staffing structure of the program is organized to ensure that the needs of individual children are met, and to maintain positive interactions and constructive activity among the children and staff.

6. The quality of the early childhood experience for children is affected by the efficiency and stability of the program's administration. Effective administration includes good communication, positive community relationships, fiscal stability, and attention to the needs and working conditions of staff members.

7. The indoor and outdoor physical environments should be designed to promote involvement in the daily activities and easy, constructive interactions among adults and children.

8. The health and safety of children and adults are protected and enhanced. Good programs act to prevent illness and accidents, are prepared to deal with emergencies should they occur, and also educate children concerning safe and healthy practice.

9. Children are provided with adequate nutrition and are taught good eating habits.

10. Ongoing and systematic evaluation is essential to improving and maintaining the quality of an early childhood program. Evaluation should focus on the program's effectiveness in meeting the needs of children and parents.

Source: From B. Willer *Reaching the Full Cost of Quality in Early Childhood Programs.* (1990). Washington, DC: National Association for the Education of Young Children. Published with permission by NAEYC.

guidelines for Developmentally Appropriate Practice. In their guidelines, Bredekamp and Copple (1997) stated

> Play gives children opportunities to understand the world, interact with others in social ways, express and control emotions, and develop their symbolic capabilities. Children's play gives adults insight into children's development of new strategies. . . . Research demonstrated the importance of sociodramatic play as a tool for learning curriculum content with three-to-six-year-old children. (p. 14)

■ Creating the Context for Play for Preschoolers

There are many different ways to consider the teacher's multidimensional role. For the sake of clarity, these roles have been integrated in a step-by-step plan that begins with planning and then moves to evaluation and intervention in a dynamic, spiraling cycle that is continuously changing. These four main areas include planning, observing, guiding, and evaluating. Each topic will include a variety of subtopics.

Planning and Organizing for Play

This is the first and most important step and a role that many teachers relish. Planning and organizing involve orchestrating time, space, materials, and preparatory experiences. Organization is influenced by the teacher's constant and ongoing assessment of play. If she notices an interest in dinosaurs, she may choose to make papier-mâché dinosaur eggs and place them in the outdoor sandbox to simulate a dig for fossils. Adding books on dinosaurs and materials for a fossil hunt will stimulate both play and learning. When time, space, materials, and preparatory experiences are optimal, play flourishes.

Time

Time is a crucial element. Preschool children need time to become involved in play that involves more sophisticated play scripts. Some teachers think that children should be moved every 15 minutes. When teachers do this, they interrupt play to the extent that the children never become involved in mature play and never develop the ability to concentrate and sustain social interactions. This teaches the child to hop from one topic to another. Research indicates that children need at least 30 minutes to become engaged in play (Johnson, Christie, & Yawkey, 1999). Preschool programs by their very nature should be structured around play, and long periods of play are necessary for the development of concentration skills.

Physical space

Preschool children need adequate space in which to provide a variety of activities. Research suggests that 30–50 square feet of useable space per child will facilitate play. Less than 25 feet per child leads to increased aggression (Smith & Connolly, 1980). Space should be set up so there are clear paths and boundaries. When children build with blocks, they need to be located away from the pathway or exit. Low shelves can be used to separate different play spaces. The room needs to have a clear pathway to an exit for safety purposes. Children need clear boundaries, but they also need to be able to integrate materials when engaged in complex play. The room should have areas that are wet and dry, quiet and noisy, and that provide space for one or many, that are private and public, and that have hard and soft surfaces. Teachers who have limited space may want to consider innovations such as a loft that will increase the space available.

Materials

Selecting, rotating, and storing materials has a major impact on play. The teacher must decide what materials are developmentally appropriate for

Adults encourage play when they create the context for preschool play.

the group. Is this a good match for the age, level of development, and culture represented in the classroom? Three-year-olds will enjoy building with plastic and cardboard blocks, but four-year-olds will enjoy unit blocks with accessories.

Materials need to reflect the culture of the classroom. Using food such as rice as a material may be offensive to parents who see this as a grievous waste of food. Check to see if the children need more stimulating materials. What is going on during play? Are new materials needed to add interest or do materials need to be placed in storage? The use of prop boxes can facilitate storage and frequency of use. Prop boxes are boxes that are used to store materials or props for play that relate to a specific theme. For example, masks, gloves, and other medical supplies can be added to encourage hospital play. Prop boxes are decorated so the teacher and children know the content of the boxes just by looking at the boxes. If materials are too difficult to retrieve, they may not be changed as needed. Materials include purchased materials such as puzzles, stacking toys, stringing toys, nesting materials, and real materials. Real materials are defined as any materials that adults use for non-play purposes including both manufactured items (kitchen items, hats, and clothes) and natural materials (sand, water, mud, clay, and wood). Materials make such a difference that many preschool teachers joke about spending their mornings at the "local preschool store" (a yard sale). A list of some materials that are interesting are included in Figure 5–2.

FIGURE 5–2 Play Materials for Preschoolers

Basic play materials for preschool and kindergarten children:

- a full-length, unbreakable preschool mirror mounted on wall or in sturdy stand
- dolls of various ethnicities, including those of the children in the program, with clothes and caregiving accessories (such as bottles, blankets)
- a variety of dress-ups (with increasing levels of role-relevant details) and supporting props for various themes
- a variety of hand puppets
- materials for constructing play scenes, including blocks and human and animal figures
- a variety of sturdy vehicles for use with blocks
- sand and water play materials for exploration and experimentation (measures, strainers, tubes, funnels) and materials for fantasy play in sand and water
- construction materials, including large and small unit blocks, large hollow blocks, and a variety of other small materials for construction
- a variety of puzzles (fit-in, framed, jigsaw), with number of pieces appropriate to children's ages
- beads for stringing (size depends on age), Peg-Boards,™ pattern-making materials (pattern blocks and tiles, weaving materials) for older end of age range
- dressing, lacing, and stringing materials to learn simple self-help skills and beginning sewing activities
- specific skill-development materials that include activities related to matching, sorting, and ordering by shape, color, letter, number, etc.; equipment related to science and the natural world
- a variety of games such as dominoes, lotto, simple card games, bingo, first board games (with the outcomes based on chance, not strategy)
- a large variety of books appropriate to the ages, interests, and experiences of the group
- a large variety of art and craft materials, including both graphic and plastic materials
- a standard rhythm instrument set (and instruments such as wood xylophones if cost permits)
- recorded music (and player) for singing, moving, and playing rhythm instruments
- push-and-pull toys that support sociodramatic play (wagon, doll carriage, vacuum cleaner)
- a variety of balls for specific sports activities, such as kicking, throwing, catching, and rolling (beanbags can also be used for throwing and catching; target games for the older end of the age range)
- pedal tricycles (appropriate for children's size and age)
- outdoor and gym equipment (such as climbing gym, swings, slides, ladders, seesaw by age five) proportioned to children's sizes and capabilities; also sand and gardening tools and all-weather construction equipment

Source: From *The Right Stuff for Children: Birth to 8* (pp. 26, 42, and 81) by M.B. Bronson, 1995, Washington, DC: National Association for the Education of Young Children. Copyright 1995 by the National Association for the Education of Young Children. Reprinted by permission.

Preparatory experiences

Children need experiences and activities that will extend their play. If not, children will play and replay their existing reality. Exposing children to rich literature every day and taking them on field trips gives children a basis for imitating, representing, playing, and replaying newly acquired knowledge. This provides an excellent opportunity to integrate academics with play. Children need exposure to new ideas to optimize play.

Observing

Observing provides the teacher an opportunity to look at the total picture. As a skilled observer, the teacher will see many levels of play skills. Some children will be engaging in a great deal of symbolic play. Others may be just walking around. Another may be engaged in associative play or one may still play alone. By observing the action that is occurring, the teacher will know where and when to act. The skilled teacher notices that the book center is empty or that the house materials need to be rotated. Teachers who are skillful know when to intervene and when to walk away. The teacher's knowledge of play is reflected in her observations. Time to watch play is an important and often overlooked responsibility.

Guiding Play

The teacher assumes a variety of roles during play. She may position herself in or out of the play frame (Johnson, Christie, & Yawkey, 1999). The term *play frame* has been used to describe an episode of play that has a definite beginning point and a definite ending point. Teachers in the play frame assume four major roles, as described below, and interact in a variety of roles within these different roles.

Parallel play

Parallel play occurs when the teacher is near the child, but not engaged with the child. In this situation, the teacher can model play and serve as a source of security. Many teachers use this technique when a child is sitting alone, is new, or is timid. The teacher is involved in the play but not as an interactive player. This technique is equally useful for stimulating children to cross gender lines. For example, female teachers who engage in parallel play in the block area will notice more girls moving into the block area. In the same way, a male preschool teacher who cares for a baby doll in the house area might notice more boys caring for baby dolls. Teachers frequently use parallel play to foster social concepts and interactions.

Co-play

The preschool teacher becomes a co-player when she engages in play with the child. She is careful to follow the child's lead and exit the play in a way that fits the play. **Co-play** is useful for extending play when it has become repetitive. The teacher must be careful to enter and exit naturally.

Noticing Maria and Tony involved in another play episode that has led to fights during the past week, the early educator moves over to the play area. She knocks on the pretend door and asks if she can visit a while. After she joins the children, the children ask if she wants to eat pizza with them. She agrees. Maria begins setting the table. The adult asks if she can help prepare the pizza. Tony replies, "No, the man of the house cooks." Maria responds, "Not in my house." The adult interjects, "Yes, I can help. I will help set the table while the pizza is cooking. Can we take turns cooking and setting the table? I will get the plates. Who will help me set the table?"

Careful interjection as a co-player allowed the children to consider other roles as valuable. The teacher did not admonish the children who reflected different cultural perspectives, but focused interest on other aspects of the play.

Play tutor

A **play tutor** serves as a play leader, model, and guide to scaffold children to a higher level of play. As a leader, the teacher leads and directs the play as children follow her directions and suggestions. When the adult models play, she demonstrates behaviors that should or could occur during play episodes. She guides children when she scaffolds them to a higher level of play. For example, in the scenario above, the teacher is co-playing by following the child's lead, she sets the table but is not changing the flow of the play. If she had said, "In some homes, everyone cooks. Let's pretend that men are cooking in our kitchen today. You cook and I'll wash the dishes." Then she would have been taking a more active role to change the flow of the play. The adult provides a scaffold or support when she interjects additional information or materials that extend or expand play. If she had confronted the child as a spokesperson for reality by saying, "Men cook, too," then the pretend may have stopped. As a co-player following the child's lead, the play stayed at the same level. When the teacher intervenes to lead children to more sophisticated or mature play, then the teacher served as a tutor. This technique is used most in therapeutic settings or with children who have delays. This is especially important with children who have had limited experiences or developmental delays. Several commercial programs are available to support teachers and parents who work with children who have play problems. Current research at Yale University is extending this line of research. Jerome and Dorothy Singer, in conjunction with Harvey Bellin at Media Group, have been involved in creating a program designed to assist adults in facilitating pretend play. See Figure 5–3 for additional details.

Spokesperson for reality

Inside the play frame, the **spokesperson for reality** can add to the depth of the play by extending and expanding it. Paradoxically, she can also stop

FIGURE 5–3 Pretend Play Facilitation

Video-based Play Training to Enhance School-Readiness Skills

by Harvey F. Bellin, Prof. Jerome Singer, and Dr. Dorothy Singer

Background

A significant percentage of American children, especially children from low-income families, enter kindergarten unprepared to learn. Extensive research, including studies by Prof. Jerome Singer and Dr. Dorothy Singer, Directors of the Yale University Family Television Research and Consultation Center indicates make-believe play, a natural feature of early childhood development, peaking at ages three to five, can be an effective means of strengthening children's ready-to-learn skills.

Intergenerational play between children and adults is mutually reinforcing, and can be an effective means of engaging untrained parents and other caregivers as full partners in children's development. Parents and other caregivers of poor children are among those least likely to know of or have access to effective training in skills-enhancing play. Under United States Department of Education grants, Harvey F. Bellin, President of The Media Group of Connecticut, Inc., collaborated with Prof. Jerome Singer and Dr. Dorothy Singer of Yale University to address this need by developing a series of video-based training programs of easily replicated, playful learning games.

Learning Through Play for School-Readiness Program

Learning Through Play for School-Readiness (1997–1999) is a video-based program that trains parents and teachers to engage three-to-five-year-old children from low-income families in six intrinsically motivating learning games that have been shown to produce measurable gains in children's key school-readiness skills. Each game presents a simple, age-appropriate story narrative designed to strengthen specific skills such as vocabulary and language usage, counting, fine motor control, and social/emotional growth.

The Restaurant Game, for example, is a make-believe narrative of a birthday party at a restaurant. By playing the roles of the birthday person and waitstaff, children practice sequencing (doing things in order), new vocabulary and language usage, counting (paying the bill with pretend dollars), social skills (politeness, sharing, taking turns), and color and shape recognition and fine motor skills (pretend writing and drawing shapes for place mats to decorate the restaurant). The two-part, 26-minute training video features inner-city parents, teachers and preschool children, rather than professional actors, playing each learning game. Testing confirmed that this approach empowered viewers with the sense that the games are fun, are easy to do, and require no special training. The Facilitator's Manual includes comprehensive guidelines for conducting training sessions and handouts of instructions and materials for playing games. Results of two years of testing successive versions of the program with samples of low-income parents and preschool teachers of several hundred inner-city children in three cities (New Haven, Atlanta, Los Angeles) indicated:

- Low-income parents and other caregivers were able to understand the value of the program's educational objectives, and were able to engage preschool children in playing the program's skills-enhancing games.
- After children played the learning games for just two weeks, they showed measurable gains in school-readiness skills such as vocabulary, numbers, and cooperative behavior, when compared to a control group.
- Training both parents and teachers of preschool children resulted in increased gains in children's school-readiness scores.
- The training can be replicated in geographically diverse low-income communities.

Twenty-seven hundred free copies of the completed program were disseminated to Head Start centers, Ready-to-Learn Directors of PBS stations, state agencies, public libraries, and other organizations that serve low-income communities, and resulted in the training of significant numbers of parents and teachers of at-risk preschoolers from poor families.

Circle of Make-Believe Program

The next program, *Circle of Make-Believe* (2000–2002), is designed for use by untrained parents and other caregivers of three-to-five-year-olds anytime, anyplace, in any child care setting—families, home care, preschools and child care and Head Start centers. It presents seven make-believe learning games to strengthen key school-readiness skills, including:

- Emergent Literacy: alphabet letter recognition, language usage, enhanced vocabulary
- Math and Reasoning: counting, numbers, shapes, sequencing, spatial relationships
- Social/Emotional Skills: politeness, cooperation, emotional literacy, sharing
- Motor Skills: fine motor skills for writing/drawing and large motor movements

FIGURE 5–3 *(continued)*

In *The Store Game*, for example, children play the cashier and customers of a make-believe store. By buying and selling merchandise, they practice alphabet letters (choosing items to sell with the same first letters), new vocabulary, counting and social skills such as politeness. Children use simple hand puppets (faces drawn on socks) in the *Counting Game* to practice correspondence counting of ten objects and ten fingers. In the *Where Is My Kitten Game?* children use a "kitten" puppet (cat face drawn on a paper plate) to practice words that describe spatial relationships. The *Grumbles Game* enables children to practice emotional literacy and skills for making friends.

The program also models scaffolding skills, such as encouraging children to verbalize and providing positive reinforcement, through which parents/caregivers can foster the development of children's school-readiness skills.

The training video is designed for presentation to preschool children, rather than adults. It features inner-city preschool children with their parents or teachers, playing the skills-enhancing learning games. The video is punctuated with digital animations and real-time, interactive challenges to young viewers that reinforce the learning objectives.

The printed manual of comprehensive guidelines and materials for playing the learning games is written in simple, clear language for untrained parents and other caregivers, including those with limited literacy skills and those for whom English is a second language.

The program was tested with urban and rural low-income children in their homes, home care, preschools, and Head Start centers. In the first year it was tested in Connecticut inner cities and in the second year in a diverse national sample of parents, home care providers and teachers of preschoolers from low-income families in Alabama, California, Connecticut, Maryland, Minnesota, Ohio, Wisconsin, and Wyoming.

Participants received no prior training. They simply used the program to play the learning games with children in their care for two weeks, and then reported the results. National testing resulted in these findings:

- On a 1–5-point scale, in which 5 = Extremely Useful and 1 = Not Useful, participants rated the program a mean score of 4.4. Over half (57%) gave the program a perfect score of 5; and 84% scored the program 4 points or better.
- Adults' rating of whether children enjoyed the games was 4.24 (mean) on a 1–5-point scale in which 1 = Not at all, 5 = Very Much.
- Children continued to play the learning games on their own initiative without adult intervention in 90% of national test sites. They incorporated the games into their play activities and improvised alternate versions.
- Pre- and postintervention ratings of children's skills reported by parents, home care providers, and teachers indicated improvements in children's skills for a full spectrum of cognitive and behavioral measures after children played the learning games for just two weeks. Children's largest gains were in Numbers and Letters and Shape Recognition.
- Children in home care showed the greatest improvements. They gained nearly a full point on a 1–5-point scale for the key readiness skills of Numbers (0.98 point gain) and Letters (0.94 point gain).
- Qualitative feedback from national testing in diverse communities reinforced participants' positive quantitative assessments. This is a representative example of feedback from a Birmingham, Alabama, home care provider:

Children can identify with the people in the video—parents, teachers, children. Instruction easy to understand. When you watch the video if you need to refer back to a game you can use the booklet. The material used everyday household items—hurrah! I have put away gimmicky toys that can be used only one way and fail to challenge the children's imaginations. I brought out household items. Games also helped me to open a new avenue for building partnerships with parents.

A New Video-based Program of Emergent Literacy Skills

Under a new 2003–2005 United States Department of Education grant, Bellin, Singer, and Singer are developing a video-based program that applies playful approaches tested and refined in the previous programs to focus on strengthening the emergent literacy skills of at-risk children from low-income families.

The program will target key emergent literacy skills such as phonological awareness (the ability to detect and manipulate the sound structure of oral language), emergent writing, naming alphabet letters, vocabulary, comprehension, and print knowledge (how to use a book, understanding that English text runs from top to bottom and left to right across a page). It will also train parents and other caregivers in ways to foster children's emergent literacy skills, such as frequent shared book reading and trips to the library and a home literacy environment of age-appropriate picture books.

(continued)

FIGURE 5–3 *(continued)*

Bellin, Singer, and Singer developed and tested a prototype of the video-based program, *The Lost Puppy Game*, that presents a playful make-believe narrative in which preschoolers use emergent literacy skills to help a sad, lost puppy find his way home. The prototype program was tested with three-to-five-year-olds in the care of their parents and home care providers. The results were quite encouraging:

- With no prior training in the program's use, all participating low-income parents and home care providers, including those for whom English is a second a language (21% of parents), could easily use the program to engage children in their care in the emergent literacy learning game.

- Participants rated the program's effectiveness a mean score of 4.17 on a 5-point scale in which 1 = Not Useful and 5 = Very Useful. Seventy-five percent of participants rated the prototype program a score of 4 (Useful) or 5 (Very Useful) on the 5-point scale.

- Preschool children from low-SES families enjoyed and eagerly played the learning game an average of 4.6 times/week in sessions averaging 20 minutes (62.2%) or 30 minutes or more (33.3%).

- After playing the learning game with parents/caregivers, 80% of children continued to play the game and practice skills in the game on their own without any adult intervention.

- After playing the game for just two weeks, preschoolers showed gains in targeted emergent literacy skills, such as print knowledge—a 48.9% mean gain in the percentage of children knowing the meaning of "author," a 33.3% mean gain in those knowing the meaning of "title," and a 30.6% mean gain of children who understood "borrow" (as in "borrow" library books).

- Children also showed gains in knowledge of alphabet letters (15.8% mean gain), and emergent writing skills (12.1% mean gain).

- Qualitative feedback indicated additional gains in children's knowledge that text is read top-to-bottom and left-to-right, and in their motivation to use libraries.

- Adult participants also showed gains in their skills to foster children's emergent literacy. For example, the percentage of parents reporting they had never taken their children to a library decreased by 19% from a pre-intervention mean of 44% to a postintervention mean of 25%.

- A mean of 81.8% of participants reported gains in children's emergent literacy skills, and 68.2% reported gains in their own skills for fostering children's emergent literacy.

Summary and Conclusions

Make-believe play, a natural feature of early childhood development, can be an effective, intrinsically motivating means of strengthening children's ready-to-learn skills and of engaging parents and other caregivers as full partners in children's development. But parents and other caregivers of young children from low-income families, who are at increased risk of starting school unprepared to learn, are least likely to know of or have access to effective training in skills-enhancing play.

Programs developed by the authors have demonstrated the efficacy of easily replicated, video-based training to empower parents, home care providers, and teachers of preschoolers from poor families to engage children in playful learning games that can result in measurable gains in school-readiness skills. They are continuing to develop additional programs and will explore the applicability of newer technologies such as DVD and Web-based learning to increase the number of at-risk preschoolers who can benefit from learning through play for school readiness.

Related Reading

Singer, D. G. & Singer, J. L. (2004). Encouraging school readiness through guided pretend games. In E. F. Zigler, D. G. Singer, & S. J. Bishop-Josef (Eds.), *Children's play: The roots of reading* (pp. 175–188). Washington, DC: Zero to Three Press.

Singer, D. G., Singer, J. L., Plaskon, S. L., & Schweder, A. E. (2003). A role for play in the preschool curriculum. In Sharna Olfman (Ed.), *All work and no play: How educational reforms are harming our preschoolers* (pp. 59–101). Westport, CT: Greenwood.

Singer, J. L., Singer, D. G., Bellin, H. F., & Schweder, A. E. (1999). *Learning through play for school readiness: Report, Year Two.* Prepared for United States Department of Education Early Childhood Institute. Unpublished manuscript. Yale University, New Haven, CT.

FIGURE 5–3 *(continued)*

Whitehurst, G. J., Storch, S. A. (2002). A structural model supporting home literacy activities with African American children. In B. Bowman (Ed.), *Love to read.* Washington, DC: National Black Child Development Institute.

For Additional Information

Visit the Media Group of Connecticut Web site: **http://homepage.mac.com/mediagroupct/**

To purchase *Learning through Play for School Readiness* or *Circle of Make-Believe,* contact Instructional Media Institute: 203/544-0018

Source: Used by permission of Harvey Bellin, The Media Group of Connecticut; Jerome Singer and Dorothy Singer, Yale University, New Haven, CT.

the play. It depends on how the teacher interjects her statements. For example, Robert and Whitney were playing together in the art area. They were pretending that everything they touched was magic. "I'm touching the glue and it's magic." "The glue touches you and it's magic." Whitney jumps up and holds the bottle over Robert's head, saying, "It's magic, it's magic." If the teacher interjects abruptly and reminds Whitney that glue should be used on paper, not people, she stops the play. If she does not intervene, he will have glue on his head. If time permits, the teacher may be able to co-play and say, "Let me add the magic to my paper." This allows the play to continue. If time does not permit, the teacher must intervene as the spokesperson for reality. Even though the play has stopped, Robert does not have glue in his hair. These decisions are the most difficult to make. Sensitive teachers will consider social, cultural, and historical factors when making the decision.

Outside the play frame

Teachers guide play from inside the play frame by careful interactions. Guidance can also be offered outside the play frame. If a child is hitting another child, the teacher must intervene. In Maslow's (1959) hierarchy, health and safety are the first basic considerations. The teacher who does not intervene sends a message that this behavior is acceptable. Safety and health issues always take precedence. Allowing children to hurt other children sends a message that it is acceptable to hurt other children. This message should not be heard by either the child inflicting or the child receiving the pain. Strategies for guiding play from outside the play frame have been suggested by Van Hoorn, Nourot, Scales, and Alward (1999). These roles include artist apprenticeship, guardian of the gate, peacemaker, spectator, matchmaker, storyteller, and scribe. Suggestions for assuming these roles are listed below.

◆ The artist apprenticeship facilitates play by moving materials and props. Moving a phone from the house area to the block area may allow the constructor to phone his make-believe space ship.

◆ The guardian of the gate protects the play by facilitating careful entry into the play.

◆ The peacemaker helps resolve conflicts by offering alternatives.

◆ As spectator, the teacher serves as an audience and offers feedback when needed.

◆ The teacher serves as matchmaker when she suggests that specific children play with other children.

◆ The storyteller provides a platform for play reenactment. Vivian Paley devoted much energy to defining the role of the storyteller in her book, *Walley's Stories* (1981). This aesthetics-based approach allows children to reenact their play as a story, thus developing their literacy skills.

◆ The role of the scribe is an extension of this method and uses art instead of stories. These roles extend, expand, and support play. The teacher uses pictures and captions to share the children's play.

Evaluating Play

Evaluating play provides teachers with opportunities to document both play and learning using authentic, ongoing assessment. Information gained through assessment can be used to guide changes and interactions. Additional observations can provide information concerning the consequences of the changes. Evaluating play involves looking at the centers and the play that is occurring at each center. First, a list should be made of all centers in the room. A tally of children in each center will reveal which centers are most popular. The number of children visiting a center should be monitored and less popular centers altered. This should occur regularly throughout the year to monitor center utility. This provides an overall profile of usage, but does not provide information about the quality of play going on in the center. To examine the quality of play that is occurring requires a different lens and is discussed at the end of the chapter in Play Assessment and Documentation.

■ Extending Play through Aesthetics

> *Music gives a soul to the universe, Wings to the mind,*
> *Flight to the imagination . . . And life to everything.*
>
> —*Plato, 360 B.C.*

Preschool children explore and experience their world through music, movement, art, and story reenactment. An aesthetics-based program provides a way to embrace both play and academics. When children create art, they may be exploring the medium of paint or they may be engaged in a highly symbolic activity. They may discover ways to express their ideas, experiences, and feelings through symbols (Seefeldt, 1995). Play also uses symbols. Play and art enhance the quality of life for preschool children as they develop their ability to engage in abstraction, which is necessary for literacy.

Art

Art should be a major part of the preschoolers' daily experience in school. From painting at the easels to creating with clay, children should have opportunities for art every day. When children use large pieces of paper for drawing their play, they are engaging in writing. When children paint a picture of their pretend castle—that only they recognize—they give life to their play and use their ability to abstract. This provides an opportunity for facilitating academic skills through pretend and art.

Children go through several stages as they develop their artistic abilities. Most three- and four-year-olds are in the **basic forms stage** of artistic development (Isbell & Raines, 2003). They have better fine motor control and hand-eye coordination than they had when they were toddlers. They have moved beyond controlled scribbles and can repeat marks. It is not unusual to see a child at this age fill a complete page with similar marks. When drawing a story about their play, one child filled a sheet and said that he played in the ocean that day. Actually the child played in the water table, but perhaps that was her ocean.

Children's first exposure to materials will be reflected in their artistic ability. Some children at this age will still be in the controlled scribble stage (birth–two) and others will begin to move into a more advanced stage. The **preschematic stage** occurs from four to seven years of age and involves the use of symbols to represent ideas, thoughts, experiences, or feelings (Isbell & Raines, 2003). This stage begins in the preschool classroom and is refined in the primary classroom.

Music

Music enriches play. Incorporating music in preschool programs can be traced to the work of pioneers in early education, discussed in Chapter 2. In the 1700s, Rousseau recommended that mothers teach their children how to sing so they could recognize meter and harmony. The songs that

Children who have daily opportunities to paint can express their view of the world through art.

Froebel (1895) used in his kindergarten are still being sung today. Throughout the twentieth century, music has been a part of the preschool curriculum. Today, research supports the use of music in programs for young children (Kenny, 1997).

The preschooler's interest in music reflects both her cultural and social background. A child's background in music is soon evident in the preschool classroom. Some children enjoy classical music and recognize Bach when they hear his music. Others may enjoy and respond to jazz, pop, country, rap, or spiritual music. When parents are encouraged to bring their own music to school, it creates a climate of trust and respect for the parents' culture. It also exposes all children to a variety of music and facilitates cultural interaction. One exception is the use of music with violent or offensive language. Rap music with violent themes should never be used in a center.

Three- and four-year-olds want to clap, sing, and move. They can improvise simple melodies and sustain a one- or two-tone accompaniment to a well-known song. Music contributes to the total development of the child through the development of psychomotor, perceptual, affective, cognitive, social, cultural, and aesthetic skills (Isenberg & Jalongo, 2001).

Early educators and music

Music is limited in classrooms only by the adult. Early educators who are comfortable using music throughout the day have a powerful tool. Singing in the classroom can be developed. Linda Neelly (2002, p. 81) believes that a positive attitude can be established by recognizing that

- ◆ The art of singing is learned through singing.
- ◆ Teachers should think of themselves as singers.
- ◆ Children love to express their feelings and understandings about the world through singing.
- ◆ Teachers should think of all children as singers. No nonsingers!
- ◆ Singing with children throughout daily routines nurtures important learning connections.
- ◆ Enthusiastic teacher participation in singing encourages the development of children's innate musical ability.
- ◆ Singing is developmentally appropriate practice.

Thomas Moore, a trained early childhood educator and musician, encourages teachers to embrace music and use music to foster social relationships (2002).

Songs for preschoolers

By age three, children can name favorite tunes, recognize favorite songs, and sing. Many cultures have songs that have been passed on to the next generation identified with that culture. *Go Tell Aunt Rhody* and *This Train* are examples of songs that have been handed down in rural America. Learning songs from other cultures can facilitate multiculturalism. Learning simple songs is an exercise in both music and memory. There is a plethora of songs designed to teach concepts. Few can deny, however, the continuing influence of Ella Jenkins, who uses her music to teach children about the world through music and to enjoy music.

Movement

Most preschool children can walk, hop, run, jump, gallop, skip, and climb. Movement occurs naturally when children play. Teachers can also facilitate movement through play. A guide for best practice, *Developmentally Appropriate Physical Education Practices for Young Children ages 3–5*

Daily experiences with music create a source of knowledge for extending play.

(1992), was produced by the Council on Physical Education for Children (a division of the National Association for Sport and Physical Education). The goal of movement programs for children at this age is to produce citizens who

◆ have mastered necessary physical skills.

◆ participate regularly in physical activity.

◆ understand the cost/benefits of physical activities.

◆ recognize the long-term benefits of healthy choices. (Wellhousen, 2002)

Preschool children are in the **fundamental movement phase** (Gabbard, 1992). In this stage, preschool children are developing skills that will provide a foundation for movement later. Children at this stage should be involved in both planned and unplanned activities that occur both indoors and outdoors. Teachers should provide opportunities for children to engage in a variety of activities and develop a variety of skills ranging from skipping, hopping, climbing safely, jumping, running, to various balancing activities. A variety of levels will be apparent at this age. Some children will have difficulty standing on one foot while others are very agile.

Given the number of children in care outside the home, it is imperative that children have opportunities to develop good habits for physical health. Outdoor play adds to the child's physical fitness and love of nature. Helping children enjoy movement at this age may establish patterns that last a lifetime. The benefits of movement are further discussed in Chapter 9.

■ Play as a Medium for Learning

We see the role of play in learning as a central one, and one which also relates to all-round emotional, social and physical development. Play, along with other forms of active learning, is normally a natural point of access to the curriculum for each child at his or her particular stage and level of understanding. It is therefore an essential force in making for equal opportunities in learning, intrinsic as it is to all areas of development.

—Vicky Hurst & Jenefer Joseph, 1998

The foundation for the content areas begins at birth and develops with each passing year. Content areas refer to learning within one academic discipline such as literacy, math, science, social studies, P. E., health, music, or art. Play serves as a medium for learning during this time. Children who play with blocks learn how to build up and tear down. Children who ride tricycles learn to guide and control equipment. Children who play with baby dolls learn to nurture and care for the next generation. These are all valuable and these all form the basis for content areas. Building up and tearing down provide practice in completing a project and turning ideas into products; operating equipment prepares the child for tool usage in other areas and develops motor skills; and understanding that all humans need care is basic for social studies. Because movement, music, and art have been integrated in the curriculum, this section will consider the relationship between play and literacy, math, science, and social studies.

Language and Literacy

Language begins before birth when parents talk. After the child is born, she is immersed in language and communication develops. In the same way, literacy immersion facilitates the child's knowledge of reading. The International Reading Association (IRA) and the National Association for the Education of Young Children (NAEYC) in 1998 issued a joint paper outlining guidelines for parents and teachers to encourage literacy at different levels. Preschoolers are in Phase I (p. 40), an awareness and exploration stage. Components of Phase I are listed below.

Children explore their environment and build the foundations for learning to read and write. They

- ◆ enjoy listening to and discussing storybooks.
- ◆ understand that print carries a message.
- ◆ engage in reading and writing attempts.
- ◆ identify labels and signs in their environments.
- ◆ participate in rhyming games.
- ◆ identify some letters and make some letter-sound matches.
- ◆ use known letters or approximation of letters to represent written language (especially meaningful words like their name and phrases such as "I love you").

Teachers

- ◆ share books with children, including Big Books, and model reading behaviors.
- ◆ talk about letters by name and sounds.
- ◆ establish a literacy-rich environment.
- ◆ reread favorite stories.
- ◆ engage children in language games.
- ◆ promote literacy-related play activities.
- ◆ encourage children to experiment with writing.

Suggestions for creating a literacy-rich environment are included in the following (p. 42):

- ◆ positive, nurturing relationships with adults who engage in responsive conversations with individual children, model reading and writing behavior, and foster children's interests in and enjoyment of reading and writing
- ◆ print-rich environments that provide opportunities and tools for children to see and use written language for a variety of purposes, with teachers' drawing children's attention to specific letters and words
- ◆ adults' daily reading of high-quality books to individual children or small groups, including books that positively reflect children's identity, home language, and culture

- opportunities for children to talk about what is read and to focus on the sounds and parts of language as well as the meaning

- teaching strategies and experiences that develop phonemic awareness, such as songs, fingerplays, games, poems, and stories in which phonemic patterns such as rhyme and alliteration are salient

- opportunities to engage in play that incorporate literacy tools, such as writing grocery lists in dramatic play, making signs in block building, and using icons and words in exploring a computer game

- firsthand experiences that expand children's vocabulary, such as trips in the community and exposure to various tools, objects, and materials

For additional information, see *Learning to Read and Write: Developmentally Appropriate Practices for Young Children*, the joint position statement of the International Reading Association (IRA) and the National Association for the Education of Young Children (NAEYC).

Math

Play provides an optimal environment for supporting math acquisition. According to Kamii and Housman (2000), young children in the preoperational stage of intellectual development construct their understanding of the world through physical knowledge, logical-mathematical knowledge, and social-arbitrary knowledge. **Physical knowledge** is knowledge of the observable traits of an object. **Logical-mathematical knowledge** occurs when children construct a relationship between two objects. **Social-arbitrary knowledge** is knowledge that is socially constructed by society. Examples include reading from left to right, seven days in a week, or the alphabet. Reading skills can be described as social-arbitrary knowledge. Physical and cognitive skills can be learned through physical knowledge. Math skills can only be developed through logical-mathematical thinking. Young children must construct relationships within their mental structures. These skills can be developed through play.

The National Council for Teachers of Mathematics recommends an approach that includes manipulatives and a hands-on approach to math. Preschool children in group settings should be engaged in play that incorporates math naturally. When children set the table in the house area, they are learning patterns and counting. When they build with unit blocks, they are learning geometry. When children paint, they are developing an understanding of lines, shapes, and space. When children discuss the plan for the day, they are learning about time. All math concepts that children should know can and should be taught throughout the day during play and other natural activities. It is not appropriate for children to use workbooks or worksheets in a preschool classroom. Children learn numbers through counting with real materials, not coloring a worksheet with "1" written on it that means nothing to the child—only to the parent and teacher.

Science

Knowledge of science is also developed through logical-mathematical thinking. Preschool children should be exposed to science in a way that is both natural and playful. Einstein noted that he never lost his ability to view the world through the eyes of a child and Erikson referred to Einstein as "the victorious child" (Rogers & Sluss, 1999). He meant that children are naturally curious and open to new ideas. This disposition for science can and should be nurtured. Play provides a natural medium for science. When children explore the grass or other coverings outdoors, they are using their observation skills. When children ask "Why," they are developing their understanding of how the world works. This is the first step toward developing a scientific view of world. Teachers foster this perspective when they create a curriculum that stimulates what Jeffery Trawick-Smith (1994) calls sciencing with young children. The basic process skills of science are nurtured through play.

It is critical that children be exposed to their immediate environment rather than the environment on the latest child's video. It might be better to assist in their knowledge of one tree rather than an entire rain forest that they may never see. Children benefit by touching and feeling items before incorporating them into their mental structures. Look around the immediate environment. What can children touch? What can they feel? Children can touch leaves, nuts, shells, cacti, rocks, sand, snow, or water. Preschool children can plant seeds in the ground, watch them grow, and even harvest vegetables from the plant. Planting seeds to take home too often results in seeds that never mature. A natural realistic approach to science is the best approach. An inquiry-based approach that utilizes the child's natural environment is optimal for developing science skills.

Social Studies

Social studies for preschool children is generally integrated with literacy. Lucy Sprague Mitchell's (nd) "Here and Now" approach developed in the twenties still provides guidelines for a social studies curriculum. The **"here-and-now" curriculum** focuses on what is close to the child (Seefeldt & Barbour, 1998), which is what Bronfenbrenner (2000) and

Scientific inquiry is a natural part of play.

Pelligrini and Boyd (1993) view as the child's microsystem. Preschool children need to understand and make sense of their immediate world before they are ready to venture into the abstract. A computer in a room for a three-year-old may change what appears to be near to the child. Still, children need to represent their neighborhood on a floor map before they are ready to recite state capitals. Given that we know recall is the lowest level of knowledge acquisition, it still seems to impress adults when children can recall obscure facts about abstract situations. Often adults discover that children have memorized the days of the week but cannot understand the concept that a visitor will appear in two days. When children learn in an authentic manner that fits their learning level, their knowledge base is much more developed.

Social studies for preschoolers can occur through units and projects. Themes and units have been used for many years. This approach is developmentally appropriate when it reflects the interest and level of the children. Units are appropriate when they are created with a specific purpose in mind and the early educator is amenable to change based on the children's interest. Many resources are available to guide unit development and implementation. The Bank Street program has expertise in this area and has several themes included on their fine Web site.

When children use the **project approach,** they construct knowledge through an in-depth study of a particular subject. The project approach integrates all subject areas through exploration and play. The project approach is used as a foundation for the curriculum of the Reggio Emilia approach which was initially discussed in Chapter 4.

Although the project approach was created by Katz and Chard (1989) in the 1970s, it has been more closely associated with the Reggio Emilia approach. Additional information is available in the section on constructivism at the end of this chapter.

■ Designing Play Environments

Play centers in the preschool classroom define the play areas in a safe and orderly fashion. Children should have an established safe way to choose play areas that is fair and provides choice every day. A **choice board** provides a good way to select centers. A choice board is a board that illustrates all of the choices available in the classroom. Choice boards can be circular and children can place clothespins (having their names on them), or they can be rectangular and provide spaces for children to hang their names on pegs or hooks. There are many ways to create a choice board. The key is using a system that communicates to the child (and the teacher) that "This is an area where I will play today." Children should be able to choose another play center if they are not satisfied with their initial choice. Allocating an hour or more for center play ensures quality outcomes from play. Ringing a bell to send children to another play center disrupts play. This technique prevents the development of concentration skills. Play centers can include art, music and movement, books, blocks, house, quiet, and dress-up. A sociodramatic interest center should be rotated. With three- and four-year-olds, it is important to not overwhelm the child with too many choices and too much material. It is better to rotate play centers and materials in and out of the classroom.

Art/messy/writing center

The art center can be used for multiple purposes. The art center should be near a source of water. If it is not located on a tile floor, place plastic shower curtains or something similar under the area to facilitate cleanup. Easel painting should be available for children who choose to paint. This can be accomplished if easels remain up and materials are accessible. Painting smocks should be within reach. Hanging them on hooks close to the easels allows children to put them on by themselves. A drying rack provides a convenient place for children to dry their products. An area should be available for displaying the finished products. Tables or flat surface areas are also needed in the art area and can be used for finger painting and other activities that require drying time. Examples of great art can also be displayed in the art center. These can be collected from discarded calendars. Most preschool children enjoy the work of Monet, Picasso, and van Gogh.

Storage shelves should be close so children can select paper, crayons, markers, and paper independently. Stamps, patterns, and templates extend choices. Many centers use the art center as a writing center so children can create books and journals in this center also. Some centers include reusable materials. Adding a bin where parents can leave recyclable materials adds to the class resources and helps parents feel involved. A parent who brings newspapers on Monday can quietly leave the papers on the shelf as she departs for her job. She has contributed to the class, and the class benefits from her donation. Preschoolers have the luxury of using the old newspapers for finding letters, advertisements, or making hats. The key to the art center is organization of materials on the child's level. Be sure to use only safety scissors. An upside-down egg carton makes a good holder.

Music and movement

The music and movement center are especially important for children developing gross and fine motor skills. This area can be located away from the block or book areas. Most preschool children can climb stairs, walk up ramps, or dance to the music. Lofts with Plexiglas™ partitions and ladders encourage movement. Adding music items such as tamborines or bells in an area with mirrors encourages music and movement. Cushions are still important for climbing and tumbling. Encouraging safe movement is still very important at this age.

Book Center

Books should be included in *all* play centers located throughout the room. Book baskets can be placed throughout the center. A *book center* provides a quiet place where children can listen to a tape recording of a book, sit in a lab to listen to a favorite story, or enjoy looking at a book. Book shelves should be used to display the book with the front facing the child. This allows children to remove and return books to the shelf independently. Book centers should be aesthetically appealing. Wall hangings that reflect local and distant cultures are appropriate. Charts with poems can be placed in the center on the child's eye level. Adding puppets, flannel boards, and book props can enhance interest in the center and stimulate story reenactment.

Blocks

Blocks have been a staple of preschool environments for over a century. A variety of blocks should be available. Three-year-olds will enjoy sponge and cardboard blocks, older fours will find the wooden blocks more interesting. Adding realistic props such as a bus, barn, or house is essential for increasing the level of play of the younger children. Younger threes still benefit from toys that are more realistic. Safety mirrors and Plexiglas tables add to the interest of this area.

The block area should be placed away from through traffic. It should be in a place that will allow children to extend play from day to day. Placing the block area in a carpeted area is optimal. If tile is the only option, add a rug to the area or place one on the edge so it can be pulled out during play time. Display pictures of block structures that others have built previously on the walls.

Home center

Preschool children need an area that reminds them of home. This is an area that can include pictures of family members. They can play out being at home and act out any situation that is causing them concern. The house area should be safe, neat, and inviting.

Montessori (1914) used miniature furniture in a classroom as a way to prepare children to care for their own home. The goal of a home center in a preschool classroom is to encourage sociodramatic play. Realistic props encourage pretense. Children who are experiencing separation anxiety are often comforted by participating in play that includes going home.

Toy area

An area for play with puzzles, manipulatives, or toys should be included in all preschool classrooms. They need a place where they can engage in quiet play with a friend, an adult, or by themselves. This area should have bean bags and comfortable seating arrangements. Some centers use a cabinet without shelves. They add padding and curtains to make a safe place for children to be alone. Rotating materials such as puzzles and manipulatives increases interest.

Toys and play materials that stimulate sociodramatic play are especially beneficial. For this reason, some programs rotate their play centers. Materials and toys used to stimulate specific themes are placed in prop boxes that can be rotated in and out of the center. One box may hold materials to set up a flower shop. Other prop boxes include items for doctor, dentist, the grocery store, and the veterinarian. For additional ideas, see *The Complete Learning Center Book* (Isbell, 1995).

Preschoolers can use puppets. Children younger than three can play with puppets as stuffed animals, but they may not understand the concept of puppet. Preschoolers understand that this is pretend. Puppet play allows children to act out their feelings as they develop a concept of story. Children enjoy finger puppets as much as they do regular puppets. Puppets possibilities are unlimited.

Pretend play allows children to try on different roles.

Locomotor skills are developing, and children enjoy running, climbing, and skipping. Their fine motor skills are more developed. Blocks, puzzles, and objects that can be manipulated are appealing. Socially, preschoolers do not like games with complex rules and do not understand when they lose. Therefore, games involving active physical movements should focus on cooperative goals.

■ Integrative Play Programs

Historically, programs for young children started as play programs. Ideas for encouraging play have been presented in this chapter as possible classroom play areas. Early educators can choose how these are used and what philosophy guides their choices. Several program models are available that offer a framework for organizing the curriculum. These models generally use a philosophical base that promotes one perspective. Some centers will choose one system as a framework for their curriculum and their choice influences the type of play that occurs. An example of a *maturationist approach* is the Montessori model (1914). Programs that reflect a *cognitive approach* include the *developmental-interaction approach*, cognitive based approach, *constructivist model*, and Reggio Emilia (Edwards, Gandini, & Forman, 1998) model. Creative Curriculum (Dodge, Colker, & Heroman, 2002) is presented as a program for professional development based on a typical nursery school model. It is included here because many professional development programs use it as a training model.

The advantage of using a program model to inform all classrooms in a center is that children are exposed to a consistent approach. It is more difficult if a child is in a preschool that uses a developmental-interaction approach in one class and a Montessori-based approach in another classroom. High-quality programs use a consistent theoretical approach to guide programs in the center. Some common models are discussed on the following pages.

Good environments encourage play.

Developmental-Interaction

The developmental-interaction approach (presented in Chapter 4) is based on enhancing the development of the child through interactions with the world.

Bank Street was initially started by Lucy Sprague Mitchell in 1916 as the Bureau of Educational Experiments. Over the years, the school has been influenced by John Dewey's (1930) view of progressive education and later by Erikson's (1950) view of emotional development. The goal was to educate the whole child and included the physical, social, cognitive, emotional, and aesthetic domains. Specific emphasis was placed on progressivism and emotional health.

The learning environment

The developmental-interaction curriculum is based on progressivism and experiential learning. The curriculum basically consists of daily living activities. These involve routines and active use of materials throughout the day. Activities for preschoolers include

- ◆ Sensory experiences: Sand, water, play dough, shaving cream, and cooking projects
- ◆ Gross motor activities: Classrooms are set up so children can move in, on, under, over, through, behind, and around objects in the room and so they can be up high, underneath, or hidden. Climbing rooms are used for spatial explorations.
- ◆ Blocks: Blocks are a core material in a Bank Street classroom. Like artwork, block-building with young children emphasizes the process, not the product.

The curriculum

The preschool curriculum is unstructured with minimum day-to-day or week-to-week planning. Emphasis is placed on the knowledge and preparation of the teacher who must understand the overall principles and implement them in the classroom. Children in this program are actively engaged in activities in a democratic classroom. Social studies forms the core of the curriculum. Cuffaro, Nager, and Shapiro (2000) define social studies as ". . . the relationships between and among people and their environments, the world in which we live and our place in it. It concerns the near and far, the past and present" (p. 267). The role of the teacher is to question, plan, provide resources, and assess the relationships.

Bank Street uses the field trip as a way to introduce the child to the world. After the child experiences the field trip, a unit is used as a guide for planning activities and implementing instruction. Another area of emphasis in this program is literacy. Children, teachers, and parents are encouraged to read, write, and publish their work. For more information, visit the Bank Street Web site for a selection of available materials and teaching ideas.

High/Scope

High/Scope is a program that originally started as the Perry Preschool Project and was one of the first preschool programs established as a research model. As mentioned in Chapter 4, it is based on Piaget's child development theories that view the child as an active learner and is designed to provide action-based activities for children that foster the development of key learning experiences. The program has a consistent routine to maximize opportunities for learning. The daily routine for preschoolers includes a **plan-do-review** sequence in the morning. This is a framework for organizing play. First children plan what they are going to do and discuss how they will accomplish their task. Next, they engage in the "do" part of the cycle during work time. During this time, teachers float throughout the room, use questions to scaffold play, and monitor interactions among the children. Cleanup is a part of this phase. Attention is paid to carefully replacing materials on the shelves. Materials are organized so that children learn mathematical concepts when placing materials in their original position. Recall time is the last part of this cycle. Children review what they have accomplished and represent their work in a variety of ways. Some will dictate stories, some will tell about their work, others will draw pictures. Recall provides an opportunity for children to develop their language and literacy skills.

Large-group time provides a time for children to come together for music and movement. The key preschool experiences include the following:

◆ creative representation
◆ language and literacy
◆ initiative and social relations
◆ movement
◆ music
◆ classification
◆ seriation
◆ number
◆ space
◆ time

Though the program does not tout itself as a play-based program, the "do" part of plan-do-review that is called work time is very much a time for play. In describing the layout of the room, the program recommends four quadrants with a wet/dry, quiet/loud division with clear low boundaries. Assessment is ongoing and uses an instrument developed by High/Scope—the Child Observation Record. One key to effectiveness is maintaining a staffing ratio of no more than 10 preschoolers per staff member and group sizes that are limited to 20.

Constructivist

Many fine constructivist programs exist in the United States. As discussed in Chapter 4, the program in Reggio Emilia was selected as a model for constructivism due to the recent interest in this approach. The preschools of Reggio Emilia have been recognized by many as the best in the world. Started at the end of World War II by parents with the leadership of Louis Malaguzzi, the schools of Reggio Emilia were sponsored by the local municipal government of Reggio Emilia, Italy. Malaguzzi was influenced by the teachings of Dewey (1930) and Vygotsky (1978). He believed that children had many ways of knowing the world and described this as *The Hundred Languages of Children* (Edwards, Gandini, & Foreman, 1998). The preschools of Reggio Emilia include a curriculum that reflects the children's interest and expression of their interest as mitigated by adults and the environment. The curriculum is based on an aesthetic approach. Enjoyment of the arts is an important component of the child's world, and play has a major role in the curriculum. A typical center in a room for three-year-olds might include a block center, home area, dress-up or pretend area, computer area, book area, group meeting area, gross motor area, and an enclosed room for art and music. Each room is supervised by two teachers. The daily routine is very flexible with children's interests defining a majority of the activity each day.

Preschoolers in Reggio Emilia engage in a great deal of project work. This concept is based in part on Dewey's notion of progressive education and Katz and Chard's (1989) project approach. The projects can be teacher or child initiated. The preschoolers engage in many field trips. Like the schools of Bank Street, only three or four children participate in an outing at one time. For example, in a video produced by the Friends of Reggio Emilia, a project about the lions on the piazza is discussed. The children travel to the square to look at the lions, measure the lions with string, and observe the shadows that occur during their visit (Fu, Stremmel, & Hill, 2002). This project, which started as a field trip, can extend throughout the month as they make clay lions, paper lions, 3-dimensional lions, that develop concepts.

Creative Curriculum

Creative Curriculum (2002) is in its fourth edition which speaks to the usefulness of this text for preschool teachers. Though the program is not affiliated with a lab school or university, it uses an eclectic approach. The curriculum framework used by Dodge, Colker, and Heroman (2002, p. xiv) is composed of two areas. The first area is the curriculum framework and includes:

1. how children develop and learn
2. the learning environment
3. what children learn
4. the teacher's role
5. the family's role

The second area includes 11 interest areas: blocks, dramatic play, toys and games, art, library, discovery, sand and water, music and movement, cooking, computers, and outdoors.

    The charts for planning weekly activities are used in many programs as are the materials for parents. Creative Curriculum provides materials that are very clear. Their professional development programs provide valuable information for early educators.

Family Child Care

Family centers can choose any of the centers mentioned above or use an eclectic model by choosing different components from each program. For example, some early educators choose to use some aspects of the High/Scope plan-do-review and some parts of the Bank Street program. It is important to align the philosophy of education and the program.

■ Play Assessment and Documentation

Assessment for preschoolers is both formative and summative. Formative assessment is also called *authentic assessment* and reflects the philosophy of the program. Different program models described above use an assessment plan that matches their program philosophy. For example, Bank Street uses an approach that focuses on the child's holistic progress. High/Scope uses a Piagetian approach that looks at key elements of cognitive development. The High/Scope program uses a specific instrument created to reflect program goals and objectives. Reggio Emilia uses an assessment system based on a social constructivist view of teaching and learning. It documents the child's process of learning through documentation panels and portfolios. Reggio Emilia does not look at children in terms of norms; it focuses on children's construction of knowledge within the context of the group. Creative Curriculum includes an assessment system in their text. Some preschool programs combine different elements to create their own unique system. Assessment that occurs throughout the year on an ongoing basis is called *authentic* or *formative assessment* because it provides information that can be used to guide instruction and interaction.

Summative assessment is used at the end of a time period to determine if the child has met certain objectives and has knowledge in specific areas. Learning that occurs through play can be useful during tests. By its nature, play-based assessment can be either formative or summative. It is formative when it is used in an ongoing way to guide behavior, activities, or experiences and summative when used at the end of a program. The next section discusses play-based assessment and ways to integrate it into the curriculum to create a seamless system.

Play-based Assessment

Observing play is relatively easy. Assessing play is much more difficult. The first question that arises in assessment is, "What is the purpose or goal of the assessment?" If the goal of play-based assessment is to understand the child's level of play in order to facilitate the child's development and play skills, then examining the child's play level is essential. One way to accomplish this is to assess the child's play in a specific area such as block play (See Figure 5–4). Another instrument that is designed to measure cognitive and social levels is the Play Observation Scale (Rubin, 1989) that was explained in Chapter 1. This provides a profile of the child's play behaviors. This instrument can be used to capture a picture of the child's play at the beginning and end of a specified period of time. For example, it would not be unusual for a preschooler to engage in solitary play or to engage in constructive play with blocks. In fact, this is very typical behavior. If, however, the child was observed on three different occasions and used the same materials in the same way, then closer observations would be needed. This instrument only shows what the child is doing. It cannot be used for any other purposes.

Other informal techniques for assessing play include photo essays and documentation panels. Photo essays capture not only an image of the child, but also an interpretation of the child's play for others. Documentation panels are similar in that they also capture the child at play but they add an explanation and interpretation. The difference between a photo essay and a documentation panel is that a photo essay may be on a computer

FIGURE 5–4   Evaluating Block Play

Level of Block Play	Day 1	Day 2	Day 3	Day 4	Day 5	Total
Stage 1 Children carry blocks.						
Stage 2 Children build with blocks. They build up (vertically) or out (horizontally).						
Stage 3 Children begin putting connecting blocks with other blocks.						
Stage 4 Children connect blocks to make completed shapes.						
Stage 5 Additions are made to the connected blocks. A great deal of symmetry can be observed.						
Stage 6 Children name the structures.						
Stage 7 Children use the structure for dramatic play.						
Additional notes						

For an overview of play in the block center, the number of children engaging in each stage of block play can be tallied. This does not provide information on individual children, but rather provides a profile of what type of play is dominant during the week.

Source: Adopted from Johnson, 1984.

or paper. A documentation panel is generally on a large board designed for viewing for others and is displayed over a period of years. The panel is used to add to the history of a school.

Another way to examine the quality of the play is through the arts. Children can draw their play. They can use a mural or large sheets of manila paper (12" × 18") to create play stories. They can also use puppets to act out their play. Another possibility involves drama and is similar to Vivian Paley's (1981) method. The children act out their play. Creative teachers will discover even more ways to understand and capture children's play. Assessment during play provides a natural environment for obtaining information about the child and the child's play. Many teachers have anecdotal stories of hopping assessments that indicate that the child can not hop on one foot, yet the child hopped all over the playground! Play-based assessment has the potential to impact how we think about assessment for preschool children. More research is needed in this area.

PlayScape Reflections

Juan is in middle of his "play years" and is engaging in very sophisticated play. His construction of blocks involved some practice play as he carried and stacked the blocks. He appropriated a story he heard earlier and is acting out the story through song and movement. Juan's ability to engage in abstraction is preparing him for instruction in math and literacy. Rosalie knows that not only is Juan enjoying his experiences in the corporate child care center, but that he is also receiving a solid educational experience that will prepare him for life and school. Like many of the other parents at the center, Rosalie understands the relationship between play and learning. The teachers are fortunate that the parents in this center understand the value of play.

■ Summary

Preschool children are in the middle of the "play years," when pretense peaks. This chapter was designed to provide a way of thinking about play in preschool as a time for optimizing opportunities for pretend play. Adults create the context for play by planning for play, observing and guiding play, and evaluating play. An aesthetics approach to preschool ensures that children have natural learning opportunities as they engage in music, art, and movement. As preschoolers learn about their world, they are also learning literacy, math, science, and social studies. Special-interest areas in the preschool room include blocks, house, manipulatives, book center, and toys. Programs that integrate play include High/Scope, Bank Street, and Reggio Emila. These programs have assessment plans that reflect the philosophy of the program. Family-based child care can also implement any of the commercial models or create their own system. Play-based assessment based on an aesthetic approach uses art, drama, and music as vehicles for understanding pretend. This is an area that needs additional research.

■ Key Terms

Basic forms stage   *Logical-mathematical knowledge*   *Play years*
Choice board   *Physical knowledge*   *Preschematic stage*
Co-play   *Plan-do-review*   *Project approach*
Fundamental movement phase   *Play frame*   *Social-arbitrary knowledge*
"Here-and-now" curriculum   *Play tutor*   *Spokesperson for reality*

■ Helpful Web sites and Technology Resources

◆ **Association for the Childrenhood Education International (ACEI)**
http://www.udel.edu   The Association for Childrenhood Education International (ACEI) Web site is an outstanding site with connections to reliable sources of information, experts in the field, and new resources on childhood education.

◆ **National Association for the Education of Young Children (NAEYC)**
http://www.naeyc.org   The National Association for the Education of Young Children (NAEYC) Web site is an excellent source of information about preschool children. This site provides connections to high-quality, authentic sources of information. The NAEYC interest group, Play, Policy and Practice (PPP), also serves as a source of information about play.

◆ **Medical University of South Carolina (MUSC)**
http://www.musckids.com   The Medical University of South Carolina (MUSC) Children's Hospital hosts a Web site that provides good information about preschool play.

◆ **Bank Street College of Education**
http://www.bnkst.edu   Bank Street College has an excellent Web site that features a great deal of information as well as access to their book store.

◆ **Creative Curriculum**
http://www.teachingstrategies.com   Creative Curriculum features a Web site that provides specific information about preschool play and curriculum.

◆ **Lucille Packard Children's Hospital**
http://www.lpch.org   The Lucille Packard Children's Hospital at Stanford University Medical Center has an excellent site that encourages play.

■ Activities

1. **Inclass Lab**

   A. Design a room for a preschooler that reflects the concepts discussed in the chapter. Know the local and state fire, safety, and licensing standards. Also check on the academic standards. Draw the room on a large 6' × 6' piece of paper. When all the groups have completed their tasks, share the designs in class and display them on the wall.

   B. Look at the charts that were placed on the wall. Decide which areas would stimulate cognitive, social, and physical play. Which areas could be used for music, art, and drama? Which areas could be used for functional, symbolic, sociodramatic play, and games with rules? Do you need to address other criteria?

   C. Create a prop box outside of class. Include a graphic of the learning outcomes for children. Share the prop box and representation in class.

2. **Research and Inquiry**

   A. Visit a preschool classroom for two hours. Complete a running record of a child's play. Compose a list of the preschool child's characteristics. Identify several physical, social, and cognitive characteristics.

   B. How does play in the preschool differ from that in the infant-toddler center?

   C. The statement "Play is the child's work" is used in many preschool classrooms. Visit the library and investigate who first made this statement. Bring your answer to class and be ready to share your findings.

3. **Service Learning**

   A. Volunteer to assist in a preschool center for two hours one week. Does the center need additional play materials? Can you assist in creating an environment that fosters play?

   B. Volunteer to create a Web site for a local preschool center.

   C. Contact a local center and ask if you can present a program or play for one of their family night meetings.

4. **Family Connections**

   Create a letter that you can send home to parents that will stimulate play. The letter in Figure 5–5 can serve as a template. Add information that is unique to your geographic area and local culture.

FIGURE 5–5 Template for Letter to Parents.

Dear Parents,

Young children learn as they play. The list below contains some activities that you can use to encourage play at home.

1. *Collect the junk mail that comes to home. Let the children set up a pretend post office. They can draw pictures for relatives or friends and pretend to mail them in the junk mail envelopes. Some may even be mailed.*

2. *Get some boxes that have been discarded and allow children to use them to build pretend houses. They can drape an old sheet or blanket over the box and create a tent. The possibilities are endless.*

3. *Collect clean grocery boxes and plastic bottles. Let children set up a pretend grocery store.*

4. *Let children take coupons to the store. They can locate the item that matches the coupon and pretend to shop while you shop.*

5. *Blocks are wonderful. You can buy a variety of sizes or you can make blocks by following the directions that are attached to this sheet.*

6. *Cooking activities are wonderful. A recipe for goop just requires corn starch and water. Mix together and store any unused goop in a plastic bag in the refrigerator.*

Please contact me if you have questions about any of these activities.

Your child's teacher

5. **Play Advocacy**

   A. What are the provisions for play programs in your community? Are there any federally funded programs? What state programs are available? What does the local school system fund? Find or start a local group to support young children in your area.

   B. Ask a local clinic or community center if a display can be set up to distribute NAEYC brochures. Initiate a fund-raiser to purchase materials. Select several good brochures that relate to play and other issues related to play-based education.

■ References

Bergen, B. (2002). The role of pretend play in children's cognitive development. *Early Childhood Research and Practice, 4* (1), 1–13. Retrieved July 10, 2003, from http://ecrp.uiuc.edu/v4n1/bergen.html.

Berk, L. (1994). Why children talk to themselves. *Scientific American, 271* (5), 78.

Bodrova, E., & Leong, D. (2003). Chopsticks and counting chips: Do play and foundational skills need to compete for the teacher's attention in an early childhood classroom? *Young Children, 58* (3), 10–17.

Boston, C. (2002). *The concept of formative assessment.* (ERIC Digest). College Park, MD: ERIC Clearinghouse on Assessment and Evaluation. (ERIC Document Reproduction Service No. ED346082).

Bredekamp, S., & Copple, C. (1997). *Developmentally appropriate practice in early childhood programs.* Washington, DC: National Association for the Education of Young Children.

Bronfenbrenner, U. (2000). Ecological theory. In A. Kazdin (Ed.), *Encyclopedia of psychology* (pp. 129–133). Washington, DC & New York: American Psychological Association and Oxford University Press.

Cuffaro, H. K., Nager, N., & Shaprio, E. (2000). The developmental-interaction approach at Bank Street College of Education. In J. P. Roopnarine and J. Johnson (Eds.), *Approaches to early childhood education* (3rd ed.) (pp. 263–276), Upper Saddle River, NJ: Merrill/Prentice Hall.

Dewey, J. (1930). *Democracy and education.* New York: Macmillan.

Dodge, D. T., Colker, L. J., & Heroman, C. (2002). *The creative curriculum for preschool,* 4th ed. Washington, DC: Teaching Strategies.

Edwards, C., Gandini, L., & Foreman, G. (Eds.). (1998). *The hundred languages of children: The Reggio Emilia approach—Advanced reflections.* (2nd ed.) Greenwich, CT: Ablex.

Elkind, D. (2003). Thanks for the memory: The lasting value of true play. *Young Children, 58* (3), 46–52.

Erikson, E. (2000). *Childhood and society.* New York: Norton. (Originally published in 1950.)

Forman, G. (1998). Constructive play. In D. P. Fromberg & D. M. Bergen (Eds.), *Play from birth to twelve and beyond: Contexts, perspectives, and meanings* (pp. 392–400). New York: Garland Publishing.

Froebel, F. (1895). *The songs and music of Freidrich Froebel's mother play (mutter und kose lieder).* New York: Appleton.

Fu, V., Stremmel, A., & Hill, L. (2002). *Teaching and learning: Collaborative explorations of the Reggio Emilia approach.* Columbus, OH: Merrill.

Gabbard, C. P. (1992). *Lifelong motor development.* Dubuque, IA: Wm. C. Brown.

Hurst, V., & Joseph, J. (1998). *Supporting early learning, the way forward.* Buckingham: Open University Press.

International Reading Association (IRA) and the National Association for the Education of Young Children (NAEYC) joint position paper. (1998). Learning to read and write: Developmentally appropriate practices for young children. *Young Children, 53* (4), 30–46.

Isbell, R. (1995). *The complete learning center book.* Beltsville, MD: Gryphon House.

Isbell, R., & Exelby, B. (2001). *Early learning environments that work.* Beltsville, MD: Gryphon House, MD.

Isbell, R., & Raines, S. (2003). *Creativity and the arts with young children*. Clifton Park, NY: Thomson Delmar Learning.

Isenberg, J., & Jalongo, M. (2001). *Creative expression and play in early childhood*. Columbus, OH: Merrill.

Johnson, H. (1933/1984). The art of block building. In E. S. Hirsch (Ed.) *The block book* (pp. 8–26). Washington, DC: National Association for the Education of Young Children.

Johnson, J., Christie, J., & Yawkey, T. (1999). *Play and early childhood development*. New York: HarperCollins.

Jones, E., & Reynolds, G. (1992). *The play's the thing: Teachers' roles in children's play*. New York: Teachers College Press.

Kamii, C., & Housman, L. (2000). *Young children reinvent arithmetic: Implications of Piaget's theory* (2nd ed.). New York: Teachers College Press.

Katz, L., & Chard, S. (1989). *Engaging children's minds: The project approach*. Norwood, NJ: Ablex.

Kenny, S. (1997). Music in developmentally appropriate integrated curriculum, In C. H. Hart, D. C. Burts, & R. Charlesworth (Eds.), *Integrating curriculum and developmentally appropriate practice: Birth to eight* (pp. 103–144.) Albany: SUNY Press.

Maslow, A. (1959). Psychological data and human values. In A. H. Maslow (Ed.), *New knowledge in human values*. New York: Harper.

Montessori, M. (1914). *Dr. Montessori's own handbook*. New York: Frederick A Stokes.

Moore, T. (2002). If you teach children, you can sing! *Young Children, 57* (4), 84–85.

National Association for Sport and Physical Education (NASPE). (1992). Developmentally appropriate physical education practices for young children. A position statement of the council on Physical Education for Children of NASPE. Reston, VA: AAHPERD.

Neelly, L. (2002). Practical ways to improve singing in early childhood. *Young Children, 57* (4), 80–83.

Olson, L. (2002). Starting early. In Education Week quality counts 2002: Building blocks for success. *State Efforts in Early Childhood Education, 21*(17), 10–22.

Paley, V. (1981). *Wally's stories*. Cambridge, MA: Harvard University.

Pelligrini, A. D., & Boyd, B. (1993) The role of play in early childhood development and education: Issues in definition and function. In B. Spodek (Ed.), *Handbook of research on the education of young children* (pp. 105–121). New York: Macmillan.

Pianta, R., & La Paro, K. (2003). Improving early school success. *Educational Leadership, 60* (7), 24–29.

Plato. (1986). *The Republic.* (A. D. Bloom, Trans.). New York: Basic Books. (Original work published 360 B.C.)

Puckett, M., & Black, J. (2000). *Authentic assessment of young children: Celebrating development and learning* (2nd ed.). New York: Macmillan.

Rescorla, L. A., Hyson, M., & Hirsh-Pasek, K. (Eds.). (1991). Academic instruction in early childhood: Challenge or pressure? (*New directions for child development,* No. 53). San Francisco: Jossey-Bass.

Rogers, C. S., & Sluss, D. J. (1999). Revisiting Erikson's views on Einstein's play and inventiveness. In S. Reifel's *Play contexts revisited, Play and culture series,* Vol. 2, (pp. 3–24). Greenwich, CT: Ablex.

Rubin, K. (1989). *The Play Observation Scale.* Waterloo Canada: University of Waterloo.

Seefeldt, C. (1995). Art—serious work. *Young Children, 50* (3), 39–45.

Seefeldt, C., & Barbour, N. (1998). *Early childhood education: An introduction.* Columbus, OH: Merrill.

Smilansky, S., & Shefatya, L. (1990). Rough-and tumble-play, aggression, and dominance: Perceptions and behavior in children's encounters. *Human Development, 33,* 271–282.

Smith, P. K., & Connolly, K. J. (1980). *The ecology of preschool behavior.* Cambridge, England: Cambridge University Press.

Trawick-Smith, J. (1994). *Interactions in the classroom: Facilitating play in the early years.* New York: Macmillan.

Van Hoorn, J., Nourot, P., Scales, B., Alward, K. (1999). *Play at the center of the curriculum.* New York: Macmillan.

Vygotsky, L. (1978). *Mind in society: The development of higher psychological processes.* Cambridge, MA: Harvard University Press.

Wellhousen, K. (2002). *Outdoor play every day: Innovative concepts for early childhood.* Clifton Park, NY: Thomson Delmar Learning.

Wheelock, L. (n.d.) *My life story.* Unpublished autobiography. Cited in *Childhood Education, 76* (3) 164–169. By Catherine C. Ducharme.

Willer, B. (1990). *Reaching the full cost of quality in early childhood programs.* Washington, DC: NAEYC.

CHAPTER 6

Supporting Play in Kindergarten Classrooms

Perhaps what is needed are super programs that provide balance, giving every child a chance to succeed and to play.

—Teri Lewis, Geoff Colvin, & George Sugai, 2000

Chapter Overview

Play is the core of the kindergarten program. This chapter examines the implementation of a high-quality play program in today's kindergarten. The teacher's role, environment, curriculum, music, movement, and art are considered as they pertain to creating indoor environments (blocks, house, puzzles, toys, and literacy centers) for all children. Formal and informal assessment and documentation of indoor play are also presented in this chapter.

Objectives

After reading this chapter, you should be able to:

◆ Discuss characteristics of an effective kindergarten program.

◆ Describe five play centers found in traditional kindergarten programs.

◆ Explain how children develop language and literacy skills through play.

◆ Identify assessment strategies that can be used to used to document how children learn through play.

PlayScape

Jamal did not like kindergarten. He liked his grandmother's house and routine. He missed his grandmother and their "stories" that they watched every day. Now, he didn't know what was happening on "Days" anymore. He really wanted to go home. Another tear fell from his eye as he watched the teacher stack block after block.

"Jamal, would you like to stack some blocks higher than mine?" she quizzed.

As he started to stack these things she called blocks, he realized you could do other things. He watched as others built something that looked like a house. He could build one bigger than that!

An hour later, the lights dimmed to remind everyone that cleanup time was near. Jamal did not want to stop. He liked blocks. Grandma did not have blocks at her house. Maybe this place might be fun. . . .

Play Provocation

The provocation to play in this classroom was the combination of time, materials, and teacher interaction. The teacher allocated over an hour for play, blocks and other materials were well defined and available for use, and the teacher moved throughout the room to facilitate play. Jamal, like some children who come to kindergarten, was not transitioning well. For Jamal, play was cathartic: play provided a place where he could control the situation and gain mastery over his emotions (Erikson, 2000). A play-based program in kindergarten can facilitate a positive transition into public school. The first day of kindergarten can be overwhelming for some children and adults. If Jamal's grandmother has watched daytime television with her grandson for several years, she may be having an equally difficult time adjusting to his absence. The emotional issues surrounding this first step away from home are often complex. At the same time, the teacher must recognize the needs of children and families who have experienced preschool programs for several years. Play materials and interaction will need to provide an array of interesting, challenging experiences. The teacher must realize the variability of experiences that the children bring to the kindergarten class and provide experiences that foster play for all children. The lasting results can be powerful, as depicted in Figure 6–1.

▧ Kindergarten Programs

> *As we [have] seen many of our public-funded early childhood*
> *programs become downward extensions of public schools, we need to*
> *advocate for the children's right to play.*
>
> —Francis Wardle, 1999

The history of kindergarten can be traced to Froebel's (1887/1902) work in Germany. *Kindergarten* literally translated means "garden for children." As discussed in Chapter 2, Froebel thought children should be free to grow and develop like flowers in a garden. Froebel's influence was evident in the first two kindergartens in America, which were started by his students. He believed that Americans might have more freedom to begin a school for children than he had encountered in Europe. Margarethe Schurz (1832–1876) is credited with starting the first kindergarten in America in Watertown, Wisconsin, and Caroline Luise Frankenberg started a kindergarten class in Columbus, Ohio, even before Froebel opened his own center. Others influenced by Froebel include Elizabeth Peabody, who started the first English-speaking kindergarten, and Susan Blow, who started the first public school kindergarten in St Louis, Missouri (Froebel 1887/1902; Brostarman, 1997).

FIGURE 6–1   All I Really Need to Know I Learned in Kindergarten!

Share everything.

Play fair.

Don't hit people.

Put things back where you found them.

Clean up your own mess.

Don't take things that aren't yours.

Say you're sorry when you hurt somebody.

Wash your hands before you eat.

Flush.

Warm cookies and cold milk are good for you.

Live a balanced life—learn some and think some and draw and paint and sing and dance and play and work every day some.

Take a nap every afternoon.

When you go out into the world, watch out for traffic, hold hands, and stick together.

Be aware of wonder. Remember the little seed in the Styrofoam cup: The roots go down and the plant goes up and nobody really knows how or why but we are all like that.

Goldfish and hamsters and white mice and even the little seed in the Styrofoam cup—they all die. So do we.

And then remember the Dick-and-Jane books and the first word you learned—the biggest word of all—LOOK.

Patty Smith Hill started as a Froebelian but was influenced by G. Stanley Hall and his scientific approach to studying children. She is credited with creating the traditional kindergarten core that is still found in kindergartens today, inventing unit blocks, and writing the song *Happy Birthday to You*. She was committed to a kindergarten program that emphasized social skills. Today, full-day and half-day kindergarten programs are a part of public school systems. They are publicly funded and situated in public school buildings with primary and elementary schools.

Many of the concepts basic to the Froebelian or Hill kindergartens are disappearing as academics and workbooks replace block play and pretense. In a position paper issued by the Association for Childhood Education International (ACEI), Joan Moyer (1999) found five misunderstandings that have contributed to this situation:

1. society's emphasis on children learning more at an earlier age
2. misunderstandings about how children learn
3. large selection of inappropriate materials for this age group
4. shortage of well-trained teachers
5. reassignment of trained teachers to areas of need in the school

Better-trained educators can turn the tide, but it is more important than ever that effective programs are recognized and that low-quality programs be improved or closed. In the guidelines for appropriate practice, Bredekamp and Copple (1997) recognize certain characteristics and these are listed in Figure 6–2. Choice and play are major components of effective kindergarten programs.

FIGURE 6–2 Characteristics of an Appropriate Kindergarten

1. Children are engaged in activities that are meaningful or interactions with peers.
2. Children have access to a variety of materials and activities—i.e., block-building, pretend play, picture books, paints, and other art materials, Legos™, pegboards, and puzzles, on a rotating basis throughout the day.
3. Children can work individually, in small groups, and in whole-group activities.
4. Children complete artwork and other unique creations that are displayed on the walls.
5. Children engage in natural activities that are used as a framework for teaching basic concepts.
6. Children can participate in play in time increments of one or two hours.
7. Children have outdoor play every day that weather permits.
8. Children hear books read or stories throughout the day, not just at story time.
9. Children who have different ability levels experience success with challenging activities.
10. Children and their parents enjoy the school experience.

Source: Adapted from Bredekamp and Copple (1997).

Sensory play is an important component of kindergarten.

■ Role of Adults

> *The one thing that makes life worth living is to serve a cause, and the greatest cause that can be served is childhood education. From the first day of my kindergarten experience I dedicated my life to such service.*
> —Lucy Wheelock, 2000

The first kindergarten programs built their programs on the Renaissance-inspired beliefs of Rousseau and others who romanticized play. Kindergarteners, the name for kindergarten teachers, were committed to ensuring a play-based curriculum. Research conducted since the early days of kindergarten support the benefits of a play-based kindergarten program (Bredekamp & Copple, 1997). Unfortunately, play is not the main goal of some kindergarten programs today. Programs today reflect the current trends and needs of society. Many kindergarten teachers believe that they receive a new curriculum every time a major news story breaks. There is no denying the impact of national media coverage of school violence on the local school program. A visit to many kindergarten classrooms in rural areas will find classroom doors that are locked from the inside during the day. The children and teachers can move out freely but trespassers will find it difficult to get into the classroom. Kindergarten teachers who choose to conduct a high-quality program are faced with the many challenges in today's schools. Five-year-old children still need to play and they need a curriculum that promotes holistic growth and development.

Teachers who follow the kindergarten tradition still place play at the core of the curriculum. Programs that follow this model are described in this chapter. The implementation of any program is contingent on local and state guidelines as well as on the educational philosophy of the community, school administration, and teachers. It is the classroom teacher who must look at societal expectations, governmental regulations, and children's abilities—and then develop a kindergarten program. The kindergarten teacher of the past had to be an advocate for the existence of kindergarten. Stories abound of Lucy Sprague Mitchell's travels throughout the country as she advocated for kindergarten programs. She was even purported to wear her nightgown under her clothes so she could travel quickly and easily. In the same way (but perhaps, not to this extent) modern kindergarten teachers must be advocates for play and programs that are appropriate for young children.

■ Developing a Theoretical Foundation

Though the trend is changing, many kindergartens still have the option of creating their own curriculum. It is the philosophy of the teacher that determines how the program operates on a day-to-day basis. It is the teacher who decides which theoretical base is used to influence the classroom. Some theories and curriculum models that influence kindergarten curriculum have been discussed throughout the text. An overview of these theories is available in Figure 6–3.

The kindergarten classroom reflects the classroom teacher's interpretation of these theories. Their influence is filtered through the teacher's understanding of how children grow and develop. Each theory has implications for pedagogy. These theories were discussed in earlier chapters with the exception of Maslow's theory of basic needs. Because it is so basic to kindergarten, it is discussed in the following section and is examined in terms of its impact on play.

Maslow's Theory of Basic Needs

Abraham Maslow (1998) developed a hierarchy of needs basic to all humans. See Figure 6–4. His theory continues to provide the basis for many kindergarten programs. Children cannot grow and develop until their basic survival needs are met. Three levels of basic needs must be met before growth needs can be considered.

The first basic need for survival is physiological and psychological safety and survival. This includes food/hunger, water/thirst, and shelter/bodily comfort. These basic survival needs are shared by animals and humans. Children who do not have their physiological needs met cannot move to the next level and these deficits will impact play. This is evident in developing countries. Children who do not have sufficient food and

FIGURE 6–3 Theories That Influence Kindergarten Philosophy

Theoretical Perspective	Scholar	Implications for Impact on Play-based Curriculum Model
Maturation Perspective		
Theory of Basic Needs	Maslow (1998)	Hierarchy of needs
		Typical kindergarten program
Psychosocial Theory	Erikson (2000)	Bank Street program
		Social and emotional emphasis on the total child
Attachment Theory	Bowlby (1988)	Biological ties exist between adults and children and affect behaviors.
Attachment Theory in Infant-toddler Care	Honig (2000)	Infant and toddler care should consider attachment issues.
Constructivist Perspective		
Cognitive Development	Piaget (1962)	Constructivist-based model
		Fosnot (1996)
		DeVries & Zan (1994)
Sociocultural Theory	Vygtosky (1978)	Reggio Emilia approach
		Edwards, Gandini, and Foreman (1998)
Cognitive Adaptation	Bruner (1990)	
Multiple Intelligences	Gardner (1995)	
Other Approaches		
Ecological Systems Theory	Bronfenbrenner (1979)	Family-based relationships
		Context for play
Brain-based Research	Shornkoff & Phillips (2000)	Chemicals change in the brain according to different influences such as water and exercise.

water do not have the strength and energy required to run and jump. This is also a concern in the United States because so many children are hungry and homeless (Kids Count, 2004). In addition, some teachers restrict bathroom visits. Children who are not allowed to freely use the bathroom or who are concerned about safety issues in the classroom may not be able to play. These children will wander throughout the classroom, display onlooker behaviors, or experience play problems.

The second level of basic survival needs is the need for belonging, love, and acceptance. The need for emotional security is almost as critical for survival as food and shelter. Children who are experiencing attachment issues because a parent has left the classroom, or perhaps the home, will not fully engage in play. Eric Erikson (2000) spent a great deal of time discussing the effect of a death in the family on the play of one child in his classic book, *Childhood and Society.* The child's concern that the family

FIGURE 6–4 Maslow's Hierarchy

would forsake him because he contributed to his grandmother's death permeated his block play. Today's children are equally affected by real trauma and perceived threats. Many teachers have written about changes in play observed after the September 11, 2001, World Trade Center explosions. Teachers who are inconsistent or irritable create similar concerns for young children. When children experience emotional insecurity, play is affected.

The third level is a sense of competence, approval, and recognition from others that is unique to humans who need to develop good self-esteem. All children want to be a part of a group and seek the approval of others. This is a basic survival need that develops as children grow. By the age of kindergarten, children regularly engage in dramatic and sociodramatic play. Children who direct the play decide who will be chosen and who will be excluded. All children want to be a part of the group selected to ride the bus or sail on the boat. Those who are left out of the play often end up in tears if the teacher does not intervene. By the end of kindergarten, the need to belong can be observed in play areas when 7 or 8 children will crowd into a center as they engage in sociodramatic play while other play areas are void of visitors. Children who do not believe they belong to a group will cease active participation and will watch as others actively engage in social interactions during play. Teachers who use ridicule and sarcasm contribute to the demise of the child's self-esteem. When children lack self-esteem based on knowledge of authentic accomplishments, they cannot grow and develop.

The next levels of Maslow's hierarchy are not basic for survival but reflect the need to grow and develop into healthy individuals. The fourth level deals with the need for knowledge. When basic survival needs are met, humans need to grow by seeking knowledge. In the same way, when children have their basic survival needs met, their play grows. They may build a school bus and when an argument erupts about the nature of the bus, they will seek an authority (teacher or book) in their quest for more information.

The fifth level of need for growth is the need for aesthetics, beauty, truth, and justice. This is reflected in children's play. Children move through stages of block-building that move from stacking blocks to balancing blocks on matching structures. When someone does not play fairly, children will protest that, "That's not fair." These complex block structures and discussions of fairness do not occur in classrooms until basic survival needs are met and energy can be directed to growth needs.

The final level of growth is self-actualization towards which all humans are striving, but no one with the exception of Gandhi, Jesus, or Martin Luther King, Jr. has attained.

Children who live with adults who provide a stable, caring, environment are free to take risks. They know that acceptance is not tied to their performance. Even if their block structures fall, they are still accepted as a member of the group and can figure out why the blocks tumbled. A physiologically and psychologically safe environment provides an optimal environment for establishing self-esteem and autonomy. This serves as a basis for all curriculum implementation.

◼ An Aesthetics Approach to Kindergarten

An aesthetics-based approach integrates music, art, dance, and drama in meaningful activities. An integrated approach is

> one in which art concepts and practices are combined in relation to broad teaching and learning goals. Making such conceptual and process connections involves unifying the disciplines while at the same time recognizing that each of the fields of knowledge is different and distinct, with its own special content. (Wright, 2003, p. 262)

This is different from using a song to teach the days of the week. Rather, it integrates the structural, expressive, and process facets. Poetry and music are created as one. All areas are expressed through the arts. These are expressed as products and processes of children's integration through the following:

- ◆ music (listening, improvising, composing, learning musical literature)
- ◆ dancing (imitating, interpreting, choreographing)
- ◆ drama (role-playing, character-building, miming, story-building)
- ◆ visual arts (using art media and processes to make props, masks, costumes, structures, backdrops, using lighting and projected images) (Wright, 2003, p.265)

*Children develop
through play.*

Wright (2003) recommends using storytelling as a basis for curriculum development. Because the story has a basic structure that includes a plot, it can be extended to music and art as children create masks, costumes, and music. Storytelling is a basic component of humanity and is found in all cultures. The use of the story as a basic component of the curriculum has been explored by Vivian Paley (1981). Children draw their stories, tell their stories, and direct the production of their stories and enrich their lives as they learn. Paley's books provide a wealth of information in this area.

An aesthetics-based play program encourages the use of the arts during and after play. Music plays during block play. Stories arise and are recorded or drawn for revisiting. Opportunities to sculpt, create, and paint at the easel are a part of daily play. Dance occurs in the music center or sociodramatic center as children don costumes and move to the music. When play is over, children can draw their stories, tell their stories, and act out their stories. Integrating the arts through play enriches both.

■ Play as a Medium for Learning Content Area Curriculum

The push for academics has created a situation in which play time is being replaced by worksheets and flash cards. In Pennsylvania, the legislature has even mandated that each day a certain amount of time must be spent on specific subjects (Olfman, 2003). If play is how children naturally learn, and symbolic play is at its height at this time, then symbolic play can serve as a vehicle for learning. Knowledge of how children learn academic content through an aesthetics-based play program is featured in this section.

Language and Literacy

The variety of languages used in kindergarten classrooms has never been greater. Some children come to school as non-English speakers or with language difficulties. For these children, play provides a risk-free environment where they can play with words and acquire greater language skills. During play, children use words in a variety of ways. They make a variety of sounds as they pretend to fly, knock down blocks, or play dress-up. Literacy develops in the block center when they label their constructions, in the house area when they make up stories, in the art center when they complete visual representations of their world, in the puzzle center when they use visual clues to complete a picture or create a poster, and in the book center when they look at books. Music is a universal language: children who may not know many words to a song can still enjoy the melody.

Literacy is enriched through this approach. When children act out stories, they are developing their sense of story, which is a prerequisite reading skill. Children who use puppets to dramatize a story are learning about characterization and plot development in the story. They are also learning the concept of beginning, middle, and end of a story. Children who have opportunities to develop their play simultaneously develop their stories and literacy skills.

Language and literacy are supported through play when

- children draw, tell, and act out their play.
- play centers encourage language when children talk to each other.
- play centers encourage literacy when children draw pictures and tell or act out stories about their play.
- reading and writing materials are available in the home and block areas, costumes and materials are convenient for dress-up to encourage role-play. Props to encourage role-play (such as empty cartons and containers) are located in the house area. This also encourages children to become familiar with letters and words. Adding coupons that can be exchanged also enriches play. Prop boxes with different themes should be rotated on a regular basis.
- children's language is extended by using appropriate models and giving children opportunities to talk during play.
- children participate in author's chair, chart making, cooking, drama, documentation panels, fingerplays, guided reading, journals, poetry, reading aloud, shared writing, and storytelling.

Math

A play environment is a natural math environment. How many children can play at one center? What happens when too many people are in a center? How many plates are needed for dinner? Block center fosters the development of math concepts such as spatial relationships, symmetry, and patterning. Puzzles and toys stimulate critical thinking and problem-solving skills. Mathematic thinking involves the development of logical-mathematical knowledge. When children engage in sociodramatic play, they are creating linkages and relationships that stimulate mathematical thinking. Supporting mathematical thinking through play occurs when

◆ play centers encourage mathematical thinking.

◆ storage facilities promote storage of dishes, utensils, and other materials in order from smallest to largest.

◆ materials include dishes and utensils that encourage the development of a sense of sets.

◆ cleanup time teaches one-to-one correspondence. Shelves are labeled so children can match the block with the label when they are putting them away.

◆ different storage bins for manipulatives and other counting materials are available.

◆ pattern and bead cards as well as other materials are nearby.

◆ props in the sand and water center encourage measuring.

◆ clocks, calendars, and schedules are used throughout the day.

◆ money is used in different play centers.

Science

A play environment stimulates science learning. When children play with water in the water table, bubbles outdoors, sand and water, or paint, they are experimenting. Children are developing basic science concepts as they blow a cotton ball from one side of the table to the other side of the table. Children who carry the thermometer outdoors and back again are learning how to measure temperature. Children who pretend to camp in a refrigerator box that has been painted black and decorated with lights in the shape of different constellations begin to represent the differences between the night and day sky. These basic concepts serve as the foundation for science. When children communicate their science learning (play) through art, music, or stories, they develop a view of science as a part of their world and this may stimulate some

Children try on different roles during sociodramatic play.

children to pursue a career in science. The arts and play can be integrated to teach basic concepts by ensuring that

◆ all centers stimulate science and inquiry learning.

◆ investigative tools such as magnets, magnifying glasses, and a simple balance are available so children can use them on a daily basis.

◆ activities that cause discrepant events are available so children will be challenged to think about the experience and anticipated consequences versus reality.

◆ science is encouraged in the sand and water center by using different props.

◆ science is encouraged in the block center with pictures of unusual buildings.

◆ plants are an ongoing part of the classroom. All plants are required to be nontoxic.

◆ a variety of musical instruments are available for experimenting with musical sounds.

◆ paint and other methods of expression are available for both experimentation and communication.

Social Studies

Social studies abound in the kindergarten classroom. From the house area to the sociodramatic center to the prop box, the focus is on social studies, the study of the relationship between humans and ecology. Social studies includes economics, history, geography, and multiculturalism. Play in the kindergarten classroom lends itself to teaching social studies. Dress-up clothes allow children to try on different roles. Prop boxes with community-based themes provide additional knowledge about their world. Support for social studies occurs through play when

- ◆ play-based curriculum emphasizes a democratic classroom. When children choose their own center, they are a citizen in the classroom with all the rights and responsibilities therein.
- ◆ play-based curriculum explores different topics through themes, units, or projects.
- ◆ children listen to and share books and stories that relate to social studies.
- ◆ children participate in holiday experiences such as Martin Luther King, Jr. day.
- ◆ music is used to commemorate and celebrate holidays.
- ◆ art is available as a means of cultural expression.
- ◆ drama is a part of the program.

■ Designing Play Spaces

Environmental design is second only to adult interaction in terms of influencing play. Indoor environments will be discussed in this section and outdoor environments will be discussed in Chapter 9. The schools of Reggio Emilia refer to the environment as the third teacher in the classroom (Edwards, Gandini, & Forman, 1998). Centers provide a way to include multiple experiences for children. Some common centers include blocks, home, and special sociodramatic centers.

Blocks

Perhaps no other materials are more clearly identified with the kindergarten curriculum than wooden blocks. As mentioned earlier, plain wooden blocks have had a place in early education for over a hundred years. These materials still form the nucleus of the block center.

To encourage play, the block center should be located in an area away from a walkway; low shelves should be available for storing blocks; and shelves should be clearly labeled. A variety of props should be available to stimulate pretense and more complex play. Labeling block constructions, adding writing materials, and placing charts and pictures on the wall can also stimulate learning. Using Plexiglas tables and mirrors adds interesting dimensions to the block center.

Constructive play that occurs in this center is a combination of practice play and symbolic play. The child stacks, builds, and creates, and then pretends that the construction is whatever he wants it to be. During the process, the child may quickly revert to building again. This movement between building and pretense facilitates the child's mental agility.

The value of block play for understanding geometry and physics seems rather obvious. Recent research that supports this premise was conducted by Wolfgang and Wolfgang (2002). They found that children who engaged in high-level block play also achieved higher grades on math tests in high school. Other research supports block play as a valuable activity in the kindergarten classroom.

Home center

The home center stimulates dramatic play and sociodramatic play. **Dramatic play** occurs when the child uses symbolism to pretend. Sociodramatic play differs in that a group of children assign scripts and develop the play together. Kindergarten children are at the zenith of pretend play and can create a variety of play scripts in the home center. Prior to this age, play scripts may be less complex, less developed. **Play script** is a term used to describe the conversations and interactions that occur during sociodramatic play. Children will assign and assume specific roles. The child's knowledge of the world is fully evident during this type of play. To encourage dramatic play by all children, the house area should have materials that reflect the different cultures represented in class. Materials from different cultures can be added to the house area at different times throughout the year. Culture boxes also provide an avenue for ensuring that all children have familiar objects in the classroom.

The house area helps children understand the need for food, shelter, and clothing throughout the world. Equipment for preparing food should be available and may include a stove, refrigerator, and sink. In addition, a table for eating, cribs for lifelike dolls, and dishes should be included. Storage for all materials should be available and clearly labeled. Dress-up clothes should be available to encourage pretense and self-help skills such as snapping, buttoning, and tying. Hooks, hangers, and cabinets should be available for storing materials.

Special sociodramatic center

Establishing a special sociodramatic center allows the home area to remain a home area while the special center becomes a dentist's office. This allows the children to visit the dentist and return home and, in turn, encourages pretense among a group of children. This center should be changed every two or three weeks as the children's interest waxes and wans. Some topics that are especially interesting include a doctor's office, dentist's office, pet shop, flower shop, restaurant, grocery store, clothing store, hardware store, or veterinarian's office. Setting up centers that are familiar to children encourages pretense. A child can pretend to be a doctor who is taking a pulse or checking a heart beat with a stethoscope. In this way, the center becomes very cathartic. That is, it can help the child work through an emotion-filled situation.

Prop boxes

Prop boxes, as discussed in Chapter 5, are especially beneficial for this age group. A prop box can be used to store materials that are used to stimulate sociodramatic play. A sociodramatic center can be set up in one area of the room but prop boxes are mobile. A prop box can be taken outside or set up in the book center. Some themes that are especially interesting for prop boxes include a bank, camping, travel agency, and construction. Prop boxes for kindergarten contain more complex materials than those for preschool classrooms.

Art center

Art centers serve as the command center for play in an aesthetics-based program. The art center should provide children with an opportunity to create with paint or other sensory materials on a daily basis. The art center should be stocked with a good supply of paint, different sizes of paper, brushes, different kinds of markers, scissors that children can use, different types of play dough and other materials for creating. Stamps and stamp pads should be available for making posters. The creation of an art center that children can use with and without assistance provides a place that encourages language, literacy, writing, and creativity.

Sand and water

Montessori was the first to recognize the benefits of sensory materials for young children. A water table provides a place where children can experiment with sinking and floating boats of different sizes. The force and flow of water can be studied as water is poured and pumped. Sand provides a soothing material that can be manipulated, poured, and moved. Props can be added to encourage the development of roads and towns. Measuring materials can be used to extend play.

Toys and puzzles

This center can be used to stimulate symbolic play and simple games with rules. As the child manipulates a puzzle, a problem is solved. Knowledge of rules are established as the child plays games and lotto. Perceptual and fine motor skills are developed as the child engages in manipulating toys.

This center provides a unique setting for facilitating the development of specific skills through one-on-one play with the child.

Book center

The book center is especially important in the kindergarten class. Many teachers create a loft area that provides a quiet area for children—one that physically removes them from the rest of the room. The use of Plexiglas provides a safe translucent barrier. The book center should have a good selection of high-quality books that are changed on a regular basis. The book center can also include audiocassettes with books, flannel boards with story characters, and letters. Different books on a variety of levels should be available. Books should be available throughout the room.

Computer center

Most kindergarten centers have at least one computer. This center should be treated like any other center with children rotating in and out on a regular basis. Otherwise, one or two children will dominate the center. There are many games available though most kindergarten teachers use the computer for encouraging writing. Children can write or dictate their stories. Pictures can be added and the children can share their play experiences with their parents and other adults.

Putting it all together

How do you start and where do you start? What factors are important? For a look at how two early educators re-created a program in a traditional center, see Figure 6–5.

■ Program Models

Ideas for encouraging play have been presented in terms of individual areas and in terms of interest centers. Teachers decide how these are put together. Several programs are available that can be implemented according to the program's guidelines. These programs generally use a philosophical base that promotes one theoretical perspective. Some centers will choose one system as a framework for their curriculum, and this choice influences the type of play that occurs. Several models are included in this section. A traditional American kindergarten model based on an eclectic theoretical stance is provided as the first model. Constructivism is a commonly used approach in kindergarten. Other program models include Project Approach, High/Scope, Bank Street, Creative Curriculum, and Reggio Emilia. This list does not include all available programs but focuses on the ones that are most commonly known and that have been discussed in previous chapters.

FIGURE 6–5 In Their Own Words . . .

Enhancing Sociodramatic Play through Room Design

Pradnya Patet, P.H.D., Faculty Associate, Arizona State University
Britta Pells, Early Childhood Undergraduate Program, Arizona State University

Have you ever wondered why young children like to crawl into small spaces or turn a bunch of cushions into a trampoline? Whether or not we are consciously aware of it, we are all influenced by the organization of space and materials within it. We strongly support Kritchevsky, Prescott, and Walling (1969) who assert that "children behave in ways suggested by spatial contents and arrangement" (p. 152). In fact, we found that among other factors, a well-crafted physical environment can greatly influence children's level of play.

While the benefits of well-designed physical environments extend to all aspects of play and learning, our research focuses on pretend play. Typically, children express different levels of cognitive and social development through pretend play. These levels are related to the chronological and developmental age of the child. Cognitively, they move from functional play, to symbolic play and then role-play, leading into sociodramatic play. Socially, we see a movement from onlooker and solitary play to parallel and associative, and then finally to cooperative play. [See Chapter 1 for details.]

In our preliminary observations of the room that we redesigned, we found that the majority of the children's interactions were limited to parallel and associative play. Common behaviors observed were children imitating each other, playing alongside each other for short interrupted sessions, aggressive interactions with one another, and mundane use of play materials. Pretense was limited to children role-playing an adult, but rarely did they get together to plan elaborate themes. These children were between ages three and five, and although it is quite common to find such behaviors at this age, we were curious to see if any room arrangement might trigger a change, taking play to higher levels.

There were two key themes that kept resurfacing after the room makeover was completed. First, we found that designing an area to resemble a real context provided a holistic feel and, therefore, enhanced the children's level of pretense, leading them towards sociodramatic play. Second, small, well-defined, and uncluttered spaces proved to be havens in which children's conversations reached sophisticated levels and consequently enhanced their sociodramatic play. Despite our primary emphasis on physical environments, we find it imperative to conclude with a brief discussion of the complementary relationship between physical environments and active teacher involvement in facilitating sociodramatic play.

Designing an Area to Resemble a Real Context

Originally, the wall opposite the main entrance housed the kitchen in one corner and a loft in the other with dress-up props squeezed in between. The whole area served as a "closet of props" for the kitchen, clothes, and accessories as well as a water table and toys. Therefore, none of the materials were completely explored. In order to create a stage for sociodramatic play, we removed the dress-up area and relocated it to another part of the room and rotated the loft stairs towards the kitchen.

The loft, in its new position, looked more like a den, which now contained the library, and felt like an extension of the kitchen. The soft pillows and fabrics on the loft reduced the noise level of the previous active play in that area, allowing children to use the space for reading as well as climbing in an appropriate and safe manner. The loft now seemed to provide children with a space to watch the play below and find a suitable time to enter. One of the children looking into the kitchen from the loft said, "Hey! They're making pancakes down there. Let's go visit!" Contexts that resemble those in the real world provide children with a holistic context rather than an isolated assortment of props.

To increase the homelike feel in the kitchen area, we included an artificial window over the sink, flower arrangements, and a Peg-Board™ backing to hang up pots and pans, oven mitts, and dish towels. We also added a real telephone and hung it on the wall over the ironing board. Apart from the enhanced aesthetic appeal of the area, we saw marked changes in the social levels that children displayed in this newly created space. They began to carry on imaginary conversations, holding the phone between their ear and shoulder while ironing dolls' clothes. The original cook-and-eat parallel play turned into cooperative play as they sat around the table and enjoyed tea parties. The following year, with a new group of children, we found play at a much higher social level even in the first part of the semester.

We also found that this holistic context can be strengthened by coordinating props in the dramatic play center around a central theme. On the first day in the new dress-up area, we chose props to go with a theatrical show theme. We set out dresses and chairs and made tickets available. Some children instantly dressed up to put on a show while others played the role of the audience and bought tickets. They even made up their own rules for proper etiquette and entry into the "theatre"!

FIGURE 6–5 *(continued)*

In our scenario, children were participating at many different levels. At the symbolic play level, children were using their fists to represent a microphone. Others role-played a performer or spectator, and still others entered the sociodramatic level when they made up rules like "You can only be here if you have a necklace on." Although our initial reasoning in moving the dress-up clothes was to make the props more accessible through clear visibility and give children more space to explore the area, what we saw was the importance of the totality of physical context. Coordinating the props to suggest a basic open-ended theme facilitates children's pretense to emerge in a significantly coherent manner and therefore takes their play to higher levels. We could never have planned for such pretense to emerge. Theme centers that have shown to be effective in enhancing sociodramatic play (Woodard, 1984) and we believe that "design" can greatly influence their appeal.

Small Havens for Intimate and Sophisticated Conversation

The need for "small havens" emerged from our observations of the room prior to the makeover. On one occasion, the teacher put a tent in the back corner of the loft to reduce the usual rambunctious play that caused her concern about the children's safety. For the short period of time that the tent was set up, there was intimate, cooperative play inside it. Girls brought in dolls and played house while they cared for their "babies." It was interesting to watch this intimate interaction taking place amidst a frenzy of children running and yelling just outside the tent. The tent offered refuge in the midst of commotion. In our makeover, we had intended for the large dress-up area to house such "havens" with props like a tent, refrigerator boxes, or even large cartons that children could crawl into when the need arose. We saw something very interesting in an area that we had not considered a haven.

To curb rambunctious behaviors around the loft, we created appropriate and safe avenues for children to climb and crawl, recognizing their physical need to engage in such activity. One of the most interesting play episodes occurred in the tiny space that we had opened up under the loft. Two girls and one boy had taken a few dolls under the loft area to play quietly. Immediately the boy created a script for play, telling the girls their roles: "Take the baby and go to sleep. I am going to the store." The girl pretended to sleep but without the baby. The boy was astounded at her lack of action; he remarked, "What's wrong with you? Why can't you even take care of the baby while I'm gone?" The play progressed to a different theme as the children assigned roles to each other—the boy was the king and the two girls were his princesses. Willingly taking on the role of the "good" characters, they also created imaginary "bad" ones. The complicated theme of good characters rescuing an innocent baby from the bad characters emerged and was played out in much detail until it was time to clean up.

Our belief that "havens" are a much-needed part of room design for sociodramatic play was certainly strengthened. It is possible that sometimes children prefer to play by themselves and may not want adults to join them in the enactment of themes for fear of being laughed at or threatened. These havens provide an escape from not only other children in the classroom, but also from the teachers when children need some private time. The importance of physical spaces that enable this kind of pretense is important—keeping in mind, of course, the need for inconspicuous adult supervision at all times.

Encouraging as these responses to the physical environment were, children slowly started regressing back to parallel play after the first few weeks. Higher levels were reached when new themes and props were introduced and adults engaged children in play. Research suggests that adult involvement in children's play can greatly enhance and sustain play or disrupt it depending on *how* the adult gets involved (Johnson, Christie, & Yawkey, 1999). We found that when adults suggest new avenues of play through the arrangement and design, it becomes easier for them to take on the supportive role of a play partner and follow the children's lead to facilitate higher levels of play. The level of the children's involvement when a purpose is introduced into the play is amazing. The children no longer wander from one area to the other, picking up a toy here and then a toy there and socializing at random. Their play becomes meaningful when an open-ended, cohesive context is suggested.

We were able to see how carefully designed physical environments can provide this context but certainly not replace active teacher involvement. Conversely, active teacher involvement can be accentuated by well-crafted physical environments that set the stage for meaningful conversations with children, thus facilitating more complex levels of play and minimizing discipline problems. We strongly agree with educators in the pre-primary schools of Reggio Emilia, Italy, who consider environment as the third educator in conjunction with the two classroom teachers. (Gandini, 1998). The sense of "inner" equilibrium that comes from being in comfortable spaces greatly increases learning opportunities. The importance of such environments for children can only be summed up in Ceppi and Zini's work which "demonstrates the belief that children have a right to be educated in thoughtfully designed spaces" (Tarr, 2001).

(continued)

FIGURE 6–5 *(continued)*

References

Gandini, L. (1998). *Educational and caring spaces.* In C. Edwards, L. Gandini, & G. Forman (Eds.), *The hundred languages of children: The Reggio Emilia approach–advanced reflections* (pp. 161–178). (2nd ed.). Greenwich, CT: Ablex.

Johnson, J. E., Christie, J. F., and Yawkey, T. D. (1999). *Play and early childhood development.* (2nd ed.). New York: Addison Wesley Longman.

Kritchevsky, S., Prescott, E., and Walling, L. (1999). *Planning environments for young children: Physical space.* In K. M. Paciorek & J. H. Munro (Eds.), *Sources: Notable selections in early childhood* (pp. 152–157). (2nd ed.). Guilford, CT: Dushkin/McGraw Hill.

Tarr, P. (2001, May). *What art educators can learn from Reggio Emilia.* In *Art Education.* Retrieved August 2002 from http://www.designshare.com/Research/Tarr/Aesthetic_codes_3.htm.

Woodard, C. (1984). *Guidelines for facilitating sociodramatic play. Childhood Education, 60,* 172–177.

Acknowledgement: We would like to thank the staff of the College of Education Preschool, Arizona State University for their active and collaborative participation in this project.

Used with permission of the authors, Pradyna Patet and Britta Pells.

Typical Kindergarten Program

A traditional model that has developed in America over the years includes routines and activities that are familiar to most who have attended kindergarten or who have had children in kindergarten in the past few years. This approach was designed over the years to develop "the whole child" and uses a holistic view of the child that considers cognitive, social, language, and physical development.

The day usually begins with a morning meeting that includes some form of group sharing (show and tell) experience. Songs, fingerplays, and nursery rhymes are usually included in the group meeting. This is followed by play that occurs both indoors and outdoors. Afterwards lunch is served midday, children listen to a story, and then take a nap. When they get up from naptime, they play, sing songs, and leave. There are different curriculum approaches that emphasize various aspects of the program, but all follow some sort of variation of this approach.

A routine helps children because young children view the routine as the rule. When thinking about the day, some activities can be viewed as routine activities that occur every day. Other activities may be nonroutine activities that require a special plan. Based on Maslow's theory, routines help children establish a sense of safety and security. One caveat: this is not to suggest that a rigid time line should be imposed in kindergarten. *In kindergarten, flexibility is the key.* A typical kindergarten schedule would be:

1. morning greeting
2. morning meeting
3. center play
4. outdoor play

Movement is a critical component of morning meetings.

5. lunch
6. story time
7. rest
8. center play
9. recess
10. afternoon circle
11. afternoon farewell

These are explained in more detail in the following section.

Morning greeting

Children should be able to enter the classroom on an individual basis as they arrive at school. When children wait in a hallway, cafeteria, or auditorium, they are physically uncomfortable, and the result is crowd control when the children walk to their room. Children should be able to enter the room individually, greet the teacher and other children, put materials in their own cubby labeled with their name, put away outer garments or other materials, and then select a math game, book, manipulative, or other activity. Providing children with a regular schedule facilitates the child's physiological and psychological safety and contributes to the development of autonomy and self-concept. Autonomy is the aim of education (Kami & Houseman, 1999). **Autonomy** is a term used to describe behavior that is independent and self-reliant.

It is important that children are allowed to choose from several activities in the morning. Transitions in the morning and afternoon are the most problematic. Providing children with choices minimizes possible behavior issues and enhances the child's developing self-esteem.

Morning meeting

Kindergartens have long been identified by circles and sharing time. The morning meeting was initially designed to provide a time for children to come together as a group, share their news, show and tell, or discuss the events for the day. Over the years, it has changed with some morning circles lasting for two hours—much longer than most children can sit still! A morning meeting is more important than ever. Children need to come together for a short meeting. They need to have an opportunity to share. Show and tell is effective and will not digress into "bring and brag" if the teacher sends a letter to parents stating the guidelines for show and tell. (First guideline, expensive toys should not come to school.) Children do not, however, need to sit for two hours. Limit the meeting to 20 minutes or less. Let the children choose their centers by putting their name by the center. This can be done as they come into the room or as they leave the circle. Move children out of the circle using a transition activities. It is never safe to just let a group of children run to their centers because they will soon learn that the fastest runner gets his favorite center.

Transition activities

Transition activities are activities that provide a mechanism to move groups of children from one place to another or from one activity to another. Transitions are advantageous because they provide cues about the next upcoming activity. Children know what to expect and have a plan for performing this activity. Some transition activities include calling all children who are wearing certain colors to line up, giving children the upper case or lower case letter and ask for the matching letters to line up.

Morning centers

Centers should have signs with words and picture symbols hanging in the room so the children can see their centers. They should also have a system for selecting centers. Any system will work as long it is systematic and fair. When children have an opportunity to move to centers of their choice, they are more engaged and can develop more sophisticated and complex play.

Centers that are traditionally found in a kindergarten class include block, house, art, sand, water, book, wood, toy and puzzle, computer, and a sociodramatic center that changes through the use of prop boxes. These were discussed earlier in the chapter. Children should be allowed to stay in the center for an hour. It is never appropriate to ring the bell and require children to move to another center. When children are forced to move frequently, they do not develop concentration skills during play. They learn *not* to concentrate. At the same time, children should be allowed to move from center to center. Some routines may be needed for cleanup. Some teachers insist that they return to help clean up at the end of the center time. During center time, the teacher can float throughout the room. Going from one center to another allows the teacher to monitor and participate in the play. This is also a time that an additional teacher or adult can work with small groups. Small-group activities can include cooking, art, painting, and even assessment activities. Some classrooms will have snacks set up for children who are hungry during playtime. Children should not be forced to participate in activities unless they choose. Again, every child does not have to participate in every activity every day. It is more important that children are allowed to choose activities. Ten minutes before play is over, move throughout the room and begin to give children a signal that play will soon be ending. Give a five-minute warning also. When it is time for cleanup, put on some classical music or other music that is pleasant. Refrain from using a loud sound to signal cleanup as some children may be sensitive to abrasive sounds.

Transition

When children clean up their centers, they can use the bathroom, wash their hands, and return to the morning meeting area. This is a good opportunity to sing songs and do fingerplays.

Morning recess

Outdoor play has always been a traditional part of the kindergarten schedule. Children benefit from outdoor play with their friends. They develop physical and social skills when they engage in active play. They also develop cognitively and morally when they participate in games. These are desirable outcomes for children. The teacher should monitor the play and move throughout the playground. It is never appropriate to talk to other adults, supervisors, or teachers while the children are playing. This is a time when accidents can happen quickly. Adults must be vigilant when the children are on the playground. Some centers can be set up on the playground. These are discussed in more detail in Chapter 9. Generally, recess should last for at least 15 minutes up to an hour. *Safety note: Prior to going outside, children should be checked to ensure they have appropriate attire for cold weather and are covered with sunscreen if they are in a warm climate.*

Transition

Always use a signal to move children indoors. Moving around the playground like a train provides a fun way for children to join the line and prevents the power struggle that ensues when children don't join a line. When children reenter the room, they can use the bathroom, wash their hands, and prepare for lunch. They can draw pictures or write in their journals while waiting for everyone to use the bathroom. Use a transition activity to move the children to the dining facilities.

Lunch

Teachers should eat with children. This allows them to monitor and model good eating habits. Some teachers of kindergarten classes in public schools leave the children during lunch for a duty-free lunch hour. Frequently, the issues that they face when they return negate the benefit of being away from the class. Some classes are allowed to eat in the room. When this occurs, the teacher can play music while the children dine, brush their teeth, and then move to journaling, books, or other activities as they finish.

Story time

This is a good time for reading books aloud. This time should last between 15 and 40 minutes, depending on the interest of the children. After the story, children can get their cots or towels and transition to rest time.

Rest time or naptime

Rest time or naptime is an important part of the kindergarten day. Children should not be required to maintain a day that is equal to that of an adult. Rest time provides a time for relaxation. Turn down the lights, play soft music, and allow children to rest with a stuffed animal or doll that they bring from home. This is a good time to play classical music. Some children prefer to look at books during this time. Again, children can have choices, but rest should be encouraged for at least 40 minutes. Gently begin to wake up children who are asleep five minutes before the lights go on.

Give children the opportunity to go to the bathroom and get a drink of water.

Afternoon center time/recess

Depending on the length of the day, children will be able to have afternoon centers or afternoon recess or both. Guidelines similar to those used in the morning should be followed.

Daily schedules ensure daily play.

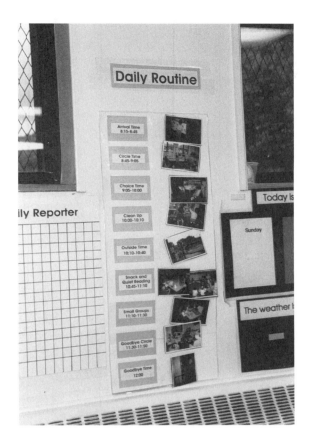

Afternoon meeting

The afternoon meeting provides a time for stories, songs, drama, and farewells. Again, the end-of-day meeting should not last longer than 20 minutes. Just as each child is greeted individually in the morning, the teacher should bid each child farewell in the afternoon. This also allows the teacher time to check the child's transportation home. The children should check their cubbies as they leave. The children should be able to stay in their classroom or play on the playground until they leave for the day. It is never appropriate to place young children in a cafeteria or auditorium to wait for buses unless there are activities available.

Overview

This is an overview of a traditional kindergarten class for one day. It is generally adjusted to reflect the philosophy and interests of the teacher, the guidelines of the state, and local school rules. It is the teacher who translates these so that the child experiences an appropriate play-based program in kindergarten. Some teachers are influenced by constructivism which was discussed earlier in Chapter 4 and is discussed in the section on constructivism in this chapter.

Half-day Program

A less-than-full-day program could include:

1. morning greeting
2. morning meeting
3. center play
4. outdoor play
5. lunch
6. story and circle
7. dismissal

The same activities that are included in the full-day program are included in the morning program. It is difficult to avoid the wish to include more in a half-day program, but it is advisable to ensure *quality* experiences rather than quantity. Suggestions for preparing for the first day of either whole-day or half-day kindergarten are available in Figure 6–6.

Constructivism

Constructivism is based on the notion that children construct knowledge as they interact with their world. Constructivism has three different interpretations: cognitive, social, and symbolic constructivism. **Cognitive constructivism**, based on the work of Jean Piaget, emphasizes the child's internal construction of knowledge. **Social constructivism**, influenced by the writings of Lev Vygotsky, emphasizes the child's construction of knowledge through interaction with more knowledgeable others. **Symbolic constructivism**, informed by the work of Jerome Bruner, focuses on the child's construction of knowledge through symbolic systems such as narratives.

Early childhood education has been most influenced by cognitive constructivism based on the work of Piaget. A book that reflects this philosophy is *Moral Classrooms, Moral Children: Creating a Constructivist Atmosphere in Early Education* by Rheta DeVries and Betty Zan (1994). This book describes how teachers can establish a classroom that fosters the child's intellectual, social, moral, emotional, and personality development. A constructivist model differs little from the traditional kindergarten model

FIGURE 6–6   Tips for Encouraging Play on the First Day of School

1. Plan for the experienced as well as for the novice players. Some children have attended preschool and are ready for this experience. Others have never stayed away from home for an entire day. Each child in the class brings a cadre of experiences to the class.

2. Open a limited number of centers. Too many materials can overstimulate and confuse the children. Some centers that are inviting on the first day include blocks, house, manipulatives and puzzles, and art (play dough). Using a limited number of materials will allow you to monitor the interactions and float throughout the room.

3. Label each center in the room so the children know where to go. Hang signs above each center. Make sure the signs are large enough to be seen (14" × 14") and can be suspended by fishing twine. Using white cardboard with pictures of the center creates a visually appealing effect. In some schools, fire codes prohibit hanging items from the ceiling. If this is the case, put the signs on the wall near the center.

4. Take the children on a tour of the centers. Let them look at the center and examine the materials, and help them develop a list of classroom rules. Help them consider the value of putting materials away when center time is over. Help them understand that this room is their home during the day and that neither teachers or custodians can pick up toys for so many children. Make sure shelves are clearly labeled so children can easily replace materials when they finish.

5. Develop a system for moving children to the centers. If you don't have a transition plan, the children can fall over one another in their rush to get to their favorite center and disputes can easily erupt over who was at the center first. Establishing routines the first day can eliminate problems throughout the rest of the year. Some teachers put smaller versions of the center signs on a chart and allow children to select their center. Having a deck of cards with each child's name and picture on it allows children to see a fair system for selecting centers as they establish a democratic classroom. This system allows children to select the first center on a rotating basis.

6. Ensure that children have at least an hour for play. Children cannot engage in deep play unless they have uninterrupted time for play. During the first day, the teacher will be able to note who plays well and who watches. Children who are observing but not playing may need additional assistance or time.

7. At the end of the play time, go around the room and give the children a ten-minute warning that it is time to end their play. Then give them a five-minute warning. Finally, give a signal by dimming the lights or ringing a chime that play time is over for the day. Remind them that they can return tomorrow for more play.

described in the preceding section. It depends on how the individual teacher interprets and implements the program. If those having a behaviorist view of learning use the schedule described in the traditional kindergarten, they might be very directive in how they implemented the centers and activities. In contrast, someone influenced by a constructivist pedagogy would focus more on giving the children opportunities to make choices about their centers and activities. Classrooms that use a constructivist philosophy focus on sociomoral and cognitive issues and the establishment of mutual respect and cooperation between the teacher and child. Many teachers who use a constructivist approach also use the project approach which is described in the following section.

Project approach

The project approach is grounded on a constructivist approach and the belief that children construct knowledge through interactions with the world. The project approach uses the project as the curriculum organizer.

Vygotsky's sociocultural theory serves as a basis for this approach. The focus is on learning through social interactions with more capable peers. The child moves from a point of knowing with the assistance of others to appropriating the information as his own. During the project, inquiry will develop as well as critical thinking skills and creativity. The project approach provides a venue for facilitating social development, cognitive development, and parent involvement.

The project is divided into three parts, Phase I, Phase II, and Phase III, (Helm & Katz, 2001). The project begins with a provocation which stems from the adult or child. This can take on many forms. One project began when an adult left an envelope on a desk filled with clues. The children tried to solve the mystery by following the clues which led them on an exploration of the building. Responsive teachers who listen to children can generally seize the moment when the provocation occurs. For example, in one kindergarten class, the children were looking at a book about bread that someone brought for show and tell. The children were discussing the different kinds of bread that they eat and were amazed at the different types in their classroom. The teacher used this as a provocation and started a KWL (Know-Want to Know-Learn) chart about bread. A KWL chart provides a good instrument for organizing the project as children can see what they knew, what they want to know, and then, what they learned. See Figure 6–7 for a sample chart. The most important aspect of using the project approach with young children is keeping it appropriate.

After discussing what they wanted to know about bread, they listed their questions. This served as the impetus for the study. The children worked in three groups. One group worked on the first question, the second group considered the second question, and the third group attempted to answer the last question. The first group talked to everyone to find out how many different kinds of bread people in class ate. After they made a list, they decided to make a loaf of bread. The class met and decided on the type of bread. The team that was working on the question "How do you make bread?" was in charge of the cooking project. A field trip to a local bakery and grocery store supplied the materials. A bread center was established where children could create, bake, sell, and sample bread. The children were able to engage in symbolic play as they engaged in role-play and pretend.

After the children began to tire of the center, they reviewed their chart. What did they learn about the bread? What did they learn about the cooking process? What were additional outcomes of this experience? Children can communicate their acquired knowledge through music, art, drama, and stories. Some teachers document the experience through pictures or video. Children can use digital photography, art, music, or stories to communicate their knowledge. For additional reading, see Katz and Chard (2000), *Engaging Children's Minds: The Project Approach,* or *Young Investigators: The*

FIGURE 6–7 KWL Chart

Phase I	Phase II	Phase III
What do we KNOW about this topic?	What do we WANT to know?	What did we LEARN?

Project Approach in the Early Years by Helm and Katz (2001), and *The Power of Projects: Meeting Contemporary Challenges in Early Childhood Classrooms—Strategies and Solutions* by Judy Helm and Sallee Beneke (2003).

High/Scope

High/Scope was originally developed as a preschool program but has been adapted for kindergarten in many systems. The High/Scope program was designed as a cognitively based program. It places more emphasis on cognitive development than on sociomoral development. The High/Scope program differs from the traditional program in that it uses a plan-do-review approach. This process was explained in Chapter 5. Research supports the legitimacy of this approach (Barnett, 1995). Children in the High/Scope program made significant gains over children in programs using a more academic approach. After over two decades, the differences are still evident. For these reasons many kindergartens structure their programs around this approach.

Developmental-interaction

As discussed earlier, the name *developmental-interaction* is generally used to refer to a model that has been used by Bank Street since the 1920s (Cuffaro, Nager, & Shaprio, 2000). Kindergartens that use this approach focus on the democratic views put forth in this program. This program more than any other uses the work of John Dewey to influence the classroom climate. Respect for the child as a person and citizen is evident in all aspects of the program. The focus is on learning through daily experiences with the indoor and outdoor environment through experiential activities. The indoor environment consists of art; sensory experiences; music, movement, and gross motor experiences; blocks; and outings. Outings or field trips are a regular feature of the curriculum and occur in groups of two or three. Though the goals are somewhat similar to a constructivist approach, the influence of Erikson and Dewey are prevalent.

The underlying philosophy of Bank Street is developmental-interactionist that emphasizes that children develop through social interactions with the world and others. This approach is markedly different from a constructivist approach because the developmental interaction curriculum is more directive and focuses on literacy.

Kindergarten teachers influenced by the directive interaction approach assist the child in establishing social and emotional health. Home visits and the use of attachment objects to ease the home to school transition are techniques that have been used in programs directly or indirectly influenced by Bank Street. The source of the Bank Street curriculum is social studies and this fits well with educational goals for kindergarten. Social studies focuses on the "here-and-now" curriculum for kindergarten, which places the emphasis on the child. For example, units can be developed on the topics "Me," "My Family," or "My Neighborhood." Units provide a venue for teaching social studies and revolve around experiences in the classroom and community. Books created by children and teachers in the Bank Street program reflect authentic experiences used in activities. An example can be found on their Web site.

Creative Curriculum

High/Scope and Bank Street have models that conduct and disseminate research. Creative Curriculum consists of professional development and books that outline how to implement the system. The approach is based on an eclectic approach that combines Piaget, Maslow, Erikson, and Dewey. Information designed for preschool and kindergarten is available in Chapter 5.

Reggio Emilia

Reggio Emilia is an approach named after a town in northern Italy where it originated and is based on the principles of a social constructivism. The philosophy is based on the work of Dewey and Vygotsky as interpreted by Loris Malaguzzi (New, 2003). At first glance, the program may look like a traditional kindergarten schedule. Children play in centers, outdoors, eat, rest, and have group meetings. The program is different, however, because the children are not following a routine; they are following their interests and research. In addition, interactions between the adults and children are different from those found in most kindergarten classrooms. Children in the Reggio Emilia program receive more scaffolding when completing projects than is typically observed in most kindergarten classrooms. For example, during center time, the patio door may be open to provide indoor and outdoor play together. If a child is painting a picture

Effective documentation captures the child's view of the world.

of a flower, the child will be encouraged to look closely at the flower to capture the reality of the flower and will be encouraged to do it over until it reflects the child's best effort. This is very different from the American kindergarten. Children in the Reggio Emilia program work in groups. Not every child participates in every activity. The focus is on the completion of the final project by the group.

Assessment in the Reggio Emilia–influenced schools is very different and has the potential to impact kindergarten throughout the world. Assessment includes **portfolios** and **documentation panels**. Each child has a portfolio that moves with the child through the program. Portfolios contain samples of the child's best works. Documentation panels can be based on the work of one child or a group. The documentation panel illustrates how the child or group of children developed a project. There are many ways to illustrate how they are constructing knowledge. The schools of Reggio Emilia subscribe to a philosophy that every child has a hundred languages and a hundred ways of knowing. Their assessment process reflects a hundred ways of assessing and documenting their knowledge. This reflects a social constructivist approach to assessment and is vastly different from traditional kindergarten that focuses on developmental norms.

For additional information, see *Authentic Childhood: Exploring Reggio Emilia in the Classrooms* (Fraser & Gestwicki, 2000), *Teaching and Learning: Collaborative Exploration of the Reggio Emilia Approach* (Fu, Stremmel, & Hill, 2002), or *Early Learning Environments That Work* (Isbell & Exelby, 2001). Of course, the classic, *The Hundred Languages of Children: The Reggio Emilia*

Approach—Advanced Reflections (Edwards, Gandini, & Foreman, 1998) is always recommended as a starting point.

■ Toys, Puzzles, and Materials

Toys and materials add depth and breadth to the kindergarten classroom. Toys should provide children with the opportunity to turn knobs, manipulate pieces, and have fun while developing their fine motor, perceptual, and critical thinking skills. Good puzzles stimulate children's problem-solving abilities as they learn the mathematical concept of part to whole. The classroom should have a variety of toys and materials that can be replaced on hooks, labeled shelves, or containers. It is especially important at this age to have a variety that meets the needs of those who are still in sensorimotor play stage, those who are engaged in dramatic or sociodramatic play, and those who are ready for games with rules. Some children will be ready for Cherry-O™ or Candy Land™ while others will still need to play with tactile toys. The key is variety.

■ Assessment

Unfortunately, the misuse and abuse of evaluation has had more effect on the play of young children than any other factor in the past decade. Assessment in kindergarten includes a variety of formative and summative instruments. Generally a **screening instrument** is used at the beginning of kindergarten. A screening instrument is designed to reveal the need for additional evaluation, nothing more. Many young parents will buy materials for their young children based on their belief that these materials will prepare the child for the "kindergarten test"! These screening instruments were never intended to be used as entry tests but, sadly, many schools will set a certain score as the entrance score for kindergarten admission. Given that most screening tests are criterion-based tests that are based on the mastery of the items on the test, this is a complete misuse of the instrument. This is most unfortunate because the children who need kindergarten the most are blocked from entrance. Few who originally recommended the use of a quick screening instrument could have imagined this use and abuse of the test scores. Other screening instruments include the Gesell, the Brigance, the LAPP, the McCarthy, and the Peabody language screen. All should be used appropriately.

Formative Assessment

As discussed in Chapter 5, **formative assessment** refers to assessment that occurs throughout the year and includes instruments that provide feedback that can be used to guide curriculum. Checklists, rating scales, and anecdotal records can be used for formative assessment purposes and can also be used to assess play. Play assessment has two dimensions. The child's play level can be assessed at regular intervals. What is the child's level of block play? Does the child engage in symbolic play? Does this child engage in sociodramatic play with other children? Asking these questions provides a profile of the child's play level.

Another dimension of play assessment involves the use of play to access other areas. The child's ability to use language, count, recognize letters, hop, skip, and write his name are skills that can be assessed through play. Block play provides a proper setting for understanding the child's sense of symmetry, patterning, and spatial relationships. A checklist can be used for sampling the child's play level at different points throughout the year. This provides a picture of the child's ongoing growth and development. The child's dictated stories can be used to gain a sense of the child's literacy development. These strategies are useful in developing a holistic profile of the child. When used in this way, this is called authentic assessment. **Authentic assessment** is a term used to describe ongoing assessment that provides an overall picture of the child's growth and development.

Digital technology is beginning to impact assessment. Portfolios are beginning to replace report cards in many kindergarten classrooms. Teachers can capture activities in the class on a daily and weekly basis and add these to the portfolio. This technique emanates from the art community, but it has been used successfully in the schools of Reggio Emilia and many high-quality programs throughout the world. Play provides a good avenue for capturing the child's developing skills. A series of pictures created while the child engages in water play may reveal the child's discovery of the physical properties of water in a way that would never be evident using other tools. This captures the essence of the child's thinking and reflects Vygotsky's view of assessment. *Assessment will change as assessment tools and techniques become more sophisticated and play may arise as the perfect platform for capturing a profile of the child's thinking. Understanding how the child is developing an understanding of the world is more valuable than comparing the child to others.*

This is not intended to denigrate screening instruments. When used appropriately, screening tests provide a great deal of information in a short period of time. The key is the appropriate use of the instruments.

Summative assessment refers to assessment that is used to provide information about how much the child has learned over a period of time. It is summative in nature and provides a summary of what the child has gained. Many schools administer group standardized tests at the end of kindergarten. This is not appropriate for this age group. Their attention span and perceptual skills are not well developed at this age. If a standardized test is administered, it should be given on an individual basis. Five-year-olds are not physically, cognitively, or socially ready to take group standardized tests (Bredekamp & Copple, 1997).

PlayScape Reflections

Jamal and his family may have a difficult time adjusting to daily school attendance at first. Using an ecological systems approach will help the teacher understand Jamal within the context of his home and culture. She may want to ensure that some of the play reflects some of the experiences at home. She may even want to take a picture of his play so he can show his grandmother what he is doing at school.

The teacher who understands attachment theory will encourage Jamal to bring a toy or stuffed animal from home. Pictures of Jamal's family will also serve as a reminder that he is loved by his family. He can play in a center, visit the family board, and then return to his play.

Providing a curriculum rich in play opportunities will allow Jamal to develop a foundation for learning complex concepts. Sociodramatic play will allow Jamal to develop his ability to engage in interactive social play using symbolic words and gestures. If he is playing the role of the baby, he will be expected to act out that role as both he and his peers recognize it. Misunderstandings are also opportunities for learning. His skills as a risk taker will develop during play and allow him to take chances when he encounters new material in school. His ability to engage in abstraction will serve him well as he looks at a symbol and connects it to a sound and meaning. Though Vygotsky (1978) first warned of the possible abuses inherent if the public viewed play as a way to develop instructional skills, it may be important for Jamal's family to understand this relationship so they see play as a valuable part of Jamal's life.

The curriculum used in the kindergarten classroom will also affect Jamal's entry into formal education. If the teacher uses a constructivism-influenced curriculum, Jamal will make choices that will facilitate the development of autonomy and his sense of self. If Jamal is in a class that communicates that his play is unacceptable, he may withdraw and wish for the safer days at home. For Jamal, his play experiences in the kindergarten classroom are pivotal for success in school.

■ Summary

Kindergarten programs have existed for over one hundred years and continue to be an important part of the child's public school education. Teachers assume responsibility for ensuring that children meet state and local guidelines through programs that reflect the child's age, stage, culture, and interest. Play centers in most kindergarten classrooms include blocks, house, art, book, sand and water, computer, sociodramatic, and toys and puzzles. Knowledge of the content material in the areas of literacy, math, science, and social studies is acquired through play. Program models that can be used to guide kindergarten programs include High/Scope, Bank Street, Creative Curriculum, and Reggio Emilia. Toys and ancillary materials are important in the kindergarten classroom. Assessment in kindergarten involves both formative and summative assessment. Children entering kindergarten go through a battery of tests prior to entry. Screening assessments include the Brigance, LAPP, McCarthy, and Peabody. Child observations occur every day and consist of anecdotal notes, checklists, and rating scales. Documentation using current technology has changed how some teachers are communicating with parents, documenting play and learning. Summative assessment occurs at the end of the year when some kindergarten children take a test for first grade.

■ Key Terms

Authentic assessment
Autonomy
Cognitive constructivism
Constructivism
Documentation panels

Dramatic play
Formative assessment
Play script
Portfolios
Screening instruments

Social constructivism
Summative assessment
Symbolic constructivism
Transition

■ Helpful Web Sites and Technology Resources

◆ **American Library Association**
   http://www.ala.org   The oldest and largest library association in the world supports this site. It is designed to promote the highest-quality library and information services and public access to information. Both teachers and children will find this site helpful.

◆ **Bank Street College of Education**
   http://www.bnk.st.edu   The Bank Street College of Education at Columbia University in New York has a Web site that offers research-based information on activities and experiences. They also feature a book corner with reviews of current publications, recommendations, and activities designed to extend the reading experience.

- ◆ **Creative Curriculum**
  http://www.teachingstrategies.com/   Creative Curriculum hosts this Web site and provides samples of their materials.

- ◆ **National Museum of Play**
  http://www.strongmuseum.org   Located at the Strong Museum this museum houses an extensive collection of toys. The Web site provides a collection of activities and links to the Smithsonian.

- ◆ **Smithsonian Museum NASM**
  http://www.nasm.si.edu/   The Smithsonian sponsors this Web site and provides an array of educational materials.

- ◆ **School Improvement Research Series**
  http://www.nwrel.org   The School Improvement Research Series is produced by the School Improvement Program of the Northwest Regional Educational Laboratory under a contract with the Office of Educational Research and Improvement U.S. Department of Education.

■ Activities

1. InClass Lab

A. In small groups, discuss the current influences that are impacting play in kindergarten classes in your area. Depict these graphically in terms of the microsystem, macrosystem, exosystem, mesosystem, and chronosystem discussed in Chapter 1. Display your chart in the classroom.

B. Discuss the impact of early entry into kindergarten on play. Contrast the impact of delayed entry into kindergarten. How can teachers create play opportunities that ensure challenging experiences for both children?

2. Research and Inquiry

A. Visit a local kindergarten classroom. Watch the children during play time. What activities are the children selecting? What is the most popular center? What is the least popular center? What factors are contributing to the different levels of interest in the two centers.

B. Interview two kindergarten teachers. Ask them to explain their philosophy of teaching. How are they alike? How are they different?

FIGURE 6–8   Template for Letter to Parents

Dear Parents,

Young children learn through play. The list below contains some activities that you can use to encourage play at home. Some of these can be purchased and others can be made.

Games that can be purchased

Cherry-O   Candyland   Uno

Games that can be made

Checkers   Bingo   Number cards for simple card games

A recipe for simple play dough is included on the back of this sheet.

Please contact me if you have questions.

Your Child's Teacher

3. **Service Learning**

   A. Volunteer in a kindergarten classroom for two hours. Are some children more engaged than others in play? Can you facilitate their interaction with others? Were you successful? Why or why not?

   B. Create a toy that might be used in a local kindergarten classroom. What factors affected the design. What safety features were considered?

4. **Family Connections**

   A. Create a letter for parents that discusses home play activities. The one included in Figure 6–8 can be used as a template.

5. **Play Advocacy**

   A. What is the state and local policy for kindergarten attendance? Do children spend a whole day or half day in kindergarten? Are groups advocating for a whole day kindergarten? Why or why not?

   B. Do the local schools require tests at the beginning and end of kindergarten? If so, how does this impact curriculum and play?

■ References

Annie E. Casey Foundation (2004). *Kids count data book: State profiles of child well-being.* Baltimore, MD: author.

Barnett, W. S. (1995). Long-term effects of early childhood programs on cognitive and school outcomes. *The Future of Children, 5* (3), 25–50.

Bowlby, J. (1988). *A secure base: Parent-child attachment and healthy human development*. New York: Basic Books.

Bredekamp, S., & Copple, C. (Eds.) (1997). *Developmentally appropriate practice in early childhood programs*. (Rev. ed.). Washington, DC: NAEYC.

Bronfenbrenner, U. (1979). *Ecology of human development: Experiments by nature and design*. Cambridge: Harvard University Press.

Brostarman, N. (1997). *Inventing kindergarten*. New York: Harry N. Abrams.

Bruner, J. S. (1990). *Acts of meaning*. Cambridge, MA: Harvard University Press.

Cuffaro, H. K., Nager, N., & Shaprio, E. (2000). The developmental-interaction approach at Bank Street College of Education. In J. P. Roopnarine and J. Johnson (Eds.), *Approaches to early childhood education* (pp 263–276). (3rd ed.). Upper Saddle River, NJ: Merrill/Prentice Hall.

DeVries, R., & Zan, B. (1994). *Moral classrooms, moral children: Creating a constructivist atmosphere in early education*. New York: Teachers College Press.

Du Charme, C. C. (2000). Lucy Wheelock: Her life and work, *Childhood Education, 76* (3), 164–177.

Edwards, C., Gandini, L., & Foreman, G. (Eds.). (1998). *The hundred languages of children: The Reggio Emilia approach—Advanced reflections*. (2nd ed.). Greenwich, CT: Ablex.

Erikson, E. H. (2000). *Childhood and society*. (3rd ed.). New York: Norton. (Originally published in 1950.)

Fosnot, C. (1996). *Constructivism: Theory, perspectives, and practice*. New York: Teachers College Press.

Fraser, S., & Gestwicki, C. (2002). *Authentic childhood: Exploring Reggio Emilia in the classroom*. Clifton Park, NY: Thomson Delmar Learning.

Froebel, F. (1902). *The education of man*. (W.N. Hailmann, Trans.). New York: Appleton. (Originally published in 1826, copyright 1887.)

Fu, V., Stremmel, A., & Hill, L. (2002). *Teaching and learning: Collaborative explorations of the Reggio Emilia approach*. Columbus, OH: Merrill.

Fulghum, R. L. (1988). *All I really need to know I learned in Kindergarten*. New York: Villlard.

Gardner, H. (1995). *Frames of mind: Multiple intelligences*. New York: Basic Books.

Helm, J., & Beneke, S. (2003). *The power of projects: Meeting contemporary challenges in early childhood classrooms—strategies & solutions*. New York: Teachers College Press.

Helm, J., & Katz, L. (2001). *Young investigators: The project approach in the early years*. New York: Teachers College Press.

Honig, A. (2000). *Secure relationships: Nurturing infant/toddler attachment in early care settings.* Washington, DC: NAEYC.

Isbell, R., & Exelby, B. (2001). *Early learning environments that work.* Beltsville, MD: Gryphon House.

Kami, C., & Housman, L. (1999). *Young children reinvent arithmetic: Implications of Piaget's theory.* New York: Teachers College Press.

Katz, L. and Chard, S. (2000). Engaging children's minds: The project approach. Stamford, CT: Ablex.

Lewis, T. J., Colvin, G., & Sugai, G. (2000). The effects of pre-correction and active supervision on the recess behavior of elementary students. *Education and Treatment of Children,* 23 (2), 109–121.

Maslow, A. (1998). *Toward a psychology of being,* (3rd ed.). New York: Wiley. (Originally published in 1962).

Moyer, J. (1999). The child-centered kindergarten. Association for the Education of Young Children position paper. Retrieved January 10, 2004, from http://www.acei.org/cckind.htm

New, R. (2003). Reggio Emilia: New ways to think about schooling. *Educational Leadership,* 60 (7), 34–39.

Olfman, S. (Ed.) (2003). *All work and no play . . . How educational reforms are harming our preschoolers.* Westport, CT: Praeger.

Paley, V. (1981). *Wally's stories.* Cambridge, MA: Harvard University.

Piaget, J. (1962). The stages of the intellectual development of the child. In S. Harrison & J. McDermott (Eds.), *Childhood psychopathology* (pp. 157–166). New York: International Universities Press.

Shornkoff, J., & Phillips, D. (2000). *From neurons to neighborhoods: The science of early childhood development.* Washington, DC: National Academy Press.

Vygotsky, L. (1978). *Mind in society: The development of higher psychological processes.* Cambridge, MA: Harvard University Press.

Wardle, F. (1999). In praise of developmentally appropriate practice. *Young Children,* 54 (6), 4–12.

Wolfgang, C., & Wolfgang, M. (1999). *School for young children: Developmentally appropriate practices.* (2nd ed.). Boston, MA: Allyn & Bacon.

Wright, S. (2003). *The arts, young children, and learning.* Boston, MA: Allyn & Bacon/Longman.

Supporting Play in Primary Schools

Play is the child's most useful tool for preparing himself for the future and its tasks

—*Bruno Bettelheim, 1987*

Chapter Overview

Play takes on new dimensions in the primary grades as cognitive, social, emotional, and physical dimensions develop through music, movement, art, and content areas. Toys, games, adults, and peers for children in schools and after-school settings add an extra dimension. Creating environments indoors (blocks, games and manipulatives, art, literacy, and writing centers) and outdoors (recess) for primary age children will be examined. Opportunities for observing and assessing play will also be presented in this chapter. The relationship between play and content areas such as literacy, math, science, and social studies will be featured in this chapter.

Objectives

After reading this chapter you should be able to:

◆ Explain the impact of development on primary play.

◆ Identify strategies for supporting play in the primary classroom.

◆ Describe play centers in a primary classroom.

◆ Develop plans for creating a project.

◆ Describe a play-based assessment system.

237

> ## PlayScape
>
> *The astronauts were ready to land. "Ground control, can we land now?"*
> *Control to space ship: "The technicians are checking the atmosphere now.*
> *Over and out."*
>
> *Astronauts move about in the space shuttle preparing for landing. They are*
> *checking their pulse, calculating the distance from the shuttle to the landing*
> *spot, and checking the air supply needed for exploring on the moon once*
> *they landed. "Can we land now?"*
>
> *Control to astronauts: "Yes, prepare to land. Check all systems."*
>
> *This did not occur at, NASA it occurred at Goldsboro Magnet Elementary*
> *School located in Florida. Students have a model lab that facilitates their*
> *play. As they dramatize the entire aeronautical experience, they are play-*
> *ing **and** they are learning.*
>
> ## Play Provocation
>
> The provocation to play is the model station complete with artificial
> moon for landing, videos, a planetarium, and a computer room that
> simulates the one at NASA. The children are engaged in play. It does
> not look like play in the preschool classroom, but it *is* a type of play.
> Play for this age is different and reflects a more sophisticated level of
> physical, cognitive, social, and emotional development. Some might
> even argue that it is not play. In this chapter we explore the multiple
> dimensions of play in the primary grades as well as the controversial
> issues surrounding primary play.

■ Primary Play

Primary play reflects characteristics typically found in school age children. Three major characteristics that impact play include (1) a need for
order, (2) a need to belong, and (3) a sense of self (Hughes, 1999). In the
cognitive domain, the child is developing logical thought and has a *need
for order* and structure (Piaget, 1962). Socially, the child wants to be accepted by his peers and has a *need to belong to a group*. The child is in what
Erikson described as the industry-versus-guilt stage (Erikson, 2000). The
child needs to develop confidence and a sense of self-esteem, which affect
the type of play that occurs in the primary years.

Symbolic play decreases during the primary years and the use of games-
with-rules increases. Primary play is dominated by games. As children

develop a sense of self and become more interested in belonging to groups, games become more important. Using primary play to foster academic development enables children to learn naturally.

■ Role of Adults

The role of the adult changes in the primary grades. Adults still have a role in supporting play. Creating the context for play requires that adults use their knowledge of children's development and interests to guide program development. For example, they must know that children at this age are in the **concrete operational stage** and that somewhere around the age of six, the child's vision is developed sufficiently to focus on print. Combining a newly acquired focus on text and the development of logical thought enables children to engage in complex cognitive tasks. Teachers must be ready and capable of supporting and challenging them. Adults support play by

- ◆ providing opportunities for budding talents in diverse areas.
- ◆ designing games.
- ◆ encouraging creative dramatics.
- ◆ providing appropriate intervention on playground.
- ◆ providing activities that provide legitimate play-based learning experiences.

Adding materials enhances the experience and creates new possibilities. Figure 7–1 includes a variety of basic play and learning materials that can extend the play for primary-age children.

■ Play as a Medium for Learning

Looking for play in primary school through the same lens as in preschool may create a situation that provides an incomplete picture of play in the primary classrooms. Play at the primary level involves more inquiry and exploration and less pretend play. The context for play in a preschool classroom might include blocks and a house area, whereas the context for play in a primary classroom might include blocks but may also include materials necessary for conducting science experiments and completing project work.

Aesthetics

Primary classrooms that use an aesthetics-based approach integrate content to extend the child's learning experience. Combining music and

FIGURE 7–1   Basic Play and Learning Materials for Primary School Children

- small figures that may be used in fantasy scenes and constructed models
- materials for enacting real-life activities (buying and selling, checking out books, sending letters), and materials (to make props and costumes) for plays and performances (role-play materials); a variety of puppets provided or made by children (characters appropriate to children in the group)—to replay familiar stories and give performances and shows
- a variety of materials for constructing play scenes and models—to be used with blocks or construction materials (ages six and seven)
- a large variety of puzzles (jigsaw, three-dimensional), including 50- to 100-piece jigsaws, map puzzles
- a large variety of specific skill-development materials, including printing and book-making materials, math manipulatives, measuring equipment, materials for learning about money and telling time, science materials (including those related to weather, the solar system, plant and animal life, and basic human anatomy), and computer programs
- complex pattern-making materials (mosaic tiles, geometric puzzles) to develop spatial, mathematical, and artistic understanding
- a variety of games to develop interaction skills, planning, using strategies, and an understanding of rule systems; simple reading, spelling, and math games; guessing or deductive games; memory games; simple card games; and beginning strategy games (games may be created by the children)
- a large variety of art and craft materials, including both graphic and malleable materials appropriate for practicing skills and producing products
- recorded music for group singing, moving, and rhythm activities, and equipment for listening and recording
- a variety of balls and equipment for specific sports activities, such as kickball, and materials for simple target games
- complex outdoor and gym equipment (may include climbing gym, swings, slides, ladders, seesaws), especially for ages six and seven, for acrobatics

Source: From *The Right Stuff for Children: Birth to 8* (pp. 26, 42, and 81) by M.B. Bronson, 1995, Washington, DC: National Association for the Education of Young Children. Copyright 1995 by the National Association for the Education of Young Children. Reprinted by permission.

math, art and literacy, movement and social studies, or music and science increases possibilities for neurological connections. Gardner's theory of multiple intelligences suggest that children have many ways of knowing the world (Gardner, 1983). By using an aesthetics-based approach, opportunities for understanding are optimized. When children combine music and movement through play, they can dramatize history by acting out stories from long ago. Children who are able to paint pictures after visiting an aquarium or draw pictures of foliage observed on an outing develop not only knowledge and skills, but also a disposition for learning.

Music

Primary-age children are predisposed to enjoy music and can learn through integrating music with other content areas. Budding talents begin to emerge at this age. Children can learn simple tunes, play simple instruments, and develop their talents. They are ready to perform, create,

Music is a part of an aesthetics-based play program.

and respond to music. The relationship between music and reading has been discussed on the Web site of the Music Teacher's National Association. The use of symbols for music and symbols for reading requires similar abstract thought. Children who may not read easily may sing easily. This realization has led to the integration of music with different areas. For example, when music plays softly in the background during writing time, children can be observed tapping or nodding to the beat of the music. It relaxes, comforts, and stimulates the children as they write. This is an aesthetic approach that integrates music, writing, and play.

Music also bridges cultures. Children who have a special knowledge of a culture or ethic group can share music and enhance the sense of community in the classroom.

Movement

Movement and motor development are especially important at this age. Developing gross and fine motor skills enable primary children to develop content-related skills. For example, children enjoy games that involve movement and learning such as tossing games that require them to add the number of tosses. Children also enjoy dancing and moving to music. Dance provides an opportunity for children to act out feelings and emotions.

When movement is a part of the curriculum, other benefits are often realized. Obesity rates have doubled since 1970 (Elliot, 2002). Encouraging movement is more important than ever. Outdoor play provides an excellent way to encourage movement.

Art

Appreciating and creating art is an important but often overlooked part of the primary classroom. Children who can begin their day with music and art have opportunities to integrate them into their work throughout the day. Children can paint, draw, use clay and other materials for modeling, make puppets, create collages, use papier-mâché, and engage in a variety of creative activities. Different opportunities are available when educators use different tools, mediums, and materials. Tools for painting can range from brushes to feathers, sticks or string, or even paintbrushes. Materials that can be used for painting can range from bubble plastic to cloth. The medium can range from paint to glue. Changing the tools, medium, and materials alters the experience and optimizes opportunities.

Literacy

The goal of fostering literacy in primary classrooms is paramount in most school systems. The actions taken to accomplish this goal, however, do not always have the desired effect (Hall, 2000). Combining play and literacy provides a better approach for encouraging literacy in the primary school. Play is self-motivating to children, in part, because they direct it. In the same way, literacy activities should be meaningful to children. This

Art is a part of an aesthetics-based play program.

can be accomplished through a play-based literacy program that focuses on meaningful, real-life activities.

In an effective literacy program, children should have

- ◆ daily experiences of being read to and independently reading meaningful and engaging stories and informational texts.

- ◆ a balanced instructional program that includes systematic code instruction along with meaningful reading and writing activities.

- ◆ daily opportunities and teacher support to write many kinds of texts for different purposes, including stories, lists, messages to others, poems, reports, and responses to literature.

- ◆ writing experiences that allow the flexibility to use nonconventional forms of writing at first (invented or phonic spelling) and over time move to conventional forms.

- ◆ opportunities to work in small groups for focused instruction and collaboration with other children.

- ◆ an intellectually engaging and challenging curriculum that expands knowledge of the world and vocabulary.

◆ adaptation of instructional strategies or more individualized instruction if the child fails to make expected progress in reading or when literacy skills are advanced. (IRA/NAEYC, 1998, p. 42)

The National Association for the Education of Young Children and the International Reading Association have developed a position paper on reading instruction in the primary grades, mentioned earlier in Chapter 4. Using the arts to extend the reading program optimizes learning for children who have many, multiple ways of knowing.

Math

Math instruction at the primary level uses a hands-on approach to foster the development of mathematical concepts. As children develop more logical-mathematical thinking skills, they become proficient with math. The National Council of Teachers of Mathematics (NCTM) established national standards that are used by many states as guidelines for developing state requirements in math. Susan Sperry Smith (2001) notes that "In order to prepare today's students for the twenty-first century, it is necessary to provide a wide variety of opportunities for each child to experience a challenging math curriculum" (p. 15). These standards include context and process standards. The context standards focus on the knowledge that students know at each level and include: (1) number and operation, (2) algebra, (3) geometry, (4) measurement, and (5) data analysis and probability. The process standards emphasize the process of acquiring and using knowledge to solve problems. Process standards include problem solving, reasoning and proof, communication, connections, and representation. See the NCTM Web site for additional information.

NCTM recommends an emphasis on number operations and geometry during the primary years. Patterns, measurement, and data collection add to understanding and should be integrated in all activities. Play provides a natural venue for math.

There are two ways to approach math instruction through play. One is through planned activities, experiences, and games that stand alone. The other is through integrated play themes which are discussed in the second part of this chapter. It is important to note that teachers must make a special effort to ensure math instruction interests and involves girls. This has been a focus for a decade and has been effective. In the Third International Mathematics and Science Study (TIMSS), the United States is one of three countries that does not realize a gender bias in the test scores. Both girls and boys scored equally well on general math knowledge (U.S. Department of Education, 1997a, 1997b).

Planned activities, experiences, and games must be meaningful, reflect real life, and be appropriate for the primary-age child. Math materials should be placed in the room so children can always obtain math manipulatives or games. Blocks should be part of the math program in primary schools because children can see the concepts of geometry and physics. When children are building with triangles and half circles, they are learning geometry through block play. Legos™ are interesting for both boys and girls. Games placed on a table provide an opportunity for children to play games while waiting for the teacher to start the class. Games provide the best venue for primary-age learning.

Games can be used to teach first, second, and third graders using the same materials. For example, two children get number cubes (dice) from the shelf and scrap paper from the bin. One child begins by rolling the number cubes. The numbers are 4 and 3. If she is in first grade, she would write them down on the paper and add them together. If in third grade, she might multiply the numbers. When the play time is over, the children can spin a game board that is divided into "higher" or "lower". If the spinner lands on "higher," the child with the highest number wins. If the spinner lands on "lower," the child with the least wins. This provides both children an opportunity to win and lose.

Constance Kami (2000) has documented the use of games with children from first to sixth grade. Her research has found that children who play games instead of completing worksheets can complete computation just as quickly and also have a better grasp of mathematical concepts. She has written a series of books with classroom teachers that describe how to develop a Piagetian game–based approach for each grade level. These books can be used as a framework for developing a play-based math curriculum.

Science

Science and play have always been linked. Science is a way of experiencing the world. Many of the most renowned scientists play with their ideas (Rogers & Sluss, 1999). One goal of science instruction is to encourage inquiry as a way of investigating the world. Inquiry-based learning includes describing objects and events, asking questions, constructing explanations, testing explanations, and communicating results to others. Primary-age children are natural scientists who ask "Why?" The National Science Education Standards recognizes inquiry as a central tenet of science education. They further assert that it must be developmentally appropriate, interesting, relevant, inquiry based, and integrated with other subjects. Play provides a natural vehicle for understanding scientific principles.

Centers are an important part of the primary classroom.

Primary-age children have certain attributes that predispose them to science. First, they are naturally curious. They want to know how and why everything works as it does. Books that contain *Everything You Want to Know about the World* answer questions about the color of grass or why the wind blows and are very popular. Second, they enjoy order and delight in collections of stuff. They create collections out of anything and collections hold a great place of fascination. As they collect and sort, they are classifying materials and they are developing a sense of self. Third, many are developing budding talents that will affect a career choice. In a recent conversation with a scientist, he indicated that his interest in science was stimulated by a teacher in the second grade who routinely did science projects. Fourth, children want to belong at this age, so interacting with each other to solve problems provides a positive social outlet.

Science learning can occur through themes, units, or projects or it can be included in a play program, as discussed at the end of the chapter. Themes or units are designed by teachers with set goals, objectives, activities, and evaluations. Projects are open ended and based on emerging knowledge. Projects provide an optimal opportunity for discovery and, thus, for science.

Social Studies

Social Studies, perhaps more than any other content area, is intertwined in play. Bank Street and other play schools in the 1920s used social studies as a basis for the curriculum. Today, there are three types of curriculum recommended for primary classrooms (Seefeldt, 2000): (1) the social skills, (2) the here and now, and (3) the holiday curriculum. The *social skills curriculum* focuses on the development of skills necessary to negotiate the social world. Social skills such as turn-taking, self-help skills, and following directions provide a foundation for citizenship. The *here-and-now curriculum* focuses on what is meaningful and relevant to the child. This approach can be used to integrate all content areas through play. The here-and-now curriculum is considered to be the most appropriate approach in primary school. The *holiday curriculum* is built around holidays. Many teachers refer to this as the *calendar curriculum,* and, while it offers the opportunity to familiarize children with national observances

Children need places to play and work individually.

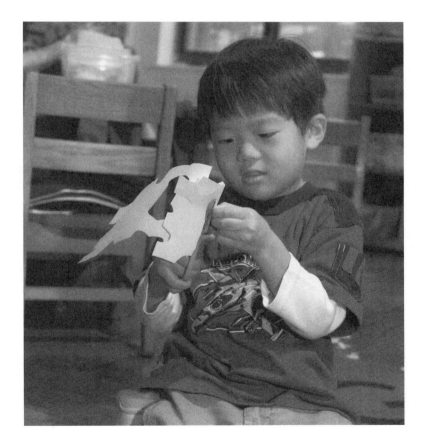

such as Thanksgiving, President's Day, and Martin Luther King, Jr., it has limits. Many who use the holiday curriculum include Christmas and Easter as holidays. These are Christian holidays, not national holidays. If religious holidays are celebrated for one culture, then all cultures represented in the room must also celebrate their religious holidays or none should be observed. Democracy is better served when parents celebrate religious holidays at home and schools celebrate national holidays.

Using play to teach social studies can be accomplished by integrating information in units, themes, or projects. For example, setting up a bank in the room allows children to role-play the job of banking employees, understand the process of money exchange, and perhaps develop an interest in economics that will last a lifetime. Children can begin to develop an understanding of needs and wants as they develop basic knowledge of a budget.

■ Curriculum Connections

One way to connect the content area in a play-based curriculum is through the use of projects. This approach, which encourages children to utilize inquiry and critical thinking skills, was explained in Chapter 6. This section contains information for implementation at the primary level.

Phase I. Planning and Organizing

The provocation for a project can come from the children, or from parents, teacher, or community. The media may also influence the children's source of topics. The teacher's role is to guide the process of topic selection. Project topics must be appropriate for the age level, meaningful, and culturally relevant. For example, children who live in the northwestern area of the United States might find topics related to trees, snow, or ice interesting, whereas children in the southern part of the United States may find the ocean interesting. Encouraging children to examine topics that are in the "here and now" also encourages identification of the local flora and fauna and this aligns with many state curriculum guidelines.

KWL

KWL charts, described earlier in Chapter 6, can be used as part of the Project Approach. The chart basically is divided into three sections that address three questions, What do we Know? What do we Want to know? And what did we Learn? The KWL chart helps organize the project and

FIGURE 7–2 KWL Chart for Project Development

Phase I	Phase II	Phase III
What do we KNOW about this topic?	What do we WANT to know?	What did we LEARN?
Oceans have beaches with sand. Fish and animals live in the ocean. The ocean makes a loud noise when the waves come in. Shells are found all over the beach.	Where does the sand come from? How many fish and animals are in the ocean? Is a whale bigger than a dinosaur? Why is the ocean blue but when I put water in my bucket, it's not blue?	

illustrate the learning that occurred. A KWL chart provides a good instrument for organizing the project. See Figure 7–2 for a sample chart.

Graphic organizers

When developing projects, children in primary grades benefit from using graphic organizers. These graphics organize children's thinking. For example, Venn diagrams are graphic organizers that have become very popular. Primary-age children can use graphic organizers that allow them to map concepts in a nonlinear way. Some refer to this as *mind-mapping*. This encourages creativity and critical thinking, and is enjoyable. Children start with a topic such as the ocean. They place it in the center of the page and then they start thinking about questions or areas of interest related to the topic. As they explore possible areas of interest, they decide which area is of most interest and use it to inform their study. This encourages thinking that is circular and many children will create one or two mind maps just for "fun." For these children, this is their play.

An example of a graphic organizer or mind map is included in Figure 7–3. The topic is the ocean. Projects that can arise out of this mind map might include natural and unnatural inhabitants of the ocean and can include technology, transportation, pollution, or the relationship between humans and the ocean. Children learn academic content such as math (depth of the ocean, size of fish, classification of shells), science (composition of ocean, classification of fish, shells, animals, or boats), and social studies (transportation, pollution, beaches around the world) as they explore oceans. They use art (painting murals and pictures of the ocean, looking at different artists' renditions of the ocean), music (creating songs

FIGURE 7–3 Graphic Organizer or Mind Map

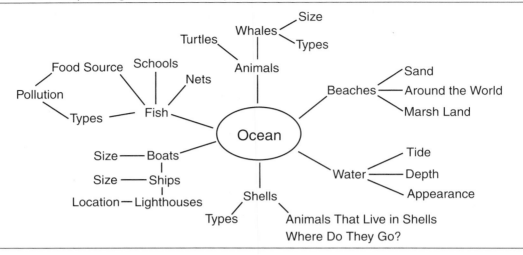

and listening to music about the ocean), and movement (creating dances). The graphic organizer provides a venue for children to expand their creative and creative-thinking skills.

Phase II. Implementing the Project

After the initial planning has occurred, the children can begin an investigation to answer their questions. For example, two questions that might evolve from a study of shells are, "Where do they come from?" and "How many kinds of shells are on the beach?" To answer the first question, the teacher may want to secure a set of books about the beach, take the children to the library to research the topic, or invite a guest speaker to talk about the animals that live in shells. To address the second question, the teacher may want to take the children to the beach to explore the vast quantities and varieties of shells on the beach. Children will gain various competencies from this experience such as sorting and classification that reinforces math skills, they are exposed to the animal's ecological niche, and they have an impetus for learning more about the ocean and beach. This is "sciencing" at its best.

Project area

When the children return, they can extend their learning in the project area. The project area is an area of the room that is designated for project work. Locating it near a source of water is always a good idea. This provides an area where children can work on projects and leave their work until the next project work time. This is not required, but it does promote the use of projects in the classroom. When children can leave a project and return in three days, it extends the interest and depth of study.

Upon their return from the beach, the children in this project may want to set up a science lab complete with magnifying glasses, microscopes, science logs, and egg cartons or ice cube trays for sorting and classifying shells. For children at this age, collecting and classifying are pleasurable activities. Adding lab coats to the center increases authenticity. Children who live near the ocean have a different level of knowledge: they have intimate knowledge of shells, fish, boats, and, in some areas, marine biologists. When children bring their real world into the classroom, it extends and strengthens their thinking. Part of the reason that the projects in Reggio Emilia are so valued is because they are so intertwined with their local culture and location. They are authentic for the children. For example, they generally visit vineyards during harvest and participate in the stomping of the grapes. This is appropriate in their culture but would be meaningless to a group of children from another area. This is their culture and their world. For this reason, the schools of Reggio Emilia discourage others from trying to replicate their children's experiences. Rather, they encourage early educators to look around their own ecological niche and find areas of interests that are most meaningful and relevant to the children there.

The children should be involved in planning how to unpack the beach experience in the classroom. They may choose to develop a marine lab, create a beach sweeper, or a lifeguard station. Providing guidance in helping the children answer their questions creatively requires both keen observation skills on the part of the early educator and a commitment to inquiry-based education.

Aesthetics

Children can paint murals of their experience, create poems or haiku, or write stories about their experiences. Some may want to create a play or puppet show about fictional characters. Other children may want to know about real people who live near the beach and explore some books about people who live near the beach. Songs and music about the beach extend their interest. Some children may want to be involved in creating movement to the sounds of the ocean. Creating a diorama also provides a way to re-create the experience.

Games

Games provide another avenue for extending project work. Number games can be made with different shells. Rules can be developed that reflect the complexity of the learner's knowledge. Other possibilities include a simple bingo with different shells. They have fascinating games that they invent when they have the opportunity to do so.

When children begin to tire of the project, it is time to end it and this happens in the third and final stage.

Phase III. Project Conclusion

Encourage the children to look at their KWL chart. What did they learn? They can document their learning on the chart and/or document it in other ways. For some projects that do not generate much interest, it may be sufficient to record the information on the chart and consider other possible topics for further study. For projects that stimulate interest and involvement, outcomes can be recorded in a variety of different ways. It helps children make sense of the experience when they realize that they need to "tell their story." What did they do first, second, third? What did they learn? This helps them develop a scientific attitude for communicating findings.

In addition, they can write and illustrate books and use digital cameras to capture their experiences and (with assistance) create stories about their experiences. Other options involve performing plays, doing a mock television interview, publishing a book of poems about the experience, or displaying a mural. One class presented its project to the community during an art display, complete with refreshments and a strolling violinist. Opportunities are unlimited. One group of third graders routinely created PowerPoint presentations after a project. A parent uploaded them to the Web and they had a photo essay of learning that had occurred that year.

Project assessment

Project assessment is difficult and may be part of the reason projects are not more popular. Careful collection of data throughout the project can be used to document the child's learning. Using photo essays, documentation panels, or electronic portfolios described in Chapter 6 facilitates project assessment. Additional methods are discussed at the end of this chapter. Assessing individual contributions to group projects is one of the challenges of project work and is an area that needs more study.

■ Program Models

Primary play programs differ from preschool play programs. Though many teachers are familiar with the preschool programs of Bank Street, High/Scope, and Creative Curriculum, few are familiar with play-based models for primary school. The best-known play program was designed by Selma Wasserman. She describes a play-based program in her book, *Serious Players in the Primary Classroom: Empowering Children Through Active Learning Experiences* (1990). She takes the reader through a step-by-step description that details how to establish a play-based program in a primary classroom. Program models are discussed below in order of their appearance. This list is not exhaustive but includes some of most popular programs available. It focuses on the ones that are most commonly known and includes Wasserman's model, constructivist, developmental-interaction/ Bank Street, Creative Curriculum, and Reggio Emilia.

Wasserman's Primary Play Model

Based on Wasserman's *Serious Players in the Primary Classroom: Empowering Children Through Active Learning Experiences*, this approach identifies itself as a play program. The focus of this model is fostering the development of competent "can-do" students through playing, debriefing, and replaying. From Wasserman's perspective, play, debrief, and replay creates a systematic approach to instruction. The goal is to explore and discover the big idea. Play activities are designed to provide opportunities for exploration. Debriefing involves reflecting and reconsidering findings developed during the play experience. Replay involves reexamination and revisiting the materials. An important part of this program involves "breathing out," which is a time in the morning devoted to aesthetically based centers. Many aspects of this approach are similar to those advocated by John Dewey and many of the activities are very similar to inquiry-based instruction.

Constructivist Primary Classrooms

A constructivist approach can be established using a framework provided by DeVries and Zan in their book, *Moral Classrooms, Moral Children: Creating a Constructivist Atmosphere in Early Education* (1994). This book provides guidelines for teachers interested in establishing a program. The premise of this approach is ". . . that a sociomoral atmosphere must be cultivated in which respect for others is continually practiced" (1994, p. 1). Like Wasserman's approach, this also promotes the ideas of a democratic

The availability of centers in primary classrooms promotes a play-based curriculum.

classroom discussed by John Dewey at the beginning of the twentieth century.

John Dewey advocated action that can occur through the arts. Aesthetics should be a part of the primary play program:

> Both play and art have much in common. Both engage imagination, both require reflection, both profit from skill, both seek to generate new forms of experience, both lead to invention, and both are marginalized in the priorities of American education. In my view both children and the cultures within which they live would be better served if art and play had a more prominent place in our schools. (Eisner, 1990, p. 55)

Developmental-interaction

The developmental-interaction program at Bank Street includes a model for primary education. The primary program is grounded in the same theoretical principles discussed in previous chapters. The program for six- to eight-year-olds is referred to as the middle school, which may be confusing to those who are trying to locate primary-based materials. The curriculum for the Bank Street primary program includes social studies, reading and writing, math and science, art and shop, music and movement, physical education, and French or Spanish class.

Creative Curriculum (Primary Classrooms)

The Creative Curriculum approach for primary grades is based on the book, *Building the Primary Classroom: A Complete Guide to Teaching and Learning*, by Bickart, Jablon, and Dodge (1999). The program is based on two parts; the first includes teaching strategies and the second involves content. The teaching strategies in Part I include the following:

- ◆ knowing the child you teach
- ◆ building a classroom community
- ◆ establishing a structure of the classroom
- ◆ guiding children's learning
- ◆ assessing children's learning
- ◆ building a partnership with families

Part II includes the content area of language and literacy, mathematical thinking, social studies, scientific thinking, technology, and the arts. A learning environment using this approach includes the following areas:

- ◆ meeting areas
- ◆ arrangement of furniture and tables
- ◆ organization of supplies and materials
- ◆ display space
- ◆ personal belongings and work

Reggio Emilia

The infant-toddler and preschools of Reggio Emilia, Italy, are famous throughout the world. Some scholars have suggested using these same principles to inform practice in primary and middle schools (Fu, Stremmel, & Hill, 2002). Though valiant efforts have been made, to date there are no program models available to inform primary classrooms. Those who are interested in pursuing the application of these principles to a primary classroom are encouraged to use the basic principles of Reggio Emilia as a starting point.

■ Designing Primary Spaces

Primary classrooms present more of a challenge than do preschool or kindergarten classrooms. Children still need centers, but also need space for individual and group work. Aesthetics are equally important for the primary room. Assigning children to water plants, feed fish, or distribute daily mail teaches responsibility and reflects knowledge of the child's need for order, to belong, and to feel competent. Areas of the room should be arranged to include the following activities or areas.

Entry or exit

The entrance/exit should be safe and free from objects that might serve as a safety hazard. Spaces for hanging coats and placing personal belongings should be close to the entry to ease transition in the morning and evening. Some primary doors have designs around them to encourage interest in the room. The room should reflect that children have been involved in the process.

Large meeting space

All primary classes need a space where children can sit on carpet squares, quilts, or blankets as a group. Many teachers are using risers shaped in a U. This provides the children with a place where they can sit for class meetings when disagreements need to be resolved. The large meeting space should have a large easel available so the responses of the group can be recorded. This space is useful for a variety of activities including social studies, author's chair, poetry readings, and story reenactments. Placing a class helper chart in this area reminds everyone of daily responsibilities.

Small-group work places

Tables can be placed around the periphery of the classroom or flat desks can be pulled together for group work. When children work in groups or teams, they have opportunities to develop the sense of self which is so important for this age. Small groups can also meet in the large meeting area, on a sofa, at a small group of tables, or on the floor. Carpet remnants provide a defining area for children. Small groups provide a context for games. Children can use games when time permits. They can get them and put them back unassisted. One teacher used coffee can math games. The children knew that the games involved two or four people. In the mornings, the children would get the coffee can games, select a carpet remnant, and play until the teacher stopped them for morning meeting. The children played math games that involved addition and multiplication. They were learning and playing. The placement of the materials made it possible.

Children need a variety of places available for play and learning.

Individual work places

Because children are developing a sense of order at this age, it is optimal for each child to have a place to hang their outer garments, a mailbox for materials that are sent home and returned, and an individual desk that can be turned into groups of two, four, or eight. Some teachers prefer tables, but individual desks can be used for multiple purposes and children are able to own one desk. They can put their materials in the desk and know that they are secure. If tables are used, children need cubby areas for their personal materials. A place in the room also needs to be designated as a quiet space for one or two children. Some teachers use a decorated refrigerator box as a space ship, while others use a bean bag or couch. Bean bags and book baskets create an inviting combination.

Storage and equipment

Materials should be stored neatly. Labels can be placed on everything in the room so children can develop a sense of independence as they use materials, put away equipment, and collect materials for the next project. Think about how you will handle passing out materials, crayons, and scissors. If children keep them in a personal space, make sure they can get to them easily. When distributing materials for the entire class, pass them out by table groups or teams. Second and third graders like the use of the word *team.*

Check the room periodically for clutter and worn-out materials. Organization is the key operative term. If materials are placed within the child's work area, it should be available for their use. Placing teacher records or materials in a shelf with the children's portfolios creates problems because children do not know which is for their use and which is for the teacher's exclusive use.

Aesthetics

A beautiful place for primary children can enhance the quality of life for them. Lighting, displays, and room arrangements all contribute to the sense of orderliness and beauty or the sense of chaos. Natural light and lamps can change the lighting in a classroom. Painting walls white so hanging plants and pictures are highlighted creates a clean, uncluttered canvas for displaying art.

Display the children's work thoughtfully. Making fewer projects and displaying them creatively is better than completing daily worksheets. Bulletin board displays purchased at teacher stores may not reflect the children or the culture. Using student-created work or pictures of a project that they just completed is more appropriate. Bringing the local culture into the classroom will add to the children's sense of identity.

Interest Centers

Blocks and math center. A section of the room set up for blocks and math will reap tremendous rewards. Primary-age children benefit from play with blocks, including unit blocks and Lego™ blocks. They need math manipulatives that can be used for counting. Many children do not have regular access to Cuisenaire rods or math games, so daily use of these materials can stimulate a greater interest in math. Children who play games can keep up with the games they are playing by writing in a journal and this can used for evaluation purposes.

Book center. The idea of a class library or book center is not new. The idea of creating a comfortable place for children to read *is* new. Bean bags and wicker baskets filled with books easily create an inviting space for reading. Couches make a great place for sitting and reading. One teacher used a boat filled with cushions.

Project area. Setting aside one area of the room for projects encourages project work. Children can move to this area to work on projects, complete research, or role-play different scenarios.

Regardless of the model used, designing and creating the structure of the class is both challenging and stimulating. At one school, the principal encouraged the children to participate in designing outdoor play spaces.

FIGURE 7–4 In Their Own Words . . .

Developing Areas of Play at Clemson Elementary School
Paul Prichard, EdD
Principal, Clemson Elementary School

When it came time to build a new school, we were given the opportunity to form a building committee to help with the planning. Our committee not only benefited from the experience of the teachers and community members, but we also gathered information from our students who knew what they wanted in their ideal school. Children described their desires, and also drew pictures of many interesting structures. Children asked for the typical things like ball field, slides, and swings, but they also had more creative ideas. They asked for climbing walls, outdoor classrooms, nature trails, and petting zoos. We tried to incorporate as many of the children's ideas as possible into the new school plan. Children also suggested theme gardens patterned after some of their favorite books. They suggested *Peter Rabbit, Alice in Wonderland, A Secret Garden,* and *Harry Potter.*

We believe that the school grounds are an important part of the total school learning environment so we incorporated many of the children's ideas into our school planning. We welcomed AmeriCorp workers and Eagle Scouts to clear paths and label foliage along the nature trails. Through parent and community fund raisers we were able to finance playgrounds which were appropriate to each grade level. Kindergarten students were welcomed by a large Panda Bear and a Turtle. Swings, a sand box, climbing equipment, and slides invited students to free-play activities. The first and second grade playground starts with jungle climbing equipment guarded by a gorilla and proceeds to a desert with a large lion. Then, children step on lily pads across a swampy area to escape two alligators. Finally, the children move to climbing and sliding equipment. There is also an open area for running and chasing activities. In another area of the school, athletic fields, basketball goals, climbing walls, and sidewalk games are available for older children. We also built a music garden with percussion instruments. To accommodate animals, a barn complete with paddock was readied for animals that come to visit when the curriculum dictates.

The theme gardens offer opportunities for reading, planting vegetables, visiting with a friend, or free play. Our classrooms truly extend to the outdoor environment offering lots of opportunities for creative activities. For larger-group activities, the amphitheater is a wonderful place for puppet shows, singing, and dancing. Built around a one-hundred-year-old oak tree, it offers an idyllic source of shade and beauty.

We believe that schools should offer a wide variety of spaces for activities that promote both organized and free play. Schools should be a place where children learn about the complexities of life. Much of what we learn about relationships with others we learn through play. We believe our school makes this possible.

Source: Paul Prichard, Ed. D., Principal, Clemson Elementary School.

The process provides a powerful model for others who want to include children in the planning process.

■ Toys and Materials

Characteristics of primary-age children (developing a sense of self-esteem, order and structure, and a sense of belonging) and their dominant play interest, games with rules, are reflected in their toys and materials. Due to the variability at this age, a wide variety of choices should be available. This is the age when children will put on puppet shows for younger children, create props for dramatic productions, and make their own games or collections. While doll-play is on the wane, human beings appear in historical re-creations and dioramas. Safety concerns at this age revolve around the risk-taking behavior that is a part of establishing a sense of self for this age group.

■ Assessment

Assessment in primary school looks very different from preschool assessment. Standardized tests are a routine part of primary classes and test results are used to compare and rate schools and teachers. This is referred to as "high-stakes testing." Many believe that this is not appropriate for young children or their teachers. Each subject area has a professional society and each group has standards: International Reading Association (IRA), National Council of Teachers of Math (NCTM), National Council of Teachers of English (NCTE), National Council of Social Studies (NCSS), National Science Teachers Association (NSTA), etc. Standards recommended by professional associations are not required by law and can be used or ignored by classroom teachers in some localities. However, most states use the specialty standards as a foundation for developing state standards that are mandatory, while some states have developed their standards independent of the guidelines from professional organizations. Add to this the variation in standardized tests from state to state and district to district. The picture is pretty convoluted. Where does play fit into this assessment picture?

Play in the primary grades is different from play in the preschool years. Primary play consists of games with rules, and so play assessment will look different. Assessing play in the primary grades provides information useful in orchestrating instruction and play. Wasserman (1990), who proposed a play-based program, also recommended an assessment system based on reflection and dialogue. She also suggested the elimination of letter grades in the primary classroom. Grades would be replaced by dialogues and thoughtful conversations. Although this is an excellent idea, many public school teachers who have a teaching contract requiring them to issue grades cannot usually implement this system.

Opportunities for developmentally appropriate assessment in primary school are available and reflect the developmental level, age, and culture of the child. Primary-age children play games with more structured rules, have a need to develop self-esteem, and have a feeling of belonging. If these characteristics are used to structure a play program with an assessment system, then authentic assessment must be included. Authentic assessment at this level includes games, teamwork, portfolios, and project work. One type of authentic assessment involves the documentation processes that originated in the schools of Reggio Emilia, Italy. It can enhance communication of the learning process. These were discussed at length in Chapters 5 and 6.

Games

Games provide an excellent venue for assessing math. Using open-ended math games allows children to create their own challenge. Children who keep math journals can record their knowledge gains. Math journals can be examined for themes so that areas of strength and weaknesses can be recognized and amelioration provided as necessary. Children at this age enjoy making games. Conducting research to make a social studies game about their town or build a replica brings together play, aesthetics, and content in a creative activity that is beneficial.

Cooperative group work (teams)

Team work offers an opportunity for children who have different skills to work together to complete an assignment. Activities can include story reenactment, puppet shows for younger children, writing poems about local places, or completing science experiments that are recorded in science journals.

Portfolios

Portfolios provide a way to document progress. The child and teacher select her best work and place it in the portfolio in selected places. For example, after talking about poetry, children can choose to write poetry or conduct research and then record it in a portfolio. A portfolio for language arts is both developmentally appropriate and provides evidence of growth across the year.

Project work

Project work demonstrates science and social studies through the language arts, math, art, music, and reenactment. At the end of the project, students share their findings. Among the skills used in projects are research, writing, math and computation, communication and social interaction.

Creating an assessment program using games, portfolios, cooperative learning teams, and project work provides an overall approach that is aligned with how the child learns. This system provides an optimal way to foster learning in the primary grades.

Assessing after-school programs

Self-study assessment instruments are available for after-school programs. The School Age Care Environmental Rating Scale (SACERS) (Harms, Jacobs, & White, 1996) is designed to give a quick overview of quality in an after-school program. Evaluators who use the SACERS must have training prior to using the instrument. Tapes and workshops are available to those who choose to use this method. Areas included in the rating scale are Space and Furnishings, Health and Safety, Activities, Interactions, Program Structures, Staff Development, and Special Needs.

> ## *PlayScape Reflections*
>
> The play described in the Playscape at the beginning of this chapter reflects a view of primary play that emphasizes play as a legitimate instructional activity—as a medium for learning. Play at this level generally does not follow a program model, but rather is as individualized as the teachers who set up the programs. The assessment is equally varied. Charting participation in different aspects of the space station and evaluating reports of the play scripts are used as indicators of the student's interaction and learning. There is a sense of trust that if the students have been engaged in play that involves walking on the moon and sending a report back to earth, then the student must know how to communicate and use technology. Rather than measuring isolated skills, the student's overall performance is assessed through play.

■ Summary

Primary play was discussed in this chapter as a means of teaching and learning. The role of adults is viewed as crucial in establishing a natural environment for play. Aesthetics are important as after-school lessons in specific skill areas begin to take on an important role. Integrated learning in the content areas of literacy, math, science, social studies, health, and physical education programs are enriched through play. Models including Bank Street, High/Scope, Wasserman, constructivist, and Creative Curriculum primary curriculum encourage a holistic approach. Spaces, places, and materials in formal and informal settings are important. Authentic assessment opportunities provide a venue for capturing learning through play.

■ Key Term

Concrete operational stage

■ Helpful Web Sites and Technology Resources

◆ **Bank Street**
http://www.bankstreetbooks.com   Lesson plans, units, and sample of books written by children are available on this site.

◆ **Goldsboro Magnet School**
http://www.goldsboro.scps.k12.fl.us   Site of Goldsboro Magnet Elementary School. Click on Kids Space Station for an overview of the program.

◆ **International Reading Association**
http://www.reading.org   Official site of the largest professional association dedicated to reading instruction.

◆ **National Science**
http://books.nap.edu   National Science Education, science standards are available.

◆ **National Council of Teachers of English**
http://www.ncte.org   Official site of the professional organization of English teachers. Good ideas for second and third grade.

◆ **National Council of Teachers of Mathematics**
http://www.nctm.org   Official site of the largest professional organization of math teachers. Provides most current research and practice on mathematics instruction in the United States.

◆ **National Council of Social Studies**
http://www.ncss.org   Official site of the largest professional organization of teachers of social studies.

◆ **Music Teachers National Association**
http://www.mtna.org/home.htm   Site of the Music Teachers National Association. Includes standards and guidelines for parents.

◆ **National Science Teachers Association**
http://www.nsta.org   National professional organization of teachers of science. Focus for elementary school is second grade through fifth.

◆ **Project Approach**
http://www.project-approach.com   Web site developed by Sylvia Chard, one of the authors of a book on the project approach.

◆ **Project Approach**
http://ecap.crc.uiuc.edu   Official site of the Early Childhood And Parent Collaborative (ECAP). Information for training on the project approach is available.

■ Activities

1. InClass Lab

A. Develop a play plan for one curriculum area from first through third grade. For example, a play plan for math might include unit blocks in the first and second grade, smaller blocks and manipulatives for all grades, and games at every level. Ways to facilitate math learning through play in the house area or other centers should also be described.

B. Develop a graphic organizer for a project for second or third grade. Plan an assessment system that can be used to document learning.

2. Research and Inquiry

A. Visit a classroom for two hours that uses play in the curriculum in primary school. Now, find another classroom at the same level (grades 1, 2, or 3) that does not use play and visit this classroom for two hours. Compare and contrast your observations in the two classrooms. Based on your knowledge of theories, what theoretical orientation influenced the classrooms? Did this impact the frequency of play in these classrooms?

B. Select a grade such as first or second and investigate the curriculum of the same grade in two other countries. How is it similar? How is it different? Do they have more or less play? What influences impact their curriculum?

C. Recall the contexts of play explained in the first chapter. Compare two systems that do and do not use a play-based curriculum. Does the micro-, macro-, exo-, meso-, or chronosystem have the most impact on play? Support your response with data.

D. What is the homework policy in local school systems? Interview teachers from grades one to three. How much homework do they assign? How does this impact after-school play?

3. Service Learning

A. Volunteer in an after-school program for two hours a week. What kind of play did you observe? What are the children learning through their play?

B. Create a set of math games that can be used in an after-school program to reinforce a specific math skill.

C. Visit a local after-school program. Volunteer to organize a game shelf to encourage play.

D. Develop information sheets that provide directions and rules for non-competitive games. Distribute these to local after-school programs.

4. Family Connections

A. Ask if you can organize a Family Night Out for parents. They can plan on eating together by bringing a dish for each member of the family. During the dinner, children have time to discuss their projects and display their panels. Panels focus on the class project rather than on individual accomplishments.

B. Another family night program should involve a presentation on play in the primary grades. Providing information about development that occurs at this age can assist parents as they deal with the issues of how many extra-curriculum activities are too many, when should they become concerned about their child's playmate, and how can they support time to play at home. Be prepared to support your comments with data. Handouts with additional information or articles to support your statements should be available.

C. Ask children who have a unique music heritage to share their music with the class.

D. Plan a family night outing to celebrate artistic creations. Invite a local high school or college student musician to provide music for the occasion.

5. **Play Advocacy**

A. Create a set of games for primary school children that can be played with minimal instruction. Donate the games to a local community agency such as a clinic or homeless shelter.

B. Find out what organizations advocate for children in your state. Who advocates for children in primary school?

C. What state laws affect play in primary school?

D. How does required assessment affect play in local schools? Design an evaluation plan that will assess children's development through games and play.

■ References

Bettelheim, B. (1987, March). The importance of play. *Atlantic*, pp. 35–46.

Bickart, T., Jablon, J., & Dodge, D. (1999). *Building the primary classroom: A complete guide to teaching and learning.* Washington, DC: Teaching Strategies.

Bronson, M. B. (1995). *The right stuff for children.* Washington, DC: National Association for the Education of Young Children.

DeVries, R., & Zan, B. (1994). *Moral classrooms, moral children: Creating a constructivist atmosphere in early education.* New York: Teachers College Press.

Eisner, E. (1990). The role of art and play in children's cognitive development. In E. Klugman and S. Smilansky (Eds.), *Children's play and learning* (pp. 43–56). New York: Teachers College Press.

Elliott, V. (2002). Adult options for childhood obesity? Doctors say the high number of extremely overweight young people is serious enough to consider radical interventions. *American Medical News, 45* (20), 27.

Erikson, E. (2000). *Childhood and society*. New York: W.W. Norton. (Originally published in 1950.)

Fu, V., Stremmel, A., & Hill, L. (2002). *Teaching and learning: Collaborative exploration of the Reggio Emilia approach*. Columbus, OH: Merrill.

Gardner, H. (1983). *Frames of mind*. New York: Basic Books.

Hall, N. (2000). Literacy, play, and authentic experience. In K. A. Roskos and J. F. Christie (Eds.) *Play and literacy in early childhood: Research from multiple perspectives* (pp. 189–204). Mahwah, NJ: Lawrence Erlbaum.

Harms, T., Jacobs, E., & White, D. (1996). *School Age Care Environment Rating Scale*. New York, NY: Teachers College Press.

Hughes, F. (1999). *Children, play, and development*. Boston: Allyn and Bacon.

International Reading Association (IRA) and the National Association for the Education of Young Children (NAEYC) joint position paper. (1998). Learning to read and write: Developmentally appropriate practices for young children. *Young Children, 53* (4), 30–46.

Kami, C. (2000). *Young children reinvent arithmetic: Implications of Piaget's theory* (2nd ed.). New York: Teachers College Press.

Piaget, J. (1962). *Play, dreams, and imitation*. Norton. (Original work published in 1962.)

Rogers, C.S. & Sluss, D.J. (1999). Revisiting Erikson's views on Einstein's play and inventiveness. In S. Reifel's *Play contexts revisited, Play and culture series,* Vol. 2 (pp. 3–24). Greenwich, CT: Albex.

Seefeldt, C. (2000). *Social Studies for the Preschool/Primary Child* (6th ed.). Upper Saddle, NJ: Prentice-Hall.

Smith, S. (2001). *Early Childhood Mathematics* (2nd ed.). Boston, MA: Allyn & Bacon.

U.S. Department of Education. (1997a). National Center for Education Statistics. *Pursuing excellence: A study of U.S. fourth grade mathematics and science achievement in international context*. Washington, DC: U.S. Government Printing Office.

U.S. Department of Education. (1997b). National Center for Education Statistics. *Pursuing excellence: A study of U.S. twelfth grade mathematics and science achievement in international context*. Washington, DC: U.S. Government Printing Office.

Wasserman, S. (1990). *Serious players in the primary classroom: Empowering children through active learning experiences*. New York: Teachers College Press.

Supporting Play for Children with Special Needs

To meet every child's needs, we believe that inclusive early childhood settings must rely on an expansive view of play that is responsive to all children.

—Catherine Marchant & Cheryl Brown, 1996

Chapter Overview

This chapter explores play for children who have disabilities or developmental delays. Topics include the benefits of play for children who have special needs, techniques for making necessary adaptations, and the important role of early educators in facilitating inclusive play among children with special needs and their peers. Additional topics in-clude adaptive toys, assistive tech-nology, and transdisciplinary play assessment.

Objectives

After reading this chapter you should be able to:

◆ Recognize the benefits of play for children who have special needs.

◆ Discuss child-focused interventions.

◆ Describe some tips for successful inclusion.

◆ List some adaptations that can be made to ensure that children with special needs can play with toys and materials in the classroom.

◆ Explore the role of assistive technol-ogy in encouraging play in inclusive settings.

◆ Discuss the methods and advan-tages of transdiciplinary play assessment.

267

PlayScape

Sheena took Twila, her three-year-old who was born with Down syndrome, to preschool this morning. This was Twila's first group experience and Sheena wondered how she would interact with the other children. Would she have friends? Would the other children play with her? Though she wanted to call throughout the day to check on her, she waited. She knew she was in good hands, that this was a center that used a play-based program. Now, she couldn't wait to pick her up.

When she arrived, Twila was sitting in a chair in the home area holding her doll that she had brought to school earlier in the day. Sheena was concerned. Did she find a friend? Did she play or did she sit alone? What did Twila do today?

Play Provocation

The provocation to play in this scenario could be the doll or other materials in the room. Typically developing children are intuitively drawn to toys and materials that lead to new and creative combinations. Children who have conditions that require special consideration may need assistance with the materials or may need adaptive equipment to support their play. Children who have disabilities can and will play, but they may need additional support. Notice that Sheena, like all parents, wanted her child to find a friend and play. Perhaps Twila's friend left or perhaps she did not have a playmate today. Only the early educator knows. The role of the early educator in facilitating play among children with special needs cannot be overstated and will be thoroughly explored in this chapter.

■ Play in Early Childhood Education

The value of play for development and growth for typically developing children has been well documented (Bredekamp & Copple, 1997; Piaget, 1962). It is perhaps even more important for children who have disabilities or delays. Cook, Tessier, and Klein (2000) acknowledged that "play is probably the single most important concept in early childhood special education" (p. 31). Play can lead to increased opportunities for social interaction and cognitive growth. The nature of the exceptional status—sensory loss, motoric, cognitive, or emotional—will affect play. For children with mild disabilities, play provides an arena that brings children with and without disabilities together. This may occur at home or in inclusive programs.

For children with more severe disabilities, play provides joy for the child and a sense of normalcy for the family. This may occur at home, in inclusive preschools, or in special settings. Information in this chapter is designed for early educators in *inclusive* settings. Specialized preparation can be obtained in special education programs and is required to work with children who have severe disabilities, who are medically fragile, or who are confined to a medical setting.

Federal Guidelines

In the seventies, public schools were required by PL 94.142 to include children with special needs in **natural environments.** A natural environment is defined as an environment where the child would naturally be if the child were not disabled. For very young children, natural environments include the home as well as family-based or group child care settings. With the passage of the Individuals with Disability Education Act (IDEA, 1997), preschool programs were required to serve young children with special needs. Now, both primary and preschool programs must

All children can play.

make reasonable accommodations to meet the needs of young children with disabilities or developmental delays. Although early educators strive to deliver programs that reflect best practices for *all* children, ensuring appropriate experiences for children who have special needs may appear daunting to even the most dedicated early educator. This chapter is designed to facilitate inclusion by providing specialized information for adapting play to meet the needs of children with delays or disabilities.

Professional Recommendations

Early interventionists and early childhood special educators belong to a professional organization, the Council of Exceptional Children Division of Early Childhood (CEC-DEC). Their publication, *The Division of Early Childhood Recommended Practices in Early Intervention/Early Childhood Special Education* (Sandall, McLean, & Smith, 2000), encourages play for children who have disabilities. "Children with and without special needs have been found to be more actively involved in activities they initiate themselves, in contrast to teacher-initiated activities" (Diamond, Hestenes, & O'Connor, 1994, p. 93). Participation in developmentally appropriate practices (DAP) is recommended; DAP encourages children to make choices, values the child's interest, and emphasizes play and enjoyment. The Division of Early Childhood (DEC) acknowledges the challenge involved in ensuring that activities, play, and assessments are developmentally appropriate for children with special needs.

DEC recommendations are provided in terms of direct and indirect services. Direct services include those services that directly involve the child and family. Direct services strands consist of:

- assessment
- child-focused interventions
- family-based practices
- interdisciplinary models
- technology applications

Indirect services are those that support the delivery of direct services. Indirect supports are comprised of:

- policy, procedures, and systems change
- personnel preparation

Early intervention occurs when infants and toddlers who have disabilities or delays receive special services to facilitate the child's development in the context of the family. The delivery of both direct and indirect services

The role of the adult is essential in ensuring the child's right to play.

directly affects early educators who are caring for and educating young children with special needs.

Research Base

Play for children who have special needs may differ from that usually found in child care centers. Put a ball in front of a two-year-old who is typically developing and the child will probably try to throw, hit, or kick the ball. Piaget's (1962) research found that children develop knowledge through action. A typically developing child can construct his knowledge of the ball by throwing, touching, and rolling it. A child who has a disability may or may not react to the placement of the ball in front of him. This is why it is essential that knowledgeable adults facilitate play. The adult must know how to intervene in a way that supports play. Adaptations vary based on the individual needs of the child. Adults who assist the child will need to know the child's diagnosis and possible avenues for encouraging play (Bicker & Cripe, 1992). Play for children with special needs may not look like what is typically viewed as play; for example, a child who has cerebral palsy may engage in a rocking behavior that may even be viewed by some as a self-stimulating activity, but for this child this may be his play.

All children can enjoy play. All children have the right to experience the joy and euphoria of play, but play is more than fun. Play is a medium for learning for all children including those with disabilities (Reynolds & Jones, 1997). Research studies have investigated the value of play for typically developing children for over a century. Only recently have scholars begun to examine the benefits of play for children with special needs (Cook, Tessier, & Klein, 2000). In attempting to understand how children with special needs play, it may be useful to look at the work of Jean Piaget (1962) and Lev Vygotsky (1978). Their theories and work in the area of play have implications for early childhood special educators and are described below.

Piaget

Piaget believed that children learn as they play and that the child's play is a direct reflection of the child's cognitive abilities (Piaget, 1962). For example, if a child is chronologically seven, his play should reflect the mastery of skills typical of his age. That is, the child should be engaging in dramatic play and games with rules. If, however, the child is chronologically seven but mentally two, the child may benefit more from play designed for the stage that preceds symbolic play: practice play. Piagetians might recommend exploratory or sensory play as a way to include the child in classroom settings and provide developmentally appropriate experiences for the child. For example, they might give the child in the scenario above a tub of sand to explore. Understanding the stages of play from a Piagetian perspective enables teachers to plan appropriate activities for the child.

Vygotsky

Vygotsky, on the other hand, viewed play differently. He viewed play as a vehicle for learning (1978). He believed that children who play together engage in the highest level of abstract thought prior to formal classroom instruction. Vygotsky believed that during play, children create the zone of proximal development (ZPD). The ZPD is created when the child moves from a state of knowing with the assistance of others to a state of knowing for oneself. Anyone who has learned to ride a bicycle has experienced the thrill of riding alone as he moved through the zone. Children who have disabilities create the zone of proximal development during play with more capable adults or peers. Children who do not move through the zone of proximal development may stay in a less mature level of play. When this occurs, the play may, indeed, reflect the child's cognitive level of development. The child has not been challenged to reach his potential. By exposing children to situations that foster pretend play, children can develop their abilities to engage in abstraction.

Current research

Although Vygotsky was the first to emphasize the role of the more capable peer or adult in facilitating play, recent studies concerning children who have special needs support this premise. Odum and Brown (1993) found that children who are typically developing do not regularly include children with disabilities in play groups. More recently, Brown and Bergen (2002) found that children were included only when an adult was present. Without adult intervention, children who have disabilities or delays may not have the opportunity to experience play.

■ Influences on Play

Right to Play

Several factors have improved the state of play for young children with disabilities or delays. One influence is the recognition of the child's right to play by the United Nations Convention on the Rights of the Child (1989) and the International Play Association for the Child's Right to Play (Guddemi & Jambor, 1993). The concept that all children have the right to play is now commonly accepted. Children who have disabilities or delays are *entitled* to play. For many years, the view that dominated the landscape was that children with special needs should spend their time in direct instruction learning skills and should not use their time to play (Hanline & Daley, 2002).

Play as a Natural Environment

Another factor that has impacted play is the support provided by the Division of Early Childhood (DEC). Some children are medically fragile and can only play with play therapists in hospital settings. Because the home is a natural environment for an infant or toddler, many programs for infants and toddlers are based in the home. Early interventionists visit the child and family in the home and provide play-based programs. Other children who are more stable face the challenge of time to play. Too often, traveling from hospital offices to specialized therapy offices does not leave time for play. More recently, Individualized Family Service Plans (IFSPs) have begun to view play as a way to acquire required skills and competencies and regularly include play as a goal in IFSP plans; IFSPs will be discussed further later in this chapter. The recognition of play as a viable medium for learning has legitimized play in the lives of children who have conditions requiring special assistance.

Global Influence

Another factor influencing play for children who have disabilities or delays is American exposure to the practices of the schools of Reggio Emilia, Italy. These schools provide a model for interested parents and early educators. They have been engaged in inclusion for very young children since the 1970s and are recognized for their excellent educational programs for young children with special needs. Children who have special needs are viewed as special citizens who have **special rights** (Smith, 1998). They believe that all children have multiple ways of expressing themselves that are not always evident to adults. They focus on ensuring the child's happiness at school. This is accomplished by accepting the many ways (or languages) that children use to express themselves and by delighting in the child. The child is included when he wants to be and not when he is tired or chooses not to do so. Though following the child's lead may be more difficult when the child has a communication delay or other disabilities, this idea has the potential to change how we view not only inclusion but also the child's right to play in his own unique way.

■ Role of Adults

The role of early educators and adults in creating a caring effective environment for young children with disabilities or delays cannot be overemphasized. As noted previously, early educators work with other adults to develop a plan of action and cooperation, they create an environment that facilitates play, they intervene to support play, they foster interaction among all children, and they assess the effectiveness of their actions on the child's development. Adults make a difference in the lives of young children with special needs.

Recommendations for supporting inclusion (Sluss, 2000) are included below.

1. Remember that children with disabilities are *children first*.
2. Use ***children-first language*** when you discuss the child. Never refer to the child by the name of the disability. For example, Twila who was mentioned in the PlayScape should always be referred to as Twila.
3. Identify sources of support in the community and school system. *Create a circle of support* for the child, family, and teachers. What are the federal resources available? What are the state resources available? What other resources and support are available? Every state has an early intervention network. Find out what resources are available.

4. *Build relationships* with family members, guardians, or other adults who care for the child and serve on the IFSP team. Communication is the key to building a relationship of mutual respect and trust.

5. Maintain *confidentiality* in all issues at all times.

6. *Make appropriate adaptations* for the child. Recognize that you do not know everything you need to know to about inclusion or about the child's disability or delay. Each child is unique and each disability is unique. Ask questions about how to adapt the classroom and materials to encourage interaction.

7. Use *assistive technology* when possible to facilitate the inclusive process.

8. *Support play*. An environment that encourages play for all children creates an optimal setting for inclusion.

9. Conduct *meaningful assessments* and make changes in the program to improve learner outcomes.

10. Remember that children with disabilities are *children first and that all children can play*.

■ Supporting Play in Inclusive Settings

Given the recent support for the play of children who have special needs, early educators have an opportunity to provide play-based programs that are developmentally appropriate for all children. This can be accomplished through active participation in the development of the **Individual Family Service Plan (IFSP)** and specialized knowledge of inclusion. An IFSP describes the child's goals and indicates how they will be met. This is a team process requiring interaction among the teacher, the parents, and early interventionists. Multiple goals and objectives can be met through play when teachers and parents are aware of the benefits of play for all children. **Inclusion** is defined as the integration of children with disabilities or delays in settings with typically developing children. *Inclusive settings* are places where children with and without special needs are involved in play and other educational activities.

Early educators must be aware of three major differences in the play of children with delays or disabilities. As discussed previously, children with special needs may not always initiate play. They may not engage in play on their own. Teachers must intervene to encourage play and to foster strategies that will encourage self-generated play. Second, the nature of their special condition will affect their play. For example, a child who has cerebral palsy and is in a wheelchair may need specialized assistance in

The role of early educators is critical in assuring that play is a part of the IFSP.

motor areas but may be able to challenge anyone to a competitive game of chess. A child who has visual impairments may need special assistance to participate in the chess game but can move throughout the room with minimal assistance. *Play for children with special needs must be individualized to reflect the child's assets.* Third, their play may not look like typical play. Each child will have a unique way of playing. Teachers must know the child well enough to understand their unique play (Cook, Tessier, & Klein, 2000). These ideas are applicable to all developmental levels, infants through primary school.

Infant and Toddler Centers

Inclusion of all children in child care settings begins in the infant-toddler center. Though some children with disabilities or delays are still undergoing medical treatment or may still be hospitalized, those who can participate in a group setting should be encouraged to do so. When a parent of a child with a disability places their child in a center, it has several benefits. First, it provides normalcy for the family. They are just like other families when picking up their children from a center. The other outcome is that it allows the parent to work or rest at home. Often, parents of children with disabilities or delays do not receive any respite from 24-hour, seven-day-a-week care. It does, however, require additional knowledge and adaptations on the part of the early educators. Centers that include infants with disabilities or delays may need additional staff to facilitate inclusion. One of the ancillary benefits is that families of typically developing children interact with children who have disabilities on a regular basis. This fosters interaction between all children and families in a community setting.

Preschool Centers

Inclusion in preschool centers may be a continuation of involvement in an infant-toddler center or it may be the child's and the family's first experience in a group setting. A curriculum that is developmentally appropriate for typically developing children may need adaptations for a child with disabilities or delays. The plan for a child who has disabilities must be tailored for the individual needs of the child. The IFSP should included a plan for transitioning into the public school setting. **Transition** is a term used to describe the process that occurs when the child in a preschool setting (birth to age three) that has been under the auspices of federal guidelines and funding is moved to a preschool setting (age three) that is funded and regulated by the state educational system. Sometimes transitions are very smooth as the child moves easily from one system to another. Other transitions are very difficult as the child and family become tangled in bureaucracy. Early educators should take an active role in ensuring that transitions are appropriate and occur in a way that optimizes the child's growth and development.

Primary Settings

It is especially important at this age that teachers take a proactive role in encouraging social interactions among all children. Primary-age children have a special need to belong at this age and children who display any apparent differences may not be treated kindly by others who are trying to belong to a specific group. Relational bullying occurs and may go unnoticed by adults. Children with disabilities or delays are sometimes targeted by bullies. Adults must ensure that all children who are in group settings are safe from bullying and abuse.

■ Child-focused Interventions in Inclusive Settings

Inclusion can be facilitated through child-focused intervention. **Child-focused intervention** is a term that refers to the

decisions and practices used to structure and provide learning opportunities for children. These decisions and practices include how children are taught (i.e., the strategies, and practices used to ensure learning), when and where the instructional practices and arrangements are implemented, and how children's performance is monitored to make decisions about modifying the interventions and identification of these goals. (Sandall, McLean, & Smith, 2000, p. 29)

All aspects of the child's educational program are included in this term.

Child-focused intervention involves (1) designing appropriate environments, (2) individualizing and adapting the curriculum, and (3) using systematic procedures to optimize outcomes. The three components are discussed in the following section.

Designing Appropriate Environments

The major goal of environmental design is to ensure that children are active and engaged members of the learning community. This is accomplished by looking at different aspects of the environmental design.

Physical environment

The first and most basic requirement involves physical safety and accessibility. Classrooms must meet all guidelines established by the state and local agencies. Children must be able to play in the classroom and on the playground without endangering their health or safety. Children who cannot reach the table cannot play checkers. Children who cannot move a walker on a rug in the block center cannot play with the blocks. Children who are not mobile cannot, without special assistance, enjoy the fresh air or joy of watching a kite fly up toward the clouds. Though this seems to be a basic need, children who have disabilities or developmental delays sometimes visit learning labs during recess or center time or leave the family center during outdoor play time. Children who have disabilities need scheduled time for play as well as play spaces that are physically accessible.

Social dimension

Psychological safety is critically important. The need for physical safety is sometimes obvious, especially when working with children who have physical disabilities. Psychological safety is equally important. Children who have disabilities sometimes face a type of relational bullying that may go unnoticed by adults. For example, the other children may choose to leave a center when a child who can benefit from special assistance enters the play area. This may not be obvious to someone who is just looking across a room of children, but it is obvious to the child who is trying to enter play. Early educators must not allow this abuse to continue in a classroom. Adults must also model positive interactions with children who have special needs. They can provide a safe environment by acknowledging without reprimanding the child's play that may look very different from the play that typically occurs in the classroom. If children are reprimanded when they attempt to retrieve a ball by reaching for it with their foot, they are less likely to repeat the behavior. This may stop their play. Children who have disabilities need a psychologically safe classroom in which optimal play can occur. This should not be translated as letting the child create chaos. Rather it means that everyone must respect the rights of all children in the classroom. Understanding that play for children who have disabilities or delays may be unfamiliar to other children and adults is a crucial first step in facilitating play for children with special needs.

Play as curriculum

The environment is designed to encourage play and interactions among all children. Many IFSPs will include play activities that can occur in the classroom. To facilitate play by all children in the class, the class must be set up to encourage this. It may mean that the easels are arranged so that a child in a wheelchair can paint beside a child who is standing. It may mean that the pictures of play areas are large enough for children who are visually impaired to read, or it may mean that music starts prior to the end of play so children who have difficulty moving to new activities will have a clear indication that play is ending and other activities will occur.

Intervention

The environment is designed to encourage intervention in a child's natural environment with minimal disruption to the child's schedule. When the child meets with the early interventionist (EI), the EI is responsible for the child's safety and security. Intervention that occurs in a natural setting benefits the child because it is a natural part of the class experience. Creating an optimal environment for inclusion also involves the *delivery of instruction* and is presented in the next section.

Individualizing and Adapting Instructional Practices

Goals for the individual child who has special needs are developed by a team composed of the child's family, early educators, early interventionists and other specialists based on the child's individual disability or delay. The child's abilities are aligned with state guidelines by team members

Play is an essential part of a young child's life.

who develop an Individual Family Service Plan. Many IFSPs include play as a goal or as a means to a goal. A plan for collecting data must also be devised and approved by the team. A summary of the collected data provides a picture of the child in context and is used to guide interactions and instruction during play.

The early educator has an active role in implementing the play activities included in the IFSP. It is the early educator who makes a difference. The importance of adults during interactions among children with and without special needs has been noted in several classic studies. Harper and McCluskey (2003) conducted a study of teacher/child and child/child interactions in inclusive preschool settings. They observed interactions of 24 preschoolers (three-to-four-year-olds) during free play time. Half of the children had disabilities and half did not. The proportion of time that preschoolers spent talking to peers and to adults was negatively correlated. Whenever teachers and children initiated conversations or interactions, the child was less likely to initiate or engage in interaction with peers. Early educators who know when and how to talk to children can foster inclusion.

On the other hand, those who do not know how and when to talk to children may actually be training the child to interact only with adults.

Teachers can avert this situation by fully understanding the concept of *scaffolding* and implementing different scaffolding techniques on a consistent basis. First, all adults in the setting must understand the difference between helping and scaffolding and know when to use each appropriately. Helping occurs when the adult or more competent peer provides support that enables the child to function in the current context. For example, picking up a toy for a child who is struggling to retrieve the object from the floor may appear to be the appropriate action. This *helps* the child by placing the toy in his hand. This action enables the child to play in the current context. In contrast, *scaffolding* occurs when the more competent other *assists and guides* the child in developing a better strategy for retrieving the object. Scaffolding is an assistive strategy that can be used in the current context but enables the child to do it on his own later. In this way, the zone of proximal development is actualized as the child moves along the continuum of independence.

Using Systematic Procedures

The most important aspect of the environment is the adult—the teacher or interventionist—in the classroom. Mature play occurs when knowledgeable adults facilitate play (Reynolds & Jones, 1997). When Stanley Greenspan (1998) demonstrated a game of catch to parents of a child with autism, he demonstrated a technique that the parent(s) could use to work with their child. As they tossed the bean bag together, they facilitated the child's ability to focus on the bean bag and the child became sufficiently competent to toss and catch the bean bag on his own. The child moved through what Vygotsky calls the ZPD. That is, although he was unable to play alone when he began, he could toss and catch the object without assistance after a great deal of play. Of course, this happened gradually. It did not occur overnight. This process required adults who knew how to enhance play.

One program that features planned activities that encourage play is the *Activity-based Approach to Early Intervention* developed by Diane Bricker and Juliann Cripe (1992). Some examples of planned activities include water play, play dough, dress-up, and fire station. Activities such as these encourage play by all children in the setting.

■ Models of Program Delivery

Inclusive programs should reflect program delivery as recommended by the Council for Exceptional Children—Division of Early Childhood

(2000). DEC (Sandall, McLean, & Smith, 2000, pp. 53–54) recommends an interdisciplinary model that is comprised of

- ◆ teams including family members who make decisions and work together.
- ◆ professionals who cross disciplinary boundaries.
- ◆ intervention focused on function, not services.
- ◆ regular caregivers and regular routines providing the most appropriate opportunities for children's learning and receiving most other interventions.

These strands can be interwoven to create a model for developing a play-based program. First, all adults who interact with the child are considered stakeholders and must be involved equally in decisions and assume responsibility for those decisions. Second, everyone must acknowledge the contributions that everyone on the team makes to benefit the child. Third, the intervention must be focused on function, not service delivery. That is, interventions ". . . should be those that are necessary for the child's engagement, independence, and social relationships in the context in which he or she lives and those that are immediately useful to the child" (Sandall, McLean, & Smith, 2000, p. 49). If a child needs a piece of equipment to be able to move to the playground, then the entire team should view this as a collective goal. Fourth, learning is holistic, so intervention should be as simple as possible and fit within the context of the group setting. This view values the early educator as an integral part of the child's intervention and values play as a medium for learning. It is therefore imperative that early educators are knowledgeable in ways to enhance and foster play with all children. These guidelines should be evident in all inclusive programs for young children as described in the following sections.

■ Family-based Practices

It is imperative that families form partnerships with the adults who work with the child throughout the day and who provide intervention on a weekly basis. These partnerships benefit the child and all adults involved in the process. If a child develops an interest in playing with blocks at school, then the parent(s) may want to encourage block play at home. If the child has been playing with paper that he crushes into a ball at home, this may be viewed negatively unless the early educator knows that the child has been playing at home with crushed paper. When families and professionals work together, the child benefits and play progresses.

Focusing on the child's strengths and capabilities instead of what the child cannot do fosters a positive relationship between the family and team members. By focusing on what the child achieves, the child is measured in terms of his own abilities. Instead of using a measure that reflects typical development, the measure reflects the child and the child's individual strengths, abilities, and rate of growth. If developmental levels based on chronological age were used, the five-year-old might be expected to engage in sociodramatic play. When the child could not meet this set goal, both parents and professionals would be disappointed. By looking at the child in terms of his current level of sensorimotor play, a more positive picture is created.

■ Assistive Technology

Assistive technology has been defined as "any item, piece of equipment, or product, whether acquired commercially, off the shelf, modified, or customized, that is used to increase, maintain, or improve the functional capabilities of individuals with disabilities. Also includes instructional technology" (Sandall, McLean, & Smith, 2000, p. 165). Many teachers think of computers and computerized boards when assistive technology is mentioned, but adding knobs to a puzzle so a child can solve the puzzle is also assistive technology. Assistive technology ranges from the very simple to the very complex.

Assistive technology makes play possible.

Toys

Adults can encourage social interaction through the selection of toys. Toys for children who have disabilities may need to be adapted. For example, if an airplane on the toy shelf requires fine motor skills to manipulate, why not add another airplane that a child who is less coordinated can use. If a truck is available that requires turning a wind-up key, find another truck that can be adapted by adding a larger knob. Adaptations will need to be specific to the child's disability. In general, *toys should be accessible, adaptable, and lead to cooperative interaction.*

Accessible

Some toys in the center should be accessible to all children. Preschoolers should be able to access blocks, dolls, books, or balls without a teacher's assistance. One caveat is that some children become overstimulated by too many available materials. If this is creating a problem, rotate toys on a regular basis. A survey of the room can determine the level of accessibility of the toys and play materials. Consider the needs of the individual children. Materials for art should be accessible to children in wheelchairs. If a child has visual impairments, signs with large pictures or signs in braille can be used depending on the child's degree of impairment. Ensuring that the placement of the shelves and materials is stable will help children navigate the classroom.

Adaptable

Toys can be adapted with low-tech or high-tech changes. When most educators think of assistive technology, they think of computers and computerized systems and accessories. These are effective and necessary for some children. When these are recommended by the IFSP, someone trained in assistive technology will assist in implementing these systems. Switches are also high-technology changes that have positive results. The addition of switches allows the child to play independently with other children. He can experience cause-and-effect and this adds to his sense of accomplishment. In addition, the child has a special toy that other children may also enjoy. An electrical switch is a device that can be added to toys to allow children with limited dexterity to control them. For example, when a switch is added to a child's CD player, the child pushes the switch and the machine starts to play the music. Adding a switch to a toy flashlight allows the child to push the switch and control the electrical impulse that operates the light. In the same way, a switch can be added to a toy that requires a physical action such as a cow that moos, a jack-in-the box, or a car with wheels. When a switch is added, winding the toy is unnecessary. The action is controlled by lightly touching the electrical switch.

Kits for converting toys are commonly available in most areas and can be ordered through the Internet. Switches can also be added to a radio so the child can turn it on unassisted.

Low-tech adaptations are just as useful and can be done by adults in the classroom. Adaptations that use minimal technology include adding large knobs to puzzles, adding Velcro™ to blocks, or adding grips to crayons and markers. Simple items such as muffin pans and soft balls can be turned into a game. The muffin pan with soft, multicolored pom-poms is generally recommended as the infant's first puzzle but is equally effective with children who have motor delays. Materials for art can also be adapted for children with visual or auditory impairments. Adding aromas like vanilla to play dough extends the experience for children who have visual impairments. Putting marbles in a rubber ball allows children with visual impairments to feel the movement of the marbles/objects inside the ball. Again, it is important to emphasize that the changes should reflect the needs of the individual child.

Cooperative interaction

Toys should be selected to encourage cooperation. Balls encourage interaction between two children when they roll or toss them to each other. Wagons and toys that require two children encourage cooperation. Water play and house play are also designed to stimulate social play. Adults can select toys that facilitate social interaction. For example, if the only blocks available are soft cloth blocks, the child may be content to carry and stack—or even sit on the blocks! Placing different blocks or firefighter hats in the block center provides the child with props that can encourage dramatic or more mature play. It is critically important that children with disabilities have the opportunity to engage in more mature play with their more competent peers. Adapting materials for children who have special needs fosters inclusion.

When children play together, the play is greater than the sum of its parts. Yes, it may be water play, encouraging physical (gross and fine motor development), social (interactions with other children), and cognitive development (sensory stimulation, language development). But, it is more; it is enjoyable. Children are playing and they are having fun. This is the essence of play for all children.

■ Assessing Play

Evaluating play involves observation, assessment, and reflection. Early childhood special education has pioneered transdisciplinary play-based assessment. This occurs when a team of specialists simultaneously observe a child at play and assess different aspects of the child's play and interactions.

When planning optimal programs for children, begin by focusing on what they can do rather than what they cannot do. In the same way, when planning play, focus on what the children can do. Begin by valuing a child's unique style of play and then facilitate movement to a more mature level. In this way, adults enhance not only growth and development, but also the quality of the child's life.

PlayScape Reflections

Sheena did not know what Twila experienced during the day by looking at her. She may not be able to clearly communicate that her day was filled with play that included block and sand play. She may not be able to tell her that she saw her physical therapist, Mary Beth, who provided intervention while she was playing outdoors. She may not be able to tell her that she ate lunch with two friends. Though Sheena may not know what happened today, she has a reasonably good idea of what she should be experiencing based on her knowledge of the goals on her IFSP. She will find out exactly how much she is gaining from the experiences when she meets with her team in two weeks. For now, she is satisfied that Twila is responsive to her request to leave for the day. She gathers her equipment, checks her medicine for her allergies, and stops for a hug from Twila's teacher, Tamara, as they head home—with Sheena satisfied that she made the right choice to place her child in an inclusive center that encourages play and friendship.

■ Summary

Play is an important part of childhood for all children and is especially important for children who have disabilities or delays. This chapter focused on the role of play in early childhood special education. Factors that influence play in early special education include governmental regulations, professional recommendations, and global issues. Strategies for supporting play in inclusive settings were presented for infant-toddler centers, preschools, and primary classrooms. Suggestions for adapting toys and materials were also listed. Play can be supported by designing interventions that focus on the environment, instructional adaptations, and assessment. Family collaboration is essential for the successful development and implementation of IFSPs. When adaptations are required, assistive technology can be used to promote not only cognitive development, but also social interaction and development. The most effective assessment occurs in the child's natural environment and is referred to as transdisciplinary play-based assessment.

■ Key Terms

Assistive technology
Child-focused intervention
Children-first language
Early intervention

Individual Family Service
*   Plan (IFSP)*
Inclusion
Natural environment

Special rights
Transition

■ Helpful Web Sites and Technology Resources

◆ **Office of Special Education Programs (OSEP)**
http://www.ed.gov   Official site of OSEP. This site provides information on infants, toddlers, and children with disabilities ages birth through twenty-one. This Web site has a great deal of information about IDEA and maintains excellent links to other high-quality sites. Nonprofit agency.

◆ **Special Education Resources on the Internet (SERI)**
http://seriweb.com   Special Education Resources on the Internet (SERI) is a collection of Internet-accessible information resources of interest to those involved in the fields related to special education. This collection exists in order to make on-line special education resources more easily and readily available in one location. This site will continually modify, update, and add additional informative links. Nonprofit agency.

◆ **NECTAC site**
http://www.nectac.org   This Web site is designed for professionals and provides links to a variety of resources. NECTAC is a program of the Frank Porter Graham Child Development Institute of the University of North Carolina at Chapel Hill, funded through contract number ED-01-CO-0112 from the Office of Special Education Programs, U.S. Department of Education. Nonprofit agency.

◆ **ISEI site**
http://depts.washington.edu/isei   The ISEI Web site is located at the Center on Human Development and Disability at the University of Washington in Seattle. This site includes links to the ISEI Coordinating Committee, membership directory, publications information, and other related resources. Nonprofit agency.

◆ **Family Resource Database**
http://fcsn.org   Contains information about agencies in Massachusetts and throughout the United States that provide information and/or services to families. Nonprofit agency.

■ Activities

1. **InClass Lab**

   A. Bring at least one toy to class that can be used by children who are typically developing. How can this be adapted to meet the needs of children who have different disabilities such as blindness, physical impairments, hearing loss, or other disability?

   B. Look at the classroom design created in Chapter 6. How will this plan work for a child who has a motoric disability? What modifications will you need to make for other disabilities?

2. **Research and Inquiry**

   A. Spend two hours in an inclusive classroom. Complete a running record. What kind of play occurred in the classroom? What did adults do to encourage play?

   B. Participate in a local IFSP or IEP meeting. Did you understand all the acronyms that were used? Did you understand all the laws referenced? Was play included in the plan? If so, in what ways?

   C. Investigate programs for children with special needs in the schools of Reggio Emilia, Italy. Compare their program with a generic program in the United States. What factors impact the programs?

3. **Service Learning**

   A. Volunteer to help with the local Special Olympics.

   B. Contact a preschool teacher in an inclusive classroom. Volunteer to assist in making adaptations in the classroom or to toys or materials.

4. **Family Connections**

   A. Interview a parent who has a child with a special need. Volunteer to provide child care for the child one afternoon or evening as a way of expressing appreciation for their time. The parent(s) may accept or reject the offer based on their perceptions and/or needs.

FIGURE 8–1   Read More about Play

Blakely, K., Lang. M., & Sosna, B. (1995). *Toys & play: A guide to fun and development for children with impaired vision.* New York: The Lighthouse Inc.

Johnson, J., Christie, J., & Yawkey, T. (1999). *Play and early childhood development.* New York: Longman.

Monighan-Nourot, P., Scales, B., Van Hoorn, J., & Almy, M. (1987). *Looking at children's play: A bridge between theory and practice.* New York: Teachers College Press.

Morris, L., & Schulz, L. (1989). *Creative play activities for children with disabilities.* Champaign, IL: Human Kinectics Books.

Paley, V. (1990). *The boy who would be helicopter.* Cambridge, MA: Harvard University Press.

Paley, V. (1992). *You can't say you can't play.* Cambridge, MA: Harvard University Press.

Scales, B., Almy, M., Nicolopoulou, A., & Ervin-Tripp, S. (1991). *Play and the social context of development in early care and education.* New York: Teachers College Press.

Tertell, E., Klein, S., & Jewett, J. (Eds.) (1998). *When teachers reflect: Journeys toward effective, inclusive practice.* Washington, DC: National Association for the Education of Young Children.

5. **Play Advocacy**

   A. Attend a meeting of a local Council for Exceptional Children student meeting. What issues are similar to those discussed in other student meetings? What issues are unique?

   B. Contact your local newspaper. Do they feature articles on individuals who have special needs? Citizens who are not visible do not exist. Are citizens with disabilities visible in your community?

   C. Distribute the list of reading materials in Figure 8–1 at a local teacher's meeting or community meeting.

■ References

Bicker, D., & Cripe, J. (1992). *An activity-based approach to early intervention.* Baltimore: Brooks.

Bredekamp, S., & Copple, C. (1997). *Developmentally appropriate practice in early childhood programs.* Washington, DC: National Association for the Education of Young Children.

Brown, M., & Bergen, D. (2002). Play and social interaction of children with disabilities at learning/activity centers in an inclusive preschool. *Journal of Research in Childhood Education, 17* (1), 26–37.

Cook, R., Tessier, A., & Klein, M. D. (2000). *Adapting early childhood curricula for children in inclusive settings* (5th ed.). Englewood Cliffs, NJ: Merrill.

Diamond, K. E., Hestenes, L. L., & O'Connor, C. D. (1994). Integrating young children with disabilities in preschool: Problems and promise. *Young Children, 4* (2), 68–75.

Greenspan, S. (1998). The child with special needs: Encouraging intellectual and emotional growth. Presentation to the OSEP Early Childhood Projects Meeting. Washington, DC.

Guddemi, M., & Jambor, T. (1993). *A right to play: Proceedings of the American Affiliate of the International Association for the Child's Right to Play*, Little Rock, AK: Southern Early Childhood Association.

Hanline, M., & Daley, S. (2002). "Mom, Will Kaelie always have possibilities?"—The realities of early childhood inclusion. *Phi Delta Kappan, 84* (1), 73.

Harper, L., & McCLuskey, K. (2003). Teacher-child and child-child interactions in inclusive preschool settings: Do adults inhibit peer interactions. *18* (2), 163–184.

Individuals with Disabilities Education Act P.L. 101-476. Stat. 1103 (1990) (codified as amended at 20 U.S.C. Secs. 1400-1485) (1997).

Marchant, C., & Brown, C. (1996). The role of play in inclusive early childhood settings. In A. Phillips, *Playing for keeps* (pp. 127–140). St. Paul, MN: Redleaf Press.

Monighan-Nourot, P., Scales, B., Van Hoorn, J., & Almy, M. (1987). *Looking at children's play: A bridge between theory and practice*. New York: Teachers College Press.

Odum, S., & Brown, W. (1993). Social interaction skills intervention for young children with disabilities in integrated settings. In C. Peck, S. Odum, & D. Bicker (Eds.), *Integrating young children with disabilities into community programs* (pp. 39–64). Baltimore: Brooks.

Piaget, J. (1962). *Play, dreams, and imitation in childhood*. New York: Norton.

Reynolds, G., & Jones, E. (1997). *Master players: Learning from children at play*. New York: Teachers College Press.

Sandall, S., McLean, M., & Smith, B. (2000). *DEC recommended practices in early intervention/early childhood special education*. Longmont, CO: Sophis West.

Sluss, D. (2000). *Towards inclusion in early education (TIES) training manual*. Johnson City, TN: East Tennessee State University (Grant Number HO24B60032-97).

Smith, C. (1998). Children with "Special Rights" in the preprimary schools and infant-toddler Centers of Reggio Emilia. In C. Edwards, L. Gandini, & G. Foreman (Eds.), *The hundred languages of children*. (pp. 199–214) Greenwich, CT: Ablex.

Vygotsky, L. (1978). *Mind in society: The development of higher mental processes*. Cambridge, MA: Harvard University.

CHAPTER 9

Outdoor Play for Young Children

There's no way we can help children to learn to love and preserve this planet, if we don't give them direct experiences with the miracles and blessings of nature.

—*Anita Olds, 2001*

Chapter Overview

The outdoor environment provides rich opportunities for play. Adults can support outdoor play by understanding different types of play that occur outdoors, activities that promote play, and interactions that encourage cognitive, social, emotional, and physical development. This chapter is designed to provide information necessary for supporting outdoor play with an emphasis on rough-and-tumble play.

Objectives

After reading this chapter you should be able to:

◆ Describe the benefits of outdoor play.

◆ Identify different types of playgrounds.

◆ Discuss major types of play that occur on playgrounds.

◆ Differentiate outdoor play for infants and toddlers, preschoolers, and primary-age children.

◆ Explain the benefits of rough-and-tumble play.

◆ Investigate assessment in outdoor environments.

291

> ## *PlayScape*
>
> *Exiting the school, Phillipi could feel the excitement of the children around him. When they reached the outdoor playground, they ran. Some went to the equipment, some to the trees, some to the grassy area, and a few to a covered area. He noticed the boys challenging each other to play toss. They chose teams and he noticed the leadership skills of William. The girls had already started jump rope games complete with the latest chants. Others played chase. The morning recess provided just the right break in the morning. He could make it until lunch if he could just get a chance to play.*
>
> ## *Play Provocation*
>
> The scenario could have occurred in 1790, 1890, 1990, or 2004. Children need little provocation to play outdoors. Though culture does influence chants and games, high-quality playgrounds and play spaces provide children with optimal challenges that encourage developmentally appropriate outdoor play. Infants and toddlers enjoy touching and moving everything. Preschoolers want to run, climb, and jump. Kindergarteners begin making their own pretend games. Primary-age children begin to play exclusively with their own gender, pay attention to rules, and develop their own sense of competency in physical areas. Outdoor play is natural for young children. Adults who support outdoor play optimize natural opportunities for play and learning.

■ Benefits of Outdoor Play

> *Man is perfectly human only when he plays.*
>
> —*Friedrich Schiller, 1954*

Playing outdoors benefits children in all areas. When children play outdoors, they have more opportunities to run and play with friends. Locomotor skills are developed and social interactions are promoted. Young children benefit from fresh air and the opportunity to explore natural environments, touch grass, look at clouds, and watch leaves fall or flowers bloom. Jean-Jacques Rousseau wrote of the benefits of nature over three centuries ago. Current research supports outdoor play for growth and development (Frost, Wortham, & Reifel, 2001). A study that looked at four dimensions of play—physical versus constructive play, change and stability

Nature creates a natural laboratory for learning.

continuum, freedom and control dimension, and differences in adult-child interactions—found that outdoor play is more open than indoor play (Stephenson, 2002). This supports the need to ensure outdoor play opportunities for all children.

Outdoor play is unique in that it

◆ *provides opportunities to engage in freely chosen play*. Children can choose when and where they play during outdoor play. Though adults control indoor activities, children can freely choose their outdoor play. They can choose rough-or-tumble, pretend, or games with rules. This may be the only time during the day when they can control their activity level.

◆ *creates a unique environment for learning*. Outdoor play areas create an environment with multiple opportunities for learning. It is difficult to understand wind or the movement of clouds from reading a book. The value of actual experience was emphasized by Dewey (1930) over a century ago. Many schools are creating outdoor laboratories to encourage interaction with natural environments.

◆ *encourages different levels of social participation as children self-select playmates*. Children can choose to play with a group, with a friend, or alone. During a game of chase, all children may participate. During a game of jump rope or tag, a smaller group may play in isolation. When children are on the playground, they can freely choose to play with boys, with girls, or with no one. This is the richness of outdoor play.

Children can disengage if they so desire. They can sit alone and stare at the sky if they choose. They select their level of social engagement.

◆ *develops standards of morality during interactions with peers and more competent others.* Children transmit cultural norms during play with peers. Younger children who play with older children learn the rules of the society and alter them to meet their needs. Piaget (1997) observed this social interaction on the streets of Geneva, Switzerland. Children who were not told the rules at the beginning of games learned them as they interacted with others. Sometimes the rules changed, but the children knew who could and who could not change the rules—and when. Outdoor play provides a context that encourages children to compromise and collaborate as they become members of the group.

The mechanism for transmitting cultural norms during outdoor play occurs through chants, rhymes, and rituals used during games. In their classic studies of children during outdoor play, Opie and Opie (1959) found that children used chants and rhymes that dated back to the seventeenth and eighteenth centuries though adults had not shared these with them. Children on the playground transmit their songs, chants, and rhymes to each other. These are not transmitted from adults to children, but rather from child to child. Outdoor play creates a special context for the transmission of children's culture.

◆ *encourages physical movement and good health.* One of the most important roles of recess is to improve the level of physical fitness in today's child. "Recent surveys have discovered that 40% of our young children have significant cardiac risk factors including obesity, high blood pressure, high cholesterol, and an inactive life style" (National Association of Early Childhood Specialists in State Departments of Education, 2003). Many children are not getting enough exercise to develop healthy hearts and lungs. Another cause for concern is obesity. In October 1999 the Agriculture Department released a report that revealed a record 10 million American children—or one in five—are overweight, and that a record 8% of the children are already overweight by preschool age (National Association of Early Childhood Specialists in State Departments of Education, 2003).

Other organizations concerned about the state of childhood obesity have recommended increased levels of activity and, specifically, outdoor recess. These organizations include the American Medical Association (2004), the American Heart Association (2004), National Center for Health Statistics (2004), and the American Academy of Child and Adolescent Psychiatry (2004).

■ Play Spaces

Although outdoor play seems natural and spontaneous, the quality of play can be enhanced through high-quality inclusive playgrounds and the support of adults. A look at a community or school play space provides a mirror of the community. Some areas have play spaces that reflect the most current research and equipment. They invite children to enter, run, and play. Other regions have playgrounds with two or three pieces of equipment on an asphalt surface—or none at all. Children play because there are no other places to play. Even worse, some communities have no places that are safe for young or old. Cars parked on vacant lots, drug dealers on the corner, and unsafe streets cause children to stay indoors behind locked doors. These children only see the outdoor world as they travel to and from their homes. These differences make a real and visible difference in the daily lives of the children. If we are to create an educated citizenry appreciative of nature and the natural environment, children must have outdoor experiences that enrich their lives.

Outdoor play areas range from unstructured open spaces where children happen to gather to fenced-in, heavily supervised playgrounds. The full continuum is described below. For a full review of the history of playgrounds, see *Children's Play and Playgrounds* (1983) by Joe Frost and Barry Klein, and *Play and Child Development* (2001) by Joe Frost, Sue Wortham, and Stuart Reifel.

Natural Play Spaces

Natural play spaces are identified as those areas that are not defined by adults but provide a space for children to play. For example, a local park may have open areas that are not defined as playgrounds but that children use for running, tumbling, and chasing. The National Park Service has many open areas that provide space for play that are not specifically designed as playgrounds. Too often, outdoor play is equated only with outdoor playgrounds. High-quality playgrounds provide a well-defined, safe environment for children, but this should not define how we view outdoor play. Many modern schools are including outdoor areas that expand their classroom activities. Though these do not fit the definition of a playground per se, play occurs.

Defined Play Spaces

Defined play spaces are just that. They are areas that are set aside for children's play. This is the precursor of the traditional playground. Defined play spaces are used by groups like the !Kung tribe in Africa. Adults throughout the world realize the child's need to play and some set aside space for play. David Elkind (1981) warned of the disappearance of play spaces and playgrounds in urban areas three decades ago. Defined play spaces still exist in some communities, but too often defined play spaces have given way to soccer fields, tee-ball and little league, or other sports activities. In America, noncompetitive play does not enjoy the same level of support as competitive sports.

Traditional Playgrounds

Traditional playgrounds first appeared in the 1920s (Frost, 1992). G. Stanley Hall is considered the founder of the American playground movement. He believed children should be encouraged to play out their natural evolution from monkey to human by swinging on equipment like the monkey bars. Though spaces with equipment can encourage play, too often playgrounds include monkey bars, a slide, and swings over asphalt surrounded by a chain link fence. This type of playground only encourages limited movement. More often than not, these playgrounds encourage accidents. The National Program for Playground Safety (NPPS) (2003) reports that over 200,000 children are injured on playgrounds every year. The NPPS has launched a campaign to remove animal equipment from the playground. Animal toys look like plastic models of lions, zebras, horses, etc., that are placed on large coil springs. The springs will not remain in the ground and children fall when they attempt to ride these, or worse, they fly through the air when the coil comes out of the ground. Because they can rock back and forth, they can receive a very severe fall when they are tossed through the air. Unlike children, these asphalt playgrounds with iron equipment are almost indestructible.

Contemporary Playgrounds

Contemporary playgrounds encourage a great variety of play. These playgrounds generally have diverse ground coverings and an assortment of equipment designed for a variety of ages and levels. Contemporary play structures are generally made of wood and have tire swings, slides with platforms at the top, and areas for climbing. These playgrounds include driving areas for tricycles, wagons, and buggies, and shaded areas that provide a variety of physical challenges. Some modern designs look very colorful and contemporary but on closer inspection are really very traditional. Playgrounds that are the most appropriate for children have the following characteristics. They

- ◆ have been checked for safety using the NPPS guidelines which can be found on-line.
- ◆ include a variety of ground coverings that meet safety standards.
- ◆ create multiple opportunities for movement.
- ◆ encourage play for all children who have multiple skill levels. Slides have a variety of levels and ladders with platforms and steps are available.
- ◆ facilitate different kinds of movement. The child can move up and down, sideways, tumble, climb, crawl, and jump.
- ◆ encourage creative pretense. Good equipment is open ended and encourages sociodramatic play.
- ◆ include materials that are translucent and provide places where children can look at and talk to other children through a variety of openings.

Community or Adventure Playgrounds

The adventure playground movement started after World War II in the Scandinavian countries and spread throughout Europe reaching England in the 1960s. Today, Denmark and other Scandinavian countries still lead the world in playgrounds, but England is making headway. In contrast, there are very few adventure playgrounds in America today.

The adventure playground movement started in Copenhagen, Denmark, with spaces that allowed children to build, tear down, and build again. Adventure playgrounds employ an adult who is the play leader. The leader is available to assist in the play and ensure a supply of materials. The area for the playground ranges between a half acre and four acres. Animals live in many of these and some resemble a small farm with growing plants, flowers, and greenhouses. The children and adults are encouraged to work in these areas and many families grow vegetables.

Unlike playgrounds with either a chain link fence or no fence, adventure playgrounds are enclosed by a wood fence that has a gate wide enough for a truck to enter. These fences do two things, first they shield the public from messy play because when children are building, the playground may be cluttered. Second, they provide privacy for children at play. Given America's obsession with safety, it is amazing that more playgrounds are not enclosed by wood fences. A building for storing materials and rainy day play is always available and bathroom facilities are located within the building.

Inclusive Playgrounds

A recent trend in America has been the development of playgrounds designed for children with disabilities or delays. This is the result of the American with Disabilities Act of 1990 and the 1997 IDEA amendments (Individuals with Disabilities Education Act, 1997). All children with disabilities have the right to access any public facility. As public areas, playgrounds should be free and open to everyone. All playgrounds should be inclusive, this has been set aside as a separate category because new playgrounds provide access for all children and are designed to allow simultaneous play with typically developing peers. Inclusive playgrounds are designed to allow children with disabilities or delays to access areas so they experience play with other children. Paved walkways are parallel with steps for climbing. This allows friends to move along the playground together. Similarly, sandboxes are built so that children in wheelchairs can play alongside others in the sand. Several nonprofit groups are dedicated to establishing inclusive playgrounds. Kaboom! and Boundless Playgrounds are two nonprofit groups that are involved in creating playgrounds for all children. See Helpful Web Sites and Technology Resources at the end of this chapter for their Web sites.

Theme-based Playgrounds

Some playgrounds have been developed around a theme with specific learning outcomes in mind. The idea is that children will enjoy the outdoor play and learn content material incidentally. One example of this concept is the Science Playground in Flushing Meadows Park, New York. It is the largest science playground in the Western Hemisphere with 30,000 square feet of space. "The science play ground is packed with exhibits that invite not only hands on, but whole body participation through the use of giant slides, whisper dishes, water play areas, light activated kinetic sculptures, and a teeter-totter that balances a dozen children" (Hymes-Dusel, 1999, p. 51). Another type of themed playground is built around a story. One example is the Underhill Playground, which is also in New York. This playground uses the theme of a Russian folktale and activities are designed to encourage pretense during physical movement.

Pay for Play

The term *theme based* is also used to refer to commercial parks such as Disneyland. It is also used by manufacturers of playground equipment to

Playgrounds provide a mirror of the community. This playground is located in a rural area that emphasizes play.

describe large pieces of equipment that depict a theme such as a pirate ship. These are not the same as the science playground. The difference is that theme playgrounds are areas that provide children opportunities to grow and learn through the process. Commercial theme parks are designed for entertainment. Theme-based equipment is designed to encourage one type of play only, whereas parks such as Underhill provide a vast array of opportunities for the child to expand the theme. It expands rather than restricts play.

Different playgrounds provide experiences that optimize social, cognitive, and physical development. Adults make a difference in how this occurs and their important role is discussed in the next section.

■ Role of the Adult

> *Too much money and uniformed thought is often spent on fixed play apparatus. It must not be forgotten that this is only furniture and no matter how ingenious it may be, it alone does not make a playground.*
>
> —*Arvid Bengtsson, 1974*

Adults have a major role in fostering outdoor play. They may serve as a source of information for chants during jump rope, keeper of the rules for tag or basketball, or guide as children discover how to climb up and down safely. Adult roles can be categorized into four areas: organizer, observer, supervisor, and evaluator (Seefeldt & Barbour, 1998). Above all, the adult is responsible for the safety of the children on the playground.

Organizer

Organizing materials for outdoor play involves surveying the area, observing play, and considering goals for outdoor play. Plans for moving materials in and out will be necessary when setting up additional activities. Children should have appropriate materials and sufficient time for play. In some climates, organizing to go outside may require time to put on boots and coats. In other climates, sunscreen may be needed. Some teachers take play crates outside. Play crates contain materials that can be used to stimulate play. For example, one play crate might be filled with different balls, while another might contain different kinds of sheets and coverings for pretend buildings. Other teachers will set up a special project outside such as using water to paint the building. These activities provide choices for children.

Observer

Observing provides the teacher an opportunity to look at the total picture. As a skilled observer, the teacher will see many levels of play skills. Some will be engaging in a great deal of symbolic play. Others may be just walking around. Another may be engaged in associative play; one may still play alone. By observing and recording the action that is occurring, the teacher will know where and when to act. Taking time to watch outdoor play is an important and often overlooked responsibility.

Supervisor

Keeping children safe and healthy is, of course, critically important. Someone must be assigned to routinely check and perform maintenance on the playground and any equipment used by the children. Ensuring that children are using materials in a safe manner is of paramount importance. Figure 9–1 has a checklist that can be used to check the playground for unsafe equipment or materials. Physical safety is the first basic need recognized by Maslow (1959) and is necessary for high-quality play (Rogers & Sluss, 1992).

Adults charged with children's safety must monitor the overall play scene. Are the perimeters safe? Are there any adults nearby who should not be on the playground? Does litter need to be removed? Is the equipment safe? As supervisor, the adult can walk around the playground and both observe and interact with children on a one-to-one basis. Pushing a child on a swing, helping a child climb a slide, and interacting with children agitated over ownership of a ball all add to the richness of the play experiences.

Adults should avoid talking to other adults when supervising groups of children on the playground. If an accident occurs, the adult in charge will need to provide a description of the incident and this is difficult to do if the accident was not observed.

Evaluator

Evaluating play can provide insights that may be less obvious in the classroom. Children who cannot skip when asked to do so in a semiformal assessment have been observed skipping and hopping later during recess. Outdoor play provides early educators with opportunities to observe, monitor and assess, evaluate, and then develop new plans for more complex play. Additional information is provided later in this chapter under the assessment section.

■ Safety Issues for All Children

Sun Safety

Safety issues are especially poignant for infants and toddlers. The American Academy of Dermatology recommends special caution with infants and toddlers. Minimize exposing infants under the age of six months to direct sunlight. A covered pram is recommended for outings. Older infants and toddlers should be covered with sunscreen thirty minutes prior to going outside. Be sure to check for allergic reactions prior to using the sunscreen. Parents can be asked to provide their child's sunscreen. Recommended sunscreen for this age is a UVA- and UVB-absorbing or-blocking product with an SPF of at least 15 (Geller et al., 2002). Encourage children to wear hats, sunglasses, and sun protective clothing. Schools in some climates may want to limit outdoor time between 10 A.M. and 4 P.M. Overexposure to the sun is a major concern at this age, so monitor carefully how long children are exposed to direct sunlight. Additional information is available on the Web site of the American Academy of Dermatology.

Playground Safety

Play areas must be safe havens for children. Playgrounds should be fenced in, with sturdy, safe equipment and shock absorbent surfaces (Rogers & Sluss, 1992). The unique needs of the children must be considered also. If children are allergic to bees, an extra adult should be present with necessary supplies. Too often, children who have allergies are forced to stay inside the building. Adults must take responsibility for ensuring that all children can experience the outdoors. Some teachers ask parents to come by the school for the outdoor time and parents will plan their work schedule so they can ensure their child has a safe experience. Adults who care will find creative ways to overcome barriers to play as seen in Figure 9–1.

FIGURE 9–1   Public Playground Safety Checklist

**Consumer Product Safety Commission
Public Playground Safety Checklist**
CPSC Document #327

Is your public playground a safe place to play?

Each year, more than 200,000 children go to U.S. hospital emergency rooms with injuries associated with playground equipment. Most injuries occur when a child falls from the equipment onto the ground.

Use this simple checklist to help make sure your local community or school playground is a safe place to play.

Public Playground Safety Checklist

1. Make sure surfaces around playground equipment have at least 12 inches of wood chips, mulch, sand, or pea gravel, or are mats made of safety-tested rubber or rubber-like materials.
2. Check that protective surfacing extends at least 6 feet in all directions from play equipment. For swings, be sure surfacing extends, in back and front, twice the height of the suspending bar.
3. Make sure play structures more than 30 inches high are spaced at least 9 feet apart.
4. Check for dangerous hardware, like open "S" hooks or protruding bolt ends.
5. Make sure spaces that could trap children, such as openings in guardrails or between ladder rungs, measure less than 3.5 inches or more than 9 inches.
6. Check for sharp points or edges in equipment.
7. Look out for tripping hazards, like exposed concrete footings, tree stumps, and rocks.
8. Make sure elevated surfaces, like platforms and ramps, have guardrails to prevent falls.
9. Check playgrounds regularly to see that equipment and surfacing are in good condition.
10. Carefully supervise children on playgrounds to make sure they're safe.

You can also view our other playground safety publications.

Brought to you by the U.S. Consumer Product Safety Commission and KaBOOM!, a national nonprofit organization committed to building safe playgrounds for America's children through the KaBOOM! LET US PLAY campaign. For more information, call toll-free 1-888-789-PLAY or visit the KaBOOM! Web site at www.kaboom.org.

Consumers can obtain this publication and additional publication information from the Publications section of CPSC's Web site or by sending your publication request to info@cpsc.gov.

This document is in the public domain. It may be reproduced without change in part or whole by an individual or organization without permission. If it is reproduced, however, the Commission would appreciate knowing how it is used. Write the U.S. Consumer Product Safety Commission, Office of Information and Public Affairs, Washington, D.C. 20207 or send an e-mail to info@cpsc.gov.

In the following section, information specific to age groups is provided. Just as indoor play is different for infants and preschoolers, outdoor play is equally unique for the developing child.

Safety First Tip: NO climbing structures should be placed on asphalt.

■ Designing Outdoor Play Environments for Infants and Toddlers

Infants and toddlers need fresh air every day. Outdoor play allows them to experience a different learning environment. Grass and natural materials are intriguing to toddlers. Slides and tunnels provide opportunities for movement that might not be possible in the indoor environment. Infants and toddlers need and benefit from daily outings and outdoor play.

Play spaces for infants and toddlers should be separated from preschooler's play spaces. The area must be partially shaded to prevent overexposure to sun and allow for play on rainy days. The area should include sensorimotor activities such as sand and water. Placing a sheet on the grass creates a sensory experience for infants and toddlers. Activities such as painting, bubbles, and play dough are enjoyable activities that can occur outdoors. The play area should be small and secure so children feel safe and comfortable. The ground cover should include a variety of surfaces. Equipment with low ramps and stairs permit children to practice their walking and climbing skills as they improve their gross motor skills. Karyn Wellhousen (2002) describes four principles for designing outdoor spaces based on the work of Joe Frost (1992).

1. *Safety and comfort* are the most important aspects to consider when looking at play spaces. Infants and toddlers who are just developing vertical stability should be separated from preschoolers.

2. *Provide for a large range of movements.* Frost (1992) advocates play areas that are "gentle for crawling, kind for falling, and cool for sitting" (p. 260). Infants and toddlers need places that allow them to develop in a safe environment. Play areas that include places for both low-mobile and high-mobile children generally include a variety of coverings including grass, sand, and indoor/outdoor carpet.

3. *Plan for sensory stimulation.* Wind, sunshine, grass, rocks, and trees are primary gifts of nature. When these are not available, use sand and water experiences, wind chimes, and art activities.

4. *Offer a variety of novel and challenging activities.* Adding empty boxes that children can safely climb into is always interesting. Scarves allow children to catch the wind. Play centers that are moved outside are always exciting.

Examples of Infant-Toddler Play Places

Infant-toddler play areas should be separate from those designed for older children. Features that should be included in the infant-toddler playground include:

◆ shady area

◆ sandbox

◆ grassy area

◆ place for locomotor play such as running, climbing, and rolling

◆ mounds

Additional materials may include:

◆ blankets or soft materials for sitting on grassy areas

◆ empty boxes

Safe enviroments provide optimal opportunities for developing locomotor skills.

Types of Play on Infant-Toddler Playgrounds

The outdoor playground encourages a different kind of play than that found inside. Play happens as toddlers run, jump, climb, crawl, and slide down. Climbing is a primary interest of toddlers. Outdoor play areas can provide a safe place for climbing and exploring. Toddlers also enjoy running and engaging in rough-and-tumble play. Infants engage in exploratory, sensorimotor, and locomotor play outdoors. Infants and toddlers do not initiate group play at this age. They still tend to play alone or interact with a caregiver. Interactions that occur generally are caused by intersections rather than mutual reciprocity.

Climbing is an activity that is seldom discussed in the literature, but it is a natural activity. Although it is seldom valued, it is an activity that older infants and toddlers engage in as often as possible. By taking advantage of the child's interest in climbing, we can use the child's natural interest to enhance developing motor skills. Climbing requires a certain combination of thoughts and motions. First, the child must have the desire. Some children are more interested in climbing than are others. Children who enjoy climbing need little motivation other than a higher surface! Second, they must have the skills and strength to pull themselves up and then push their larger head and body onto the supporting structure. By the age of two, almost all children are able to climb (Readdick & Park, 1998). Playgrounds that have climbing structures, low slides, and low stairs with handrails encourage children to develop climbing skills. Of course, a soft padded surface is necessary to ensure safety. Readdick and Park (1998) recommend that heights be limited to 1 foot for each year of life. So, a climbing structure for a twelve-month-old would be a stair that is a foot high. Structures for two-year-olds would be no higher than 2 feet. Because they love to climb, never place any equipment near fences that will allow them to climb over the fence. Most fences are made of chain links and this a perfect climbing fence. Wood is a better choice for playgrounds for infants and toddlers.

Safety for Infants and Toddlers

Be aware of sun safety. Infants under six months should not be exposed to direct sunlight. Young children should have a play area that has a shelter or tent covering the area to prevent direct exposure to the sun's rays. Infants and toddlers must be carefully supervised and should never be left unattended outside.

Preschoolers enjoy climbing when structures are designed to encopurage a variety of movements.

■ Designing Outdoor Play Environments for Preschoolers

Preschoolers need outdoor time and fresh air every day. This age group benefits from outdoor play as the children acquire competency in locomotor abilities, problem-solving, negotiation skills, and social interactions. Preschoolers enjoy acrobatic activities that are difficult to do inside. Playgrounds also provide opportunities for different types of play. Preschoolers have moved beyond the need to climb and are beginning to engage in rough-and-tumble play. Rough-and-tumble play is "composed of the following behaviors: play face, run, chase, flee, wrestle, and open-hand beat. Young children benefit from rough and tumble play . . . children often alternate between victim and victimizer" (Pelligrini & Boyd, 1993, p. 115). Preschoolers are only beginning this stage and rough-and-tumble play occupies less than 5% of their time. It is important not to confuse rough-and-tumble play with aggressive behavior. Rough-and-tumble may be frowned on inside but acceptable outside.

During social interactions, children can choose playmates. Interventions are necessary when children purposefully exclude other children. Responsive teachers are careful to intervene without interfering. For example, when a child is being excluded from a group, the adult can physically move over to the group and join their play. Bring the child who is excluded into the entire group and then watch for an appropriate time to exit the play.

Preschoolers need room to run, jump, skip, hop, gallop, and play with their friends. The space should be enclosed with a fence to ensure safety. An adult should be assigned to check the equipment and play area on a daily basis. A shelter is needed to shield the children from the sun and to serve as a play place on rainy days. Equipment should include tire swings, low slides, climbing apparatus, sandboxes, water tables, and equipment with wheels for pulling, pushing, and riding. The space should include a variety of surfaces with a paved riding area for tricycles, wagons, and pull toys. Large blocks also work well outside. Old tires make wonderful swings when attached correctly and can be used to reinforce areas for climbing and sitting.

Designing Preschool Play Spaces

Areas for preschoolers should be more complex and challenging than those of infants and toddlers. The complexity level should be greater and should allow for more diversity and independent play. Seven different zones recommended by Esbensen (1990) for preschoolers are included in Figure 9–2.

Types of Play on Preschool Playgrounds

The most dominant play during the preschool years is pretend. Though some rough-and-tumble play may be evident, pretend play is at its peak. When children are outdoors, they can pretend that they are flying like birds, running like dogs, or rescuing someone from a monster. They are less egocentric and may engage in associative and cooperative play during

---

FIGURE 9–2 Seven Zones on Playgrounds

Different zones provide interests and challenges:

1. Manipulative/creative
2. Projective/fantasy
3. Focal/social
4. Social/dramatic
5. Physical
6. Natural
7. Transition (to tie zones together)

Source: Ebensen, 1990.

this time. Rudimentary games may be evident but are short-lived due to the episodic nature of play at this age.

Safety Issues

Though preschoolers need less supervision, they still need supervision. Children at this age are testing their abilities and do not have the necessary skills to assess risks. It is incumbent upon teachers to ensure their safety during outdoor play. As with younger children, they need appropriate clothing and sunscreen when outdoors. Many schools give children snacks and ice cream at this time but this is unwise. If children use their time eating, they miss their play time. When they finish, they cannot wash their hands and sticky hands can cause accidents when using equipment. When ice cream and food are eaten and papers deposited outdoors, bees and other insects are attracted. For children who are allergic to bees, this makes outdoor play risky. Keeping snacks and ice cream indoors minimizes these problems.

■ Designing Outdoor Play Environments for Primary-age Children

Primary-age children need equipment for swinging, sliding, and climbing with their friends. They are beginning to play group games and need space for playing jump rope and group chase games. They can still benefit from sandboxes and enjoy spaces that allow them to dig in the dirt.

Play Spaces

Though equipment should be more complex and challenging, as with preschoolers, primary-age children need opportunities within the seven zones listed in Figure 9–2. Playgrounds for primary-age children should have more space for group games that include running and throwing. Adults should also ensure that girls and boys have access to equal space. Too often, boys tend to dominate the space on the playground and girls spend their time in one corner of the playground.

Types of Play on Primary Playgrounds

Typically developing primary-age children are capable of playing structured games and enjoy doing so. They can concentrate on play for a longer length of time than can preschoolers, and they can select group leaders. The dominant play at this age involves games and exploration. Games evident on the playground may include running games like red rover, jump rope games with chants and rhymes, different kinds of ball games, hopscotch, and tag. Many adults recall games they played as children though they can remember little else from that time period. Adults must be aware that some children may be ostracized at this time. Teachers must pay attention to those children who are not included in the games. Without forcing children to play—which does not work anyway—teachers must be creative in how they create opportunities for all children to participate in outdoor play.

Safety Issues

Safety issues are a concern at every age. Children at the primary age are establishing their self-esteem. In an attempt to demonstrate their skills, they will sometimes take risks that place them in danger. Children also need to be protected from the sun and should wear appropriate footwear and attire outside.

Primary children face different issues during outdoor play. Issues surrounding recess will be explored in the following section.

■ Recess

> *Recess is the right of every child. Article 31 of the United Nations Convention on Children's Rights states that every child has the right to leisure time. Taking away recess, whether as a disciplinary measure or abolishing it in the name of work, infringes on that right.*
> —Audrey Skrupskelis, 2000

The term **recess** is generally applied to a block of time when children are allowed to go to a defined play area and engage in self-selected physical play for a specified amount of time. Within a decade, recess has disappeared in many schools throughout the United States. In 1989 over 90% of the principals in districts throughout the United States reported recess in their school. Ten years later, only 40% had recess (Kieff, 2001). Where did it go and why? The focus on academics has created a situation that eliminates any activity that can not be tested. Music, art, and movement are not included on standardized tests and have been the first areas eliminated from the schedule. Recess is not a test item so it has been eliminated in many schools. In one research study of a school district, Olga Jarrett

(2003) found that recess occurred every day in predominantly affluent suburban schools, but was eliminated in urban schools with African-American populations.

The American Association for the Child's Right to Play has launched a movement to support the child's right to play outdoors every day. Two states, Virginia and Michigan, passed laws requiring schools to allow children to have a recess period for play. NAEYC supports the reinstatement of recess and notes that recess benefits instruction in the following ways:

1. It is an appropriate outlet for reducing stress in children.
2. It allows children the opportunity to make choices, plan, and expand their creativity.
3. It releases energy.

If these sound familiar, revisit the classical theories of play in Chapter 2. The innate nature of play suggests that the need to play is a biological need, and eliminating recess does not eliminate the child's need to play. It only eliminates an appropriate context for play. Bogden and Vega-Matos (2000) found that discipline problems and disruptive behavior were minimized as a result of recess. The National Association of Early Childhood

Outdoor play spaces encourage play rituals and transmissions of culture from one generation to the next.

Specialists in State Departments of Education recommend the following advocacy actions (2003):

- ◆ Support policies which require recess time to be part of the preschool and elementary school curriculum.

- ◆ Ensure and support additional research on the effects of recess on the developmental domains (social, emotional, physical, and cognitive), and on the effect of recess on academic achievement.

- ◆ Develop policies and resources necessary to support an awareness of the importance of recess and of active, free play in the development of the young child.

- ◆ Support research on the benefits of recess and its possible restorative role for children with attention disorders.

- ◆ Support research and professional development that facilitate every educator's skills in observation and assessment of the developmental growth of children through the play process.

■ After-school Programs

These programs hold a special challenge for all educators. After-school programs are designed for primary-age children who do not have alternative care at home. Creating an interesting curriculum is filled with obstacles. Children have been in structured programs during the day and are tired, all ages are put together, and few activities are planned. Too many times, children are expected to stay in a large field without equipment or materials and just play. Some children may create games that involve chase but, needless to say, this often deteriorates and aggression and hostility erupt. Adults in charge then might decide that children cannot play well outside and take them in for a video where they are forced to sit, watch passively, and perhaps eat a snack. On the other hand, if these programs were not available, many children would be in self-care or "**latchkey children.**" Latchkey children is a term used to describe children who are at home without adult supervision for an hour or so before their parents return from work. Today, one in five children are in self-care while their parents work and this number is increasing. This is a dangerous situation for over five million children in America (Lamorey, Robinson, Rowland, & Coleman(1998). After-school programs are better alternatives. Planned programs with proper adult supervision provide enriching experiences for young children. Outdoor play should be a part of this experience.

Outdoor experiences and play should be as carefully designed for after-school, multiage programs as they are for children during school hours. To ensure optimal educational experiences for children during this time, adults must plan their outdoor experiences following many of the same rules used to implement play during the school day, as explained in earlier sections.

In designing outdoor spaces in after-school programs, use the same guidelines described in the previous section on establishing a playground for school. One caveat is that many playgrounds are overcrowded. The program should limit how many children can be on the playground at one time. Perhaps they can rotate in and out so that not too many children are on the playground at one time.

■ Assessing Outdoor Play

Outdoor environments provide an optimal opportunity for assessing play and the child's development. Assessment can be used to evaluate physical, social, and cognitive development by examining play taxonomies discussed in Chapter 1. These include physical development (gross and fine motor skills), social interaction (solitary, parallel, associative, and group play), and cognitive development (sensorimotor or functional, constructive, pretense or dramatic play, and games with rules). These taxonomies provide tools to examine different aspects of the child's play. Combining methods can provide a profile of the child's play.

Planning for Assessment

The first step involves planning. Decide how you will use the information. Appropriate assessment is conducted for a purpose. The data collected should be used to change or improve programs for young children. Next, decide if you are observing skills. If so, do you plan to make changes based on your assessment? If you choose to observe the child's play level, always focus on play that is dominant for the child's age group. For example, if you are observing four-year-olds, the dominant play should be pretend play though some sensorimotor and constructive play will be occurring. You may even see some rough-and-tumble play. If you only see sensorimotor play, then you may want to look at the playground again. What are the impediments?

Outdoor assessment provides a unique context for observing play. The playground is different from the indoor classroom. When beginning informal assessment, limit assessment to one or two behaviors per class or limit observations to one child. If you are assessing skill development such as jumping, use a checklist to write down the names of all the children in the class. Then slip a 1" × 2" pack of yellow memo notes along with a pencil into your pocket. As you walk around the playground, pay attention to who is jumping. When you see someone jumping, write the name on the memo slip. Later in the day, check off the child's name. Some teachers choose to put a square for each child on a file folder and place sticky notes on the file folder. Some teachers will take a picture of the behavior. Either system works. If this is done throughout the week, the entire class can be assessed for jumping skills without a single test situation. Deciding what and how you will assess is the first step. The next step involves assessment.

Play Assessment

If you are assessing play behaviors, use the Play Scale (Figure 9–3) to record play behaviors for five minutes. Do this for two weeks and average the data. When this is done throughout the year, it provides a powerful picture of the child's play.

The process of watching one child involves watching his movements during one outdoor play period. Doing this requires another adult on the playground to supervise the other children. This is a valuable process for several reasons. First, by focusing on observation and assessment only, the adult can more fully analyze the child's total play by combining the physical, social, and cognitive behaviors together for a total picture of the play experience. This is especially valuable for children who have play problems or are exhibiting other atypical behavior.

Physical movement

First, examine the child's physical play. All children should engage in movement outside. Is the child's level of movement congruent with his age, stage of development, and culture? Can children move, climb, run, skip, hop, jump, and move in a variety of directions? Does the child have a sense of balance or does he seem to be unstable at times? Does the child engage in smooth, fluid movements or are his movements jerky and uneven? If there are signs of inconsistencies with his age mates, then an additional report requesting additional testing might be needed.

Social interaction

Second, consider the child's social play. Outdoor play provides a perfect place for assessing social interaction. Again, set up a system for either class observations or individual observations. If you select two children per day, look at their play with their peers. Do they have friends or are they playing alone? Can they play with other children or are they constantly seeking

FIGURE 9–3 Play Scale

	Sensorimotor Play	Symbolic: Constructive	Symbolic: Dramatic Play	Games	Other
Unoccupied					
Onlooker					
Solitary Independent Play					
Parallel Play					
Associative Play					
Cooperative Play					

Rough-and-tumble Play _____

_____

_____

Adapted from Piaget (1965), Parten (1932), and Rubin (1989).

adult attention? Children who report behaviors of others or what is called tattling are often seeking adult attention and approval. Find out why the child needs adult interaction. Can you assist the child in finding playmates? Are some children demonstrating leadership skills by organizing games? Have you seen these behaviors in the classroom?

Cognitive development

Though more difficult to observe, this also manifests itself on the playground. Very young children should engage primarily in practice or functional play on the playground. The infant-toddler playground will be filled with children engaging in practice play such as emptying sand buckets over and over, climbing up and over a low ramp, and repeatedly moving in different ways. This is typical behavior for this age. Preschoolers will begin to engage in pretend play. Place a large empty box on the infant-toddler playground and they will fill it with materials. As soon as it is filled, they will empty it again. Place the same large box on the preschoolers' play area and it becomes a boat, a car, or a space ship.

The element of pretense has begun. Take the same box to the primary playground and it becomes a clubhouse and only those who follow the rules can enter. Look at the child's play. Engaging in practice play in preschool is fine, but when children are still exhibiting this type of play in primary school, there may be a reason for concern. Use the Play Scale (Figure 9–3) to get an overall sense of the child's play.

Multiple Measures

Other data collection techniques are available. These include running records, checklists, narratives, portfolios, and documentation panels. Refer to Chapter 6 for a review of portfolios and documentation panels. Narratives and running records are discussed in the next section. A **running record** is exactly what the name implies, it is a running record of observed behaviors. After watching the children to develop a sense of their physical, social, and cognitive play levels, take a look at each child for one play period. As indicated earlier, this will require another adult on the play space. Complete a running record on the child. That is, write down everything you see the child do during the play period. This will provide an in-depth view of the child's social interaction with peers, communication, and skill level. Information gained from this technique cannot be garnered using any other method. Running records are used to write narratives of the child's play experience.

Assessing Primary Play

Assessing primary play is more difficult than assessing preschool play. A system for observing primary play has been developed by Anthony Pelligrini (1998) based on the work of Humphries and Smith (1987). He used the following behaviors in a matrix.

passive/noninteractive
passive/interactive
adult-directed
adult-organized
aggressive
rough-and-tumble play
vigorous behavior
games
object-play
role-play

These behaviors can be used to record observations and frequency of student behavior. Watching behaviors over a period of time can provide a powerful tool for understanding children.

PlayScape Reflections

Phillipi, like many other children his age was excited to be outside. The playground provided a good variety of appropriate choices. As in years past, the girls continue to occupy a smaller amount of space on the playground than the boys. Though Phillipi cannot speak English as well as others in his class, he excels on the playground in games of competition. He found a way to be accepted by the other children in the class. When the children return to the class they are more likely to sit and concentrate. Though Phillipi may not excel indoors, he excels outdoors. Children have always benefited from outdoor play, and all children should continue to benefit from outdoor play on a daily basis.

■ Summary

Outdoor play has never been more important than it is now. More children are obese and overweight than at any other time in history. This chapter provides an overview of outdoor play, playgrounds, and the play that occurs in these play spaces. The importance of safety on the playground was emphasized and a checklist for playground safety was available for use by students. Specific suggestions were offered for encouraging infant-toddler, preschool, and primary-age outdoor play. High-quality playgrounds for after-school programs are needed. The importance of play assessment was examined as was the important role of the adult.

■ Key Terms

Contemporary playgrounds   Natural play spaces   Recess
Community playgrounds   Latchkey child   Running record
Inclusive playgrounds   Theme-based playgrounds

■ Helpful Web Sites and Technology Resources

◆ **After-school Programs**
http://www.afterschool.gov   This is an excellent site on after school programs. Sponsored by the federal government and designed for educators, there are also links for children.

◆ **American Association for the Child's Right to Play**
http://www.ipausa.org   Contains a USA Network of Recess Associates in every state. Free materials are available at this site.

◆ **Boundless Playgrounds**
http://www.boundlessplaygrounds.org/   Boundless Playgrounds is a nonprofit group committed to ensuring that children of all ability levels can play together. This Web site provides a step-by-step guide for developing an inclusive playground.

◆ **California Early Childhood Protection Curriculum**
http://www.dhs.ca.gov   The California Early Childhood Protection Curriculum is available for use by early educators.

◆ **Centers for Disease Control and Prevention**
http://www.cdc.gov   U.S. Department of Health and Human Services, Centers for Disease Control and Prevention. (2000, February). *School Health Index for Physical Activity and Healthy Eating (Elementary School): A Self-Assessment and Planning Guide.* [The document can be downloaded from the CDC Web site.]

◆ **International Play Association**
http://ericps.ed.uiuc.edu   Includes information to support recess in primary schools. Links to other information about recess are included. **http://www.ncsu.edu/ipa/**   International Play Association home site. Great information about play. This is an international site and provides information about the state of play throughout the world.

◆ **National Program for Playground Safety**
http://www.uni.edu   National Program for Playground Safety Web page. The site has a tremendous amount of information available about playground safety.

◆ **Playground Design**
http://www.ecdu.gov.   This is an excellent site designed by educators that includes the necessary information for planning and developing safe play spaces for young children.

◆ **Skin Cancer News**
http://www.aad.org.   This site is sponsored by the American Academy of Dermatology. A fact sheet is included that can be shared with parents.

■ Activities

1. InClass Lab

A. Design play activities for an infant-toddler, preschool, and primary play area. Be sure to include some art and water activities. How will you set up the area? Consider cleanup. How will this be implemented?

B. Think about the activities that you planned in the activity above. How will you store and or transport materials to the playground?

2. Research and Inquiry

A. Visit a local primary school during recess. Complete a time sample of one minute each on three boys and three girls using the Play Scale in Figure 9–3. Compare and contrast their play.

B. Visit and describe at least three different playgrounds. What factors contribute to making them different?

3. Service Learning

A. Visit a local playground. Use the checklist to inspect the playgrounds for safety. Report any safety concerns to the playground supervisors.

B. Volunteer to help clean up a playground on a community cleanup day.

C. Make a list of safety precautions that teachers should follow to ensure safety on the playground. Include information about sun safety. Create brochures or order some from the National Program for Playground Safety (NPPS). Distribute the materials to local PTAs.

4. Family Connections

A. Contact the International Play Association for information on the International Play Day.

B. Take the information to a local parent's group, student group, or community group and invite them to sponsor the day in the community.

5. Play Advocacy

A. Survey local schools concerning recess in your community. If recess is at risk in your community, join an action group that is supporting school recess.

■ References

American Academy of Child and Adolescent Psychiatry. (nd). Facts for Families. No. 79. *Obesity in children and teens*. Retrieved January 10, 2004 from www.aacap.org/publications/factsfam/79.html.

American Heart Association. (nd). *Overweight children*: AHA recommendations. Retrieved January 10, 2004 from www.americanheart.org/presenter.jhml?identifier=4670.

American Medical Association. (2003, Dec. 1). *AMA calls on physicians to help combat obesity*. Retrieved January 10, 2004 from www.ama-assn.org/ama/pub/article/1616-8203.html.

Bengtsson, A. (1974). *The child's right to play*. Sheffield, England: International Playground Association.

Bogden, J. F., & Vega-Matos, C. A. (2000, March). Fit, healthy, and ready to learn: A school health policy guide. Part I: *Physical activity, Healthy eating, and tobacco-use prevention*. Alexandria, VA: National Association of State Boards of Education.

Dewey, J. (1930). *Democracy and education*. New York: Macmillan.

Elkind, D. (1981). *The hurried child: Growing up too fast too soon*. Reading, MA: Addison-Wesley.

Esbensen, S. (1990). Play environments for young children: Design perspectives. In S. Wortham & J. L. Frost (Eds.), *Playgrounds for young children: National survey and perspectives* (pp. 49–68). Reston, VA: American Alliance for Health, Physical Education, Recreation and Dance.

Frost, J. (1992). *Play and playscapes*. Clifton Park, NY: Thomson Delmar Learning.

Frost, J., & Klein, B. (1983). *Children's play and playgrounds*. Austin, TX: Playscapes International.

Frost, J., Wortham, S., & Reifel, S. (2001). *Play and child development*. Upper Saddle River, NJ: Merrill/Prentice Hall.

Geller, A., Colditz, G., Oliveria, S., Emmons, K., Jorgensen, C., Aweh, G., & Frazier, A. L. (2002). Use of sunscreen, sunburning rates, and tanning bed use among 10,000 US children and adolescents. *Pediatrics, 109*, 1009–1014.

Humphries, A., & Smith, P. K. (1987). Rough-and-tumble play, friendship, and dominance in school children. *Child Development, 58*, 201–212.

Hymes-Dusel, J. (1999). A closer look at playgrounds centered around a theme. In M. Guddemi, T. Jambor, and A. Swkrupskelis, *Play in a changing society* (pp. 51–52). Little Rock, AR: Southern Early Childhood Association.

Individuals with Disabilities Education Act P.L. 101-476. Stat. 1103 (1990) (codified as amended at 20 U.S.C. Secs. 1400–1485) (1997).

Jarrett, O. (2003). Urban school recess: The haves and have nots. *Play, Policy, & Practice Connections. Newsletter of the Play, Policy, and Practice Interest Forum of the National Association for the Education of Young Children,* 7 (1), 2003.

Kieff, J. (2001). The silencing of the recess bells. *Childhood Education,* 77 (5), 319–325.

Lamorey, S., Robinson, B., Rowland, B., & Coleman, M. (1998). *Unlocking doors for children and their families* (2nd ed.). Thousand Oaks, CA: Sage.

Maslow, A. (1959). Psychological data and human values. In A. H. Maslow (Ed.), *New knowledge in human values & Bros* (pp. 119–136). New York: Harper & Bros.

National Association of Early Childhood Specialists in State Departments of Education, Retrieved October 12, 2003 from http://ecap.crc.uiuc.edu/websites/naecs.html.

National Center for Health Statistics, *Prevalence of overweight among children and adolescents: United States, 1999–2000.* Retrieved January 10, 2004 from www.cdc.gov/nchs/products/pubs/pubd/hestats/overwght99.htm.

National Program for Playground Safety. Retrieved October 23, 2003 from http://www.uni.edu/playground/home.html.

Olds, A. R. (2000). *Child care design guide.* New York: McGraw Hill.

Opie, I., & Opie, P. (1959). *The lore and language of schoolchildren.* Oxford, England: Claredon Press.

Parten, M. (1932). Social participation among pre-school children. *Journal of Abnormal Psychology,* 27, 243–269.

Pelligrini, A. (1998). Play and the assessment of young children. In O. Saracho and B. Spodek (Eds.) *Multiple perspectives on play in early childhood education* (pp. 220–239). Albany: SUNY Press.

Pelligrini, A., & Boyd, B. (1993). The role of play in early childhood development and education: Issues in definition and function. In B. Spodek's (Ed.) *Handbook of research on the education of young children* (pp. 105–121). New York: Macmillan.

Piaget, J. (1997). *The moral judgment of the child.* New York: Simon and Schuster. (Originally published in 1965).

Readdick, C., & Park, J. (1998). Achieving great heights: The climbing child. *Young Children,* 53 (6), 14–19.

Rogers, C., & Sluss, D. J. (1992). Young children and play. *ChildCare ActioNews,* 9 (4), 1–3.

Rubin, K. (1989). *The Play Observation Scale.* Waterloo, Canada: University of Waterloo.

Schiller, F. (1954). *On the aesthetic education of man.* New Haven, CT: Yale University Press.

Seefeldt, C., & Barbour, N. (1998). *Early childhood education: An introduction.* Columbus, OH: Merrill.

Skrupskelis, A. (2000). An historical trend to eliminate recess. In Clements, R. L. (Ed.) (2000), *Elementary school recess: Selected readings, games, and activities for teachers and parents* (pp. 124–126). Boston: American Press.

Stephenson, A. (2002). Opening up the outdoors: Exploring the relationship between the indoor and outdoor environments of a centre. *European Early Childhood Education Research Journal; 10* (1), 29–38.

Wellhousen, K. (2002). *Outdoor play every day: Innovative concepts for early childhood.* Clifton Park, NY: Thomson Delmar Learning.

CHAPTER 10

Current Trends and Issues

Play is the child's response to life.

—*Anonymous*

Chapter Overview

Supporting play in group settings has been examined throughout this book and is examined in this chapter in terms of the impact of trends and issues. Trends are considered using an ecological perspective that examines global, national, community, and family trends. Four major issues that are currently affecting play are technology, media influences, toys, and violence. As play and play policies change in response to societal influences, research can be used as a source of information for advocacy efforts.

Objectives

After reading this chapter you should be able to:

◆ Identify factors in the ecosystem that are affecting play.

◆ Discuss major issues currently impacting play.

◆ Develop a play policy plan.

◆ Discuss the future of play.

PlayScape

As the teacher walked over, Selma and Harry looked up from their block play. They had just finished putting the finishing touches on their block structures. The grass blocks were glowing a bright shade of green against the bright buildings. As Harry put the last grass block in place, he told Selma to "Put the metallic block here, Selma." Selma responded, "Okay, turn on the day lights, not the nighttime lights." As the teacher watched, she contemplated: how much should she interject. Slowly she spoke. "You know you don't see as much grass in the cities. Sidewalks and highways are more common. If you want to change the environment block from grass to concrete, you can push this button. Do you want to look at some tech samples of cities?" Both Harry and Selma shook their heads. "This is a pretend city, let's just pretend the grass blocks are concrete. Let's just pretend the skylights are on and the night lights are off." Harry laughed and said, "We're pretending!" She replied, "Okay, but let me know if you want to look at some samples." As the teacher walked away, they laughed and continued to play.

Play Provocation

The children are engaged in block play. Blocks serve as the impetus for play as the teacher attempts to guide their play. The blocks described in this scenario do not exist. In trying to consider the issues that young children and teachers will encounter in the next five years, technological advances will certainly influence play. Perhaps new blocks will be designed that allow children to create different environmental systems. New materials and toys can encourage activity or passivity. In fact, there are already classes with block computer programs but with no blocks in the room! Children will always be fascinated by new materials and will always engage in pretend play—or will they? Many are concerned about the influence of today's culture on the young child's play (Levin, 1998). This chapter is designed to examine current trends and issues that will impact play in the twenty-first century.

■ Current Trends

So powerful is the urge to play, to move outside the limitations of the immediate moment, the here and now, the status of smallness, weakness, ignorance and powerlessness, that children even in the most terrible circumstances insist on playing.

—June Factor, 1993

In the first chapter, the contexts of play were examined using an ecological lens. This approach looked at the political and economic forces that impact young children and their play. This chapter returns to this perspective in an examination of global, national, regional, and community trends and their subsequent impact on play.

Global Trends

The impact of war, poverty, and disease are factors that influence play throughout the world. Children in countries that are being ravaged by war, poverty, or disease have limited opportunities to play. Still, we know that children will use their last energy to engage in play. After touring refugee camps, Liv Ullman noted that "Children who are too sick to move, who must be carried out of their house, will play in the dirt. With their last breath, they play" (Rogers, 1989). AIDS is raging in several countries in Africa and having an impact on children's daily activities. Children in many countries still face the peril of stepping on land mines when they play. Many international organizations such as UNICEF are providing assistance. One organization, the United Nations Educational, Scientific, and Cultural Organization (UNESCO), encourages families in impoverised areas to work together to provide child care that is low in cost and efficient (Allen, 2002).

Children in more affluent nations have more opportunities to play. Mobility and communication provide access to information at an unprecedented rate as they create the global village. Early educators in countries throughout the world travel to different locations to study play for young children. Teachers from centers in 44 countries have visited the schools in Reggio Emilia, Italy. Others travel to Norway to study their programs for infants. During a program that the author attended with Constance Kami (1996), teachers from America sat next to teachers from Japan as they talked about how young children make sense of the world through play with games. Teachers communicate via the Internet when they return to their own centers. As teachers acquire new information, they change how they view their centers and the play that occurs therein. *The interface between countries and culture will continue to evolve and influence play as we experience the reality of the global village.*

National Trends

Shifts in the demographics of children under eight have created a major impact on early education. Over the past decade, the demographics of the preschool and primary population changed. More children are entering the country from different countries bringing with them different cultures and styles of play. Many children are non-English speakers and ESL (English as a Second Language) is a standard part of many classrooms (Okagaki & Diamond, 2003). *Teachers must understand diversity and multiculturalism to fully ensure an appropriate environment for all young children.*

An informational trend is affecting play as the Internet grows. Organizations such as the National Association for the Education of Young Children, International Association of the Child's Right to Play, and the National Program for Playground Safety are capable of providing more information. Anyone seeking information can find research and support within a matter of minutes. Information through books and journals is plentiful.

At the same time, a national crises is occurring in the health of our youngest citizens. As mentioned in Chapter 9, obesity is creating a national discussion of the need for physical movement through recess and play. The focus on the need to play will, most likely, exacerbate within the next 10 years. This national discussion will impact state and local programs.

Community Trends

Neighborhood

Changes in neighborhoods have altered play. In the past, children played in neighborhoods after school, often without adult supervision. Today's neighborhoods may not always be safe, so young children are supervised by adults all the time. They watch television, play games on a computer, or participate in organized activities. The days of roaming through the neighborhood, climbing trees, and wading through a stream have disappeared in most areas of the United States. Children who climb, play with mud, or visit sites in the neighborhood do so under the watchful eye of a parent or early educator. The transient nature of neighborhoods suggests that this trend will continue, thus limiting the freedom to participate in unsupervised play.

To combat this trend, many neighborhoods are developing play places for young children. Neighborhood groups throughout the nation are involved in building playgrounds. Kaboom and Boundless Playgrounds are two nationally recognized groups that are dedicated to establishing playgrounds for all children so that children with special needs can play side by side with typically developing children. The influence of constant adult supervision on the transmission of children's games, songs, and chants is, at this point, unknown.

Families

In the past, young children played with members of the family or siblings. As mentioned previously, many families are smaller. The structure of families has changed over the past 20 years. Young children live in nuclear, single, extended, and blended families. More children live in single-parent homes than in any other structure and single-parent families tend to be under-funded families (Ramsey, 2003). Children who are raised in families without male role models may not experience the benefits of rough-and-tumble play. In addition, the only other young children that they encounter are in group settings. For this reason, many parents are developing play groups two or three times a week. Other changes in the family unit include the increase of grandparents who are serving as parents. As family structures continue to change, play will also change.

■ Current Issues

Young children are experiencing changes in their culture that will affect how they view the world. Notice a four-year-old using a computer that his grandmother will not touch. Watch the five-year-old use her cell phone or Barbie digital camera. Walk through an exhibit filled with art based on the World Trade Center explosion. How will these changes impact children's play? Some are concerned that changes in technology and constant media coverage of all topics are creating a culture that threatens to erode childhood. At the same time, technology provides a link between children and grandparents that offers possibilities never before imagined. Early educators must be informed and serve as both a conduit and filter for information.

Four issues that are currently creating concerns among educators and the public are (1) technology, (2) media influences, (3) toys, and (4) violence. These issues will be considered in this section.

Technology: Ready or Not

Perhaps no other area has created as much conversation and consternation in the early childhood education community than technology. Viewpoints range from complete avoidance to a computer-based curriculum. Early educators are faced with questions. Should I encourage computer usage? Should I refuse to place a computer in my classroom? Will children be forced to choose between computers and play? These are real issues that teachers are currently struggling to answer. The impact of technology on play is a major concern and is already evident in children's play. One colleague shared the following story.

A grandmother reminisced about her experience as a child of watching one of the first telephone operators use a headset and telephone. She recalled that as a child the operator let her put the headset on and dial numbers. She never forgot the magic of that moment. She said she wanted her grandchild to have a similar experience. She was elated when she found a headset that looked like the one she remembered from her childhood. Her granddaughter was equally delighted when she opened the gift. The grandmother later observed the child at play. She had the headset on and was engaged in pretend play. As the grandmother moved closer to the granddaughter, she heard her say, "Hello, Welcome to McDonald's. Can I take your order, please?"

Those who work with young children understand the child's use of headphones. The child was engaged in pretend that reflected her knowledge of reality. In Piaget's terms, she subordinated reality to fit her schema. Vygotskians might point to her social knowledge. The child's experiences with headphones had occurred at fast food restaurants. Even though grandmother had shared her stories about operators and headphones, the child was more familiar with McDonald's restaurants. This child's pretense reflects *her* understanding of her world.

The difference in technology at the beginning and at the end of the twentieth century is startling. At the beginning of the century, technology included new inventions such as telephones, cars, and airplanes, which were reserved for the very few wealthy. At the end of the century, technology includes televisions, computers, and digital phones that are commonly used by a majority of Americans. A survey found that 83% of middle-income homes in America with children between the ages of two and seventeen have a computer. Among low-income homes, 69% own a computer (CPB, 2003). When over half of all children have computers in their home, technology is a daily part of a child's life. Technology has changed rapidly over the past century and will continue to change in the future. These changes will, no doubt, impact play.

Current state of technology

The impact of technology on children can be either positive or negative. It is negative when children access unsafe sites or when teachers isolate children in front of a computer screen for mindless drills. On the other hand, it is very positive when children can take pictures of their play, write about their play, and access additional information that extends their activity. It is the teacher's knowledge that makes the difference. The National Association for the Education of Young Children recognizes the appropriate use of technology in the classroom and supports professional development in the area of technology so early educators will have the necessary knowledge to be effective (Hyson, 2003). "Rather than being merely an enrichment or add on to the curriculum, technology has

These children can connect to classrooms on the other side of the continent. How will this impact their play?

taken a central place in early childhood programs. Candidates demonstrate sound knowledge and skills in using technology as a teaching and learning tool" (p. 38).

Techniques for using technology appropriately have been suggested by Douglas H. Clements and Julie Sarama (2003). They recommend the following.

Planning

- ◆ Use technology only after adequate professional development on the appropriate use of computer hardware and software in education (more than 10 hours).

- ◆ Begin with professional development, then decide on curriculum modifications, software, and hardware—in that order. This avoids waste of time and money.

- Choose high-quality software.
- Promote thoughtful, slow adoption and incremental improvement. Have reasonable expectations of what technology can do and an appreciation of the importance of the total educational environment.

Arranging the classroom setting

- Place two child seats in front of the computer and one at the side for adults. This will encourage social interaction.
- Place computers close to each other to facilitate sharing of ideas among children.
- Locate computers centrally to invite other children to pause and participate in the computer activity.
- Strive for a 10:1 ratio (or better) of children to computers to encourage computer use, cooperation, and equal access by girls and boys.

Teaching

- Be active! Guide children's learning of basic tasks, then encourage experimentation with open-ended problems. Encourage, question, prompt, and demonstrate, as appropriate. Conduct whole-group discussions about strategies.
- Use open-ended software. Designate projects rather than merely asking children to explore freely.
- Make sure children with special needs are accepted and supported at the computer. Offer them initial training so they can demonstrate programs for others. (Clements & Sarama, 2003, p. 37)

Technology and play

Technology can be used to extend, expand, and document play. Documentation panels created in the schools of Reggio Emilia used technology to capture the essence of play. These panels also illustrate the joy involved in play and provide evidence of learning that occurs when children play. Many schools in America are starting to use this concept. In the schools of Reggio Emilia, they recognize the hundred languages that children use and view both technology and play as languages that children use. Putting them together gives children a powerful mode of expression (Fu, Stremmel, & Hill, 2002).

Strategies to enhance the appropriate use of technology to support play and development are listed below.

1. Integrate technology into the classroom. It is optimal to place a computer in the writing center so that children see this as a means of communicating. A separate computer center can also be established. If the computer center is in a separate center, treat it like a center. Digital cameras should be available throughout the day to capture play and learning. Many children see pictures as a natural part of their activity. Some schools have limited funds but are using disposable cameras. Others have encouraged children to take cameras home and record what they do at home. It is easier for children to share their view of the world when using technology.

2. Select appropriate hardware and software.   Use funds wisely. Many companies will donate used equipment. A list of appropriate software is included on the International Society for Technology in Education (ISTE) Web site. Violent games are never appropriate. Some programs waste the child's mind. Flash cards are still flash cards even though they are colorful and flashing! Computer programs should challenge and enrich, not stifle.

3. Use computers appropriately.   Time is important. It is not appropriate to force children to stay at the computer station. At the same time, children who are engaged in interactive play with the computer should not be stopped after 10 minutes. Time spent in front of a computer screen or television is often called **screen time** and should be limited. The effect of overexposure to computer screens is not known, but the effects of passive activities are well documented. It is alarming to know that some companies are targeting babies as an audience for products. Recommended computer use for each age is listed below:

Infants and Toddlers	Infants and toddlers can benefit from the adult's use of technology to create books, posters, and document growth and learning through portfolios. Infants and toddlers should *not* use computers.
Preschoolers	Like infants and toddlers, three- and four-year-olds can benefit from adult's use of technology. Creating books, documenting play and learning for portfolios are valuable activities. In addition, adults can create a record of group activities. Preschoolers can use cardboard replicas in their house area. If a computer is available, some games can be used with older four-year-olds.
Kindergarten/First Grade	Five- and six-year-olds can use computers for creating books, playing games, and

	writing stories. The computer should be a center that is available as needed.
Second/Third Grade	Children who are seven and eight are ready to use the computer on a regular basis to create books, play math games, write stories, and conduct simple research.

It is important to recognize that information technology should reflect best practices. Using a computer with two-year-olds is not appropriate but may be appropriate for kindergarteners. When technology is used, it must be developmentally appropriate for the age, stage, and culture of the child.

4. Integrate technology in the curriculum.   Include pictures of computers and digital cameras in picture boxes. Include technology props in prop boxes and house areas. What are programs that develop skills in math, science, literacy, and social studies?

5. Involve parents.   Many classrooms are setting up Web sites so the child can show the parents what they did at school that day. This is a wonderful way to connect the family to the classroom. In the same way, some classrooms even have a camera attached so parents will know what is going on at the school throughout the day.

6. Continually update your knowledge.   Computer literacy depends on staying current. Those who thought they would wait until the fad passes are in trouble. Computers are a part of everyday life. Keeping current involves reading the latest information and participating in training workshops. Teachers who play with computers and explore a variety of programs are more knowledgeable and can help their students become comfortable with new experiences and learning opportunities.

Impact of technology on play

The impact of technology on play has the potential to be very positive. It also has the potential to be very negative. Technology can be a powerful force in early childhood education if it is used appropriately. It is legitimate to be concerned that the rush to put computers in the classroom has raced ahead of the research. At this time, we really do not have sufficient evidence to know the long-term implications of technology in the classroom and subsequent impact on the young child and their play. The impact of the media on children is, however, well documented and is fully discussed in the next section.

Media

Since the placement of the first television set in a home, the impact of television and media has transformed our culture. The average child spends 35 hours per week either watching television or playing video games (Levin, 1998). Before kindergarten, they will have spent over 4,000 hours watching television (Levin, 1998). They will spend more time in front of a television than in school. During cartoons and children's programs, they will observe more than 20 acts of violence per hour: prime time has 5 acts per hour, and by the end of elementary school, they will have witnessed 8,000 murders and over 100,000 other violent acts (Levin, 1998). The influence of the media cannot be denied, nor can the effect of this onslaught of violence be ignored. The American Medical Association (1996) recognized seven effects of media violence on children. It

1. causes an increase in mean-spirited, aggressive behavior.
2. causes increased levels of fearfulness, mistrust, and self-protective behaviors toward others.
3. contributes to desensitization and callousness to the effects of violence and the suffering of others.
4. provides violent heroes whom children seek to emulate.
5. provides justification for resorting to violence when children think they are right.
6. creates an increasing appetite for viewing more violence and more extreme violence.
7. fosters a culture in which disrespectful behavior becomes a legitimate way for people to treat each other.

Impact of media on play

The effects of overexposure to violence is affecting how children play. Diane Levin (1998) is concerned that

> Many children seem to use playtime to imitate the violence they see on the screen rather than to develop creative, imaginative play of their own making. In addition, these children often impose this violent content and behavior on the play of others. In such a situation the quality of play (and therefore, learning) is undermined for all children in early childhood classrooms. (p. 15)

Children transmit their moral code through play (Piaget, 1965). Watching others play games has always provided a venue for learning games.

Children who are overexposed to violence are developing a moral code from the media and it is a morality based on a culture of violence. The outcome is a change in society and culture resulting in activities that occur in the context of the macrocosm over which teachers have little control.

Obviously, the power of the media in shaping culture cannot be denied. This can also be a positive influence. On television, Fred Rogers influenced generations. One story bears repeating. A well-known professor shared that as a child, he came home every evening to an empty home. Reared in a single parent home, he watched Mr. Rogers every evening until his mother returned from work. Mr. Rogers served as the male influence in his life. When he learned of the September 11, 2001 attack, he went home and after being overcome by disbelief and grief, he turned to *Mr. Rogers's Neighborhood* just as he had done so many times as a child. Just sitting and listening to Mr. Rogers's soothing voice made it easier for him to cope with the violence. The calming effect and wisdom of Fred Rogers was transmitted through the media of television. Similar stories were shared about the influence that Mr. Rogers had on both viewers and those who knew him personally. His wisdom transcends generations and is now recorded for future generations. This is the positive influence of the media. Unfortunately, it pales in comparison to overall media programming.

Early educators must be knowledgeable about the impact of the media. Mr. Rogers would encourage teachers to find ways to use the media in appropriate ways. Another issue closely linked to the media is toys and is discussed in the next section.

Materials and Toys

Toys are miniature replicas of objects in the child's physical and social environment.
—James Christie, James Johnson, & Thomas Yawkey, 1999

Materials and toys provide a reflection of society. Concern is currently being expressed about the effect of the media on children's materials and toys. Nine of the top ten toys in 2002 were related to television shows or movies (Levin, 2003). When a new movie is released, new toys are produced, and new ad campaigns launched to sell toys at fast food restaurants. Children play out this reality during play in the house area. Children who have parents who wisely avoid eating at fast food restaurants and or buying these toys, are left out of the group during conversations and play. This creates a culture of consumerism based on the latest movie and advertisements.

Another concern inherent in the manufacturing of toys is the nature of the toys themselves. Toys that are *unidimensional* only have one focus and can only be used in predetermined ways. Toys that are developed specifically for a movie or television show have only one use. It is difficult to do very much with an action hero figure other than play out scenarios that involve action heroes. In most of the book, *multidimensional toys* or open-ended toys such as blocks, house items, sand, water, and art materials have been discussed (Christie, Johnson, & Yawkey, 1999). Open-ended materials can be used for any purpose. The only limit is the child's imagination.

The impact of this change can be examined by looking at a list of materials and toys that are used in play. These can be divided into a taxonomy of open-ended to structured.

Unidimensional toys have only one option for play.

1. *Natural or real materials* are materials that are real and that adults use on a daily basis such as mud, water, clay, food, wood, clothes, utensils.
2. *Construction materials* are materials that can be used to build and create. These include unit blocks, hollow blocks, sponge blocks, cardboard blocks, tinker toys, interlocking plastic units, wood, nails, and hammers.
3. *Toys* are materials that stimulate play and include replicas of people and animals, vehicles, and homes and places. This includes bicycles and wheeled vehicles.
4. *Educational materials* are materials that facilitate skills such as stringing beads, puzzles, nesting materials, books that talk to children, computer programs, and robots.

Most of the toys influenced by the media are designed for more structured play. This is the reason for the concern among some educators.

Toy safety

Another current concern is toy safety. The National Safe Kids Campaign found that in 2001, at least 25 children ages seven and under died from toy-related injuries. The same year, an estimated 202,500 children ages fourteen and under were treated in hospital emergency rooms for toy-related injuries. The biggest danger is latex balloons for children under three. Riding toys are responsible for the most injuries between three and fourteen.

Violence

Perhaps no other issue is impacting children more than violence. Violence transcends political and national borders. It is a concern in Miami, in New York City, and in neighborhoods, schools, and families in both rural and urban America. Since the September 11, 2001 attack on the World Trade Center, few are exempt from the reality of violence and its subsequent impact.

Children who grow up in violent neighborhoods, attend dangerous schools, and go home to abusive homes are at risk to grow into abusive, violent adults. But even children who live in safe neighborhoods, attend safe schools, and grow up with nonabusive parents may be at risk. When children are surrounded by violence on television, play with toys that encourage violence, and play computer games, they are immersed in an environment that James Garbarino refers to as **"social toxicity."** Social toxicity is a term he used to refer to the social and cultural "poisons" that surround the child (Garbarino, 1999). To combat the effects of violence on children, Levin (2003) suggest guidelines to help children use play to work out violent and disturbing content.

- ◆ Watch children as they play to learn more about what they know, what worries them, and what they are struggling to understand.
- ◆ Remember that for many children it is normal and helpful to bring into their play graphic aspects of what they have seen and heard.
- ◆ If the play gets scary or dangerous, gently intervene and redirect it. For example, ask children, "How could people help each other?" Or provide toys such as rescue vehicles and medical equipment.
- ◆ Help them come up with ways for extending the play. Try to follow the children's lead in the roles that you take rather than taking over.
- ◆ After the play, talk to children about what they played. Reassure their safety. Answer questions simply. Clear up confusions.
- ◆ Try to teach alternatives to the harmful lessons children may be learning from the violence they bring to the play. (p. 104)

Some children will need additional intervention and can benefit from play therapy.

■ Play Research

Now, perhaps researchers can derive as much pleasure from their serious investigative efforts as children do from engaging in this mutual topic of interest—play!
—Kenneth Rubin, Greta Fein, & Brian Vandenberg, 1983

At the beginning of the twentieth century, play research was influenced by the emphasis on empirical research and focused on the physical and social aspects of play. During the second half of the century, research examined the benefits of play in terms of development. Cognitive development and social pretend dominated the literature during this time. As we move into the twenty-first century, the study of play is being influenced by new information in the area of research methods, cognitive development, social and emotional development, and physical development.

Research Methods

The state of play research was dealt a blow by omission from the fifth edition of the *Handbook of Child Psychology* (Eisenberg, 1998). Though play held a prominent role in the fourth edition of the *Handbook of Child Psychology*

(Mussen, 1983), it is markedly missing from the fifth edition. Those interested in play theory must turn to the *Handbook of Research on the Education of Young Children* (Spodek, 1993) for the most recent overview of play in a major research volume, and this source is a decade old.

A movement away from the laboratory and into the classroom started during the past decade and is continuing to gain momentum. The focus on the teacher as researcher is continuing to affect how some teachers view their role in the classroom. Naturalistic settings provide rich environments for gathering data and are gaining in popularity. These settings affect research and the data that is gathered.

Another change in research is the role of play in the study. In the past, many studies looked at behaviors that occurred during play. More recent studies are using play as an intervention for performance outcomes in the areas of social interaction, math, and literacy.

Cognitive Development

Research on Theory of Mind (TOM) has begun to change some previously held beliefs about the child's ability to understand concepts. As discussed in Chapter 2, Theory of Mind refers to research that looks at the child's ability to understand what others are communicating in terms of intentionality. Research in this area emphasizes the role of culture on cognitive development.

Another area of interest is brain-based research. The latest findings confirm the plasticity of the brain. Children have over a 100 trillion synaptic connections at eight months of age but lose these as the infant interacts with his culture. By the age of ten, the typical child has 500 million connections (Shornkoff & Phillips, 2000). Those that were not used were eliminated. As we know more about the brain, additional information will help clarify the role of play in establishing neurological connections. This presents an exciting area of research.

Social and Emotional Development

Information regarding social interaction and emotions is changing in terms of play. The use of play as a way to assist children who are experiencing cognitive, social, or physical difficulties or delay continues. In one article, Riihela (2002) investigated children's play as the origin of social activity. One ongoing study that is being conducted at Yale University by Drs. Jerome and Dorothy Singer uses play as an intervention for facilitating play skills that may impact developing reading skills. (See Chapter 5.)

Physical Development

Health issues have never been more important. Many organizations are turning to play as a way to decrease the number of obese children. Play research in the next decade may be conducted by the medical community rather than early childhood educators. Another area that is impacting development is the number of children who are living with grandparents. Children who live with octogenarians are certainly affected by their physical limitations. How does this affect the physical development of children who are living with them? The need for intergenerational studies has never been greater.

■ Play Policy

At the same time that the research literature on the value of play appears to be expanding geometrically, the presence of play in early childhood classrooms has been dwindling impetuously.
—*Doris Fromberg, 1990*

When early scholars of play discussed the benefits of play, they based their comments on their studies of previous research and personal observations. As we enter the twenty-first century, we know more about the benefits of play than at any other time in history. Indeed, Brian Sutton-Smith has spent a lifetime studying play and stated that play is probably necessary for survival (1997). The recent plethora of research has validated the real benefits of play. Though we know more about the value of play for young children, early educators are being challenged to focus on skills that can be measured on tests and to eliminate outdoor play. Changing the public's perception of play begins with developing sound play policy that can be used to guide play advocacy efforts (Seefeldt, 1995). Ideas imitated in the first chapter serve as a foundation for developing play policy. These include:

- ◆ Play is important in the lives of young children.
- ◆ Play and development are reciprocal and progressive. Play contributes to growth and development and these, in turn, enhance play. Both follow an orderly progression from simple to complex.
- ◆ Play promotes good physical and mental health.
- ◆ All children should have play places that are safe and support play.
- ◆ All children have the right to play as stated in Article 31 of the United Nations Convention on the Rights of the Child.

Play policy supports play for all children.

Though these ideas may seem repetitive to those who have read this book, these can be used to develop a play policy that can be used to inform the public. Basic advocacy steps include awareness, research, and action (Kieff & Casbergue, 2000). James Garbarino (2000) tells his students, "You can change the world . . . but unless you know what you are doing, please don't." The steps below provide information that will assist in changing public perceptions about play.

1. Awareness:
   ◆ **Develop an awareness of the needs and available resources.**
   ◆ **Investigate.** What is the current state of play in your area?
2. Research:
   ◆ **What professional organizations promote play?** Many organizations are dedicated to supporting play. International groups include the National Association for the Education of Young Children (NAEYC), Association for Childhood Education International (ACEI), International Play Association (IPA), The Association for the Study of Play (TASP), and the Parent Teachers Association (PTA). State and local groups are available throughout the United States.
   ◆ **What are other communities doing?**

3. **Action:**

   ◆ **Consider what steps are needed to make a difference and take them.**

   Plan activities in your classroom. Parents who are informed are supportive. Plan the following activities to communicate with parents:

   Home visits. Discuss the value of play during home visits.

   Group meetings. Present the benefits of play from research studies.

   Newsletters. Send articles and statements supporting play home in newsletters. Include pictures and stories relating the children's progress through play.

   Class Web pages. Many classrooms have a Web page. Teachers take pictures of children at play and explain what they are gaining from this experience. Links are included that connect parents Internet sites that support a play-based curriculum.

   Plan or participate in a local play day. Every year, AARP sponsors an international play day and many communities host activities for young children that focus on the child's need to play.

   Be politically active. Know your local representatives and discuss the child's need to play and the impact of legislating mandates on children.

PlayScape Reflections

At the beginning of the chapter, Selma and Harry were engaged in pretend play with blocks and enjoyed play most when the adult was not involved. This is very similar to what we see every day in our classrooms; it was different in that the materials reflected technological changes that have not been created yet. Based on our concerns about the influence of technological and media changes, we can only hope that children are allowed to create their interpretation of the world through materials that are designed specifically for them. Today, some manufacturers are trying to find ways to market computers to parents of babies in order to stimulate the babies. A real concern exists that these programs are not only ineffective, but that they will also produce damage that cannot be reversed. This has occurred in China when parent(s) pushed infants and toddlers to walk and crawl before they were ready. These children suffered permanent neurological damage. As we move into the twenty-first century, the challenge will be to use technology designed for adults in ways that are appropriate for children. We should not force children to adapt to technology, rather we should ensure that all technology is used appropriately with young children. In this way, modern technology enhances the child's quality of life.

■ Summary

Play does seem to open up another part of the mind that is always there, but that, since childhood, may have become closed off and hard to reach. When we treat children's play as seriously as it deserves, we are helping them feel the joy that's to be found in the creative spirit. We're helping ourselves stay in touch with that spirit, too. It's the things we play with and the people who help us play that make a great difference in our lives.

—Fred Rogers, 2003

An overview of the current state of play practice and research was presented in this chapter. An exploration of major issues included technology, media, materials and toys, and violence. The impact of current demographic and social changes were considered at the global, national, community, and local level. An overview of play research was presented as a way to understand not just the current but also the future state of play. The challenge in the twenty-first century will be to protect the child's natural style of learning through play and to encourage early educators to engage in play advocacy efforts. This book may help teachers meet this challenge.

■ Key Terms

Screen time
Social toxicity

■ Helpful Web Sites and Technology Resources

◆ **National SAFE KIDS Campaign**
http://www.safekids.org/   This site is sponsored by the National SAFE KIDS Campaign. National SAFE KIDS Campaign is a national nonprofit organization dedicated to preventing unintentional deaths of children under fourteen.

■ Activities

1. InCass Lab

A. What issues are affecting play in your community? How do you know that this issue is the causal agent? If this issue is responsible for a negative change in play, list three actions that your group can take to make a change. If this issue is responsible for a positive change in play, how can your group supply additional support or encouragement?

2. Research and Inquiry-based Learning

A. Select one area of interest (for example, recess, pretend play, or sand) and locate a study that dealt with it at the beginning of the twentieth century and one that deals with it now. What are the similarities? What are the differences?

B. Spend four hours on a Saturday morning in front of local toy store. What toys were purchased? What factors seemed to influence the purchases?

C. Use the Internet to discover how children are playing in other parts of the world.

3. Service Learning

A. Contact a local women's shelter. Ask if you can volunteer to survey and repair toys and other materials that are available to the young children of women in the shelter.

B. Talk to the local police department about their policy for dealing with young children. Some departments carry teddy bears with them for young children and are always needing replacements so they can give them to more children. What can you do to add to their collection? If they do not have a policy, can you help them start a program?

4. Family Connections

A. Ask parents to survey their children's toys and donate any unwanted toys to local charity organizations such as homeless shelters.

5. Play Advocacy

A. Find out how you can support play in early childhood education in your local area. Are there local groups that conduct activities during the Week of the Young Child? Do they write letters to support play and recess in local schools? How can you become an advocate for play on the local, state, and national level?

■ References

Allen, J. (2002). *Day care in the community: Action research in family and early childhood.* UNESCO Education Sector Monograph. Paris, France: UNESCO.

AMA (1996). *American Medical Association. Physician guide to media violence.* Chicago: AMA.

Christie, J., Johnson, J., & Yawkey, T., (1999). *Play and early childhood development.* New York: Longman.

Clements, D., & Sarama, J. (2003). Young children and technology: What does the research say? *Young Children, 58* (6), 34–40.

Corporation for Public Broadcasting (CPB). (2003). Connected to the future: A report on children's Internet use from the Corporation for Public Broadcasting. Retrieved September 3, 2003 from www.cpb.org/pdfs/ed/resources/connected/

Eisenberg, N. (Ed.) (1998). Social, emotional, and personality development, Volume 3, In W. Damon (Series Ed.) *Handbook of child psychology* (5th ed.). New York: Wiley.

Factor, J. (1993). Enriching the play environment: Creativity, culture, and tradition. *World Play Summit '93: Environments for Play, Melbourne 14–19 Feb: Proceedings.* Melbourne, Australia: World Play Summit Management Association.

Fromberg, D. (1990). A review of research on play. In C. Seefeldt (Ed.), *The early childhood curriculum: A review of current research* (pp. 42–85). New York: Teachers College Press.

Fu, V., Stremmel, A., & Hill, L. (2002). *Teaching and learning: Collaborative explorations of the Reggio Emilia approach.* Columbus, OH: Merrill.

Garbarino, J. (1999). *Lost boys: Why our sons turn violent & how we can save them.* New York: Free Press.

Garbarino, J. (2003). Introduction in Diane E. Levin. *Teaching young children in violent times: Building a peaceable classroom.* Washington, DC: NAEYC.

Hyson, M. (2003). Professional Development: "Introducing NAEYC's Early Learning Standards: Creating conditions for success." *Young Children, 58* (1), 66–68.

Kami, C. (1996). Seminar on Piaget. University of Alabama, Birmingham. AL.

Kieff, J., & Casbergue, R. (2000). *Playful learning and teaching: Integrating play into preschool and primary programs.* Boston, Allyn & Bacon.

Levin, D. (1998). *Remote control childhood? Combating the hazards of media culture.* Washington, DC: NAEYC.

Levin, D. (2003). *Teaching young children in violent times.* Washington, DC: NAEYC.

Mussen, P. (Series Ed.), (1983). *Handbook of child psychology.* New York: Wiley.

Okagaki, L., & Diamond, K. (2003). Responding to cultural and linguistic differences in the beliefs and practices of families with young children. In C. Copple (Ed.) *A world of difference: Readings on teaching young children in a diverse society* (pp. 9–15). Washington, DC: NAEYC.

Piaget, J. (1965). *The moral judgement of the child.* New York: Free Press.

Ramsey, P. (2003). The stress of poverty. In C. Copple (Ed.) *A world of difference: Readings on teaching young children in a diverse society* (pp. 86–88). Washington, DC: NAEYC.

Riihela, M. (2002). Children's play is the origin of social activity. *European Early Childhood Education Research Journal, 10* (1), 39–53.

Rogers, C. (1989). Personal Interview with Liv Ulman. Recorded for PBS pilot, *To Play.*

Rogers, F. (2003). *The world according to Mister Rogers: Important things to remember.* New York: Hyperion.

Rubin, K. H., Fein, G., & Vandenberg, B. (1983). Play. In E. M. Hetherington (Ed.). P. H. Mussen (Series Ed.), *Handbook of child psychology: Vol. 4, Socialization, personality, and social development* (pp. 693–774). New York: Wiley.

Seefeldt, C. (1995). Playing with policy: A serious undertaking. In E. Klugman *Play, policy and practice.* St. Paul, MN: Redleaf Press.

Shornkoff, J., & Phillips, D. (Eds.) (2000). *From neurons to neighborhoods: The science of early childhood development.* Publication of the National Research Council and Institute of Medicine. Washington, DC: National Academy Press.

Spodek, B. (Ed.) (1993). *Handbook of research on the education of young children.* New York: Macmillan.

Sutton-Smith, B. (1997). *The ambiguity of play.* Cambridge, MA: Harvard University Press.

Glossary

A   **accommodation**—Term used by Piaget to describe the process that occurs when children adjust their schemata or mental structures to accept new knowledge. This generally occurs during instruction when children acquire new information.

adventure playgrounds—Adventure playgrounds allow the children to engage in open-ended play or adventures as they design and build different structures. Materials and tools are available for building the play structure.

assimilation—Term used by Piaget to describe the process that occurs when the child fits information into existing mental structures or schemata. Piaget thought that play was almost pure assimilation. For Piaget, play strengthened and solidified neurological connections.

assistive technology—Any adaptation that facilitates the ability of the individual to function. Frequently used to refer to computer assistance provided to individuals who have special needs. Assistive technology can range from low-tech such as adding knobs to puzzles to high-tech changes such as adding switches or using computers to communicate.

associative play—Play that occurs when a child plays with another child. They may talk to each other, exchange toys, and play near one another, but they do not have defined roles or shared goals.

attachment—A strong emotional tie that exists between a baby or young child and caring adult who is part of the child's everyday life. The child's attachment to the adult can affect play. Children who are secure that the adult will return can engage in more complex play whereas children who are concerned that the adult will not return may not engage in play at all.

authentic assessment—Assessing children using an on-going, continuous process. Generally conducted in the classroom or on the playground on a daily basis, it is used to provide information about the child's development and involves the child, parent, and teacher in a collaborative process designed to facilitate learning.

autocosmic play—This term was coined by Erikson to describe what he viewed as the first level of play that occurs in the first year of life when the child explores, experiences, and investigates his own body as he discovers he is separate from other people. Involves a lot of repetitive play—shaking hands, shaking feet, and pulling hair.

autonomy—Typically refers to the notion that individuals are independent and self-reliant. That is, that peer influences are minimal and behaviors are based on

347

reason, not popular opinion. Piaget believed that facilitating the development of autonomy should be the aim of education.

B **basic forms stage**—A stage in the development of writing when children move beyond *controlled scribbles* and can repeat their marks on paper. It is not unusual to see a child at this age fill a complete page with similar marks.

C **chase**—Involves one child running after another child.

child-focused intervention—Child-focused intervention includes all aspects of the child's educational program: (1) designing appropriate environments, (2) individualizing and adapting the curriculum, and (3) using systematic procedures to optimize outcomes.

child study movement—A period of time in the first three decades of the twentieth century when a group of scholars simultaneously began using scientific research methods to study children. A great deal of their work still informs research today. Example: Mildred Parten's study of social interaction is as beneficial today as it was in 1932 when it was published.

children-first language—Refers to the use of language to acknowledge and respect the child with special needs first as an individual. It is never appropriate to refer to a child by their diagnosed medical condition or disability. The child is always a child first.

choice boards—Boards that provide an array of play choices available in the classroom. Children may place a clothespin, picture, or symbol/name tag next to the area to show that this is their play choice for the day. Choice boards present a procedure that is understandable and fair for the young child. This provides a venue for developing independence that leads to autonomy.

choke tube—A tube used to check the size of a toy. If the toy fits inside the tube, it could fit inside the child's throat, become lodged, and cause an infant-toddler to choke to death. Toys that are too big to go through the choke tube are considered safe. Choke tubes vary according to the child's age.

chronosystem—In Bronfenbrenner's ecological theory, the chronosystem refers to the impact of sociocultural and sociohistorical factors on the child. Examining the impact of factors over a period of time provides insight that may be available otherwise. For example, the impact of the computers on play can be observed in children who have been exposed to them since birth.

cognitive constructivism—A type of constructivism that emphasizes the child's internal construction of knowledge as the source of information. Piaget is the primary source of inspiration for this approach.

concrete operational stage—Piaget used this term to refer to the stage when children begin to develop a more organized view of the world. Conservation and logical though develop during this time which generally occurs between seven to eleven years of age.

community playgrounds—Started in Europe after World War II and known as adventure playgrounds. In America, term frequently refers to a playground built through a community-initiated effort.

constructivism—Educational approach based on the notion that children construct knowledge as they interact with their world.

constructive play—Play that occurs when children use materials to create, invent, or construct something; occurs more than any other kind of play in the classroom and leads to the development of skills and creativity.

contemporary playgrounds—Defined areas that have diverse ground coverings and an assortment of equipment designed for a variety of ages and levels. Contemporary playgrounds generally have structures made of wood with tire swings, slides with platforms at the top, and climbing ropes that provide a variety of physical challenges. In addition, driving areas for tricycles, wagons and buggies, and shaded areas are a part of the playground.

context—The social, cultural, political, and environmental factors that impact behavior. The context influences and affects play behaviors.

controlled scribbles—Type of drawing that young children make when they can control the direction of the pencil or crayon. This can be observed during play in a variety of settings.

coordination of secondary schemes (eight to twelve months)—Piagetian term used to describe a level of cognitive development that occurs during the first year of life. The child tries known actions in new situations. Because mobility is increasing, the child moves quickly from one action to another. That is, she uses a previously learned behavior in a novel setting and does so rather quickly. Pushing and pulling objects, putting hats/materials on their heads, and filling and dumping are examples of play that occurs as a result.

cooperative play—Term used by Parten to describe play that occurs when two or more children engage in interactive play with a common goal. This is a complex level of social play in which the children may assign roles and scripts.

co-play—The adult slides into the child's play to extend and expand it. As a co-player, the teacher does not take the lead, but rather follows the child's lead.

creeper-crawler—An informal term sometimes used to describe older infants who are beginning to crawl.

D   **DAP**—Acronym for developmentally appropriate practice (DAP). DAP is based on a consensus of experts. This perspective encourages children to make choices, values the child's interest, and emphasizes play and enjoyment as best practice for young children.

      DEC—The Division of Early Childhood (DEC) is a division of the professional organization, Council of Exceptional Children (CEC). Whereas CEC is committed to working with disabled individuals, DEC specifically focuses on young children with special needs and their families.

decentration—Moving from focusing on self to awareness that others exist. This generally occurs within the first two years of life. Piaget viewed this as the first step in the development of symbolic play.

decontextualization—Representing objects and actions symbolically with other objects and actions. Piaget viewed this as the second level of symbolic play. For example, an older infant may lay his head on a pillow as though he is going to sleep. He realizes he is not sleeping and may look at observing adults and smile because he knows it is not real.

developmental-interaction approach—Program model that combines Dewey's view of progressive education with Erikson's view of emotional development. The goal is to educate the whole child by fostering development through social interactions. Bank Street is the original model and is located at Columbia College in New York.

documentation panels—Large boards that are used to display evidence of children's learning, play, and other behaviors through both pictures and narratives. Idea originated in the schools of Reggio Emilia, Italy. These panels are displayed for a number of years so others can see what children are gaining from the program and understand the history of the program.

dramatic play—A type of play that involves symbolism in which one thing represents or stands for another. For example, children might choose to let a set of blocks represent a hotel or plastic teddy bears serve as money. Pretend is the essential element.

E   **early intervention**—Services provided for children with disabilities or delays (birth to age three) and their families. The goal of early intervention is to provide services in the most natural setting for the child. That is, in the place or setting the child would be in if they were not disabled. For some children who have mild disabilities, this may occur in the local child care center. Others who are medically fragile may receive services in a hospital setting.

electronic portfolio/e-folio—Similar to a regular portfolio, the e-folio provides a record and interpretation of the child's experiences in school using a computer program such as Power Point™.

ego mastery—A term used to describe a benefit of play. This occurs when emotions can be "played out" and anxiety reduced through play.

exosystem—In Bronfenbrenner's ecological model, the larger social system that surrounds the child. Though the child is not directly impacted, the child is indirectly influenced. For example, changes in child care regulations by the local government or the elimination of the parent's job will impact the child's life by affecting the microsystem. For example, if a state eliminates recess, the child will be directly influenced though they have no direct contact or control over the system.

exploration—Exploration involves gaining information: the child engages in activities that are stereotypical, require deep concentration, and have a neutral effect. Inquiry-based learning and the Project Approach are based on exploration.

exploratory play—Although purists reject this term, some use it to describe the young child's play when it is rapidly moving between play and exploration. Exploratory behaviors occur in tandem with play during the first two years of the child's life and some refer to this process as exploratory play.

F **fine motor skills**—Motor skills that develop small-muscle coordination. Generally, play that involves puzzles, manipulatives, stringing buttons, and dropping clothes-pins/marbles develop these small muscles.

formative assessment—Assessment that occurs throughout the year or set time period and uses instruments and methods to provide feedback that can be used to guide behaviors or curriculum.

fortuitous combinations—Piaget viewed this as the second level of *practice play*. The child begins to put new combinations together. For example, the child can put toys in and take toys out of the basket.

functional play—Sensory and motor exploration of people, materials, and toys; appears in infancy and is evident throughout the first two years. Smilansky used the term to describe the lowest level of play, similar to practice play described by Piaget. Functional and practice play tend to be used interchangeably.

fundamental movement phase—This is a stage that occurs during the preschool years. Children are developing skills that provide a foundation for movement throughout their lives.

G **games with rules**—According to Piaget, the third stage of play. Children develop games with rules as they become more capable of using symbolism and external rules to guide play. The rules can be changed with group consensus and can be transmitted to others orally.

graphic organizers—A method of organizing thought processes by drawing a picture with words that depict how the person is thinking about a topic. This is sometimes referred to as mind mapping.

gross motor skills—Motor skills that develop large-muscle coordination. Outdoor play provides a good arena for developing large-muscle coordination through hopping, running, skipping, and riding tricycles.

H **here-and-now curriculum**—A social studies curriculum developed in the early twenties at Bank Street that focuses on what is close or relevant to the child. It is designed to help children understand their world.

holiday curriculum—A social studies curriculum based on celebrating national holidays. Some teachers refer to this as the calendar curriculum when teachers use this to the exclusion of any other approach. If this approach is used, religious holidays should be omitted.

I **inclusion**—Placement of children with disabilities or delays in settings with nondisabled children. Inclusion should occur in natural environments where a child would be placed if they did not have a disability or special need.

inclusive playgrounds—Play areas designed to allow children with disabilities or delays to access all areas so that they experience play with all children.

indiscriminant (or *stereotypical play*)—A term used by Piaget to describe object play that occurs when the child uses an object in an indiscriminant way. For example, the child bangs the cup or throws the bottle.

Individual Family Service Plan (IFSP)—A written plan that describes the goals for a child and her family and indicates how these will be met through the delivery of services.

infant-directed speech (IDS)—A term used to describe speech that infants use to engage adults and others.

Infant-Toddler Environmental Rating Scale (ITERS)—Scale developed by Thelma Harms to rate the environment of an infant-toddler center.

integration—Piaget used this term to describe a stage in which the child uses a combination of several single schemes in a multiple-scheme play experience. For example, the child pretends to put the doll in the bed.

intentional combinations—Piaget used this term to describe the third level of *practice play*. During this time, the child engages in repetitive behaviors that are more complex than in the second stage, and these foster new play experiences in which new behaviors are deliberately combined.

K   **KWL Chart**—A chart used to organize children's thinking during project work or other class activities. It provides a graphic representation of what the children want to **K**now, what they **W**ant to learn, and what they **L**earned. This is frequently used in project work to organize the children's activities.

L   **lap babies**—A term caregivers sometimes use to describe an infant that is not mobile.

latchkey child—A child who is at home alone without adult supervision for an hour or so before their parents return from work. These children typically carry a key with them so they can unlock the door in the afternoon, hence the name latchkey.

locomotor skills—Skills involving movement such as running, jumping, hopping, climbing, skipping, rolling, creeping, crawling, climbing, stepping up and down, bounding, and galloping: the list is endless.

logical-mathematical knowledge—The type of knowledge that is developed when children construct a mental relationship between two objects; it is developed through play as children develop relationships between materials as they set the table, put the block on top of a stack, or complete a puzzle.

M   **macrosphere**—Erikson described this as the second level of play development. It begins when the child enters the social realm which involves interactions with others beyond the primary caregiver. Children develop a shared view of the world as they engage in sociodramatic play and games.

macrosystem—In an ecological systems model, the culture in which the child lives including the beliefs, behaviors, and other patterns that are handed down from one generation to another. The child's culture will impact his play and this will be further impacted when the children bring their culture from home (Macrosystem) to the child care center (Microsystem).

mere practice play—This is the first stage of *practice play* and involves simple repetitive activity that the infant engages in for pleasure.

mesosystem—In an ecological systems model, relationships between two systems, such as family and school.

microsphere—Erikson referred to this as a stage where children gain mastery over their world as they gain mastery over their toys. *Solitary play* is the primary social mode of play, and pleasure is derived from managing and manipulating toys.

microsystem—In an ecological systems model, this is the setting in which the child lives; composed of the child's family, neighborhood, schools, peers, and other factors that directly impact the child.

motherse or parentese—The high-pitched voice that adults often use when talking to infants.

mother-ground—In some parts of Africa, a term used to refer to a special area set aside for children to play.

N   **natural environment**—Describes the location in which the child would be if he was not disabled. The goal of the amendments to the Individuals with Disabilities Education Act (IDEA) is to encourage natural environments for children with disabilities or delays.

natural play spaces—Areas that are not fenced or defined by adults but provide a space for children to play and run freely.

newborns—Used to refer to infants between the time of birth and four months of age.

O   **object play**—Object play begins around four months of age when the infant's interest moves from self to play with others and objects. Interactions with objects is called object play whereas interactions with adults is called social play.

onlooker behavior—The child watches, asks questions, and talks to other children. She is observing, but fails to play. She is more engaged than in unoccupied behavior, but she is not playing. While some onlooker behavior is normal, if this occurs on an ongoing basis, intervention is needed.

Ounce Scale—The Ounce Scale provides an interactive system of documentation, monitoring, and evaluation of development for Early Head Start programs, early intervention programs, including children at risk or who have special needs or disabilities, and other home or vendor-based infant, toddler, and preschool child-care in the community.

P **parallel play**—A type of social play identified by Mildred Parten in which the child plays independently alongside other children but does not engage in conversation or play with them. Some children who are entering a new play setting will engage in this kind of play.

pay for play—Commercial playgrounds located in businesses and entertainment parks designed around popular culture.

photo essay—A technique that captures the child's play through a set of pictures that may or may not include explanations. Photo essays present a message through visual imagery.

physical knowledge—Knowledge gained by observing the physical traits of an object. Young children rely on physical knowledge to help them understand the world. For example, they believe that a penny is worth more than a dime because it's bigger.

plan-do-review—An approach used by High/Scope to structure children's play experiences. Children plan what they will play, then they play, and afterwards they discuss or review what they did and represent this work by talking about it, drawing pictures, or dictating stories. In this way, children develop skills for planning and communicating their actions.

play frame—The term play frame has been used to describe an episode of play that has a definite beginning point and a definite ending point. The play frame begins when children shift from reality to pretend play and it ends when children shift back to reality. Children use signals to communicate the beginning and ending of play.

play rituals—Rituals that occur during play that transmit cultural values through aesthetically satisfying behaviors. For example, children transmit jump-rope/clapping chants on the playground through other children, not adults.

play script—Script is used to refer to a mental structure for actions or events. Play scripts are organizing structures that store play events in the young child's memory. Young children store only short play scripts, so even though they may play for an hour, they will explain the activity in a sentence. This is their play script. This term is also used by teachers to describe the conversations and interactions during sociodramatic play.

play tutors—A play tutor serves as a play leader or model who scaffolds the child or children to a higher level of play. This technique is used mostly in therapeutic settings or with children who have disabilities or delays.

play years—The play years occur from the age of two to six when play informs the child's view of the world and pretend play reaches its peak. Fantasy and pretend play are dominant during this time.

playfulness—An attitude or disposition characterized by joy, humor, and spontaneous action. It is important to note that play and playfulness are not the same.

pleasure principle—The theory that children play because they are motivated to seek pleasure and avoid pain. Viewed by Freud as primary motivator for play and recognized by others as an outcome of play.

portfolios—This term was first used to refer to folders or containers for projects used by artists to store and display their best projects. It is now used to describe a system of storing and displaying children's work in the class. Most teachers use notebooks, but boxes can be used also. Some schools even use computers for storing electronic versions of the portfolio (e-folio). The portfolio provides a venue for capturing a sample of the child's best work or most interesting play over a period of time.

practice play—Term used by Piaget to describe the first stage of play that dominates the first two years of life. The child engages in repetition of an experience for the sheer joy of doing so. Although this is the first stage of play, it can also occur later.

preoperational thinking—Second stage of Piaget's stages of cognitive development. Children develop the ability to internally represent sensorimotor actions, yet do not engage in operational or logical thought.

preschematic stage—Stage of artistic development that occurs from four to seven and involves the use of symbols to represent ideas, thoughts, experiences, or feelings.

primary circular reactions (one to four months)—First stage of infant development in which primary circular reactions develop. During this time, touching becomes important as the infant develops the ability to use circular actions when grasping and reaching for objects. This is when the infant discovers cause and effect.

prime time—The period when the brain is especially efficient at specific types of learning.

project approach—A curriculum approach that utilizes projects as a way to organize the curriculum. Projects are divided into three sections, Phase I (introduction), Phase II (investigation), and Phase III (communication). This has been popularized by the recent interest in the schools of Reggio Emilia, Italy, because they use them for all age levels.

prop boxes—Boxes or plastic containers used to store materials or props that are related to a specific theme. Example: artificial flowers, ribbons, pots, and Styrofoam™ can be used to create a flower shop. Pictures and words on the outside of the box increase ease of access. Both teacher and children can easily find the material that will support play.

R **recess**—A block of time when children are allowed to go to defined play areas and engage in self-selected physical play. This is not the same as physical education and all children should have daily recess.

reflexive stage (birth to one month)—Reflexes rule this age and newborns spend their time watching, observing, and reacting instinctively. Brain research tells us that the child is developing and pruning synapses during this time.

rough-and-tumble play—Rough and tumble includes a combination of activities including play face, running, chasing, fleeing, wrestling, and the open-hand beat.

running record—A running record is a record of observed behaviors. The adult watches the child or targeted behavior for a specified period of time, (5, 10, 15 minutes, or whatever amount of time previously established) and writes down everything that is observed. Objective observations should be included in a narrative style. Subjective observations or personal interpretations should not be included.

S **scaffold/scaffolding**—A verbal support provided by the teacher or adult to move the child to a higher level of understanding. For example, scaffolding occurs when the more competent other assists and guides the child in developing a better strategy for retrieving the object.

screen time—Time children spend in front of a computer, game, or television screen.

screening instruments—An assessment tool designed to provide a quick screening of the child's development in order to identify children who need additional tests. Common screening instruments include the Lapp, Brigance, and McCarthy screening tests.

scribble stage—A stage of artistic development that occurs when the child begins to hold a pencil and make random marks.

secondary circular reactions stage—The time between four and eight months when infants develop reaching and grabbing skills. The joy of causing an effect is evident in laughter. Doing something for the pleasure of doing it evolves at this age.

sensorimotor play—Term used by some to describe practice play that occurs when the infant is engaged in pleasure-producing behaviors that involve exercising sensorimotor schemata. This type of play occurs during the first two years of life.

sitting and "lap" babies—Term used to refer to young infants who have very little mobility. Generally defined as the period from birth to one year.

social arbitrary knowledge—Knowledge developed during social interactions with others. Includes knowledge transmitted from other generations and other cultures. Numbers, writing, and language are all examples of information acquired as social arbitrary knowledge.

social toxicity—A term coined by James Garbarino to describe the presence of social and cultural "poisons" in the world of children and youth. Poisons refer to the profanity, sexuality, and violence routinely viewed on television and in the media.

social constructivism—One type of constructivism that emphasizes the construction of knowledge during social interactions with more capable others. Social constructivism is greatly influenced by Vygotsky's sociocultural perspective.

social skills curriculum—A social studies curriculum that is based on developing social skills necessary to navigate the social world. Many still see this as the primary goal of preschool and kindergarten.

sociocultural theory—A theory of cognitive development that considers the impact of social, cultural, and historical factors on the construction of knowledge during interactions with others.

sociodramatic play—The highest level of symbolic play in which children engage in symbolism and mutual reciprocity as they assign and assume roles. Children must agree to put the goals of the group above their own individual goals during sociodramatic play.

solitary play—The child plays alone or independently and does not interact with others. Concentrates on individual play. Although Parten initially saw this as a lower level of play, others view this as very worthwhile and view it as equally valuable.

special rights—A term used in the schools of Reggio Emilia, Italy, to describe the status of the child who, in the United States would be described as having special needs.

spokesperson for reality—A role the adult assumes to add depth to play by extending and expanding it. Paradoxically, it can also stop play.

stander and mover (one year to eighteen months)—Used by caregivers to describe a child who is a toddler and can stand alone but has low mobility.

summative assessment—Assessment procedure used to provide information about how much the child has learned over a period of time; it occurs at the end of a period of time and is generally used to determine if the child has met certain objectives and has gained knowledge in specific content areas.

superhero play—Play that combines pretend play and rough-and-tumble play. In this play, children choose to assume roles of superheroes that they watch on television or in the movies. Sometimes a group will work together to develop a theme around a common superhero.

switch—An electrical device that can be added to toys to enable children with limited dexterity to manipulate them. Kits for adding switches are commonly available in most areas and can be ordered through the Internet.

symbolic constructivism—Type of constructivism that emphasizes the construction of knowledge through language and symbols. Bruner's work provided the impetus for this approach.

symbolic play—According to Piaget, the second stage of play; occurs when a child uses an object or action to represent or stand for another; usually begins within the first two years of life.

T **tertiary circular reaction (one year to eighteen months)**—Coordination of actions that enable the infant to use active experimentation to discover new uses for materials. Example: key in outlet.

theme-based playground—Playground developed around a theme with specific learning outcomes in mind. The idea is that children will enjoy the outdoor play and learn content material incidentally.

theory of mind—A line of research that examines how young children develop their understanding of their own internal mental state alongside their knowledge of the internal mental states of others.

transition—1. Term used in special education to describe the process that occurs when a child in a setting under the auspices of one governmental agency moves to a program operated by a different system. Generally refers to moving from programs for children under three to programs for children three and older. 2. Refers to activities used by teachers to seamlessly move children from one activity to another or from one place to another.

U **uncontrolled scribbles**—Stage of artistic development that occurs when the child first begins to hold a pencil and make marks: the child cannot control the direction of the marks.

unoccupied behavior—The child moves around the room or playground but does not participate in play. Behavior does not appear to have a goal.

Z **ZPD**—A term used by Vygotsky to refer to the Zone of Proximal Development. In the Zone of Proximal Development, the child moves from knowing with the assistance of others to knowing with no assistance. Vygotsky believed that instruction and play creates the ZPD and that play allows children to reach their maximum potential.

Index